The "Better Angels" of Capitalism

Polemics Series

Series Editors
Michael Calvin McGee and Barbara Biesecker, *University of Iowa*
John M. Sloop, *Vanderbilt University*

*The "Better Angels" of Capitalism: Rhetoric, Narrative, and Moral Identity
Among Men of the American Upper Class,*
Andrew Herman

Judgment Calls: Rhetoric, Politics, and Indeterminacy,
edited by John M. Sloop and James P. McDaniel

*The Rise of Rhetoric and Its Intersections with
Contemporary Critical Thought,*
Omar Swartz

Without Apology: Andrea Dworkin's Art and Politics,
Cindy Jenefsky

FORTHCOMING

Literary Integrity and Political Action,
Kathleen Farrell

The "Better Angels" of Capitalism

Rhetoric, Narrative, and Moral Identity Among Men of the American Upper Class

Andrew Herman

Westview Press
A Member of the Perseus Books Group

To the best angels:
Heidi Tarr Henson and Oliver Tarr Herman

Copyright © 1999 by Westview Press, A Member of the Perseus Books Group

Published in 1999 in the United States of America by Westview Press, 5500 Central Avenue, Boulder, Colorado 80301-2877, and in the United Kingdom by Westview Press, 12 Hid's Copse Road, Cumnor Hill, Oxford OX2 9JJ

Library of Congress Cataloging-in-Publication Data
Herman, Andrew, 1957–
   The "better angels" of capitalism : rhetoric, narrative, and moral
identity among men of the American upper class / Andrew Herman.
      p.   cm. — (Polemics)
   Revision of the author's thesis (Ph.D.)—Boston College.
   Includes bibliographical references and index.
   ISBN 0-8133-3354-7 (hc)
   1. Upper class—Moral and ethical aspects—United States.
2. Wealth—Moral and ethical aspects—United States. 3. Rich
people—United States—Language. 4. Philanthropists—United States—
Language. I. Title. II. Series.
HT653.U6H47   1999
305.5'2'0973—dc21   98-27713
                                                                                                              CIP

The paper used in this publication meets the requirements of the American National Standard for Permanence of Paper for Printed Library Materials Z39.48-1984.

10   9   8   7   6   5   4   3   2   1

Contents

Acknowledgments

Many books have a long gestation period, but the gestation of this book has been longer than most. I began research on this project in 1985, and if someone had told me at the time that it wouldn't be published until almost the dawn of the new millennium, I would have wished them and myself dead on the spot. But here I am, still alive, in the summer of 1998, wishing and writing this book toward its telos, and it's time to give an accounting of those who were essential to its birth, life, and happy conclusion. In spite of the fact that mine is the only name that signifies authorship of this work, it is the product of the gifts that have been bestowed upon me by many people and institutions over the past thirteen years. Now that the work is "finished," it is time to return the gifts of thanks to its many benefactors.

This book had its origins in the *Study on Wealth and Philanthropy*, conducted by the Social Welfare Research Institute at Boston College. The study provided the research upon which this dissertation is based and was made possible by grants from the Thomas B. Murphy Foundation Charitable Trust. In the course of doing the research for the *Study on Wealth and Philanthropy*, I had the opportunity to work with many individuals who helped to bring that project to fruition. In particular, I would like to thank Ethan Lewis, Lynn Rhenisch, and Leslie Sarofeen for their unfailing humor, grace, perseverance, imagination, and insight in helping to manage and make sense of what was an exciting, yet often chaotic, enterprise. Without their virtue, and the virtue of many others at the Social Welfare Research Institute who helped in the management of the project, the fortune of this project would not have been possible. Subsequent to the research itself, the writing of the dissertation upon which this book is based was aided by a doctoral fellowship from the Indiana University Center for the Study of Philanthropy. I would to like thank both of these institutions, as well as Tom Murphy himself, for their generous support of my research and writing.

While I was working on the research project and the doctoral dissertation that followed, there were many who contributed their intellectual energy, spirit, and insight to the cause. In listing them here, I sincerely hope that I am not forgetting anybody. Russell Eckel, Avery Gordon, Sandra

Joshel, Jackie Orr, Joseph Mendoza, Andrew Haase, Clive Smith, Janet Wirth-Cauchon, Alex Wirth-Cauchon, and Larry Zaborsky were all participants, in various forms and at various times, in an extended conversation concerning the "better angels" of capitalism. To them is due much gratitude and respect. Avery Gordon deserves special thanks for the trip to Savannah, where I read and heard the story of the three testicles. Sandra Joshel also warrants a gesture of specific gratitude. Many years ago, when both I and this project were floundering, Sandra Joshel enlisted me in what became known, in her unforgettable words, as the "Triumph of the Will Writing Camp." The book before you had its origins in a very long and difficult tape-recorded conversation between Sandra and I in her living room. As the ideas in that initial conversation were transformed from vague thoughts to written words, Sandra graciously lended her considerable talents to the production of the first version of this book.

I must also thank the members of my dissertation committee at Boston College. Paul Breines, Stephen Pfohl, and Paul G. Schervish lent their unfailing encouragement and support during the many years it required to complete the dissertation. They were exceedingly generous in terms of their time, intellect, and patience as I struggled with the project. Both Stephen Pfohl and Paul G. Schervish deserve a special and specific gesture of thanks. It was through my friendship with Stephen, and my engagement with his uniquely infectious and persuasive intellectual passion, that I came to the theoretical and methodological positions with respect to "doing sociology" that are manifested in this book. If there is anyone to blame for my willingness to transgress the norms and presuppositions of the "discipline" of sociology, it is Stephen. And I also know that he would be proud to accept that responsibility. It is impossible for me to sufficiently thank Paul Schervish. As both chair of the dissertation committee and director of the *Study and Wealth and Philanthropy,* Paul displayed a faith in my abilities when the chips were down that was extraordinary. I also appreciate the willingness of Bill Gamson of Boston College and John Langdon of Georgetown University to serve as outside readers of the dissertation.

After leaving Boston College I carried this project with me to Drake University, and it has been with the interest and support of my students and colleagues over the past six years that I have been able to transform the dissertation into this book. I tried to subject students in my SOC 172 (Wealth, Discourse, and Power), SOC 199 (Seminar in the Sociology of Knowledge), and Honors 172 (Topics in the Social Imaginary) courses to the theories, themes, and substance of the book, and in return they taught me more about subjectivity than I could ever possibly imagined. In particular, Tanya Beer, Dan Emery, John Jordan, Shane Luitjens, Robin Kneich, Nick Mathern, Jon Rosenfeld, Adam Sitze, and Anne Wallested all gave me gifts of fortune. I would also like to thank my colleagues in the sociology department and the cultural studies program at Drake University, both past and present: Richard Abel, Gregory Crider, Robert Harriman, Deborah Jacobs, Joseph Schneider, Jody Swilky, Thom Swiss, Ronald Troyer, and Sue Wright. Without their enthusiasm and interest, as well as their willingness to dialogue with my obsessions about this project, it would have never been completed. I must also thank the Drake University Center for the Humanities, which gave me funding for course releases that enabled me to work on the book.

Outside of Drake, over the past few years there have been a number of people who gave me and this project indispensable encouragement and help. Patricia Clough, Norman Denzin, Carolyn Ellis, Charles Lemert, David Maines, and Laurel Richardson, in many and different ways, provided a space and voice to perform a critical, optimistic, and consequential postdisciplinary sociology I hope this book embodies. Moreover, John Sloop and Barbara Biesecker, editors of this series, had faith that at least this project would matter and have consequences in disciplinary spaces beyond sociology. We shall see.

Then there are the friendly folks at Westview: Marcus Boggs, publisher, who called me up at my deepest moments of despair as to whether or not this book would see the life light of day and offered me a contract; Cathy Murphy, my editor, who patiently waited for the final manuscript as I broke deadline after deadline; and Jane Raese at Westview's production center, who indefatigably fielded all my questions about obscure mnemonics that weren't covered in the Westview guide to authors.

My parents, Bernie and Jean, must also be given pride of special place in this litany of gratitude. Their support in so many ways over so many years is of such a magnitude that it cannot really be accounted for in a sentence. Suffice it to say that they are truly "better angels."

Finally, I would like to thank my wife, Heidi Tarr Henson, for the innumerable contributions that she has made, not only to this project but also to my life project as a human being. In many ways, this project has been as much a part of her life during the past few years as it has been of mine, and without her embracing of its demanding presence, it would have never been finished. Her patience with it as a cohabiting partner in our lives has been extraordinary. In addition to her patience through many, many conversations and rounds of editing drafts, Heidi made invaluable contributions to the analysis that follows. But most importantly, Heidi has given me gifts that are beyond any reckoning or return: These are the gifts of laughter, love, and hope, all of which are embodied in our son, Oliver. Without these gifts that Heidi and Oliver brought into my life, not only would this book not be finished, I would not be . . . period. They are the best angels.

Andrew Herman

The "Better Angels" of Capitalism

1

Mapping the "Better Angels" of Capitalism: Space, Place, and Story in the Moral Economy of Wealth

Rhetoric, Narrative, and the "Better Angels" of Capitalism

"Next Question!": The Limits of the Study of Wealth as Power

What does it mean to be a man of wealth and power? How is the "worth" of wealth translated into moral "worth" in the identity of wealthy men? How does this identity comprise a mythical place of masculine desire in the social imagination of the "American Dream"? What are the cultural and political implications of the moral mythology of wealth in an era of increasing economic inequality in America? These are the central themes that this book explores through an ethnographic examination of life stories of wealthy men, a historical analysis of the moral meanings of wealth and power in Western capitalism, and a mapping of different symbolic spaces in contemporary American culture in which the moral meanings of wealth and power are represented and enacted.This book has its origins in a larger research project, the *Study on Wealth and Philanthropy*, that was carried out by the Social Welfare Research Institute at Boston College from 1985 to 1988. For this project, my colleagues and I interviewed 130 "wealthy" individuals who resided in eleven different metropolitan locations across the United States.[1] The impetus and the funds for this project were furnished by a newly wealthy alumnus of Boston College who was intellectually intrigued by, as well as morally concerned with, the question of how "financially secure" individuals should use what he termed their "redundant resources." By *redundant*, the funder was referring to monetary resources that exceeded the financial needs of an individual and her or his family. In particular, the funder was keenly interested in the manner in which wealthy individuals used such "redundant" resources for philanthropic purposes.

1

In the course of the study my colleagues and I learned some very interesting things about the philanthropic beliefs and behavior of the wealthy (cf. Schervish and Herman, 1988; Schervish, Coutsoukis, and Lewis, 1994). One of our most important findings was that philanthropy among the wealthy should not be viewed as an instance of "altruistic" behavior, that is, as a practice of the unselfish giving to or care of others. This is not to say that wealthy philanthropists do not articulate or evince a concern or care for others in their giving. They clearly do, and often this care and concern for others is expressed in very emotional and moving terms. The point is that in giving the wealthy do not deny or sacrifice their self-interest or their well-being. Quite the contrary, philanthropy is always a practice of power and a source of empowerment for the wealthy individual. Philanthropy is a social practice by which wealthy individuals are able to transform their *individuality*, expressed in personal desires, cultural interests, and political-economic priorities, into a *principality* or a sovereign realm of autonomy, freedom, and control.

I am a sociologist with a critical perspective on the class structure of American society, and it was this dimension of wealth and philanthropy as power that interested me the most about the research project. To my dismay, an analytical agenda primarily focusing on *how* the wealthy were powerful was not destined to lead very far. To say that the wealthy enjoy a special degree of empowerment because of their material wealth is to proclaim precisely what seemingly everyone knows. After all, it is the correlation of wealth with power, and power with freedom, that renders its pursuit one of the categorical imperatives of the capitalist life-world.

Indeed, on more than one occasion I had this almost commonsensical understanding of wealth as power thrown in my face by some of the individuals I interviewed. I directly asked one man, a real estate developer from Chicago whom I shall call Edward Hoffman,[2] to explain what it meant to be wealthy. His response, which was blunt to the point of hostility, was as follows: "*You* know what the word means. It's *in* the dictionary and I don't have to repeat the dictionary. I think its an obvious and trivial question." I was, of course, somewhat discomfited by this terse answer, yet I pressed on. "Well," I said, "let's suppose I haven't read the dictionary, what basic definition of what it means to be wealthy would you give me?" "Look," he answered, "it's quite simple: My money enables me to do what I want to do, when I want to do it, and how I want to do it. Next question."

Now, this was an exceptional interview experience. Only a few of my respondents were so dismissive and contemptuous of my questions. Indeed, my interviews were filled with very expansive and rich descriptions of how the wealthy feel themselves to be empowered, whether it is in terms of personal life, business activity, or philanthropic involvements. Nonetheless, after this particular interview I was stuck with the nagging suspicion that Mr. Hoffman's refusal of my question was a signal that my line of inquiry was missing an important dimension of the world of wealth. Perhaps the "next question," to use Mr. Hoffman's directive phrase, needed to be a different kind of question than those entailed by an overriding concern with how and in what ways the wealthy are powerful. Perhaps I needed to get beyond the common-sense understanding of wealth as power to ask a more fundamental question.

The question that I eventually came up with is this: Upon what discursive and moral basis are the men of wealth I interviewed able to convince themselves and others of the legitimacy of their power and privilege? To put it another way: How is financial worth made symbolically equivalent of moral worth? More specifically, the questions that guide my analysis in this book are threefold. First, What are the terms of their language about themselves, their motivations, their actions, and their money that construct a representational system of identity and difference within which they come to understand themselves as people of power and privilege in a class-stratified society? Second, on the basis of this understanding, How do these individuals lay legitimate claim to and exercise sovereignty over themselves and others? And, third, How does this exercise of sovereign power, in both the accumulation of wealth and its dispensation in philanthropy, become encoded and interpreted as a demonstration of individual virtue that yields social benefit?

With the foregoing questions in mind, after the research project concluded I went back to the interviews and examined the language with which the respondents framed their identity, power, and privilege.[3] All of these questions, and the analytical concepts and interpretative methodology through which those questions would lead my interrogation of the interviews, came together in one of those moments of epiphany, or what scientists call serendipity—the fortunate making of discovery by chance. In this moment of revelation I came to see a powerful resonance between the (auto-)biographical narratives my interviewees told me and the words of two premier social theorists of the late twentieth century: Michel Foucault and George Herbert Walker Bush. It was also out of this moment that I came to understand and develop for my own purposes the central concepts that I would use to make sense of the interviews: discourse, rhetoric, narrative, and moral economy. Now, the first of many stories of the "better angels" of capitalism.

"The Magic of the Machine":
George Bush, Michel Foucault, and the Wizardry of Rhetoric

It was a sticky August night in Savannah, Georgia, and on the way to the 1988 American Sociological Association meetings in Atlanta my ex-wife and I stopped to visit some members of her extended family. During the day, I had taken the opportunity to avail myself of the coast's bright sun, warm water, and broad, clay beaches. On the beach I was reading a novel by the Argentinean novelist Luisa Valenzuela, entitled *The Lizard's Tale*. The novel was about a man who was prime minister of Argentina during the mid-1970s under Pres. Isabel Perón, just before a military coup. The plot of the novel itself is unimportant here except for one element: The source of the man's political power was that he was a wizard of black magic, and his status as a wizard was signified by the fact that he had three testicles. The fact that a man with three testicles was thought to be a wizard in some cultures was something I did not know, and it stuck in my mind.

Later that night, I sat down with my in-laws to watch the Republican National Convention. Tonight George Bush was to give his acceptance speech for his first GOP presidential nomination. As Bush started, one of the aunts of the family leaned my way and said, "Do you know why I can't vote for Michael Dukakis?" Now, being where I was (the Deep South) and given who I was with (a family of rabid Republicans), I could think of a lot of seemingly rational reasons why she wouldn't vote for Dukakis. But I was totally unprepared for the one she offered: She fixed me with shiny eyes that promised wisdom and revelation and said, "He's got three testicles . . . he's a black magician!"

I was dumbfounded. My mind spun with thoughts and images of wizardry, testicular excess, political power, the mystery and inscrutability of the American South and South America, not to mention the words and stories of the wealthy to which I had just spent three years listening. I turned my eyes to the television, hoping whatever was there would pull me out of the vertigo that had engulfed my mind. And there, staring right back at me, was George Bush. And he said:

> My approach this evening is, as Sergeant Joe Friday used to say, "Just the facts, ma'am." I seek the Presidency for a single purpose, a purpose that has motivated millions of Americans across the years and the ocean voyages. I seek the Presidency to build a better America. It is that simple and that big. I am a man who sees life in terms of missions—missions defined and mission completed.
>
> Some say this election isn't about ideology; it is about competence. . . . But this election isn't only about competence, for competence is a narrow deal. Competence makes the trains run on time but doesn't know where we are going. Competence is the creed of the technocrat who makes the gears mesh but doesn't for a second understand the *magic of the machine* [emphasis added].
>
> The truth is, this election is about the beliefs we share, the values we honor, the principles we hold dear. An election that is about ideas and values is also about philosophy. And I have one. At the bright center is the

individual. And radiating from him or her is the family. From the individual to the family to the community, and on out to the town, to the church and the school and, still echoing out, to the country, the state and the nation—each doing what it does well and no more. And I believe that power must always be kept close to the individual, close to the hands that raise the family and run the home. . . . We are a nation of communities, of thousands and tens of thousands of ethnic, religious, social, business, labor union, neighborhood, regional and other organizations, all of them varied, voluntary and unique . . . a brilliant diversity spread like stars, like a thousand points of light in a broad and peaceful sky.

Some people who are enjoying our prosperity have forgotten what it's for. But they diminish our triumph when they have forgotten what it's for. . . . The fact is that prosperity has a purpose. It is to allows us to pursue "the better angels," to give us time to think and grow. Prosperity with a purpose means taking your idealism and making it concrete by certain acts of goodness. (Bush, 1988: 13)

At that moment I understood with exquisite clarity who the real wizard was. It was George Bush. He may not be a wizard of black magic but he is a wizard of something that is central to the understanding of wealth and power, both for the wealthy themselves and society at large. He is a wizard of discourse and rhetoric. As a wizard of discourse, he is using language to successfully conjure a particular imaginary constitution of the social world, within which its members are given a particular identity. In this imaginary world, in this conjuring, a particular moral truth of what wealth means, and what it means to be wealthy, is configured.[4] And it is on the basis of this moral "truth" that power can be legitimately exercised. This relationship between discursive conjuring and "truth" is what may be called, to paraphrase Bush, the *magic of the rhetorical machine*.

Although wizardry, magic, and conjuring may be extreme metaphors for what discourse does, it is this dimension of discourse as creating the social world, and therefore enabling social action, that Foucault underscores in the following passage:

In a society such as ours . . . there are manifold relations of power which permeate, characterize and constitute the social body, and these relations of power cannot be themselves established, consolidated or implemented without the production, accumulation, circulation and functioning of a discourse. There can be no possible exercise of power without a certain economy of discourses of truth which operates through and on the basis of this association. We are subjected to the production of truth through power and we cannot exercise power except through the production of truth. . . . In the last analysis, we must produce truth as we produce wealth, indeed, we must produce truth in order to produce wealth in the first place. (1977b: 93–94)

Foucault's argument is that the production of wealth, and its use by the wealthy, was predicated upon it being inscribed with certain moral "truths" about its meaning. This is what he means when he says that "we are *subjected* to the production of truth through power and we cannot exercise power except through the production of truth." In order for economic power to be exercised, we must subjectively perceive and understand it in a particular way. That is, before power can be accumulated and wielded, it must be understood not simply as power per se but as a pragmatic form of power/knowledge that is right, true, and natural.

For both Foucault and George Bush, discourse as a social activity is *rhetorical*. The rhetorical nature of discourse is derived from two meanings that have historically been attached to rhetoric as a practice, one that is familiar and another that is less so. The familiar meaning of the practice of rhetoric is argumentation and persuasion. In this sense, rhetoric is a speech-act that is intended to mobilize people into action. Clearly, George Bush is practicing rhetoric in this sense. But as a wizard of discourse, Bush is practicing rhetoric in a second sense as well. As John Shotter (1990) and Richard Harvey Brown (1992) have argued, this second sense of rhetoric can be traced back to Vico and has influenced Nietzsche, Foucault, and other poststructuralists and has been the basis for "rhetorical turn" in the contemporary human sciences (cf. Bender and Wellbery, 1990). Rhetoric in this sense means giving form to the vague and disordered flow of human experience. Rhetoric gives shape to social reality and, in so doing, makes sense of it. This imperative of rhetoric, so to speak, is what both Nietzsche and Foucault underscore in talking about the will to truth and power inherent in language and discourse. For Nietzsche, rhetoric is "the act of ordering the chaos of life" (Whitson and Poulakas, 1993: 136). It is a creative aesthetic process that imposes form upon existence; indeed, as he argued in *The Will to Power*, it springs from a "compulsion to arrange a world for ourselves in which existence is possible" (quoted in Witson and Poulakas, 1993: 136). For Foucault, to say that discourse is rhetorical, to say that it is a practice of wizardry and conjuring, is to say that it makes possible the pragmatics of power in everyday life by punctuating the world with meaning. This understanding of rhetoric has been underscored and elaborated upon by the "critical rhetoric" movement in rhetorical studies (cf. Greene, 1998; McKerrow, 1989; McGee, 1990). From the perspective of critical rhetoric, rhetoric entails far more than the artistry of oratory and persuasion or the textual embodiments of this art: The rhetorical process, to use Maurice Charland's (1987) terms, is "constitutive" of subjectivity and identity and must be analyzed accordingly. As Barbara Biesecker states in making a strong case for materiality of rhetoric as a social practice, "It is in language and rhetoric that the social takes place" (Biesecker, 1997: 50).

Although I employ Bush's rhetorical invocation of the "better angels" in order to frame the central concern of my book, I am not primarily interested in whether or not his claims about "prosperity with a purpose" and "a thousand points of light" are empirically true. This is not a book about whether the wealthy really are philanthropically beneficent "better angels" of capitalism. Rather, my principal concern is with how such arguments about wealth, the wealthy, and philanthropy acquire and maintain their cultural "truthfulness" as part of the rhetorical machine and its magical process, that is, how such propositions become accepted as natural and right in the social imaginary of contemporary American capitalism. Bush's magical act of constitutive rhetoric is an example of what I term the moral economy of wealth.

The social "truth" of wealth and philanthropy, I argue, is produced and circulated through the discursive and rhetorical practices of this moral economy of wealth. Simply stated, the *moral economy of wealth* involves the discursive production and circulation of symbolic representations of wealth that serve to invest the behavior of the wealthy with a certain moral identity, or symbolic-moral capital, that can be exchanged for legitimacy and approbation. Through the moral economy of wealth, financial wealth is transformed into moral worth, and so-called redundant or excess resources are accounted for as signs of the bountiful surplus moral value and virtue of the wealthy. To return to the question of how the wealthy are able to take the power and privilege of wealth within themselves, I argue that it is on the basis of representations of wealth such as "prosperity with a purpose" and "pursing the better angels" that wealthy individuals are able to make sense of their power and privilege and feel legitimately entitled to use and enjoy it.

It is important to point out I am exclusively concerned with how the identity of the wealthy *men* that I interviewed are articulated with and through this moral economy of wealth. I argue that this moral economy provides these men with the basic discursive categories, linguistic repertoires, and vocabularies of motive with which they give rhetorical shape to their self-identity. In the context of the interviews, this *rhetoric of self-hood* takes a peculiar form—an (auto-)biographical narrative.[5] As a diverse array of scholars in recent years has argued, ranging from philosophers such as A. Kerby (1991), A. MacIntyre (1981), P. Ricouer (1984), and C. Taylor (1989) to sociologists and anthropologists such as R. Brown (1987), J. Bruner (1991), D. Conquergood (1993), D. Maines (1993), and L. Richardson (1990), it is primarily through the rhetorical processes of narrativity and practices of storytelling that individuals give form to personal life experiences and craft moral identities in concordance with (or in opposition to) the prevailing values of culture (this is a theme that I will explore in more detail in Chapter 2). My argument is that the primary way in which wealthy men make sense of their power and privilege is to speak about it within the context of an (auto-)biographical narrative of fortune and virtue.

Obviously, this process of shaping a coherent social identity through narrative is not the sole province of the wealthy in general or wealthy men in particular. However, the reason I chose to focus on the (auto-)biographical narratives of wealthy men in the sample is that in the course of my research I discerned that the narratives were literally and figurally engendered as a story of masculinity in relation to wealth.[6] This narrative pattern, which I term the *narrative of fortune and virtue*, divides the social world into two fundamental categories—that which is given and that which is accomplished—and posits the male individual as the primary force by which the former is transformed into the latter. Moreover, as I explore in some detail in Chapter 3, these two ontological categories are figured in the discourse of Renaissance mercantile capitalism as being, respectively, feminine and masculine. Fortune as chance and circumstance, as well as wealth, are represented as a feminine power that can spell potential chaos and disaster for men unless they are able to control it and shape it according to their desires on the basis of manly virtue. Accordingly, it is on the basis of discursively valorizing a particular set of values and behaviors with respect to the accumulation and use of wealth—which have been historically designated as being "masculine"—that the narrative of fortune and virtue enables wealthy men to construct their moral identity.[7]

More specifically, as a mythic structure the narrative of fortune and virtue naturalizes the bourgeois worldview within which autonomous (male) individuals are held responsible for their own destiny. Making seemingly "natural" that which is a historically specific social construction enables certain men I interviewed to unequivocally claim (as did one man who has born into one of the oldest wealthy families in the country) that "I am what I've been able to make" without a trace of irony or contradiction. Accordingly, this narrative pattern legitimizes the power and privilege of wealth by enabling its possessors to tell a moral tale of self-identity in which their fortune, whether it is inherited or earned, is constructed as the just desserts of individual virtue. On the basis of such moral tales, wealthy men in this study were able to lay claim to a sovereign realm of individual autonomy and social power. The rhetorical constitution of and moral claim to this realm through narrative, I will argue in the next section, is intimately related to the site or location of discourse as well as to the perspectival sight such a site engenders. Accordingly, in order to understand the rhetoric of selfhood and sovereignty of wealthy men, it is necessary to focus the analysis at the interstices of space, place, and story where the emplacement and emplotment of moral identity converge.

Emplacement and Emplotment in the Moral Economy of Wealth

A Gesture to the World: A Story of Space, Place, and Moral Identity

Seattle, 1986. Standing on the observation deck of the City Capital Club on the seventy-sixth floor of Columbia Towers, I gaze down and across the spatial inscriptions of capital upon the landscape of the city and its environs. From this height, reading the signs is ecstatically easy, and I am giddy with the power and possibilities of masterful (in)sight, that gift of perceptual power inscribed long ago into our cultural consciousness by the Renaissance rediscovery of linear perspective.[8] To the west, across Puget Sound, the Olympic Mountains rise gently from the water to a white-peaked crescendo, and to the east the Cascade Range throws up a majestic, jagged boundary to the city's sprawl. Through the cloudy haze that hugs both, I can see the scars rent upon the timberland by logging roads and the clear-cuts of Weyerhauser, one of the region's largest corporations and philanthropic benefactors. To the south lies the sprawling manufacturing complex of the Boeing Aerospace Corporation, which is prospering mightily in these days of national security state Keynesianism. Several blocks away are the offices of the Mitsubishi Bank, the Long Term Credit Bank of Japan, Ltd., and Nomura Securities International. These Japanese institutions, I surmise, play a major part in suturing Weyerhaeuser, Boeing, and this city into the new economic order of the Pacific Rim by investing in the defense-driven national debt, guiding the flow of wood products to Japan, and proposing to buy the Space Needle Park as an amusement park for Japanese tourists. Across Lake Washington, in Redmond, is the Microsoft Corporation, exemplar of the structural metamorphosis of capitalism as mode of production and mode of information.

More than a landscape of geographical space, the vista is symbolic *topos*, or place of social identity, that is "charged with meaning and possibility because it is charged, like the glance that takes visionary possession of it, with desire" (Brook, 1985: 41). There is magic in this machine of visual perspective from on high, a magic of a will to truth and power, just as there is such magic in the rhetorical machine of discourse. Indeed, the two machines, the visual and the rhetorical, are intimately connected. As Michel de Certeau describes this magic of elevated and lofty vision, "It transforms the bewitching world by which one was 'possessed' into a text before one's eyes. It allows one to read it, to be a Solar eye, looking down like a god. The exaltation of a scopic and gnostic drive: the fiction of knowledge is related to this lust to be a viewpoint and nothing more" (de Certeau, 1984: 92).

Ah, but there is more. Much more. There is more that I see and even more that I cannot see. However, at this moment, I feel that my narrative glance, my scopic lust and gnostic desire, and the "visionary possession" that they entail, are somewhat evanescent. The sovereignty of my sight and story is transitory, unstable, and insecure as it lacks the capital, prestige, and position to give it material *force* and *form* that others who occupy this vantage point will recognize as being "true."[9] My vision, as Foucault would say, has a deficit of "positivity" in the social field. Such positivity is possessed by the man standing next to me, John Norris.[10]

Mr. Norris, my host at the Capital City Club, is one of my first interviews in this city, and during the past two hours he has provided me with, literally and figuratively, a voyeuristic view of corporate and philanthropic power in Seattle. The very setting of the interview is emblematic of the network of power that Mr. Norris describes to me over an elegant lunch in the sumptuous dining room of the Club and during our formal interview session on the observation deck. I wonder if this place has been chosen because it demonstrates his position, power, and prestige, and thus gives credence and legitimacy to his words. This is not to say that Norris necessarily needs a particular setting to speak with authority. Norris, a former executive for a Fortune 500 computer firm who is now a biotech entrepreneur, speaks with a degree of confidence and assuredness that I have now come to recognize as a sign of a comfortable familiarity with worldly power and efficaciousness. Nonetheless, the site and style of discourse are central to the subtle practice of what Pierre Bourdieu (1991) terms the "symbolic violence" of language, where in speaking "one not only seeks to be understood but also to be believed, obeyed, respected and distinguished" (238).

In fact, it is the site itself about which Norris is most eager to talk. Indeed, our lunchtime conversation is devoted to discussing the rationale for and nature of the City Capital Club and its importance to the organization and stature of the local power elite.[11] Mr. Norris takes great pride in the fact that he was an organizer and charter member (he showed me a membership card that signified, in fact, that he was the first member) of this establishment, which, as he put it, was necessary for Seattle to be considered a "world-class city." For whom was such a consideration necessary and important? I wondered. Given the high price of admission ($10,000 per year for individuals), it was clear that the constituency of connoisseurs of the designation "world-class city" was quite limited. Clearly, exclusivity has its own rewards in terms of status and prestige for the members of the club and, by association, the city as well.

As Norris pointed out, however, the club had a more important function of facilitating on an interpersonal basis what Michael Useem (1984) calls the "class-wide principle" of the social organization of business interests.[12] Of course, Norris did not speak directly of this principle, as the word *class* does not figure in his discourse. Indeed, class as a phenomenologically meaningful category is effaced by an array of rhetorical phrases and tropes that constitute the representational world of the moral economy of wealth. In this particular case, Norris does not talk about the club as one (among many) sites of the formation and articulation of "class," "corporate," or even "elite" interests. Rather, as he explained to me, the club was built because there was a pressing need for a place where local and regional business and philanthropic figures could socialize, network, and formulate ideas for "community leadership." In this simple phrase, *community leadership*, the particularistic interest of class is displaced by the universal, encompassing interest of community. There is, of course, much more to this process of rhetorical displacement than a simple exchange of terms. What is important here is the relationship between such rhetorical effects of discourse and the space in which it is spoken.

And thus I return to the desire for the mastery of sight that has brought me to these august heights. Although "class" is a null category in Mr. Norris's schema of representation, the sovereign power of possession is quite manifest. After speaking quite passionately and eloquently about the necessity for corporations and wealthy individuals to be "good citizens" in the "community" through philanthropic involvement and active participation in public affairs, Norris rose from the conference table where we had been seated and went to the window. Beckoning me to join him, he gestured across the cityscape below with a sweep of his hand and said for the benefit of the tape recorder (and those who could not see his gesture), "So I am looking around from the seventy-sixth floor of the building trying to see if there is anything I have done that I have not mentioned."

Both the act and the statement, so seemingly innocuous and simple, imply much about the representation of wealth and power. Contained in the gesture are two modes of propinquity between Norris and the world that he sees. In the first mode, he is articulating a kinship with a community to which he is obligated and for which he feels responsibility. When he looks out the window, he sees his good works—material signs of his civic virtue and exemplary citizenship. Yet in specifying the vantage point from which he views the community ("I am looking out from the seventy-sixth floor"), he is calling attention to his superior position in a hierarchy that is spatial and symbolic. From this privileged position he is able to assess, judge, and govern that which exists in his field of vision. The world below is his community, not simply in terms of the community being a *space* of involvement but, more importantly, in terms of it being a topos or place of sovereignty and moral identity. It is a space that he can claim as his own, upon which he is able to inscribe his desires, values, and priorities. Thus, his gesture to the world below is not simply a gesture of inclusion ("I am part of what I see"); it is also a gesture of appropriation and possession ("what I see is part of me").

This double-encoded gesture is but one frame in Norris's own personal narrative of fortune and virtue, a narrative to which I return in Chapter 2. Yet there is much at stake in this single moment of rhetorical performance for understanding the dynamics of space, place, and story within the moral economy of wealth. What is rhetorically produced in this scene of the sovereign eye that sees—and the sovereign "I" that narrates the self—is a wealthy man who is presented as autonomous, centered, and having powers to shape self and world. In Norris, we have a person whose presentation of self connotes fullness, plenitude, confidence, and control. Moreover, Norris stands as author and origin of this individuality, not only because he is the enunciator of his personal biography but also because within his biography the power, regard, and status he enjoys are presented as inhering in his unique personal attributes. Accordingly, the empowerment of wealth is presumptively presented as the just reward of his individual virtue. With Norris's authoritative gesture to the world, he locates or positions his self-identity within the representational regime of the sovereign subject described by Roland Barthes:

> Representation is defined directly by imitation: even if one gets rid of notions of the "real," of the "vraisembable," of the "copy," there will still be representation for so long as a subject (author, reader, spectator or voyeur) casts his gaze towards a horizon on which he cuts out the base of a triangle, his eye (or his mind) forming the apex. [Representation] will have as its dual foundation the sovereignty of the act of cutting out [*découpage*] and the unity of the subject of that action. (Barthes, 1977: 69, 76–77)

In casting his gaze across the landscape as he tells his narrative of fortune and virtue, his identity fills the triangle anchored by the apex of his eye, extending to the base formed by the spatial limits of the visual horizon. As his story unfolds toward the telos of his narrative, his gesture to the world, the space of the city, is constructed as a place of sovereignty and moral identity. Thus, in the moral economy of wealth, the rhetoric of selfhood involves the intertwined process of location and narrative, or emplacement and emplotment.

Whose Story Is This Anyway?
"Character" and the Truth Effect of Narrative

What is occurring in this scene is more than a recitation of an individual biography. Here is the rhetorical invocation of discourses of wealth that form the grounding upon which Norris's sovereign self is built. Within the context of the moral economy of wealth, Norris is speaking as more than a singular wealthy individual with a unique and interesting story to tell: He is also speaking as a narrativized embodiment of the ideal masculine bourgeois figure. As such, in addition to seeing Norris as the central character in his own (auto-)biographical narrative, we must also view him as an exemplary *character* in Alasdair MacIntyre's sense of the word. MacIntyre (1981) maintains that the moral life of a culture is constructed through narratives that provide a dramatic scripting of social visions of virtue. Central to such narratives are the characters who enact these communally shared notions of virtue. For MacIntyre (1981: 28–29), characters are

> the moral representatives of their culture and they are so because of the way in which moral and metaphysical ideas and theories assume through them an embodied existence in the world. *Characters* are the masks worn by moral philosophies. . . . A character is an object of regard by the members of the culture generally or by some significant segment of them. He furnishes them with a cultural and moral ideal. Hence the demand is that role and personality be fused. Social type and personality type are required to coincide. The *character* morally legitimates a mode of social existence.

In a similar vein, Robert Wuthnow (1990: 19–20) argues that such characters, or "figural actors," are the principal means by which discourse and ideology are linked to practical reason and action. If ideology is the symbolic and discursive patterning of social reality in terms of what exists, what is right, and what is possible, then characters or figural actors represent appropriate models of behavior within the ontological and normative context provided by ideology. For example, a number of such characters are crystallized in George Bush's invocation of "the better angels": the indefatigable seeker of the truth, interested in only the "facts"; the intrepid, risk-taking entrepreneur; the steward-philanthropist; the citizen-volunteer; the civic-minded businessperson; and so on—all representing ideal models of sovereign masculinity in capitalist society. Wuthnow contends that in order for such characters to provide affectively compelling models of behavior they must meet two criteria. First, they must have a "generality and openness" that allows them to be applicable to a wide range of concrete, localized situations in everyday life. Second, they must have a material embodiment in exemplars that are found in everyday life that confirm the possibility of certain moral values being enacted.

Norris and the other wealthy men I interviewed provide such embodied examples of characters who are discursively constructed in the moral economy of wealth. Perhaps this is a rather large burden to place on one individual and his story. But the point is that his *story* is not really *his* story alone. As social psychologist Rom Harré (1984) argues, one of the primary ways in which a person's social identity is formed is through the process of individual appropriation of definitions of selfhood from the public sphere of the social imaginary. Norris's personal narrative is scripted and performed in concordance with the positively valorized modes of thinking and behavior that are given unity and coherence by their embodiment in particular moral characters in the discursive field of the moral economy of wealth. Moreover, his story is given credence and respect by virtue of the fact that he becomes, in assuming the character mask of an ideologically defined figure of virtue, publicly recognizable as a living testament to the moral "truth" of wealth. This process of *character embodiment* and *recognition* is central to the way in which the narrative of fortune and virtue operates: what de Certeau (1984) terms a "scriptural economy" of discourses. It is through the narrative of fortune and virtue that the discourses of the moral economy of wealth come to bear on wealthy men as individuals and render them identifiable by having a place and meaning in the social imaginary. To borrow a phrase from Richard Harvey Brown, the wealthy men I interviewed should be analyzed as "emblems of a larger social text," and their (auto-)biographical narratives as stories that are simultaneously inscribed upon and recounted by them (1987: 146). It is the double logic of tropic exchange between the personal narratives of these men and the social text of the moral economy of wealth that produces the *vraisemblance* of the narrative of fortune and virtue.

Vraisemblance is a key concept in the structuralist and poststructuralist analysis of narrative and refers to the verisimilitude, or "reality effect," of a story. As Jonathan Culler (1975: 142–143) explains, *vraisemblance* "involves establishing a relationship between words and world, which serves as a guarantee of intelligibility. . . . When a character performs an action, [we] give it a meaning by drawing upon a fund of human knowledge which establishes connections between action and motive, behavior and personality. Naturalization proceeds on the assumption that action is intelligible, and the cultural codes specify this intelligibility." In other words, in constructing and interpreting stories both teller and listener draw upon what phenomenological social theorists call the "natural attitude" of taken-for-granted, common-sense assumptions of what characters might legitimately do, think, and say "in reality." My point here is that the intelligibility ("truthfulness") of personal narratives of fortune and virtue is dependent, in large measure, upon the conformity of presentations of self with hegemonic typifications of capitalist virtue that are congealed in the characters who circulate in the moral economy of wealth. What is put under erasure in this rhetorical practice is the fact that the natural knowledge of such characters (and the motives, values, and behaviors that inhere in them) is itself a discursive construction and an authorial artifact of narrativity. Steve Pile and Nigel Thrift succinctly describe this process: "Identity is a fiction which must continually be established as truth. Indeed the practice of authority is revealed in the moment when identity is considered as truth and forgets that is has been authored at all" (1995: 49).

In the moral economy of wealth, this moment of the fictive authorship of truth and its forgetting entails a profound tautology. We infer the virtue of wealthy men from the correspondence of their motives and actions to those of figural characters, forgetting how the presentation of self is always-already discursively framed in terms of the figural embodiments of virtue. We are then gratified when the individual's story provides a "real" concrete example of how a virtuous life of wealth can be lived. De Certeau (1984: 148–149) describes the tautology that is inherent in the scriptural economy of discourse:

> The credibility of a discourse is what first makes believers act in accord with it. It produces practitioners. To make people believe is to make them act. But by a curious circularity, the ability to make people act . . . is precisely what makes people believe. Because [discourse] is already applied with and on bodies, "incarnated" in physical practices, it can accredit itself and make people believe that it speaks in the name of the "real." It makes itself believable by saying: "This text has been dictated for you by reality itself." People believe what they assume to be real, but this "reality" is assigned to a discourse by a belief that gives it a body inscribed by the law. The law requires an accumulation of corporeal capital in advance in order to make itself believed and practiced. It is thus inscribed because of what has already been inscribed: the witnesses, martyrs, or examples that make it credible to others.

These figuring processes of the moral economy have important implications for the way one approaches the analysis of wealth and masculinity. Obviously, in order to analyze the moral identity of wealthy men, it is important to have a detailed understanding of how they enjoy a special degree of power and efficacy in everyday life because of their wealth and thus represent what has been termed the "sovereign individuals of capitalism" (Abercrombie, Hill, and Turner, 1986). Indeed, the mundane materiality of the empowerment of wealth in everyday life is the point of departure in Chapter 2. However, this analysis does not takes us very far beyond a common-sense understanding of wealth as power. Unless we shake loose our understandings, that is, of wealth as power and of the men who possess it as powerful, we shall end up affirming and accepting the valorization of these individuals as the embodiments of capitalism's sovereign ideal. A critical analysis of the character masks that are proffered to us by the moral economy of wealth, and their instantiation in a multiplicity of narratives of fortune and virtue, must be performed. Otherwise, we will unreflectively inhabit the mythical world where the language of wealth inscribes a particular configuration of desires and values and, in so doing, proscribes others from being imagined and enacted.

Identity, Difference, and the Logics of Representation

The primary goal of this work is to participate in this task by engaging in a critical analysis of the narrative grounding and structure upon which Norris's story and gesture, and the characters and ideological universe the gesture evokes, is authorized to make its (i.e., the gesture's) claim of sovereignty. At the core of that gesture is Norris's figurative inscription of his presence upon the world that he sees. Indeed, the very "essence" of the sovereignty we have been discussing is its immanent presence and fullness. And that is the nub of our problem, for within the borders of the triangle of representation described by Barthes there can be nothing but presence, a plenitude of identity for the person who is able to appropriate and claim the view. Yet what Barthes does not mention is that the sovereignty that the person claims does not originate solely in that particular act of claiming. Rather, the presence and identity of the sovereign subject are made possible only on the basis of exclusions that hold at bay that which exists outside the borders. As Chris Weedon (1987: 25) argues, "The effect of representation, in which meaning is apparently fixed, is but a temporary retrospective fixing." The fixing of such borders through representation delimits the moral space inhabited by the "better angels" of capitalism, marking the boundary between excess and surplus, and is rhetorically constituted by the (auto-)biographical narratives of fortune and virtue.

This brings me to the poststructuralist de-centering of the subject about which Jacques Derrida has been so helpful. Poststructuralism challenges the notions of self and identity that have dominated Western culture since the Renaissance. Rejecting the Cartesian conception of the self as *cogito*, as a unified center of awareness and reflexivity that is ontologically prior to society, poststructuralism views the self as being constituted in and through language, discourse, and the symbolic order. The privileging of the rational, centered *cogito* constitutes part of what Derrida (1973) calls the "metaphysics of presence" of Western philosophy and culture. For Derrida, the positing of an essential self-same presence and identity is a rhetorical illusion that is produced on the basis of occluding or effacing the process of what he calls "alterity" and *différance*. In brief, *différance* is a neologism that denotes two processes: to differ and to defer. Derrida argues that the presence, meaning, and identity of an object or subject are not defined by anything intrinsic or essential to their nature. Rather, the qualities that we ascribe to words, things, and persons are constituted on the basis of the difference of elements in a signifying system from one another and the ceaseless deferral of any fixed resting point of these differential meanings along the signifying chain. It is this process of signification that Derrida terms "alterity." As Barbara Johnson (1981: ix) explains, "*Différance* inhabits the very core of what appears to be immediate and present. . . . The illusion of the self-presence of meaning or of consciousness is thus produced by the repression of the differential structures from which they spring." It is this *production* of meaning through difference, and the effacement of that difference, that is at the core of the moral economy of wealth.

To argue that the sovereignty and virtue that the wealthy men I interviewed claim for themselves are artifacts of difference is to foreground the social, historical, and institutional discursive contexts that serve to "fix" the moral "truth" of wealth. Further, to say that this truth is constituted on the basis of difference is to give notice to the fact that this truth is heterogeneous, multivocal, and contradictory. The effect of the narrative of fortune and virtue, and the discourses that compose it, is to efface this heterogeneity so that certain understandings of wealth, power, virtue, individuality, community, citizenship, philanthropy, and so on are privileged as being right, true, and natural. Yet as Derrida argues, that which is present in the system of representation bears the "trace" of the differential elements that compose it.[13] Thus, it is the task of deconstructive social analysis to locate these traces, to show how presence is constructed on the basis of what has been prohibited, to ferret out the contradictions that are embedded within a regime of representation, and to "pursue them to rupture" (Yates, 1990: 276).

Although the Derridian critique of representation has its roots in a philosophical critique of logocentrism and the metaphysics of presence, its thrust is toward a critical understanding of the materiality of rhetorical processes of representation as power/knowledge. In Gayatri Spivak's (1988) influential piece on the depictions and voicings of postcolonial subjects at the margins of imperial power "Can the Subaltern Speak?", she points to the dual dimension of representation that is crucial for understanding those white American men who speak from its center. In an innovative reading of *The Eighteenth Brumaire of Louis Napoleon*, she observes that in the German text Marx uses different words to capture two distinct yet related senses of "representation": *darstellung* and *vertretung*. *Darstellung* connotes representation as re-presentation, the rhetorical and tropological depiction or patterning of "reality." *Vertretung* connotes representation in the more narrow political sense of standing in for or working for another's interest. According to Spivak, it is imperative to account for what she calls the "complicity" of these two modes of representation.

To move towards such an accounting one must move towards theories of ideology—of subject formations that micrologically and often erratically operate the interests that congeal the macrologies. Such theories cannot afford to overlook the category of representation in its two senses. They must note how the staging of the world in representation—its scene of writing, its *Darstellung*—dissimulates the choice of and need for "heroes," paternal proxies, agents of power—*Vertretung*. (1988: 279)

To reframe this argument for purposes of my project, Spivak is calling our attention to the magical processes of Bush's rhetorical machine of the "better angels," through which the private virtue of individuals comes to be identified with public justice in the social imaginary of capitalism. For my purposes, the "micrologies" to which Spivak refers are the personal narratives of the wealthy men I interviewed. These narratives perform the world of wealth and power and the scene of its writing as (auto-)biography. Within these narratives, the experience of wealth and power is articulated in a such a way that the individual is able to present and perceive himself as being virtuous. This narrative production of virtuous self-identity is not the result of intentional dissembling or mendacity on the part of the respondents. Rather, my argument, following the lead of Maurice Charland (1987), is that the discursive field of the moral economy of wealth provides a structure of signification that requires that the interviewees' narratives end in an affirmation of virtue and therefore constitutes their moral identity. As Charland argues, "Subjects within narratives are not free, they are *positioned* and so constrained. All narratives have power over the subjects they present. The endings of the narrative are fixed before the telling" (Charland, 1987: 140). Moreover, it is in the rhetorical construction of the virtuous, sovereign self at the microlevel of individual biography that the claims to macrological and institutional positions of power in business, philanthropy, and government are ultimately grounded. By being representations of virtue as individuals, they are able to collectively stand as virtuous representatives—heroes, paternal proxies, and agents of power—of the commonweal.

Ethnography, Genealogy, and Cartography

My methodological position is that the analysis of the moral identity of wealthy men must be situated at the intersection of space, place, and story in the everyday life-world. In order to conduct this analysis, I employ a heterodox methodology that combines new strategies of ethnographic interpretation of narrative and culture, the genealogical analysis of rhetoric and discourse, and the cartographic mapping of the spatial and symbolic landscape. This methodology, I hope, offers a compelling perspective for the postdisciplinary cultural analysis of emplacement and emplotment through which spaces of everyday life become places of moral identity.

At core of my analysis of the masculine moral identity of men of wealth is the critical interrogation of the rhetorical practice and processes through which this identity is produced, the (auto-)biographical narrative of fortune and virtue. This narratively patterned rhetoric of selfhood helps wealthy men make sense of their power and privilege and lay legitimate claim to a sovereign realm of self-mastery. It is through the narrative trajectory of emplotment that individuals and communities are emplaced in spatio-temporal and symbolic locations of social identity. The intertwined dynamics of emplotment and emplacement of the narrative of fortune and virtue rhetorically configure mundane *spaces* of wealth and power, such as the family trust, the business enterprise, the local community, or the philanthropic foundation, into *places* of social identity in which moral virtue is enacted and embodied. Moreover, the narrative of fortune and virtue is perhaps the quintessential story of masculine personhood and individuality in a capitalist culture, and it entails a profoundly seductive logic of a metaphysics of presence and sovereignty. In his gesture to the world, Norris was performing a scene of seduction in which those who listened to his story were asked to believe, indeed, *desired* to believe, that his sovereignty was right, true, and natural. As Ross Chambers argues, seduction is an intrinsic part of the power/knowledge of narrative as it recruits the desire of the narrattee to believe in the authority of narrator and the *vraisemblance* of the story he or she tells:

> All narratives are necessarily seductive, seduction being the means whereby they maintain their authority to narrate; and if it that is so, then the duplicity of seduction, whereby narrative conforms to the (projected) desire of the other in order to bring about its own desire to narrate, is *constitutive of the narrative situation as such*. If "authority" and "seduction" are in a sense interchangeable, so too are "seduction" and "duplicity". (Chambers, 1984: 218; emphasis in original)

In order to rupture the circuit of authority and duplicity, I believe it is necessary to embrace an approach to the analysis of moral identity that transgresses, or at least dis-locates, the metaphysics of presence and sovereignty inscribed in the narrative of fortune and virtue's seductive logic of emplacement and emplotment.

One possible strategy for dis-locating the hegemonic logic of emplacement and emplotment in the narrative of fortune and virtue is to embrace an analytical strategy and writing practice that Ann Game calls a "methodology of multiplicity" (Game, 1991: 190). For Game, this methodology entails foregrounding not only the act of narrating self-identity as an act of artifice and authorship but also the very act of writing about the self as a practice of fictionalizing through which the author is written as she or he writes. What Game is suggesting here is a ritual of fictionalizing, of storytelling, that displaces the pretensions to truth of realism and empiricism. For Game, what is crucial to this methodology of multiplicity is that the subject who writes explicitly gives notice to the alterity, the relations between self and other that Derrida articulates through the concept of *différance*, through which the subject is produced and sustained in writing. For Game, multiplicity entails an articulation of and dialogical movement between the multiplicity of stories encountered in everyday life and embodied in the scene of writing. As she argues:

> In terms of a methodology of multiplicity one of the key strategies has been to read stories against and with one another. Any specific instance can be read in relation to a number of stories, without being reduced to single story. By a setting up a dialog, which includes everyday stories, it is possible to rewrite stories, the narrative of the culture. Stories frequently take the form of stories of origins, but it has been argued that they are fruitfully read as "originary" in this sense of being generative *in the now*. This relates to Freud's argument about the temporality of psychical processes and the effectivity of the past in the present. Thus a rewriting of stories, in part, consists in bringing this temporality to light—a rewriting of "origins." Despite the structure of stories, they are not in the past; they refer us forward. (1991: 190; emphasis added)

There are two facets of Game's strategy for storytelling, of writing and rewriting the social, that are pertinent to my project. The first is that in engaging the multiplicity of stories of self and other we are always situated and in movement amid stories, always in-between rather than fixedly here or there. Or perhaps a better way of saying it is that through the strategy of multiplicity we rewrite *where we are* in order to understand *how we got there*. Through such rewriting, I would argue, it is possible to disrupt the seeming fixity and essential "truth" of the hegemonic logic of emplacement and emplotment in the narrative of fortune and virtue. As a strategy of ethnographic interpretation and writing, the methodology of multiplicity entails articulating the (auto-)biographical narratives of wealthy men with a polyphony of voices, texts, and stories in the contemporary moral economy of wealth: stories of myself engaged in the rituals of research and writing; stories of wealth, power, and sovereignty in the popular culture; and stories of those who comprise the "other" at the margins of the moral economy of wealth whose very lack of wealth, power, and sovereignty is crucial to sustaining the metaphysics of presence of the narrative of fortune and virtue.

In addition to embracing multivocality and multitextuality in telling the stories of the moral economy of wealth, I also want to focus on the second facet of Game's methodology, which is to engage in a rewriting of stories of origin in terms of how they are "generative in the now." My desire in this book is to articulate or link together the practice of dislocative storytelling with a genealogy of how particular locations of subjectivity are conjured through storytelling. One primary means by which I will attempt to displace the logic of emplacement and emplotment embodied in the narrative of fortune and virtue is by deploying the genealogical analysis of rhetoric and discourse as an interpretative analysis of stories of place or location.

The genealogical analysis of the narrativity of location and place begins, of course, with Foucault. In an interview conducted not long before his death in 1984, Foucault was asked why he spent so much time interrogating the history of institutions such as the prison, the clinic, and the asylum rather than directing his prodigious intellect toward contemporary social problems. Foucault (1988: 262) responded by saying, "I set off from a problem expressed in current terms today, and I try to work out its genealogy. Genealogy means that I begin my analysis from a question posed in the present." Indeed, Foucault (1979: 31) himself had already posed and answered that question in *Discipline and Punish* when he wrote: "Why [genealogy]? Simply because I am interested in the past? No, if one means by that a writing of the history of the past in terms of the present. Yes, if this means writing a history of the present."

It is this fundamental distinction between a history of the past and the history of the present that is often lost upon the Foucault-inspired practitioners of the so-called new historicism in cultural studies (cf. Vesser, 1989). Genealogy is not concerned with how the past has led to the present, particularly if the present is conceived of or assumed to be an inevitable telos of the past. Rather, genealogy is always located in the present. As Charles Shepardson (1995: 50) insightfully argues, "Genealogy always *begins* from within a particular situation, and may perhaps be more properly understood as an act-an act aimed at the present, rather than a knowledge serenely directed elsewhere, towards the past, the place of the other, where it can be contained." Genealogy differs from the assumptions of intellectual history and historical sociology in two key respects. First, it does not share the ideological assumptions that the "history" of discourse or institutions is linear and progressive. Rather, the genealogical story is one of discontinuous transformation and mutation in patterns of social thoughts and practices in Western culture. The story of Western culture is not one of progressive enlightenment and the cultivation of truth; it is one of a will to power and domination whereby particular conceptions of individuality, autonomy, community, nationality, race, gender, sexuality, modernity, and so on are produced and struggled over through discourse. For every single "truth" concerning the nature of the individual and the workings of society that is enshrined in the history of social thought, a multiplicity of competing truths are marginalized and silenced. Thus, in constructing a genealogical analysis, one focuses not simply on the enduring "truths" of Western society but also on the competing "truths" over which they triumphed. Accordingly, *genealogy* is an intellectual exercise in the practice of memory-work whereby the conditions under which prevailing, contemporary conceptions of self and society emerged are recovered and critically interrogated.

This means that genealogy as a history of the present is not only located in the present; it is also about locations in the present. As a practice of memory-work, genealogy seeks to interrogate the epistemological assumptions and ontological categories that are the foundations of identity embedded in the present of the late-twentieth-century West. This means that genealogy is concerned with how we are located or placed within the social imaginary of contemporary society or, more specifically, with the positions of enunciation from which we speak and construct narratives that organize our present experience. Thus, from a genealogical perspective, emplacement and emplotment are always-already linked together. As such, the genealogy of space, place, and story is absolutely essential to the critical analysis of the narrative of fortune and virtue and the moral economy of wealth.

The emplacement and emplotment of moral identity entails a rhetorical process through which imaginary topoi are conjured and sustained. These topoi are places of "common sense" and shared meaning where individuals and social groups locate and define their identity.[14] My genealogical examination of different topoi in the moral economy of wealth entails two moments in this rhetorical conjuring of space, place, and identity. Following Dick Hebdige's (1987: 14) insightful analysis of the rhetorical conjuring of place and identity through music, I will call these moments, respectively, the "evocative" and the "invocative." The *moment of evocation* is constituted by the (auto-)biographical narratives that are contained in the interviews with my wealthy male respondents. In this moment of rhetoric, these individuals are attempting to create for themselves, as well as for those who would be the audience for their stories, a topos, a place of identity where wealthy men are, at one and the same time, virtuous men. Yet this evocative moment of the conjuring of place in the present simultaneously involves a *moment of invocation*, or the calling forth or summoning of places of wealth and virtue conjoined that have been created in the past.[15] In this regard, the basic premise of this book can be restated as follows: If you want to understand how the "better angels" of capitalism are able to take flight and soar in the moral economy of the present, it is imperative to understand, on the basis of the genealogical analysis of the discourses of wealth and virtue, how they were given their wings in the moral economies of the past.

The final part of my methodology of multiplicity is to link my analyses of the narrative of fortune and virtue and its genealogy to the broader social terrain, both literally and figuratively, in which the moral economy of wealth operates. I want to situate my analysis of emplacement and emplotment in material as well as symbolic space. In recent years, there has been growing recognition of the need, to paraphrase the subtitle of Edward Soja's influential book, *Postmodern Geographies* (1989), to reinsert space into critical social theory and analysis. Soja offers a compelling critique of one of the key canonical texts of sociology, Mills's *The Sociological Imagination* (1959). Working within the social ontology of C. Wright Mills's twin concepts of "history" and "biography," sociologists have forgotten that not only do they entail a narrative emplotment that is constructed in time but that they also are constructed and unfold in geographical space. Soja rightly points out that for the "sociological imagination" geographical space only provides the background setting, the "milieu" for history and biography. Indeed, whenever space is evoked in ethnographic writing, it is generally done so only to set the scene for the narrative rather than as a site that is both constitutive of as well as constituted by narrative. Once again, emplacement and emplotment, space and story, are intertwined.

Perhaps the best evocation of this relationship between emplacement and emplotment in spatial terms is provided by de Certeau (1984: 113): "Space is a practiced place," he says, a location that is actualized as a site of social practice through stories and narrative. As Kathleen Stewart explains the logic by which narrative and the cartographic are conjoined in such spatial stories, "Picture how, in story, world is mediated by word, fact moves into the realm of interpretation to be plumbed for significance, how act moves into action and agency, and how the landscape becomes a space in-filled with paths of action and imagination, danger and vulnerability" (Stewart, 1996: 27). Moreover, as Soja also argues, this relationship between space, place, and story is an often ignored dimension of Foucault's own genealogical project. As Foucault said in one of his later interviews, "Space is fundamental to any form of communal life; space is fundamental to any exercise of power" (1984: 252). For Foucault, the genealogical project should strive not only to articulate formations of discourse and subjectivity in a history of a present but also to link the places where discourse is enacted and embodied in space as a site of practice.

Accordingly, I engage in a critical cartography of the situated and ambivalent character of the moral truths of wealth by examining multiple locations of their enactment. Inspired by Walter Benjamin's Arcades

Project (cf. Buck-Morss, 1989), as well as by contemporary work in the critical analysis of spatiality and representation, I map the connections and passages between an array of different spaces for the performance of the moral identities of wealth and power in the landscape of capitalist culture. My own cartography includes: autobiographical reflections on my travels in the "field" during the course of research and in my role as interlocutor of the life-stories of wealthy men; ethnographic interpretations of different sites of wealth and power, such as an elite dining club in a Seattle skyscraper, Andrew Carnegie's law library at Drake University, and Mount Auburn Cemetery in Boston; and conversations with patrons of working-class bars as they consume televised spectacles of wealth, fortune, and virtue, such as *Wheel of Fortune*. These explorations allow me to connect the rhetorical practices of wealthy men in the present—and the genealogical history of the moral economy of wealth—with different symbolic and material spatial contexts in contemporary American culture within which the dream of sovereign self-mastery and masculinity is imagined and embodied in ways that contradict the very meaning of this dream itself.

Mapping the Analysis of the "Better Angels"

These three different modes of analysis, the ethnographic, the genealogical, and the cartographic, will be used in concert to map the moral economy of wealth and the moral identity of contemporary men of wealth in the United States. In order to do this, my analysis will proceed in the following manner.

My substantive analysis of the moral economy of wealth begins in Chapter 2 with a consideration of how wealth as empowerment is experienced in the everyday life-world of wealthy men. Here I argue that wealth provides spatial and temporal empowerment through which wealthy men construct autonomous realms of freedom and sovereign self-mastery, or "principalities," that embody their personal goals and desires, or "individuality." However, as I suggest above, the view that the possession of wealth itself entails empowerment is a core assumption of both common sense as well as sociology and has serious limitations in understanding how power itself is rhetorically constituted as moral identity. Accordingly, in the second part of Chapter 2 I move from a consideration of wealth as power in terms of capacity to the question of how the empowerment of wealth is morally made sense of by wealthy men through the flow of power/knowledge. Here I argue that the empowerment of wealth in the everyday is dependent upon a particular narrative form that enables wealthy men to know and make sense of their power as a sign of virtuous moral identity. By examining two very different (auto-)biographical narratives of wealthy men, I explore in more detail how the intertwined dynamics of emplotment and emplacement in the narrative of fortune and virtue constitute the primary form of this power/knowledge in the moral economy of wealth. The teleology of this narrative of fortune and virtue is a coherent self-identity that enables these men to make moral sense of their power and prestige as right and legitimate.

The narrative of fortune and virtue is the dominant narrative of masculinity in Western capitalist culture. In order to understand its efficacy as a form of power/knowledge, it is necessary to locate it in the historical context of its origins and consider how it is generative of the moral identity of wealthy men in the present. Chapter 3 is devoted to this genealogical analysis. Niccolò Machiavelli was the foremost interlocutor of the narrative of fortune and virtue as a modern story of masculinity and power. Machiavelli's social and political theory was based on ancient Roman concepts of *fortuna*—the material conditions of life provided by chance and necessity—and *virtù*—the courage, discipline, and will of individual men to overcome *fortuna*. I argue that his understanding of fortune and individual virtue provides the basic terms for understanding the relationships between the moral worth and virtue of men, the ownership of property and the accumulation of wealth, and philanthropy and civic participation.

In Machiavelli's social ontology and cosmology, the masculine individual was placed at the center of the world and given license to create a realm of autonomy and power by imposing his will upon the chance and chaos of fortune. For Machiavelli, as a story that emplotted the creation of the sovereign masculine self, the spatial landscape within which the narrative of fortune and virtue was to be emplaced and enacted was primarily political. Masculine autonomy was to be found within the realm of the city-state and maintained through the public-minded virtues of civic republicanism. The narrative of fortune and virtue provides more than an Ur-script for the performance and presentation of the bourgeois self. It also contains figural characters that enact the moral drama of the triumph of virtue over fortune. For Machiavelli, there were several such figures, two of which are relevant for my analysis: the Founder, the creator of social and political order; and the Citizen, the active contributor to civic life and the collective life of society. These two characters represent different polarities in the discursive field of moral economy of wealth, providing two contrasting models of virtuous behavior that coexist uneasily in the social imaginary of capitalism as they embody the contradictory relationship between heroic individual autonomy, civic virtue, and the accumulation of property and wealth.

In Chapter 4 I examine the emergence of the marketplace as one of the dominant symbolic and material spaces within which men of wealth enact the narrative of fortune and virtue and locate their moral identity. My analysis is framed by a question that has been directed toward the activity of money-making and wealth accumulation in Western culture since antiquity: How much is enough? From Aristotle through Aquinas, from Machiavelli and the Renaissance civic humanists to the progenitors of the "Protestant Ethic," this question could never be answered on its own terms. Rather, it could only be answered by reference to another question: What is the rationale for making money? The answer to both questions, I argue, is provided by a moral calculus that is embedded in the language and discourse of the market as a space of social activity and a place of ethical purpose. I argue that the Scottish Enlightenment engendered a new ethical language of virtue that enables modern men of the marketplace to morally account for their wealth. Thus, I engage in a genealogical analysis of the moral space of the "marketplace" as it is invoked in the rhetoric of selfhood of several wealthy men I interviewed as well as in the discourses of Adam Smith, David Hume, and other figures of the Scottish Enlightenment that effected a major transformation in the narrative fortune and virtue. The discursive terrain upon which fortune and virtue operate shifts decisively from the political to the economic, where the marketplace became the space where the narrative of fortune and virtue was to be emplaced and emplotted. In this brave new world of "commercial society," the goddess Fortuna is banished and the circumference of her wheel of fortune is straightened into a road that stretches to an ever-receding horizon that marks the developmental progress of this society's drive toward opulence and wealth. Further, this road is traveled by a moral character, *homo mercator* or "Market Man," whose virtue is no longer "civic" (as with the Citizen) or "heroic" (as with the Founder) as these terms were understood by civic republicanism. Rather, this character's virtue is circumspect and private, conjured in the context of the marketplace of commercial society, and consists of acts of self-interest that have the unintended yet happy consequence of producing public justice through the creation of private wealth. Through the conjuring of a moral character whose virtuous conduct is appropriate to the marketplace, the notion of civic virtue and heroic *virtù* are transformed and mutated into a new narrative configuration.

In Chapter 5 I examine the distinctively American transformation in the narrative of fortune and virtue, which was an intrinsic part of the triumph of industrial capitalism in the nineteenth century. My primary focus here is on the emergence of a distinctive discourse of philanthropy. I move from a concern with the discourses that pertain primarily with the production and accumulation of wealth, and its concomitant autonomy and freedom, to those discourses that construct the moral obligation and duty of the wealthy to others and society at large. Although the wealthy in America had always been exhorted to acts of charity in order to be "good Christians," during the nineteenth century there emerged a number of discourses that recast the meaning of benevolence for the upper class. According to older Christian discourses of charity, benevolent behavior was a matter of individual conscience. In contrast, the new discourses of philanthropy articulated beneficence as a duty and moral responsibility of the wealthy *as a class* in capitalist society. I will discuss two variants of the new discourse of philanthropy: the steward-citizen model of the Brahmin aristocracy of Boston and the steward-entrepreneur model of the Gilded Age robber barons, best exemplified and articulated by Andrew Carnegie. I will also explore how these models are invoked in the (auto-)biographical narratives of two contemporary philanthropists.[16]

In Chapter 6, I bring the forgoing analysis of the moral economy of wealth and its embodiment in the mythological narrative of the American dream to bear on the cultural politics surrounding the increasing inequality of wealth and income in the United States. For George Bush, the trajectory of the narrative of fortune and virtue ends with the ascent of the "better angels" of capitalism: the men of wealth who know that "prosperity has a purpose." However, as the so-called American century draws to close, it has become abundantly clear that those for whom the prosperity of capitalist wealth has seemingly no purpose are vast and increasing. If a democratic form of civil society is to survive in America in the next century, I contend that we must conjure and imagine a different narrative of social being and becoming. Moreover, I argue that elements of this dream can be found in conceptions of fortune, virtue, and selfhood that have been part of Western culture and the American dream yet have been historically marginalized by the hegemonic dream of self-mastery inscribed by the moral economy of wealth. In these conceptions, individuality entails interdependence, autonomy encompasses community, and sovereignty designates a realm of sharing and gift-giving. In the end, I argue, we need to imagine and enact a narrative in which, *in* the end, we are all better angels.

Notes

1. In order to be included in the sample, an individual had to have a minimum net worth of $1 million and an annual income of $250,000 or more. These criteria, although relatively modest, put all of our respondents safely within the top 1–2 percent of the population in terms of wealth and income distribution. Most of our sample commanded financial resources far in excess of these minimum criteria, with 47 percent of the respondents having assets of $5 million or above. Other demographic characteristics of the sample include the following: 60 percent were men, 40 percent were women; 52 percent inherited wealth, 48 percent earned it through their own business activity; and 97 percent were Caucasian. For further

description of the sample as well as the methodological procedures of the research, see Schervish and Herman (1988).

2. With one exception, the men in this study have been given pseudonyms and their geographical location has been changed in order to protect their anonymity.

3. I would argue that a lack of attentiveness to the politics of the language of wealth implied by these questions constitutes a serious deficiency in contemporary studies of the wealthy in general and their philanthropic activity in particular. Two particularly noteworthy examples of such work are Odendahl (1990) and Ostrower (1995). Both offer a very cogent analysis of the power of the wealthy in being able to pursue their own vision of the "public good" to their class advantage. However, their analysis is marred by an insufficient attention to the particular language of civic virtue and moral obligation that is characteristic of the American capitalist class. From their perspective, the language of citizenship and civic responsibility that is so prominent among the wealthy is materially ephemeral to their class power rather than, as is my perspective, materially constitutive of it. It is this perspective, and the analysis that flows from it, that represents the major contribution of this work to the study of wealth, class, and philanthropy.

4. To say that the production of *truth* is a function of the *imaginary* is not at all a contradictory proposition. I use the term "imaginary" in the sense employed by Cornelius Castoriadis (1987), that is, as a designation of the space of signification and semiurgy within which both sociohistorical and psychic-biographical worlds are created or "imagined." Thus, the "social imaginary," as Castoriadis terms it, is not a representational space that reflects or distorts the "real" but is constitutive of it as truth. In other words, the imaginary is fictive but not false and is thus both symbolic and material.

5. I designate the interview narratives as "(auto-)biographical" for two reasons. The first is to emphasize their peculiar status as stories of the self. The interview narratives are joint productions of the interaction between interviewer and interviewee. Thus, even though interviews involve a biographical narration of the self by the respondent, they are not strictly "autobiographical" in the sense that they were not initiated or "solely scripted" by the individual. The second reason stems from the theoretical premises of this book. The notion of an autobiography that is "scripted" entirely by the self is a myth, as the ability to conjure a moral self-identity is dependent upon discursively constructed subject positions in the social imaginary. Thus, the notion of a centered subject who is the sole author of his or her "autobiography" needs to be decentered and problematized as the self is spoken as much as it speaks.

6. However, in making this argument concerning the narrative of fortune and virtue, and in offering a rationale for dealing only with the wealthy men we interviewed, I want to state most emphatically that I am not endorsing either an "essentialist" ontology, such as that of Gilligan (1982), or a "standpoint" epistemology of gender, such as that of Harstock (1987, 1990) or Smith (1987). As poststructuralist feminists such as Patricia Clough (1994), Rosemary Hennesey (1993) and Chris Weedon (1987) have cogently argued, what essentialist and standpoint feminists argue (although they protest otherwise) is how "experience" of the "real" is constituted through discursively constructed subject positions that are articulated with different existential locations within structures of

power. My analysis of the moral economy of wealth that follows is focused on these interstices between the discursive and the existential, although it is more concerned with the former rather than latter. My primary concern here is with how the narrative of fortune and virtue and its constituent discourses enable men to make moral sense of their wealth and power. In other words, my argument is that the masculine character of the moral truth of wealth rooted in discursively constructed subject positions is bounded by particular conceptions of fortune and virtue and not by any notion of sex as moral destiny or experience as being an incorrigible index of the real.

7. Three additional questions need to be addressed regarding the relationship between the individuals I interviewed and the narrative of fortune and virtue: Is it only the wealthy men we interviewed who articulate their identity through this masculine narrative of fortune and virtue? Did *all* wealthy men we interviewed do so? And, finally, to the extent that wealthy men do speak themselves through the language of this narrative, how did they learn it? The answer to the first question is negative and is congruent with the position concerning the discursive nature of masculinity elaborated in note 6 above. One does not necessarily have to physically be a man in order to find a comfortable subject position within the masculine configuration of the narrative of fortune and virtue (though this is unusual). Accordingly, there were a few women who articulated their moral identity through its language and vocabulary. However, most of the women we interviewed drew upon different configurations of discourses, such as those concerning domestic virtues of the private sphere, benevolent femininity, and the ethic of care, in order to articulate their moral identity. Early on in this project, I ascertained that a genealogical analysis of comparable size and scope would be needed to render the "feminine" rhetoric of the virtuous wealthy self intelligible (for starters in this direction, see Benhabib, 1993; Ginzberg, 1991; McCarthy, 1982, 1991). Thus, I decided to exclude the women in our interview sample from my analysis. By the same token, the answer to the second question is also negative. There were a few men who attempted to craft a moral identity with terms other than those of the discourses I examine here. Accordingly, I am not claiming that all men of wealth are smoothly interpellated into the subject position constructed by the discourses that I analyze. But this does not vitiate the thrust of my argument and analysis, which is aimed toward elucidating the dominant and hegemonic positions within the moral economy of wealth. Finally, with respect to the last question, the focus of my analysis is on the language of wealth itself and not on the socialization processes by which such language is learned. Accordingly, I make no claims concerning how or how well this language is learned.

8. The importance of the development of linear perspective to the epistemological centering of the modern bourgeois subject cannot be overestimated. John Berger (1973) points out that "the convention of [linear] perspective, which is unique to European art and which was first established in the early Renaissance, centers everything on the eye of the beholder. It is like a beam from a lighthouse—only instead of light traveling outwards, appearances travel in. The conventions called those appearances *reality*. Perspective makes the single eye the center of the visible world. Everything converges onto the eye as to the vanishing point of infinity. The visible is arranged for the spectator, as the universe was

once thought to be arranged for God" (16). As I argue in Chapter 3 in relation to the discursive figuring of the bourgeois subject in Florentine Renaissance capitalism, there is a definite connection between the development of linear perspective, the emergence of mercantile capitalism, and the narrative of fortune and virtue that figured and bound individual biography to the history of the state and economy. As Victor Burgin (1987) has argued, it is on the basis of the dominant specularity of this "monocular perspective," and the egocentric world it creates, that the subject of mercantile capitalism is "free to pursue its entrepreneurial ambitions wherever trade winds blow"(25).

9. I emphasize the words *force* and *form* to draw attention to the necessity of taking both into account in the course of analyzing the workings of narrative. Referring to the structuralist emphasis on the morphology of narrative that has dominated much critical work in this area during the past three decades (e.g., early Barthes, Genette, and Greimas), Jacques Derrida (1978: 4) provocatively suggests that "form fascinates when one no longer has the force to understand force from within itself." What Derrida means by force are the discursive dynamics that give rise to and shape particular narrative structures, as well as to the energies within a narrative that compels one to tell it and another to listen to it.

10. In claiming a deficit of authoritative sovereignty for my vision, I am giving notice to what Foucault (1972: 50–55) terms the "enunciative modality" of discourse. For Foucault, the truth value of discourse (or, as in the case here, a story) is as much a function of how things are said or written as what is said or written. More specifically, the power of discourse is dependent upon the institutional status and position of those who speak as well as the site from which they speak. As an entrepreneur, philanthropist, and, above all, member of the club, Norris is sanctioned to proffer his discourse and vision of the world and have it accepted as a privileged perspective. That is, after all, why I am at this site and in his presence.

11. I use the phrase *power elite* as defined and elaborated by G. William Domhoff (1970, 1979, 1983). For Domhoff, the power elite consists of the leadership vanguard of the upper social class that is able to exert hegemonic influence and control over the social, economic, and political institutions of a community (which can be defined either locally or nationally). Although Domhoff's definition of the "upper social class" encompasses the Marxist focus on structural positions of ownership and control within social relations of/in production, it has the virtue of also including a Weberian concern with the institutions and rituals of social closure (such as elite schools, social clubs, formal and informal networks of association, etc.) that give social classes cohesiveness and cultural identity. At one level, the Capital City Club may be seen as a site of social closure. However, as Norris described its purposes, such socializing and socialization functions seem to be secondary to facilitating the articulation of business interests in the community (see note 12 below). For a overview of recent literature on the composition and organization on the American upper class see Mintz (1989).

12. Useem argues that, historically, there have been three modes of conceptualizing the social organization of the capitalist elite: the "upper-class principle," the "corporate principle," and the "classwide principle." The *upper-class principle* places the locus of elite power in a matrix of institutions and practices, such as private schools, social clubs, philanthropic networks, and family-controlled

businesses, that serve to reproduce the status and cohesiveness of a select number of established wealthy families. According to this principle, political-economic behavior is primarily driven by the interest of preserving the social boundaries of the upper class by protecting the intergenerational transfer of wealth and status. The *corporate principle* narrowly locates the power and interest of capitalists within the organizational confines of particular large corporations, and political-economic behavior is governed by the desire to maximize the profitability and competitive position of the firm. Finally, the classwide principle, according to Useem, subsumes the other two within its logic. The *classwide principle* locates the hegemonic center of capitalist power within a transcorporate network of interlocking company directorates, business associations, governing bodies of nonprofit organizations, and acquaintanceship circles. Useem argues that this principle fosters political-economic activity that is guided by the aggregated interests of the business community and is thus able to transcend the more narrowly defined interests of either the upper social class or particular corporations.

13. My use of the concept of *trace* here may connote more of a residual presence of forgotten or repressed discourses than Derrida's own definition would allow. As he explains (rather enigmatically) in *Speech and Phenomena,* trace is "not a presence but is rather the simulacrum of presence that dislocates, displaces, and refers beyond itself. The trace has properly speaking, no place, for effacement belongs to the very structure of the trace" (1973: 142). For Derrida, the differential relations of what he calls "radical alterity" that compose presence or identity are never present to consciousness, as presence continually effaces these relations. In deploying the concept, I wish to inflect it with a Gramscian emphasis on "trace" as an archaeological metaphor for the ideological sediment of "common sense," which for Gramsci (1971) is the "product of the historical process to date which has deposited in you an infinity of traces without leaving an inventory" (324).

14. The argument that rhetoric is centrally concerned with topoi or common places in the social imaginary is hardly original. The association between rhetoric and the "common place" goes back to Aristotle's *Rhetoric.* However, in Aristotle and the classical tradition of rhetoric, the meaning of *topoi* or topics as "common places" is limited to a shared source of arguments for persuasion (cf. Barilli, 1989; Vickers, 1988). I want to emphasize the formative and productive, as well as the strictly argumentative, dimensions of rhetoric as a social practice. Thus, the topos of the moral economy of wealth is not simply a resource for rhetorical argument about wealth and the wealthy but is also an imagined place created through rhetoric. I am indebted to the work of Michael Billig (1991) and John Shotter (1983, 1989), which has enabled me to evoke this dimension of rhetoric as a central part of my analysis.

15. It is important to emphasize, once again, that by insisting on a link between these two moments of rhetorical conjuring I am not implying that there is necessarily an explicit socialization process whereby the wealthy men in my sample were specifically taught the discourses through which they evoke and invoke places of virtue. The focus of my analysis on how such topoi become *common* places, or hegemonic orderings of sense and identity in the moral economy of capitalism, and not how particular wealthy men as individuals learn the language of such places through which they speak and constitute their identity.

16. There are two points I would like to make about the scope and validity of the genealogical dimension of my analysis. First, I should note that this particular genealogical history of the present of the narrative of fortune and virtue is not, and not intended to be, exhaustive or comprehensive in scope. There are several figures and moments in the history of the moral economy of wealth that are either relegated to the background or not considered at all. There is a strong argument to be made that any genealogical of the moral "truth" of wealth should consider the contributions of, for instance, the possessive individualism of Hobbes and Locke, the call to communitarian citizenship of Tocqueville, or the character of the rational, calculating, economizing individual of neoclassical marginalism. My response to such an argument, following Foucault, is that a genealogy of discourses is not a search for essential pristine meanings or their ultimate point of origins but a tracing of the historical trajectory of the struggles and alliances between discourses through which meaning is created and sustained (Foucault, 1977). The genealogy I am undertaking here is intended to be a "case history" or "effective history" of the narrative of fortune and virtue, as opposed to a "history" in the traditional disciplinary sense of the word and the practice (cf. Cousins and Hussein, 1984; Dean, 1994 Minson, 1985). Histories and case or effective-histories operate according to different criteria of validity. Histories attempt a reconstruction of the past and are therefore governed by the evidentiary standard of exhaustiveness. In contrast, case histories are governed by the standard of intelligibility. They seek to render intelligible particular dimensions of the past, not in terms of the way they "really were," but in terms of the conditions under which they discursively emerge and exist so that we can understand their efficaciousness as constructions of the moral "truth" of wealth in the present. My selection of Machiavelli, Adam Smith, David Hume, Samuel Atkins Eliot, and Andrew Carnegie has been guided by the principle of intelligibility, and I believe that for the purposes of my analysis they sufficiently represent the most fundamental and important nodal points in the moral economy of wealth and the narrative of fortune and virtue. Second, it is important to note that in arguing that the narrative of fortune and virtue configures the rhetorical self-presentation of wealthy men I am not contending that there is a cause-and-effect relationship between the forms this narrative assumes in the thought of Machiavelli, Smith, and Carnegie and how they are manifested in the biographies of my respondents. The validity of my argument does not rest upon whether or not the interviewees heard of, read, invoke, or in any way were directly or explicitly influenced by these people or their ideas. Rather, the validity of my argument depends on whether or not I can reveal a resonant affinity between the language of wealthy men and the discursive field and narrative pattern that my genealogy seeks to uncover. What this resonance involves is not a linear relationship between history and the present but an evocation of how history is embedded in the present. When such a resonance is heard, it reveals a "shared code, a set of interlocking tropes and similitude that function not only as the objects, but as the conditions of representation" (Greenblatt, 1986: 46). In acoustic terms, resonance is the prolongation of sound produced by sympathetic vibration. This notion of resonance provides, I think, an apt metaphor for understanding the purpose of this genealogy, for it entails lending a critical ear to the voices of the past and trying to discern the sympathetic

vibrations that echo them in the present. As cultural critic Greil Marcus (1989: 33) has argued, "If one can stop looking at the past and start listening to it, one might hear echoes of a new conversation; then the task of the critic would be to lead speakers unaware of each other's existence to talk to one another." This is precisely the intent and goal of my genealogy of the emplacement and emplotment of the narrative of fortune and virtue: to engage in a conversation with those who speak the language of wealth, both past and present, and to bring them into conversation with one another.

2

Story Spaces of Identity:
Wealth, Power, and Narrativity
in the Everyday

Stories are not just practical and symbolic actions: they are part of the political process. Stories ooze through the political stream. Power is not so much an all or nothing phenomenon, which people either have or don't have, and which resides either here or there. Rather, it is best viewed as flow, a process, a pulsate-oscillating and undulating throughout the social world and working to pattern the degree of control people experience and have over their lives. . . . Power is a process that weaves its way through embodied social life and everything in its wake. Stories live in this flow of power.
—Ken Plummer (1995: 26)

We do not tell stories, we live them; they do not simply describe reality, they constitute it, not as God might, from outside, but as part of reality's very stuff.
—Ann Game and Andrew Metcalfe (1996: 76)

My substantive analysis of the moral economy of wealth begins with a consideration of how wealth as power and empowerment is experienced, and how that experience is narrated or storied, in the everyday life-world of wealthy men. This is an obvious starting point, as it is the power of wealth in a capitalist society that is at the core of its seductive charm and allure, the fount of the regard and esteem given to men of wealth, as well as the source of envy and resentment often felt toward them. It is also, as George Bush argued, the basis of "prosperity with a purpose" that allows the "better angels" to take flight. My interviews were filled with very expansive descriptions of how wealthy men feel themselves to be empowered, whether in terms of personal life, business activity, or philanthropic involvement. Accordingly, the first section of this chapter is based on these descriptions of the mundane, quotidian uses of wealth in the ethnographic interviews. Here I argue that wealth provides spatial and temporal empowerment through which wealthy men construct autonomous realms of freedom and sovereign self-mastery, or "principalities," that embody their personal goals and desires, or "individuality." Moreover, this empowerment of wealth enables

wealthy men to create not only a world of social engagement and practice of their own making in the form of business enterprises, philanthropic foundations, or political influence but also a world that sets the
conditions of social practice for others.

However, it is important to recall how Edward Hoffman responded
when asked about the meaning of wealth as power: "*You* know what the
word [wealth] means. It's *in* the dictionary and I don't have to repeat the
dictionary. It is an obvious and trivial question." The news that wealth is
a resource of power in everyday life, and that wealthy men understand
themselves to be powerful, is hardly earth-shattering. But beyond the
obviousness of the fact that wealth is intertwined with power, there is a
more important analytical issue at stake, which is how wealth as power
as storied. As Ken Plummer eloquently states in the first epigraph
above, power is best understood not simply as a manifestation of resources or capacities that people either have or don't have but as an om-
nipresent proccessural flow that is embodied in the conduct of social
life. That is to say, to paraphrase Foucault, power isn't simply repressive
or coercive; it is productive and constitutive of all forms of embodiment,
identity, and agency—whether those of the privileged or the marginalized. From a Foucauldian perspective, one of the principle ways in
which power is manifested and flows through the social is through
rhetorical practices of knowledge and discourse, of which narrative is an
important form.

Accordingly, in the second section of this chapter I move from a consideration of wealth as a resource of power to the question of how the
meaning of wealth is constituted with the flow of power/knowledge. For
Foucault, the couplet of power/knowledge means being able to do something (power) only as you are able to make sense of it (knowledge).
Knowing and doing are dynamic processes, processes that are narrativized in stories that as Plummer says "live in this flow of power." Consequently, I argue that the empowerment of wealth in the everyday is dependent on a particular narrative form that enables wealthy men to
know and make sense of their power as a sign of virtuous moral identity.
I conclude by positing that the primary form of this power/knowledge in
the moral economy of wealth is the narrative of fortune and virtue. Moreover, not only do stories live in the flow of power/knowledge; as A.
Game and A. Metcalfe point out in the second epigraph, they give life
and shape to moral identity. Through living the stories we tell, the flow
of power/knowledge is transmuted into the form of the subject. As both
flow and form, the narrative of fortune and virtue constitutes a *story
space*, a particular articulation of emplotment and emplacement, that is
the basis for the rhetorical performance of the wealthy masculine self as a
virtuous masculine self.

"It's Obvious":
The Banal Truth of Wealth as Power in the Everyday

Agency, Power, and Wealth

For Hoffman, the positive correlation of wealth and power is so "obvious," "trivial," and commonsensical that it is not worthy of comment or elaboration. To say that the possession of wealth entails power is, in a word, banal. However, for those interested in the micropolitics of subjectivity and moral identity, in how power is embodied and enacted by wealthy men in the everyday, the banality of this power is precisely the place to start. As Foucault (1983: 210) argues: "Everybody is aware of banal facts. But the fact that they are banal doesn't mean they don't exist. What we have to do with banal facts is to discover—or try to discover—which specific and perhaps original problem is connected with them."

The specific, and perhaps original, problem with Hoffman's banal truth of wealth, I would argue, is the very incorrigibility of the common-sense understanding of wealth as power, an understanding that has also dominated Western social and political theory for centuries. That is to say, the truth of this understanding is so seemingly obvious that it is rarely scrutinized or questioned. Accordingly, I will begin my examination of the relationship of wealth and power by questioning its obvious and banal "truth" on its lexicographic, commonsensical, and sociological terms.

Following Hoffman's directive and looking up the meaning of *wealth* and *power* in my dictionary, this is what I find:

> **wealth** *n.* 1. a great quantity of valuable material possessions or resources. 2. The state of being rich, affluence. 3. A profusion or abundance. (Morris, 1978: 1451)

> **pow•er** *n.* 1. the ability or capacity to act or perform effectively. 2. *often plural.* A specific capacity, faculty or aptitude. 3. strength or force exerted or being capable of being exerted, might. 4. the ability or capacity to exercise control; authority. (Morris, 1978: 1027)

Taking the lexicographical as an index of the banal truth of wealth and power, as Hoffman would have me do, wealth is intertwined with power because it is a possession or resource that enhances the ability and capacity of individuals to act effectively in the world by exercising control and authority over self and others. It is this capacity for worldly efficaciousness that makes wealth, as my dictionary defines it, a "valuable material possession or resource." It is also precisely this attribute of wealth that Hoffman underscores when he says, "It's quite simple: my money enables me to do what I want to do, when I want to do it, and how I want to do it."

A similar yet somewhat more expansive explanation of this relation-ship between wealth and power was provided by Nicholas Whimster, a relatively young owner of a software firm, who succinctly explained:

> Well, I guess it [wealth and money] can't provide happiness. But it sure can do a lot. I think probably security. It provides power. You know, when it gets down to it, the whole ball game is about power. Money just provides power. If I say to my secretary, "No, don't go to lunch," she doesn't go to lunch. That's power. And that's what money buys. You can buy what you want. You can get people to do what you want. Money to me buys a comfortable way of life. You know, security and an ability to do the things you would like to do.

The commonsensical and lexicographical truth of wealth as power is also reflected in sociology. In sociological terms, whether from a Marxist or Weberian perspective, wealth becomes power because it is a resource for individual and social *agency*. Further, because it is distributed unequally among individuals and social groups, wealth constitutes one of the pri-mary axes of social stratification and inequality. For Michael Mann (1986: 6), the power of agency is expressed as the "ability to pursue and attain goals," and as both Hoffman and Whimster say, wealth and money en-able them to pursue and attain their wants and desires, to do whatever it is they would like to do. Anthony Giddens takes this notion of power one step farther by arguing that power is "the capacity of the individual agent to 'make a difference' to a preexisting state of affairs" (1984: 14). And for Hoffman, Whimster, and other men of wealth in the study, wealth is most assuredly a resource for making a difference in the fabric of everyday life, for themselves and for others.

In our original writing on the subject of wealth and power based on our research, Paul Schervish and I (1988, 1991) tried to deepen and ex-tend this particular sociological understanding of wealth as a resource of power in terms of Giddens's theory of social structuration.[1] For Giddens (1979, 1984), social structure has only a "virtual" existence, existing only at moments in time and space when embodied by individual agents en-dowed with a relatively high degree of reflexive self-consciousness. In contrast, agency cannot take place without the rules and resources of so-cial structure, such as wealth, that both enable and constrain individual and collective agency. According to Giddens, structure is "dual" because it is the medium and the outcome of agency. Structuration theory em-braces this notion of duality in order to accentuate the creative potential of human agency in relation to institutional existence.

In this respect, Schervish and I argued that an analysis of the unique characteristics of the wealthy in general (and not just wealthy men) reveals their privileged position in the process of structuration, not only in relation to social structure as medium (by having greater command over rules and resources) but also, more importantly, in relation to structure as outcome. In the creation and extension of principality through what we called *hyperagency*, the wealthy create structure in the form of institutional settings and organizational relations that further enhance their capacity for agency. It is not that the wealthy individual can single-handedly transform or create the broad structure encompassing society. But they can and do carry out this creative moment of structuration as a matter of course in their daily practices of work, business, family, philanthropy, and consumption. Whether inherited or earned, the possession of capital provides a set of material opportunities that places wealthy individuals apart from other people in society. In essence, the wealthy are able to translate ownership and control of wealth into a practice of hyperagency whereby they generate and govern a substantial portion of (rather than accommodate themselves to) the institutional environment in which they live.

In one of his more famous statements, Marx argued that even though people indeed make their own history they are not able to choose the conditions under which they do so. Although Marx was referring to collective agency, as C. Wright Mills (1959) argued, the same dictum basically holds for individual actors as well. However, the capacity to "make history," as well as the degree to which one is subject to institutional constraint, is not equally distributed across individual agents in society. The wealthy, it turns out, do "make history" for themselves and others. As a social practice of individuals, *hyperagency* refers to the enhanced capacity of wealthy individuals to exercise effective control over conditions under which they will engage in social action and, additionally, to set the boundaries or conditions for the historymaking potential of less empowered individuals. This capacity, to use Giddens's words, to "make a difference" in the dynamics of structuration may be mundane, as in Whimster's power to command his secretary not to take lunch, or spectacular, as in Ted Turner's recent $1 billion gift to the United Nations.

Regardless, for most individuals in a society with unequal distribution of wealth and power, their agency is limited to choosing among and acting within the constraints of positions effectively controlled by others. Among the most significant "others" in this scheme of historymaking capacities are those who own and control wealth as a power-resource. This process of worlding, the act of creating one's own principality as a realm of effective control in which one's individuality is materialized and realized, sets the wealthy apart from other individuals in society. The hyperagency of the wealthy can be summed up as follows: They create themselves by creating the world rather than finding themselves by finding a place in the world made by others. In terms of the practices of hyper-agency attendant upon the possession of wealth as a resource of power, Schervish and I argued that there are two principal forms of empower-ment: temporal empowerment and spatial empowerment.

Temporal Empowerment.   As Benjamin Franklin (1840: 87) inveighed in one of the canonical maxims of the modern capitalist *mentalité*, "Re-member that *time* is money." The pronouncement is simple, but its socio-logical import in terms of the structuration of modern society is pro-found. As Brian Adam (1990), Henri Lefebvre (1991), and John Urry (1995) have argued, in modern societies, where the experience of time has become quantified, measured, and subject to the disciplining rhythms of capitalist rationality, time becomes a scarce and valuable re-source. We organize our everyday lives by calendrical and clock time, which in turn structures time as a finite resource to be used, allocated, de-ployed, or wasted. As Adam (1990: 120) points out, "Social time needs to be conceptualized in terms of relations of power to the extent that clock time *as* time has become an independent, context-free value, a social and economic reality that structures, controls, disciplines, and provides norms for our social life." As such, time is a resource of power and agency.

It is precisely this status of time as resource of power that Franklin gives notice to in his pronouncement. Of course, time is not really the ex-istential or ontological equivalent of money for the simple reason that time, unlike money, cannot be saved. However, what money can do is to enhance one's control as to how time is organized and spent. As temporal empowerment, money and wealth enable one to appropriate time, in-cluding one's own and that of others. As Brendan Dwyer explains, his desire to be able to autonomously appropriate and allocate his time was a prime factor motivating his accumulation of wealth:

> My goal in the fifties, sixties, and early seventies was to rise as far as I could within the company, but at the same time, to accumulate assets that would produce an income independently of my own earnings. Why was this im-portant? Because in my own framework, assets independent of my own earnings let me determine how I would allocate my own time. If I'm em-ployed, some other authority, the one who is paying for my time, deter-mines how my time's employed. I've always had the feeling that I was a bet-ter judge of how I spent my time than somebody else. Now, that's the way I felt about it.

As Dwyer makes clear in this statement, autonomy and sovereignty over time as a resource is intimately connected. To the extent that he was

working for someone else and did not have wealth and income independent of his employment, his employer was sovereign over Dwyer's time,
thus constraining his temporal autonomy. By the same token, wealth enables its possessor to be sovereign over the time of others: When Whimster tells his secretary not to take lunch, she doesn't go. This ability to
control the time of others, such as accountants, personal assistants, advis-
ers, and other employees, allows the wealthy to more autonomously and
creatively allocate their time to do, as Whimster says, "the things you
would like to do."

Such examples highlight the practice of temporal empowerment in the
present. However, a unique feature of wealth as a basis for temporal empowerment is that it enhances the ability to extend one's will over significant stretches of time connecting past and future. A clear example is the
inherited wealthy's practice of managing the reproduction of family life
by arranging for the intergenerational transfer of wealth through trusts
and other intrafamily mechanisms of inheritance. As interviewee Norman Stryker explains, his parents set up charitable and family trusts that
structured the subsequent generations deployment of wealth:

> We've given away three-quarters of a million to a million. And when some
> trusts, twenty-year charitable trusts, began to fall in, my parents gave to al-
> ready-taken-care-of grandchildren instead of to the Stryker Fund. So that cut
> back on the amount of money they had to give away. And so there was the
> decision to either cut back giving and perpetuate the Stryker Fund or keep
> on giving the same amount and spend it out, spend the capital out, and the
> decision was to spend it out. That was the way my parents set it up. That
> was unchangeable at that point.

But in addition to extending family and opportunity over time, temporal
empowerment entails more basically the ability to extend one's self into
the future. As I discuss in more detail later in this book, business enterprises and philanthropic organizations are often set up to institutionally
incarnate the will and desire of wealthy founders in terms of social, political, and cultural agendas, extending principality and individuality well
past mortality. Scanning the temporal horizon, the wealthy articulate a
range of possible trajectories for practices in different spheres of activity,
the possible futures not only for individuals and families but also for the
businesses and organizations of which they are part.

Spatial Empowerment. Like time, space is the medium and outcome
of the process of social structuration and, like time, is a fundamental form
and practice of social power that is enhanced by the possession of wealth.
Spatial empowerment is the geographical counterpart of temporal

empowerment. It is embodied in what Lefebvre (1991) terms "spatial practices": social relations of power that produce and form the material sites, locations, and zones of everyday life. Through spatial practices, space is appropriated, deployed, and marked for specific social purposes and thus becomes concretized in the built environment and landscape.

In terms of hyperagency of wealth, spatial empowerment as spatial practice materially marks the territorial boundaries of the extension of an individual's principality. As such, spatial empowerment refers to vertical power exercised within spatial locales and horizontal power exercised across spatial locales of social life, primarily manifested in the organizations and institutions that the wealthy own and control. In exercising spatial power, the wealthy direct and coordinate monetary and human resources of organizations, strategically mobilizing their use as material extensions of will and symbolic incarnations of presence. The confluence of the material and symbolic in the spatial practices of wealth is underscored in the following statement by Benjamin Ellman, a midwestern retail entrepreneur:

> The company was built around me. Everybody in the United States thinks about this company as me personally. I once felt that was wrong, and that there's no way you can be successful in business if things revolve around one individual and you want to grow larger. That's not necessarily true. Look what's happening today. What's happening today with Lee Iacocca and other people. Individuals who are heading up businesses are becoming more connected with their businesses.

In this statement, Ellman is giving notice to wealth (as embodied in his firm) as a resource for the spatial practice of autonomy and individuality. To be "connected" to his business is to be able to construct and inhabit it as an institutional zone or territory of self-identity: He is a personification of the company and the company is a personification of him. Implicit in this statement is how his company isn't simply a spatial embodiment of his individuality; it is also a domain for the spatial practice of sovereignty whereby he rules others. This dimension of principality, which is manifested in the spatial practices of wealth as power, is made explicit by other wealthy men.

"The most important thing money gives me is power to get through time and red-tape barriers," explains real estate magnate Graham Reynolds. Connecting spatial to temporal empowerment, he explains how wealth enables him to reduce the time and distance for getting things done: "I can pick up the phone and call a congressman who's heard my name, and I can have the impact of 1 million votes on the issue with a phone call. You always have the upper hand in negotiating, and it allows you to do in one-tenth the time what it would take somebody else ten times the time because of the credibility he'd have to develop." The same is true for another real estate developer, David Stephanov, who also "picks up the phone" to set his will in motion. Exemplifying his "Golden Rule: them with the gold makes the rules," Stephanov describes how spatial empowerment, in addition to extending himself into the world, enables him to bring the world to himself. "When I want something, [politicians] come here and meet me for breakfast, and I tell them what I want. When I have to convey a message to the governor, he comes here, or he'll have one of his top two or three aides come down, and I'll tell them what I think should be done. And then we go from there." Whether running a business, exercising executive power in a corporation, or disbursing the funds through a family foundation, the wealthy command actors and resources to carve out their principality on a daily basis.

The Symbolic Alchemy of Appropriation: From Wealth as Power to the Power/Knowledge of Wealth

The incorrigibility of the banal truth of wealth as power, whether expressed in the language of common-sense, lexicographic definitions or sociological concepts such as "hyperagency," is based on its undeniable resonance with the way the experience of power is expressed by wealthy men. Certainly, when one learns how Brendan Dwyer, Benjamin Ellman, and David Stephanov describe the power attending the possession of wealth in temporal and spatial terms, Hoffman's initial comment makes a good deal of sense: Men of wealth can do what they want do when and where they want to do it, requiring others to sink or swim in the wake of their spatial and temporal empowerment. Wealth is power—period. The more wealth one has, the more capacity one has to be an especially empowered social agent, a hyperagent. End of story.

The problem with this view of wealth and power is not that it is banal or untrue but that its banal truth is partial. The equation of wealth as resource with power as agency is not the end the story but rather is the beginning. The partiality and limitation of this view are manifold. First, as Barry Hindess (1996) argues, this view of the correlation between power and wealth assumes that this relationship is quantitative: Wealth is a discrete resource that enables individuals to pursue goals and be agents, and the more wealth one possesses the more power one has. Quantity, in turn, engenders quality—the quality of sovereign individuality. Sovereign individuality is the praxeology, or the logic of rational social action that articulates means and ends, of the autonomous individual. Within this praxeology, the autonomous individual owns himself as property, is author over his own goals and desires, is able to pursue them by rationally applying the means or resources of wealth and money to desired ends, and is thus able to extend his individuality and principality in time and space.

There is no question that wealth as a discrete resource of power is a fundament of sovereign masculine individuality in capitalist culture. However, what is left unscrutinized and is assumed by this view of wealth and power is the very transformation of quantity into quality, of wealth into sovereign individuality. There is a subtle alchemy at work in this transformation, a magical transubstantiation of wealth not simply into power but into social and moral identity as well. How, for example, does Benjamin Ellman's company become a symbolic incarnation of his identity, an identity within which the individual and the corporate are elided, thus erasing the work of his employees in constructing this monument to himself? This transformation, I want to argue, is *not* an automatic consequence of the possession of wealth itself. Rather, it is the outcome of the narrativization of the experience of wealth and power and the rhetorical construction of moral identity based upon such stories. However, it is a transformation that this prevailing view of wealth as power is ill-equipped to understand.

Another limitation of the conventional view of power is that it reifies wealth as an object. Money and wealth are assumed to be objective resources that are fungible and value-neutral; they can be applied to any conceivable goal or end. Indeed, value-neutrality and fungibility constitute their very "worth" as material resources of power, a point underscored by both Marx and Georg Simmel (a point I follow up in Chapter 4). However, this perspective elides the quantitative and qualitative by embedding money and wealth in a utilitarian praxeology of instrumental or functional rationality. That is to say, the reasons *why* particular goals or ends are pursued, as well as the moral and cultural values used to formulate them and account for actions taken, are irrelevant since wealth is a resource of power and agency irrespective of the social context and moral specificity of the goals. But as Viviana Zelizer (1994) argues, this utilitarian perspective ignores the fact that in the context of everyday social life money and wealth are laden with symbolic meanings that qualitatively "earmark" them as having distinct social purposes and having a distinct moral valence or worth. There are, for example, monies for bribes, gifts to friends and family, courtship, divorce, personal loans, donations and bequests, and so on, each of which are constituted as having particular moral meaning for creating, maintaining, or dissolving specific social relations. There is money that is "clean" or morally good, such as wages from work, and there is money that is "dirty" or morally corrupt, such as bribes or blackmail. What is true of money in general is true of wealth as well. There is wealth embodied in real estate, property, homes, luxuries, and businesses, and there is wealth earmarked for investment, consumption, inheritance, and philanthropy. These are not just functional accounting categories but moral ones. Rather than being a value-neutral means in a logic of instrumental rationality, money and wealth are constitutive of and constituted by a praxeology of substantive rationality. As Zelizer points out, "Detached from its qualitative distinctions, the world of money becomes indecipherable"(1994: 24–25). What is to be deciphered, therefore, in the analysis of the confluence of wealth and power on the one hand, and morality on the other, is how the latter constitutes the former as being *appropriate*.

Finally, and most importantly for my purposes, the conventional view of power presumes a priori a stable and coherent subject who is able to deploy money and wealth in the pursuit of desired ends or goals. Wealth is transformative not of the subject himself but only of the subject's capacity for agency.[2] But if money and wealth are symbolically constructed as having qualitative moral worth as well quantitative value, then so too is the subject who possesses and deploys wealth. As I argue in Chapter 1, the moral economy of wealth constitutes a discursive field of knowledge that defines and marks not only the qualitative worth of wealth but also the qualitative worthiness of those who are wealthy. As with the symbolic earmarking of money, the symbolic marking of the worth of the wealthy man is a matter of appropriateness. In examining the meaning of appropriateness, we can begin to discern the subtle alchemy of power/knowledge that transforms the quantity of wealth into the moral quality of sovereign individuality.

Hoffman, as it turns out, was not entirely wrong. There is much to be learned about the moral meaning of wealth and power by reading the dictionary. However, the words that will move us beyond the dominant understanding of wealth as power are not *wealth* or *power* but two related words, *appropriate* and *property*. According to my dictionary, *appropriate* has three meanings (Morris, 1978: 64). When pronounced @-'prō-prē-@t, it means "suitable for a particular person, condition, occasion or place; proper; fitting." When pronounced @-'prō-prē-āt, the word means either "to set part for specific use" or "to take possession of or make use of exclusively for oneself, to make one's own." As Steve Jones points out,

all three meanings are derived from the Latin root of "property," which is derived from the Latin *proprius*, meaning "one's own." The word *property* was a doublet of *propriety* in More's *Utopia*. In current usage the former is used make reference to ownership; the latter refers to a standard of behavior harkening back to the Latin *proprius* and its derivative *proprietas*, meaning proper signification with words. (1992: 118)

Intriguing are the intertwined meanings of *property* and *propriety*, of ownership and standards of behavior, in the word "appropriate" and its implications for how wealth is productive of sovereign individuality and principality. As I argue above, the praxeology of sovereign individuality entails that the autonomous person is able to "@-'prō-prē-āt" wealth as property, to make it one's own and set it apart for particular uses in order to create individuality and principality, a self-identity and social world of engagement and agency that is also one's own as a form of property. However, my dictionary and Jones suggest that the capacity for sovereign individuality is not only contingent upon the possession wealth as property; it is also contingent upon the *propriety* of wealth and those who possess it. In other words, I want to argue that in order to "@-'prō-prē-āt" wealth in the service of individuality and principality, the wealthy man must be understood by self and others as being "@-'prō-prē-@t." That is, he must be "suitable" and "fitting" for the "condition, occasion, or place" of the empowerment of wealth. And, as Jones suggests, whether not one is "@-'prō-prē-@t" for the appropriation of wealth as one's own is a matter of the "proper signification of words." Thus, to wield wealth as a resource of power requires the rhetorical elaboration of a discourse and narrative of "appropriation" in all senses of the term.

Consider the following statement by John Norris, the man whose proprietary gesture to the world from the top floor of Columbia Towers figured prominently in Chapter 1 and whose (auto-)biographical narrative I examine below. In his interview, Norris makes an important distinction between wealth and money as a resource of power, on the one hand, and the propriety and moral legitimacy of wealth as power, on the other. He says:

> Money obviously gives very wealthy people power whether they deserve it or not. A lot of the times that power is misused. Obviously, money gives you a certain feeling of confidence and security whether it came to you from one avenue or another. Eighty percent of the people who inherit money, at least in my observation—that's too high of a percentage, I guess, maybe 60 percent—would probably starve to death if they didn't inherit it. Forty percent who inherit it do good things with it because they respect and understand it. That's an arbitrary number but people that I see that have inherited money, six out of ten wouldn't make it if their name was Smith and they do very little good with it. The other 40 percent—again, they are arbitrary numbers, but plus or minus 10 percent—they do good things with it because they understand it and they are not the nouveau riche; the money has been around in the family for a long time. Nouveau riche gag on most of the money. When I say "nouveau riche people" I mean that wealth has come to them over the last fifty years instead of over the last one hundred and fifty. Money has come to them because of post–World War II lucky breaks. It sounds like

I am bitter, but I am not because some, mainly the 40 percent that inherited it over any time frame, do wonderful things with it and have a deep regard and respect for their wealth. Most of the nouveau riche aren't very involved in the community. Probably intellectually, they don't know how to handle it.

This statement is an important and interesting example of the symbolic alchemy of the moral economy of wealth at work. First, Norris starts off with a straightforward invocation of the conventional understanding of money and wealth as power: wealth gives its possessor security, confidence, and power regardless of the source of the wealth. Yet very quickly he moves his discussion of wealth as power to the moral terrain of substantive rationality. The mere possession of a quantity of wealth does not necessarily entail the qualitative constitution of valorized moral identity. A lot of wealthy people, Norris argues, do not "deserve" their money and power because it is "misused." What does he mean by this?

Clearly, for Norris, a significant number of the wealthy (60 percent of inheritors and most of the nouveau riche) are not deserving of their money because they do not use it appropriately. As Norris says, his quantitative categorization of the wealthy into those who use their money and power appropriately and those who do not may be "arbitrary," but his qualitative moral evaluation and symbolic marking of the deserving and the undeserving wealthy are not. The propriety of wealth and power, in this context, is constituted by proper goals, to "do good" and "wonderful things with it," especially through philanthropic involvement in the community. This appropriate use of wealth and conduct of the wealthy is in turn dependent upon a particular mode of "understanding" wealth: The deserving wealthy are said "to do good things with it because they respect and understand it" or because they "have deep respect and regard for their wealth." The precise meaning of phrases such as these will be the subject of subsequent chapters. But the important point is that they highlight how the appropriateness of the power of wealth is contingent upon the wealthy understanding their money, and themselves in relation to their money, in a particular moral way. For Norris, the moral identity of the wealthy man is produced through a framework of articulating knowing and doing, through propriety and power. After all, he says, the wealthy who "intellectually don't know how to handle" their money "gag" on it. They become dysfunctional, corrupted by their money, and they are unable to do good with it. To adumbrate what follows below, without this intellectual framework, those with fortune cannot be virtuous because they cannot manage the flow of money and wealth through their selves or materially territorialize it in the world because they cannot symbolically account for it with the proper signification of words.

What is fascinating about Norris's statement is how remarkably Foucauldian it is. For Norris, as well as Foucault, the production of subjectivity and social practice is a function of the flow of power/knowledge, or *pouvoir/savoir*, as "know-how." But the questions of how know-how operates as a productive field of power, a field that in turn disciplines and channels the flow of money and wealth, and how this field is embodied and enacted by men such as Norris through narrative remain to be examined. In broaching these questions, I can do no better than to quote at length Barbara Biesecker, who in turn quotes Gayatri Spivak, because of the exquisite clarity of their explanation of what power/knowledge means and how it works. "But what, exactly," Biesecker (1992: 357) asks, "does it mean to say that power relations are, above all, productive? . . . Gayatri Spivak provides us with an answer . . . [and] warns us that we miss what may be one of Foucault's most enabling insights when we translate *pouvoir* only as *power*":

> It is a pity that there is no word in English corresponding to *pouvoir* as there is "knowing" for *savoir*. *Pouvoir* is of course "power." But there is a sense of "can-do"-ness in *pouvoir*, if only because, in its various declinations it is the commonest way of saying "can" in the French language. If "power/knowledge" is seen as the only translation of *pouvoir/savoir*, it monumentalizes Foucault unnecessarily. You know how we use *savoir* in *savoir-faire, savoir-vivre*? Try to get some of that homely verbness into *pouvoir*, and you might get something like this: if the lines of making sense of something are laid down in a certain way, then you are able to do only those things with that something which are possible within and by the arrangement of those lines. *Pouvoir/savoir*—being able to do something—only as you are able to make sense of it. (Spivak, quoted in Biesecker, 1992: 357)

Biesecker then goes on to extend Spivak's interpretation of the meaning of power/knowledge as follows:

> On this reading of Foucault, power names not the imposition of a limit that constrains human thought and action but a being-able that is made possible through a grid of intelligibility. Power is a human calculation performed within and inaugurated by the "lines of making sense" that are operative at a particular historical moment or, as Spivak put it, a "can-do"-ness whose condition of existence is an orientation in time and space. (1992: 358)

By Norris's own account, in distinct contrast to the wealthy who do not know how to understand their wealth and do good with it, he has "know-how" in abundance and is therefore a "can-do" man of wealth. Immediately following his indictment of the unknowing and undeserving wealthy, Norris says the following about his own philosophy and practice of philanthropy:

> Giving is fun, and more and more people have to recognize that even if you are disposed to do it, you don't have to wait until you die; that the needs are now and tomorrow and the day after tomorrow and you ought to be able to plan your resource distribution so that you can do it and see what good it does and reap the joy and fun of seeing something happen. I don't believe in doing it when you do die. I believe in doing it now.

As a description of the praxeology of philanthropy, Norris's statement practically oozes know-how and Spivak's can-do-ness. Philanthropy obviously requires money and resources, but it also requires a disposition to give. Moreover, this disposition to "do it" must be acted upon in the present, because Norris knows how it does good in the present and knows how it provides him with the opportunity to "see what good it does and reap the joy and fun of seeing something happen." Clearly, Norris is articulating a substantively rational social logic, a way of connecting means with ends that embodies qualitative distinctions of moral value: It is better to give than not to give; it is better to give now than when one is dead; and when one gives now one is a more worthy individual and has more fun to boot because one can see the good one has done. This statement describes the spatial and temporal empowerment of wealth as well as its concomitant production of individuality and principality. Spatially, Norris can make "something happen" in society by shaping its material terrain; temporally, he can make things happen in such a way that addresses needs in the present and the future.

In this sense, Norris exemplifies Biesecker's claim that as *pouvoir/savoir* "power is a human calculation." But, of course, there is more to power as *pouvoir/savoir* than the calculation of means and ends inherent in the praxeology of social action and agency. As Biesecker goes on to say, following Spivak, this calculation is made possible only on the basis of particular "lines of making sense." Norris's can-do-ness is enabled by his know-how of propriety and power, and this know-how operates as a "grid of intelligibility" that makes sense of himself, his wealth, other wealthy people, and the world in a particular way.

But what precisely is this grid of intelligibility that provides lines of sense-making? As Biesecker points out, it entails an epistemological and ontological mapping of the social, a map that provides "an orientation in time and space." For Foucault and others who have followed his interest in the regimes and technologies of selfhood and subjectification that comprise practical forms of power/knowledge (cf. Minson, 1993; Rose, 1996), any historical epoch and social formation has multiple, overlapping, and often contradictory grids of intelligibility that are produced through discourse and embodied in the conduct of everyday life. Yet one of the most fundamental modes of producing lines of making sense, of providing a grid of intelligibility that orients the subject in time and space and simultaneously maps the self and the social, is narrative. Norris isn't just giving us a description of his experience of hapless inheritors who would starve without their inheritance, or of venal and greedy nouveau riche who gag on their fortunes, or the empowerment, joys, and pleasures of giving money away in the present. He is telling us a story of these experiences. More importantly, the story that he tells—and the (auto-)biographical narrative that is evoked in the telling—do not reflect his experience. Rather, the narrative and its performative telling constitute his experience and, in so doing, bring to bear a grid of intelligibility and lines of sense-making that construct the propriety of Norris's wealth and power and valorize his moral identity as a sovereign "better angel" of capitalism. Accordingly, I now turn to the temporal and spatial dynamics of narrative and how the intertwined dynamics of emplotment and emplacement produce a story space of appropriate power and moral identity.

Story, Space, and Moral Identity

One of the most exciting and fruitful developments during the past decade or so in human sciences in general, and interpretive ethnography in particular, has been the turn toward the analysis of narrative and storytelling as a fundamental form and practice of the constitution of personal and social identity. The theoretical and methodological approaches to narrative and identity are many and varied, ranging from the formal, structural, and textual to the dynamic, situational, and performative.[3] Debates rage as to which approach is most appropriate for both interpreting narrative identity and practice as well as the staging of the interpretive analysis itself (cf. Denzin, 1996). My own approach is heterogeneous, based on several theoretical perspectives on narrative and methods of interpretation. But, as Kathleen Stewart argues, the common ground of most approaches to narrative and storytelling as form and practice of power/knowledge is the fundamental premise that:

> narrative is first and foremost a mediating form through which "meaning" must pass. Stories, in other words, are productive. They catch up cultural conventions, relations of authority, and fundamental spatio-temporal orientations in the dense sociality of words and images in use and produce a constant mediation of the "real" in a proliferation of signs. They mark the space of a searching or scanning, the space of sheer meaning, the space of a positioned subject. (Stewart, 1996: 30)

Accordingly, my path through the thicket of approaches to narrative analysis will by guided by concern with: first, how narrative works as a productive mediating form that gives meaning to identity; second, how narratives embody cultural conventions and relations of authority in order to produce a spatio-temporal grid of intelligibility, or the emplotment and emplacement of moral identity; and, third, how these narrativized lines of moral sense-making comprise the story space of the positioned subject of sovereign individuality, which is the story space of the "better angel" of capitalism that embodies the know-how of wealth and the can-do-ness of power.

Narrativity and the Mediation of Identity

When Stewart speaks of narrative as a form through which meaning must pass, she is foregrounding the function of narrative as epistemology, a fundamental phenomenological framework for knowing and sense-making. Indeed, as Dwight Conquergood points out, the importance of narrative as epistemology is grounded in the very meaning of the word:

> The word "narrate" . . . traces its lineage from the Latin *narrare*, "to tell," and the Latin *gnarus*, "knowing," both derivative from the Indo-European root *gna*, "to know." The shared and intertwining etymological roots of storytelling and knowledge underpin narrative's epistemological connection. Narrative is a way of knowing, a search for meaning, that privileges experience, process, action, and peril. Knowledge is not so much stored in storytelling so much as it is enacted, reconfigured, tested, and engaged by imaginative summonings and interpretative events in light of present situations. Active and emergent, instead of abstract and inert, narrative knowing recalls and recasts experience into meaningful signposts and supports for ongoing action. The recountal is an encounter, often full of risk. (Conquergood, 1993: 337)

In this eloquent account of the epistemological character of narrative, Conquergood offers several important insights about how narrative works as power/knowledge, as an articulation of know-how and can-do-ness. First, although the form of narrative and its performance in storytelling are analytically distinct, they cannot be isolated from one another: The knowing is in the telling, and both make up the process of narrativity. Second, as a way of knowing and telling, narrativity doesn't simply report or store past events and experiences, it actively and creatively arranges and constitutes them as being meaningful in the context of the present. This underscores the temporal dimension of narrative as an epistemological grid of intelligibility. Without narrative, as philosophers such as A. Kerby (1991), T. P. Kemp (1989), and P. Ricoeur (1984) have argued, there would be no experience of time as memory. Both individual (auto-)biography as well as collective and public narratives of history are always-already configured from the perspective of the present. As Game and Metcalfe describe the temporal lines of sense-making that narrative enacts, "Beginnings are always written from hindsight: they are stories created later, from the perspective of what we have become, through which we constitute our sense of what we are. . . . If the past is another country, it is colonized through stories" (1996: 70). Third, as Conquergood points out, the manner in which we narratively configure the meaning of past events and experiences constitutes the condition for individual and social agency in the present and future. Knowing who we are, and what we have become, is the ground for knowing what to do (Somers and Gibson, 1994: 61).

All of this means that narrativity isn't simply an epistemological form and process; it is simultaneously a form and process of constructing the ontology of identity in terms of social being and becoming. Paul Ricoeur makes a strong case for the inextricable connection between the epistemological and ontological dimensions of narrativity when he writes that "our own existence cannot be separated from the account we can give of our selves. It is in telling our own stories that we give ourselves an identity. We recognize ourselves in the stories that we tell about ourselves. It makes very little difference whether these stories are true or false, fiction as well as verifiable history provides us with an identity" (quoted in Kerby, 1991: 40–41).

From a poststructuralist perspective, given the epistemological and ontological creativity of narrativity as a form of power/knowledge, we can push Ricoeur's point even farther and say that the storied self *is* a fiction. By saying the storied self is a fiction, I do not mean that identity is nothing more than a tissue of lies or falsehoods, that it is lacking in "truth." Rather, I mean that the "truth" of identity produced through narrative is a "fiction" in the root meaning of the word. "Fiction" is derived from the Latin root *fictio*, which means a "making" or "fashioning." Thus, through narrative and storytelling, self-identity is creatively fashioned and given shape and coherency. It is the coherency of identity that is the "truth effect" of narrative and its rhetorical performance in storytelling. From this perspective, as Jonathan Ree argues, "the concept of narrative . . . is not so much a justification of the idea of personal identity, as an elucidation of its structure as an inescapable piece of make-believe" (quoted in Frith, 1996: 122). Thus, the "truth" of narrative identity is one of rhetorical verisimilitude rather than empirical veracity. As such, narrative can be understood as *techné* in the Heideggerian sense, as both the instrument and activity of casting the self and the social into sense through storied practices of make-believe. Narrativity, then, is a cultural technology of identity that links together story, the self that narrates, the self that is narrated, and the real or imagined audience in order to produce the "truth" of identity.

To understand narrativity as a creative technology of making and fashioning identity, as a practice of make-believe, illuminates its status as a technique of power/knowledge. Here we can begin to discern now narrativity embodies relations of authority. For Foucault, technologies of selfhood, such as narrativity, are also technologies of power because they are pragmatic modes of subjectification, of giving shape and form to the identity and agency of individuals by *subjecting* them to particular regimes of knowledge and conduct. A technology of power, he writes,

> applies itself to immediate everyday life which categorizes the individual, marks him by his own individuality, attaches him to his own identity, imposes a law of truth on him *which he must recognize and have others recognize in him*. It is a form of power which makes individual subjects. There are two meanings of the word *subject:* subject to someone else by control and dependence, and tied to his own identity by a conscience or self-knowledge. Both meanings suggest a form of power which subjugates and makes subject to. (1983: 212; emphasis added)

This double process of subjection is precisely what narrativity as a cultural technology of make-believe does: It marks out the individual as having a identity that is recognizable to self and others. Accordingly, as Peter McClaren argues, narrativity is a form and practice of epistemological and ontological "violence" in that it embodies and enacts "dominative systems of knowledge and structures of intelligibility that construct forms of social life" (1995: 90). As a storied practice of a will to knowledge and truth of identity, narrativity is also a will to power. Recall what I argue in Chapter 1: Moral identity is rhetorically constituted through the twin moments of *evocation* and *invocation*. Although we are able to creatively evoke our identity through the cultural technology of narrative, we do so largely on the basis of invoking cultural conventions or paradigms of plot, story lines, themes, setting, and characterizations that are part of a hegemonic narrative social imaginary. That is, in order to recognize in ourselves—and have others recognize in us—the "truth" of our identity, we must subject ourselves to and within the prevailing and "already-articulated" narrative frames and devices of our culture (Maines, 1997: 2). The authorship of our self-identity through narrative thus depends on our complicity with or resistance to the authority of what McClaren calls "society's treasured stock of imperial or magisterial narratives" (1995: 91).[4]

The "magisterial" is that which is superior, masterful, commanding, and authoritative. Those who are able to author their identity through magisterial narratives, such as the wealthy men in this study, are valorized as the living embodiments of the morally superior, masterful, and authoritative and are thus commanding of belief in the "truth" of their moral identity. They speak, as does John Norris, with authority and as authority. This process of producing the magisterial subject of moral authority through narrative is precisely what Plummer is referring to when he says that "stories live in the flow of power." It is also what Game and Metcalfe mean when they say that stories are not just told; they are lived and embodied. But precisely how is the magisterial truth of moral identity produced through narrativity? How does narrativity create a story space for the appropriation and propriety of wealth and power? As I have been arguing, the will to truth and power of narrativity as a grid of intelligibility and line of sense-making is enacted through the intertwined processes of emplotment and emplacement.

Emplotment, Emplacement, and the Moral Subject of Narrative

If there is one aspect of narrativity that diverse theories and analytical approaches agree upon, it is the centrality of emplotment.[5] The reason is simple: Without a coherent plot, that is, a structured direction or trajectory to a story, there is no coherent story. Stories, whether they are personal stories of individual identity, popular media narratives, or public narratives of history, must have a point or central theme that unfolds in their telling in order to make them compelling and believable. And it is the emplotment of narrative that gives stories their point.

Many accounts of emplotment can be extremely complex (e.g., Ricoeur, 1984). At the risk of glossing over some of the important nuances of emplotment, my own account will be rather minimalist and parsimonious, tailored to the purpose of understanding the narrativity of moral identity in stories of the self. At root, emplotment entails the configuration of the diverse welter of experiences of life into a coherent temporal sequence and meaningful order. In terms of the narrative of self-identity, emplotment provides logical connections between different experiences so that one's life story becomes an "event" through which past and present are causally linked. Through emplotment, one's past experiences are selected, organized, and given a historical trajectory or direction so that they necessarily and inexorably lead to the present, which is the temporal location from which such stories are told. Accordingly, the trajectory of emplotment is fundamentally teleological. The teleology of emplotment, argue Game and Metcalfe, is absolutely essential for narratives to have a point and to be compelling. "Beginnings and endings," they write (1996: 70), "are cultural creations, the start and conclusion of stories. They are connected teleologically so that the beginning inevitably implies an end that returns to the beginning. In stories, events 'unfold' as manifested destiny, and a story that fails to return is likely to be received as a failed story, pointless or unsatisfactory." Emplotment thereby becomes the process through which individuals explain and evaluate, or tell the how and why, of their life as an unfolding story. Further, as M. Somers and G. Gibson (1994: 60) explain, emplotment also entails the "selective appropriation" of experiences in constructing narratives of social identity. Our lives contain a vast array of experiences, not all of which are commented upon, explained, or evaluated in the telling of our stories. It is through the deployment of particular themes of emplotment, such as "risk," "opportunity," "hard work," "success," "doing good," and "respect and regard for wealth," that men of wealth such as Norris thematically organize their experiences into a coherent plot.

The manner in which emplotment works as trajectory, teleology, and theme to provide the means of historical explanation and normative evaluation of a life story underscores, once again, the importance of narrativity as a cultural technology of power/knowledge. As Alan Feldman explains, *"The event is not what happens. The event is that which can be narrated. The event is action organized by culturally situated meaning"* (1991: 14). The construction of one's life as an "event" is a fiction, an imposition of a culturally shared narrative form upon the flux of life in order to make it meaningful and coherent. Moreover, as I argue above, it is not simply the story of one's life that is rendered coherent through emplotment; it is the coherency of one's identity as well. The self is narrated at the same time as the event. As Kerby argues (1991: 33), through the emplotment of narration, we performatively assert our identity. Through the telling of our own life stories, we become, to use David Maines's words, a "self-abstracted person" (1993: 23). The "I," as symbolic interactionists are fond of saying, is an "index word" that locates the self in time and space (Jenkins, 1996: 39). In the context of storying the self, the "I" who is indexed is not simply the individual who is narrating but, more importantly, is also the "I" that inhabits the narrative as a character, a narratively constructed *persona*, who is united with his or her "manifested destiny" (to use Game and Metcalfe's words) through teleological emplotment. An important dimension of the teleology of emplotment is that it does more than unite the character or persona of the self-narrative in the temporal flow from past to present; it also binds our narrativized character to an imagined and projected future as well. The point of narrative emplotment is to provide not only a grid of intelligibility that explains and evaluates our past in terms of the present but also an explanatory and evaluative context for agency in the present that is oriented toward projected goals in future. These imagined ends provide a telos or provisional closure, a point of destination that forms the continuity and coherency of our storied identity over time.

But again, it is important to emphasize that this narrative coherency of the self is a fiction, a forming and folding of the self into a recognizable identity, and it is thus the enactment and embodiment of power/knowledge. As I argue in the Chapter 1, in telling our stories we are not only bound to the self-abstracted character of the narrative; these self-abstracted characters are bound to the discourses of the cultural narrative imaginary that gives us exemplary characters and emplotments to mimetically invoke in evoking our identity. As Feldman argues:

> If the self is the referential object of the life-history recitation, then it is inter-pellated by the discourse and cannot be prior to it. No discursive object exists outside of, or prior to, discursive formation. The self is always the arti-fact of prior received and newly constructed narratives. It is engendered through narration and fulfills a syntactical function in the life history. The rules of narration may perform a stabilizing role in the cultural construction of truth, but then both self and truth are subordinate to the transindividual closures of narrative (spoken or written). (1991: 13)

This is no less true of wealthy men like Norris than it is of ourselves. The difference though, is that the moral economy of wealth valorizes their narratives as being magisterial. This brings me to the issue of the relationship between narrativity and moral identity. For philosophers such as A. MacIntyre (1981), C. Taylor (1989), and A. Kerby (1991), it is the way we inhabit our self-narratives as a character whose story unfolds from past to present and into the future that constitutes the fundament of moral life and identity. For Kerby, the emplotment of narrativity, in all of its dimensions discussed above, that comprises the "virtue of narrative":

> Human action is valorized action, if only because it involves choice and de-liberation, and it is narration that carries over to explicit consciousness ac-tion's implicit moral tenor and attempts to preserve it. . . . Without narration the past would sink into the obscurity of forgetfulness where everything is equal. Narrative, however, not only delivers over the past but is also the medium of our aspirations and desires, imaginatively expressing, in stories we tell ourselves and those that we hear and read, a possible future with its attendant joys and hardships and possible selves. The stories that we tell are part and parcel of our becoming. They are a mode of vision, plotting what is good or bad for us, what is possible and what is not—plotting whom we may become. But in the telling we seem also to be immediately involved in generating the *value* of a certain state of affairs or course of action, of judging its worth, ethical or otherwise. . . . In the sphere of social action this valoriza-tion understandably takes the form of moral judgment and critique, con-tributing to the ethical realm of our existence. (1991: 54)

What Kerby is underscoring here is the essential link between narrativity and the praxeology of substantive rationality in everyday life. There can be no social action, no articulation of resources and goals or means and ends, without bringing to bear categories of moral value upon the conduct of everyday life, which is reflexively understood as a deliberate emplotting of one's life story. Emplotment is the tissue that connects the memory of past actions with the interpretation of present situations, which are in turn projected forward into the future along possible plotlines of choice and action. Arguing along similar lines concerning the relationship between virtue and narrative, Ricoeur (1991a) maintains that it is the emplotment of narrative that provides a dynamic and quotidian form of *phronesis*, which is the Aristotelian concept of ethical knowing, judgment, and practical reasoning. By relating the plots of our own life story with the emplotments of culturally shared narratives we learn the causal connection between ethical action and moral consequence and thus script our own lives in concordance within an emplotted praxeology of substantive rationality: "We learn how reversals of fortune result from this or that conduct, as this is constructed by the plot in the narrative. It is due to the familiarity we have with types of plot received from our culture that we learn to relate virtues, or rather forms of excellence, with happiness or unhappiness" (1991a: 23).

As Ricoeur points out, from an Aristotelian perspective, "virtue" is a mode of conduct that embodies "excellence," and in conducting ourselves and judging ourselves according to such standards of excellence we emplot our lives toward good fortune and the fulfillment of happiness. Thus, for Ricoeur, the "virtue of narrative" (to use Kerby's words) in constructing moral identity consists precisely in its status as a *narrative of virtue*, a storied evocation and account of our trajectory toward fortune and the telos of happiness. Of course, the precise meaning of "virtue," "fortune," and "happiness" as artifacts of power/knowledge, particularly in the context of the (auto-)biographical narratives of wealthy men, remains to be examined and scrutinized. But the important point here is that the teleology of the narrative of virtue and fortune gives a subject's moral identity its fictive coherence over time and comprises what MacIntyre terms the "unity of a life" (1981: 197).

There is another, perhaps more profound dimension to this relationship among narrative, ethics, and moral identity: the spatial dimension of narrativity as a practice of emplacement, of locating and orienting the subject in symbolic, moral, social, and material space. The spatial dimension of narrativity is most often implicit or latent in the foregoing accounts of its dynamics, yet it is crucial to understanding how narrative operates as a grid of intelligibility that is the basis of moral identity. One of the ways in which Ricoeur, for example, describes the deontology of narrative is by saying narrativity "makes life habitable" (1984: ix). Here, Ricoeur is drawing on Heidegger's translation of the Greek word *ethos*.

According to Heidegger, *ethos* does not simply refer to ethics manifested in the conduct and character of subjects; it also refers to the "dwelling place" or "lodging" of subjects (Chambers, 1994: 95). As a form of *phronesis* or practical ethical reasoning, narrativity performs or furnishes a location or place of habitation in everyday life from which the world is made morally meaningful. By making self and world temporally coherent and morally meaningful, the emplotment of narrative is simultaneously an emplacement in a symbolic topos of collective cultural identity.

Yet the emplacement of narrative entails more than the conjuring of stable locales of personal and moral identity; it also performs a dynamic orientation and movement in moral space. This aspect of narrativity has been elaborated upon by Charles Taylor (1989). For Taylor, moral identity is inseparable, indeed, inconceivable without taking into account the subject's location and orientation in moral space, which is both a symbolic and social topos in which conceptions and categories of moral value are elaborated and embodied. Taylor maintains that there is an

> essential link between identity and orientation. To know who you are is to be oriented in moral space, a space in which questions arise about what is good or bad, what is worth doing and what not, what has meaning and importance to you and what is trivial and secondary. . . . To lose this orientation, or not to have found it, is not to know who one is. And this orientation, once attained, defines where you answer from, hence your identity. . . . But to speak of orientation is to presuppose a space-analog within which one finds one's way. To understand our predicament in terms of finding or losing orientation in moral space is to take the space which our frameworks seek to define as ontologically basic . . . the space of questions must be *mapped* by strong evaluation, or qualitative distinctions. (Taylor, 1989: 28, 29)

For Taylor, one's location and orientation in moral space is mapped by what he calls "axes of strong evaluation," cultural categories of virtue, happiness, fulfillment, and worth, all of which are constitutive of the telos of the "good life," providing the criteria for *phronesis*, choice and action. This mapping of moral space in turn provides subjects with a guide, so to speak, for dynamically moving through moral space on the basis of the narrative emplotment of our life stories as an ongoing "quest" for the good life. As he argues:

> The issue of our condition can never be exhausted for us by what we are, because we are also changing and becoming. . . . In order to make minimal sense of our lives, in order to have an identity, we need an orientation to the good, which means some sense of qualitative discrimination, of the incomparably higher. Now we see that this sense of the good has been woven into

my understanding of my life as an unfolding story. But this is to state another basic condition of making sense of ourselves, that we grasp our lives in a *narrative*.... It has often been remarked that making sense of one's life as a story is also, like the orientation to the good, not an optional extra; that our lives exist also in this space of questions, which only a coherent narrative can answer. In order to have a sense of who we are, we have to have a notion of how we become, and of where we are going.... Because we cannot but orient ourselves to the good, and thus determine the direction of our lives, we must inescapably understand our lives in narrative form, as a "quest."(Taylor, 1989: 47, 51–52)

Thus, for Taylor, the emplotted trajectory of one's moral life as narrative is simultaneously and necessarily an emplacement in the ethos and topos of moral space. In this respect, Taylor's argument is indispensable to the analysis of the rhetorical construction of the moral identity of wealthy men through their (auto-)biographical narratives that I want to pursue. Yet for all of Taylor's insights into a narrative as a spatio-temporal and ethico-moral grid of intelligibility, his argument has two severe limitations. First, as in the abstract philosophical treatments of narrativity I discuss above, there is a tendency to drift away from or efface entirely how narrativity operates as a historically and socially contingent form of power/knowledge. The attributes of narrativity, especially in terms of the formation of moral identity, are assumed to be universal, applicable to all times and places.

For Taylor, the emplotment-emplacement of the subject in moral space through an orientation and movement toward "the good" is an "inescapable framework" without which "undamaged personhood" is not possible. Taylor (1989: 64) recognizes that reigning cultural definitions of what constitutes the good life and from which we derive categories and measures of moral worth, which he calls "hypergoods," "are generally a source of conflict." However, he is surprisingly silent as to how the mapping of moral space privileges some forms of moral identity and personhood, rendering them magisterial and inflicting considerable damage to persons who do not "measure up" to prevailing understandings of moral worth. Taylor's self in moral space is an undifferentiated and ahistorical subject, reflexively aware of his or her own identity as he or she grasps it as narrative form yet blissfully ignorant of how narrative as form valorizes particular emplotments and emplacements of moral identity while devalorizing and deauthorizing others.[6] Thus, as I argue, it is essential to foreground the emplotment and emplacement of narrative as a technology of the self that is also a technology of power. As a technology of the self, narrative is a rhetorical and material practice of giving form to the ethical subject in action. This rhetorical practice of the ethical subject is also a practice of power/knowledge that "determines the conduct of individuals and submits them to certain ends or domination," thus rendering the subject visible to self and others as a target of ethical governance and discipline (Foucault, 1988: 18). Accordingly, in order to understand the moral identity of the man of wealth, it is imperative to understand the historically specific processes through which the technologies of the ethical subject of the sovereign individual have emerged.

This emphasis on the emplotment and emplacement of narrativity as technology of self and power also foregrounds its status as material social practice, not simply a representational or symbolic one. In this respect, Taylor's (as well as Kerby's, and Ricoeur's) philosophical consideration of the relationship between narrative, space, and moral identity is deficient. For Taylor, the emplotment and emplacement of moral identity in social space is pretty much identified as finding one's location in and movement through moral or spiritual space. Space is therefore primarily metaphorical or symbolic space. In order to understand how narrative operates as a rhetorical form of power/knowledge that enables men of wealth to engage in the practice of appropriation in all senses of the term, it is imperative to explore how narrativity articulates or connects the symbolic space of the ethical subject of sovereign individuality with the material sites and locales in which this subject is enacted, embodied, and performed.

The story space of the sovereign individual of wealth is a dynamic instance of the mapping processes that L. Grossberg (1993), following G. Deleuze and F. Guattari (1983), calls the "territorialization machine" of culture. Grossberg argues for a mode of cultural analysis that foregrounds the "territorialization" of cultural practices through which "spaces" (what Grossberg defines as "fields of social activity") are constructed and articulated with "places" within which people are located in terms of identity, affect, and empowerment. This "territorialization machine"

distributes subjectivity and subject positions in space. A territorializing machine diagrams lines of mobility and placement; it defines or maps possibilities of where and how people can stop and place themselves. Such places are temporary points of belonging and identification, of orientation and installation, of investment and empowerment. Such places create temporary addresses or homes . . . such places or homes do not pre-exist the lines of mobility, the space. They are not origins. They are the product of an effort to organize a "limited space" as Deleuze and Guattari describe it. They define forms of empowerment or agency, ways of going in and going out. Around such places, maps of meaning, and desire and of pleasure can be articulated. A territorializing machine attempts to map the sort of place people can occupy and how they can occupy them. It maps how much room people have to move, and where and how they can move. . . . It maps the ways in which

people live the always limited freedom to stop in and move through a field
of force. (Grossberg: 1993: 14–15)

From this perspective, social space is a malleable field of sites of identity
and agency produced primarily and mapped through rhetorical practices
of narration and storytelling. It is through the *emplotment* of narration
that individuals and communities are *emplaced* in spatio-temporal locations of common identity. These two processes converge as an instance of
the territorialization of space. Moreover, Grossberg clearly and correctly
foregrounds the workings of territorialization as an instance of
power/knowledge as it lays down upon social space a grid of intelligibility that allows people to locate themselves and move through space,
thereby appropriating it as a place of empowerment and moral identity.

However, this conceptualization of space, place, and identity is much
too simple and neat, as there are several aspects to their interrelationship
that add considerable complexity to the task of cultural analysis. This
complexity is compounded by the fact that we lack, as Lefebvre (1991)
has argued, a sufficiently elaborated vocabulary of space to avoid redundant and confusing uses of the terms *space* and *place*. That is to say, the
analysis of the dynamics of space, place, and identity is often con-
founded by a lack of sufficiently precise concepts. But try we must, so
here are a few caveats and refinements to the foregoing that should help
us better understand the relationship of space and place and, ultimately,
the story space of the ethical subject of sovereign individuality.

First, space is multidimensional and, as Kirby (1995) points out, operates simultaneously at a number of different articulated "registers": the
physical space of landscape; the material space of the built environment;
the geopolitical space of nation-states, regions, and municipalities; the
semiotic or symbolic space of language and signification; the somatic
space of the body; and the psychic space of subjectivity, desire, and affect.
What I want to argue is that in order for the men in this study to "@-'prō-
prē-āt" wealth as a form of empowerment as well as to be understood by
self and others as being "@-'prō-prē-@t" their (auto-)biographical narratives must align and imbricate these registers of spatiality in a concordant way so that the individual is sovereign over each and all. If not, I
want to argue, appropriation fails.

Second, spaces are not empty spaces, the mere scenes for, backdrop to,
or containers of the social practices that create places. Rather, each register of space is the very medium through which place is created and is inseparable from it. Furthermore, as Doreen Massey (1993a, 1993b) has argued, space and place are dynamic social processes and figurations, not
static and stable synchronic entities. The emplotment and emplacement
of narrativity are instances of what Lefebvre (1991) and de Certeau (1984)

have termed embedded "spatial practices" that map and organize location and movement in social space. Using vehicular travel and walking
as metaphors for the way in which stories provide a cartographic grid of
intelligibility for social space, de Certeau writes:

> In modern Athens, the vehicles of mass transportation are called *metaphorai*.
> To go to work or to come home, one takes a "metaphor"—a bus or a train.
> Stories should also take this noble name: everyday, they traverse and orga-
> nize places; they select and link them together; they make sentences out of
> them. They are spatial trajectories. . . . Every story is a travel story—a spatial
> practice. . . . These narrated adventures, simultaneously producing geogra-
> phies of action and drifting into the common places of an order, do not
> merely constitute a "supplement" to pedestrian enunciations and rhetorics.
> They are not satisfied with displacing the latter and transposing them into
> the field of language. In reality they organize walks. They make the journey,
> before or during the ime the feet perform it. . . . In relation to place, space is
> like the word when it is spoken, that is, when it is caught in the ambiguity of
> an actualization . . . space *is a practiced place.* Thus the street geometrically
> defined by urban planning is transformed into a space by walkers. In the
> same way, an act of reading is the space produced by the practice of particu-
> lar place: a written text, i.e., a space constituted by a system of signs. (1984:
> 115–117)

The space of the street or sidewalk is both the medium and effect of the
stories that produce the former as one's residence ("This is where I live")
or the latter as the pathway of journey ("This is where I have been and
where I am going"), just as the space of the words in the book is the
medium and effect of its reading in our imagination. Thus, place can be
understood as the "*performance* or *enactment* of spatialization," a performance that is based on the everyday competence of people to understand
how a particular space is to be performed (Shields, 1991: 53). For example, the emplotment of de Certeau's "spatial stories" requires the competence to "read" and "understand" their language, syntax, and grammar
in order for emplacement to occur. A map, for example, will only function as a guide to the extent that one is able to "read" it as a representational story; otherwise one will not be able to locate oneself or move
within it. It is on the basis of such stories or representations and their performance that space is appropriated as what Lefebvre (1991) terms " concrete" or "human" space, a space full of places of social practice and
identity. Moreover, it is on the basis of such spatial stories, and the story
spaces they perform, that men of wealth are able to engage in the practice
of appropriation.

Spatial stories and story spaces are the performance and embodiment
of what Massey has called the "power-geometry" of mapping—the

power to define and chart places and to control the pathways and flows of movement in-between. According to Massey:

> Different groups and different individuals are placed in very different ways in relation to these flows and interconnections. The point concerns not merely the issue of who moves and who doesn't, although that is an important element of it; it is also about power in relation *to* the flows and movement. Different social groups are more in charge of it than others; some initiate flows and movement, others don't; some are more on the receiving end of it than others; some are effectively imprisoned by it. (1993b: 61)

Massey is referring primarily to the capacity to shape and give form to the material spatiality of the landscape and the built environment, the spatial locations of production and consumption, and the emplacement and flows of people, money, and commodities among them. Yet the same argument about the power-geometry of space and place can and should be made about the construction and constitution of cartographies of what Derek Gregory (1995) terms the "spatial imaginary," the manner in which we emplot and emplace topoi of moral identity in material social space and the interrelationship and movement among them. As Kathleen Kirby argues, the very notion of the ethical subject of the sovereign masculine individual of capitalism is founded upon a historically contingent spatial imaginary, with its own particular territorializing machine of spatial stories, that links the subject and space in a relation of appropriation:

> The modern concept of the "sovereign self" depended upon the development of the Western spatial imagination . . . that made man able to conceive of himself as an independent actor, author of his peregrinations, master of his world. . . . Mapping, then, comes onto the scene both to reflect and reinforce a new way of conceiving both the subject and space. What kind of space, what kind of subject, does mapping perform? It organizes the landscape in such a way that some aspects of "reality" are privileged while others are silenced. Cartography emphasizes boundaries over sites . . . [and] indicates the primacy in European mapping of *ownership*. One could transfer this insight into the realm of the subject by pointing out the emphasis upon "propriety" and "own-ness" in the "one-ness" of the Enlightenment individual—as well as the subject's imbrication in the developing social form of capitalism. (1995: 42–43)

In creating territories of appropriation, the mapping of space across its different registers through narrativity is a form of power/knowledge. As a form of power/knowledge, mapping is about discipline and authorization of spatial practices, the political and moral valorization of particular meanings given to particular places that circumscribe particular performances and enactments of spatialization. I now turn to the way in which the (auto-)biographical narratives of men wealth perform, as well as fail to enact, the story space of the ethical subject of sovereign individuality in relation to the flows of wealth and power.

Story Spaces of the Ethical Subject of Sovereign Individuality

In the preceding section I argue that narrativity operates as a form and performance of power/knowledge that provides men of wealth with a grid of intelligibility of both know-how and can-do-ness that allows them to appropriate wealth as a source of empowerment and a sign of valorized moral identity. In particular, the narrative of fortune and virtue is a machine of territorialization, a spatial story that maps the story space of the ethical subject of the masculine sovereign individual of capitalism as a material and symbolic territory of propriety and power. As such, the narrative of fortune and virtue is, to paraphrase George Bush, a *magical* machine that performs the symbolic alchemy of transforming mere quantity of wealth into the moral quality of sovereign individuality, thereby rhetorically producing the moral persona or character who inhabits the territory of propriety and power—the "better angel" of capitalism.

Thus far, however, my discussion of emplotment and emplacement has remained primarily at the level of theories of narrative and spatiality. Accordingly, I want to ground the foregoing discussion in an examination of two particular (auto-)biographical narratives of wealthy men. In so doing, I will explore how the trajectory and teleology of narrative emplotment simultaneously organize and map the different registers of spatiality as places for the performance of moral identity and empowerment, thereby providing the know-how and can-do-ness of appropriation. This examination will set the stage for the genealogical analysis of the space, place, and story of the "better angels" that follows.

Although both stories are told by men of wealth, they are vastly different. One is the story of a man I have already discussed, John Norris. His story is a story of "success," of "prosperity with a purpose." His is a narrative of fortune and virtue that is productive of the autonomy and sovereignty of wealth as power that is appropriate to his identity. His narrative entails a teleological emplotment of transformation and ascension, emplaces him in the material and symbolic space of the ethical subject of sovereign individuality and principality, and gives his moral identity coherent form and virtuous positivity. As such, it is an exemplar of the rhetorical performance of the "better angel" of capitalism, the moral character or persona produced by the narrative of fortune and virtue as its manifested destiny.

The other is the story of David Schwartz, inheritor to a considerable fortune made by his grandfather and father in the retail business and whose nationwide firm is a household name. His story is also a narrative of fortune and virtue, but his is a story of "failure"—as well as a failed story. It is a story where prosperity is seemingly without substantively rational purpose. The trajectory and teleology of his story is fractured and achronic, lacking in a coherent direction or manifested destiny that is essential for him to form a coherent moral identity and thereby both "@-'prō-prē-āt" and be @-'prō-prē-@t to his wealth. Rather than being a story of ascension, it is a story of abjection. These two stories show how the narrative of fortune and virtue operates as a technology of self and power/knowledge that gives the subject coherency amid the flow of wealth and money.

"Look Them in the Eye": The Story Space of Sight and Sovereignty of John Norris

As I argue above using the insights of Game and Metcalfe, one of the primary ways in which narrativity gives coherence and form to moral identity is through the way teleological emplotment gives stories, and the self who tells the story, a "manifested destiny." By this, Game and Metcalfe mean that a story always has an imagined end or goal that fulfills a promised trajectory entailed in the story's beginning. As Kerby points out in the context of discussing the "virtue of narrative," the emplotment of narrativity functions as a "mode of vision." In the "mind's eye," so to speak, the subject "sees" and projects the emplotted trajectory that will connect the beginning and end of the story as manifested destiny. Moreover, narrativity as a mode of vision also connects the subject to the space of the social through the emplacement of the subject in terms of location, orientation, and movement. McClaren correctly emphasizes the visual dimension of narrative as a mode of spatial comportment when he writes that "narrative provides us with a framework that helps us hold our gaze, that brings an economy of movement to the way we survey our surroundings and the way we suture disparate images and readings of the world into a coherent story, one that partakes of continuity, of a fiction of stasis in a world that is always in motion" (1995: 92). Thus, the manifested destiny of stories consists of a point of departure and a point of arrival that are connected teleologically and, as such, plots and maps out an itinerary for the subject through symbolic and material space, giving both coherent shape and form.

The manifested destiny of the narrative of fortune and virtue is the ethical subject of sovereign individuality, a subject that it is able to see both self and world in a particular way and appropriate the latter as an extension of the former through the empowerment of wealth. In other words, the performance of sovereign individuality is contingent on narrativity as a mode of spatial comportment. John Norris's (auto-)biographical narrative is an exemplar of the narrative of fortune and virtue as a spatial story of appropriation, and in examining his story we can began to understand how the narrative works as a form of power/knowledge.

In the end of a story, as Game and Metcalfe say, is the beginning, and therein is located Norris's manifest destiny. In Chapter 1, I presented the end of his narrative: He gets up from the table, goes to the window, and lays claim to what he sees through his gesture to the world. But how did he get this to this place, this location in material and moral space where he is able to both "@-'prō-prē-āt" and be @-'prō-prē-@t to the view? As Norris tells the story, he knew this was his destiny as he *saw* it all along.

Foresight, Norris says, is a virtue that is essential to "success" in American society, and the necessity of foresight was a lesson that was taught to him early in his life by his father:

> My father was an engineer and he used to talk to me a lot about foresight. You know, in a kind of kidding way, but every time I didn't look ahead, he would remind me that one of the ways to be successful in our society was to try to make sure that you were looking out five or ten years just as an exercise if nothing else: Like what do you want to be doing five or ten years from now? Because he used as an example an interesting experience he had. When he got out of college with a degree in engineering, he and his closest colleague went around looking for jobs in Seattle. That was in 1916, and there weren't many jobs, but there was a little company that built airplanes out of spruce and fabric. They needed a couple of draftsman, and he was an engineer. He was not about to accept a job as draftsman. Now his closest friend decided it was a pretty good start, so he took the job because he also felt that those fabric-and-spruce–framed airplanes would amount to something some day. His closest friend, of course, was Philip Johnson, who became president of that company known as Boeing. So he used that as an example about you really have to ask yourself, "What do you see yourself doing five or ten years from now?"

For Norris, this was a cautionary tale: Unless one has the virtue of foresight, one may never see and understand the opportunities for success that are available. It was his capacity for foresight, to imagine and map the trajectory of his future emplotment, that started him on the path to "success." He explains how he ended up working for Calcucorp, one of the largest computer firms in the world:

> Well, when I was a junior in college I decided that I really wanted to work for a large company, just like I didn't want to go to small school. That's

based on the philosophy that if you go to a small school you have a small circle of friends and if you go to larger school you are going to have a larger circle of friends who will be influences on your life in a broader way than if you have just a small circle friends in a small school. So, I said, "I don't want to work for a little company. I want to work for a big one." So I wrote thirty-three letters to thirty-three large companies. I think I got about fifteen responses, and out of the fifteen there were probably eight or nine that showed some twinkling of interest, and out of that I boiled it down to three, and the one that became obvious to me was Calcucorp. So, when I got out of school I went right to work the next day for Calcucorp as a student salesman. The goal was that I just really wanted to carve out a successful career in Calcucorp, and at that point of time I was not really sure how I classed success, except that anybody can sell shoes but not everybody can sell Calcucorp machines. So, I think the first element of success was making that team.

Although making the Calcucorp team was the first definition of "success" for Norris, it was by no means the last. Once he joined Calcucorp, he began to foresee and emplot a much more grandiose trajectory of success:

Now as I went through the first year in Calcucorp as a student, because they send you to school for a year, I began to think it would be wonderful to be president of the company. And it didn't bother me to think in those terms because it was far enough away that it didn't seem overwhelming, and yet looking at the growth of the company, it didn't seem impossible. I worked for Calcucorp for seventeen years. It was a very interesting career. I had one of two "battlefield" promotions in the history of the company where they had a morale problem and instead of bringing in somebody from a smaller branch that was a manager they elected to take somebody who was here, which was me. I obviously had to have a successful sales career, but I really didn't understand all the practices of management, but they decided overnight that I would be branch manager. So that reinforced my attitude that anything can happen in Calcucorp if you perform well, and it also got me closer to that goal that, by golly, I ought to president of the Calcucorp company. From the branch manager's job here it was to Los Angeles as a regional manager then to New York as the divisional manager of all advertising, promotion, education, and the computer division, then back to the field as running the whole Northwest. I was in charge of about six hundred employees and about $150,000,000 worth of business, and I was getting closer.

I quote Norris's narrative at length without interpretation in order let the emplotted trajectory of his story emerge. Although his story is far from complete, it is already possible to discern much about how narrative works as a spatial story. Recall what I say previously about the "self-abstracted person" of narrative: The "I" that narrates the story is performing the self as a persona or character. This persona or character is given coherency through its emplotment and emplacement in symbolic and social space. The "I" of Norris's narrative indexes a character who enacts and embodies the virtue of foresight as a practice of *phronesis* or practical ethical reasoning. What the character foresees are opportunities for success: first the success of making the team, then the success of becoming the president of the company. This virtue of foresight provides Norris's character with his comportment in both moral and material space. Morally, foresight furnishes him with an orientation toward what Taylor called the "hypergood," which in Norris's story is defined as success. The company itself as an organization also provides the material social space within which Norris will pursue his hypergood. As he rises up the corporate ladder of power and authority, the material space of the company is performed as a place or ethos of moral identity, and his destiny of sovereign individuality is made progressively manifest: He is "getting closer" to the telos of his imagined emplotment.

However, Norris's story does not end here. It does end at "the top" of a symbolic and spatial hierarchy, but it is not that of Calcucorp. Eventually, Norris began to feel that he didn't want to be president of Calcucorp after all. Again, in order to let the trajectory of the next phase of Norris's teleology of success emerge, I will quote his narrative at length. He explains his decision to leave Calcucorp and start his own business:

> After becoming the manager of all fifteen districts in the United States, I began to feel that I didn't really want to leave Seattle, which was my problem, not Calcucorp's. I could run that district from my bedroom, so it was becoming less and less of a challenge, and I wasn't really interested in a new challenge which would be located at world headquarters in New York. Now you can hang on and hang on and some people might have but that's not my style. So I just did an amazing thing and resigned from the Calcucorp company. . . . There was a doctor, a vascular surgeon here who was a very interesting electronic innovator, and I had arranged to have him consult with Calcucorp for a couple of years. He founded a little company which was kind of a hobby shop, and he'd kept it going as his surgical practice grew by borrowing money from the bank. And then the bank said that is not our business. He then started to sell stock to his friends and then he ran out of friends. Finally, the thing went bankrupt, but because he was aware of my interests in life sciences because of his consulting with Calcucorp, one day he paddled up to the posh twentieth floor of the Calcucorp building where I had my office, and he wanted to know if I wanted to gamble with a little company. As I indicated earlier, I had arrived at the decision that I wasn't going to leave Seattle for corporate world headquarters. So, on a Friday night, I walked out of the beautiful twentieth floor of the Calcucorp building, and the next Monday I was president and CEO of a bankrupt little company in the medical business called Medicon. So, that's how I got started.

There are two important elements to note in the Norris narrative. First, Norris emphasizes the material space of the corporation as a locale for the performance of his moral identity. His office is "posh" and "beautiful," a sign of his power and accomplishment. Yet as he projects the future emplotment of his life toward success, he comes to a realization that his opportunities for further advancement are limited, albeit by his own choices and values. A new social space for the emplotment of success, a bankrupt company, comes into his line of sight in the form of fortuitous opportunity. Second, this opportunity entails something more than a chance for success; it also carries with it the risk of failure on a significant scale. It is a "gamble," and Norris is risking his moral identity of success by "walking out of the beautiful twentieth floor of the Calcucorp building." In order to succeed in this new enterprise, Norris must negotiate the vagaries of risky opportunity on the basis of his personal virtue. Norris describes this new phase of his narrative and fortune and virtue:

The first thing you do when you become president of a bankrupt little company is go out and raise some money. I went out and talked to fourteen well-known individuals in the community who I knew might be interested. And I could look them in the eye and say that for every dollar that I am asking you to gamble, I am gambling ten times that much just by leaving that beautiful office. It was worse than a start-up—we were bankrupt! Like any Harvard Business School case problem, the seed money is one level of investment risk, and then about two years later, if the little start up makes it through that two-year period, then you go out for a second round and that is money to grow on. We made it through the two-year period and got to the threshold of what of what we thought was going to be success, so I went out and raised more money. Of course, the company became so profitable, it was a cash generator. This little company made over $100,000,000 in profit last year. We just kept performing well enough that we split the stock 1200:1 over a period and had no debt and started to dominate our markets worldwide in the field of vascular medicine that we understood. . . . But my philosophy about Medicon—and this is a really an offshoot of Calcucorp—is that I'm not interested in all of this business school palaver about the bottom line. I think it is the most misused term in the English language, and that is the wrong focus of the corporation. A corporation's focus should be on the creation of value, so I always focused our efforts on the three values you have to create: the value you create the minute you become involved in the business, the value you create to the people who use your products and services; and third, the creation of value in the society in which you exist. Now if you create all three of those values, the bottom line will take care of itself. But I always insisted that our focus be on value, and it works. The bottom line then is a secondary thing. I'm not sitting before you and saying that I ignore the requirement that the company be profitable because without it you cannot create the values. But the three values should be the focus, not the bottom line. And if you talk to anybody in this community or industry, Medicon is probably the leading responsible corporate citizen by design, not by accident. We are very proud of that and it inspires our kids, meaning people in the business. They're proud of that, and when they walk down the street, and they say they are with Medicon, people say, "By golly, what a remarkable company." So we just started out, five of us, and we developed the basic beliefs of the company and established our basic goals and then we just really strived to accomplish them and we did. And the company dominates its worldwide markets by design, I repeat. So that was all part of this culture of corporate responsibility. I could look everybody in the eye and say, you know, I do it personally so therefore I really want the corporation to do these things. Since I am able to say that our personal lives are involved in responsibility, then obviously I have a real leg up on making sure that corporate responsibility falls into line.

Clearly, by Norris's own account, the gamble he took when he walked out of his office at Calcucorp was a successful one. Yet what were the virtues that enabled Norris to make a fortune out of a fortuitous circumstance of risk? In one way or another, all of the virtuous qualities that Norris, as moral character of his self-story, embodies are related to sight and vision. The virtue of sight and vision is manifested in two ways in Norris's story. At one level, sight is a central part of his substantive rationality of running the business enterprise. The success of the company is a function of the rational foresight of planning and organization. The dominance of the company of its markets and its role as "leading corporate citizen" was, as Norris says, accomplished "by design" and "not by accident." This success, in turn, was contingent upon seeing and focusing on the production of qualitative values (embodied in people, products, and society) rather than the quantitative criteria of the "bottom line." In these respects, Norris's virtue in constituted by entering into a field of risk and imposing order upon it through his foresight, will, and intention. His comportment in the field of social space is thus one of mastery, sovereignty, and power.

However, the propriety of his mastery in social space, and thus his location and comportment in moral space, is contingent on another level of sight and ocularity that is manifested in his spatial story as a technology of power/knowledge. As I discuss, one of the ways in which narrativity is a form of power/knowledge is that it is a technology of subjection. Narrative is a practice of make-believe through which the subject is given a coherent identity. The success of this subjection is contingent not only on the subject believing in the identity that he has made or fashioned through narrative but also on others recognizing and believing its truth as well. For Norris, his status as the ethical subject of sovereign individuality is contingent on others literally and figuratively seeing that he is what he says he is. At two points in the preceding quote he rhetorically stages this ocular dialectic of subjection and identification. When he leaves Calcucorp and asks people to invest in his bankrupt company he says, "I could look them in the eye and say that for every dollar that I am asking you to gamble, I am gambling ten times that much just by leaving that beautiful office." And again, near the end of the passage when he talks about the necessity of corporate philanthropy and citizenship, Norris says, "I could look everybody in the eye and say, you know, I do it personally so therefore I really want the corporation to do these things." By "looking them in the eye" Norris sets into motion a circuit of representation whereby the truth of his moral identity is reflected back to him by those who see and recognize his virtue. He looks them in the eye, making a presentation of himself as a man of know-how and can-do-ness—he knows what risk entails and can virtuously transform it into fortune; he knows the importance of corporate social responsibility and can do it because he does it personally. Those who are looked at look back, reflecting the truth and coherency of Norris's moral identity in the ocular mirror of their recognition. In the line of sight established between the eye of Norris and the eye of others, the metaphysics of presence of the sovereign "I" as *persona* is made manifest in his rhetoric of self.

Through the narrativization of his self as an individual who has mastered fortune through virtue, and the recognition by himself and others that he therefore embodies and enacts the moral identity of sovereign individuality, Norris has ascended to the top of Columbia Towers to appropriate its space and its view of the world as a place of his power and propriety. Yet a final gesture adds an exclamation point to his manifested destiny. Speaking about the necessity for private and corporate philanthropy in American society, he told me:

> I think society would be very sick without philanthropy and volunteerism. It would be very sick without the resource allocations and very sick without the leadership because you can't leave it to the government. Much of what we do in our society has to be supported by the private sector. All you have to do is look at the lack of success of the entitlement program in our society. They are either mismanaged or they are misdirected in most cases now. That is a broad statement, but if you look around at entitlement programs where people are becoming more and more dependent upon the government, you find that it is bad for the people involved, it takes away all the incentive to be successful at any level. So I think the private sector has to take more and more of this on, and it's not only in resources but in leadership. It's a social responsibility. . . . I don't have to have a Ph.D. to understand it. Now you'll have great scholars of government, you'll have great scholars of sociology argue the point and that is fine. But I don't see them spending 30 percent of their time doing what I am doing.

As Norris is saying this, he is looking *me* in the eye. At this moment in his performance of self, I am being directly recruited to recognize the moral truth of his sovereign individuality through sight. Moreover, an intrinsic part of this rhetorical process of subjection and identification is that I am being asked to recognize my own, subject position in relation to that of Norris. Within the story space conjured by Norris's rhetoric and narrative, private and corporate philanthropy is a virtue and government social programs are a vice. Those who argue otherwise, particularly those with a Ph.D. and scholars of sociology, don't know what Norris knows or do what he does. Accordingly, within his story space of sovereign individuality, to paraphrase Marcel Mauss (1967), Norris is "magister" and superior; I am "minister" and inferior. However, the manifested destiny of Norris's magisterial presence and my subservient lack is made possible only if the circuit of representation between the *eyes* and of the *Is* remains stable and closed. As I argue, this stability and closure of the story space of sovereign individuality is not guaranteed, either historically or in the present. In order to understand how and why Norris's story seems to be a successful one, it is necessary to examine a story of wealth that fails.

David Schwartz: The "Wild Card" Lost in Space

As I argue, one of the principal ways in which narrativity is constitutive of moral identity through emplotment and emplacement is by conjuring an ethos, a place or locale in symbolic space from which both self and world make moral sense. It is in this respect, as Ricoeur said, that narrative makes life habitable. It is in the ethos constructed by narrative that the temporal and spatial dimensions of emplotment and emplacement converge in order to produce a coherent moral identity and provide the conditions for moral choice and action. In the telling of one's life story, past experience is given a trajectory that leads to the present, setting the stage for the imagined trajectory of one's future. The ability to simultaneously make sense of *who* and *where* one was, is, and will be as a function of the teleological order of an unfolding story comprises what Game and Metcalfe termed the "manifested destiny" of narrative. But what happens when one's story of the self fails to perform the self as enacting and embodying a manifested destiny? The result is a self that is incoherent, a self that seemingly doesn't "know how" and therefore "can't do." Such a self, so to speak, is lost in space across all registers. Such a self is without an ethos, a moral place called home.

David Schwartz is a self lost in space. This is not to say that he is in a literal sense homeless. Quite the contrary: The locale of our interview is his office in a newly bought and refurbished house in an exclusive, wealthy suburb along Lake Michigan north of Chicago. Yet even when he is in his house, it is not really a home in an ethical and moral sense. As a spatial story, his (auto-)biographical narrative fails to turn this space into place, an ethos that makes life habitable. As he told me:

> Everybody has problems making money, and it ties them down. And in this world making money and making sense are rarely compatible goals. I mean very rarely. You can find a few niches. But for the most part, they are largely incompatible. . . . We just bought this house [in 1986]. This house cost close to, after all the hidden costs of repairing and stuff, probably $400,000. It's been on my mind a great deal. It's a burden because I'm a bourgeois social-ist. I work all day in this socialist organization and I come back home to a very comfortable setting and it becomes very philosophical for me. I don't make decisions to buy on whether I've got enough money or not. I make de-cisions based upon one of two things: one is that it is exemplary of what I think everyone ought to have and deserves and is possible to have on this planet; or it is exemplary of being a privileged elite. It's either one of those two, and this house is a hard one to justify on the former grounds. I mean because not everybody can live here at this stature. Making money and making sense just don't go together.

For Schwartz, finding an ethos is a matter of being able to find a map of the world, a grid of intelligibility, that brings together "making money and making sense." His "philosophical" dilemma about how he can jus-tify his house, given his morally ambiguous status as a "bourgeois social-ist," is emblematic of a larger question that he succinctly articulates as follows: "I mean how do I *fit* in this world, given my money? What mod-els are there for making sense of my wealth for what the world means right now?" This question forms the thematic organization of the emplot-ment and emplacement of his (auto-)biographical narrative as a quest for the moral identity of sovereign individuality and provides the trajectory where past, present, and future converge in the story space he is perform-ing in his house. The answer to this question is clearly an embodiment of power/knowledge, of being able to link the know-how of wealth with the can-do-ness of empowerment so that one fits appropriately in the world in terms of moral identity. Yet it is a question that he is seemingly destined not to answer. This inability is an artifact of his own story of for-tune and virtue.

What is Schwartz's narrativized manifest destiny? Where does his story begin and end? It begins and ends with an ambivalent assessment of fortune itself. As I explore in some detail in Chapter 3, the word *fortune* is derived from the Latin *fortuna*, which means (among other things), "chance." *Fortune* therefore mean chance and circumstance. Fortune may be good or ill, having positive or negative consequences. Fortune can also refer to a possession that causes someone to be fortunate, and one way fortune is materialized as a possession is wealth. As such, wealth and fortune tend to be synonymous in everyday language. In the popular imagination, wealth as fortune is viewed as an unambiguous good, a cornucopia of positive benefits and possibilities. Often overlooked in popular imaginings and desires for wealth as fortune are negative consequences that make its possessor at times feel distinctively *unfortunate*. Thus, the blessings of the good fortune of wealth can be decidedly mixed. Schwartz explains the path of his life story in relation to his wealth:

> The money fucked me up thus far. I was thrown on this long, circuitous route, largely as a result of the money and my upbringing. I don't have to think of myself as the most fortunate person around. You can't say that this is such a great benefit. I've gotten very tangled up in my life, partially because of the money, and therefore I can justify the possession of money long enough to get me off the ground so that I am coming back to a path with some momentum building. See now I am talking about a kind of entitlement here—I'm entitled to getting to the money supporting me as I disentangle from the money and the effects of the money. So you can see the potential for suspicion there because you start to say, "If the money's tangling you up, let go, and then it will let go of you." That's the counterargument. Let go of the money. Walk away from it. If you want to know what it's like to live in the real world, walk away from it. This is just another way of holding on to it. It's another delay tactic. But you know what there is to do in this world and you've got get out and start doing it.

This statement is a profound evocation of the ambivalences of wealth as fortune. His inheritance "fucked" him up by "tangling" him up in its "effects." He does not feel fortunate at all. Yet he cannot disentangle himself by giving it away—he needs it to help him see and plot out a future "path" for himself in the world so that he can both know and do "what there is to do in the world." However, transforming the possibilities of wealth as power into the propriety of entitlement does not come easily for Schwartz. In fact, it does not come at all. Of course, the question is why, or what story does Schwartz tell to account for the misfortune of fortune and the dilemma that it poses for him in terms of constructing his moral identity?

The "circuitous path" of his life is a result of the intertwined dynamics of his family background and the inheritance itself. In terms of his family background, Schwartz is referring mainly to his father, who with Schwartz's grandfather was the progenitor of the family fortune. In Schwartz's account of his upbringing, his relation to his father is extremely complex and contradictory. As he says, "I have always been swinging in-between two positions with my father. One is total adoration and compliance and whatever I could to do to take on his own lifestyle and his whole character. And the other is complete avoidance. They really are, in fact, the same thing."

Schwartz's father embodied and enacted, albeit in an eccentric manner, the ethical subject of sovereign individual of wealth and power. Schwartz describes the role of his father in his upbringing:

> My father was always a little different. He played bagpipes as a kid, which was unconventional for a Jewish boy. He was a real enthusiast, very passionate for different things at different points in life. He would take on the discipline and devour it, and they were usually exotic. For a while, we had birds in our house; we had major aviaries in this house in Brooklyn. At one point, we had five hundred birds, mostly hummingbirds and finches, flying through the rooms of this house. One summer, he got me a cow from a friend and we had a cow in Brooklyn. That was my pet cow. . . . There was a lot of structure in our childhood. We went to the equivalent of a Yeshiva day school. It was like four hours a day of Hebrew, four hours a day of English. My father was a fanatical pianist and wanted us all to play music. So he enforced it, enforced it like a zealot. At one time, he made my brothers and I form a family chamber orchestra with him as the conductor, and we would regularly have concerts for the rest of the larger family, who all lived within a few blocks of us.

Clearly, then, as Schwartz was growing up, his household was a territory for his father's individuality and principality. As Schwartz tells the story, he had troubles with his father's power and authority early in childhood: "I was the identified patient growing up. I was definitely the troubled one, the one who whined, complained, threw tantrums—that's what we called it at the time. I took on the role of the struggler in the family in relation to my father, and I maintained that role for a long time. I went into psychoanalysis at the age of eight or so and continued until I was thirteen." For Schwartz, struggling with his father entailed struggling for some sort of independence and autonomy, some grounding of identity, outside of his father's realm of sovereignty in everyday life. Yet Schwartz's struggle for independence from his father was complicated by something else his father represented aside from eccentric and overzealous patriarchal authority: money or, more specifically, his inheritance. Schwartz describes the circumstances and experience of coming to learn of his inheritance:

> In my sixteenth or seventeenth year, I remember the time I first heard about it, rumors were out. There was a change in the tax law that made it appropriate for my father to pass on some money to us. And so at sixteen years old I had a checking account with $30,000 in it, and it grew rapidly. So I never saw a ceiling to my money after I was sixteen. Also, my grandfather

started putting money into it too, and I couldn't figure it out. I mean, all along I had known we had a large house. I knew that there were some benefits from living in my family as compared with someone else's. But I hadn't faced the possibility that I would have more money that I knew what do with. It hadn't quite become clear to me. . . . It made me uncomfortable, this money I hadn't earned.

Here the problematic relationship between Schwartz's money and his moral identity begins to emerge as a theme. First, the dual meaning of fortune as both chance and wealth are clearly present. Although Schwartz understood his family was relatively privileged, he was unaware of the family's wealth. It first insinuates itself into his life as "rumor," whisperings and intimations of a fortune that seemingly befall Schwartz as if by chance rather than by design. Schwartz then points to an important quality to the phenomenological perception of wealth as fortune: In and of itself, wealth is money without "a ceiling," a limit or boundary. This has profound implications for the appropriation of wealth through discourse and narrative as power/knowledge. At one level, to say there was no ceiling to his money means that it exceeded need. At another level, to say there is no ceiling means that it cannot be accounted for. By "accounting," I mean being able to account for it through the articulation of know-how and can-do-ness. As Schwartz says, at the moment of inheritance, his wealth exceeds the limit of his ability to understand it in terms of substantive rationality: He hadn't faced the possibility that he would have more money than he "knew what to do with." Finally, Schwartz brings to the fore the question of virtue and moral legitimacy in relation to fortune: One of the ways in which wealth exceeded his capacity to account for it was that he hadn't "earned it." This makes Schwartz feel "uncomfortable" and without a habitable ethical location in relation to his wealth.

Schwartz elaborates these complexities of knowing and accounting for wealth. Reflecting on this dramatic moment of identity transformation in his life, Schwartz connects the past to the present and the future as he imagines how and whether to pass his wealth down to his children.

My father warned me at one point, "Don't continue to give away your money. You don't have that much." That much, too much, too little—it's so relative. And the fact is that my father passed on very little financial education to us, and we didn't really know what we had. And the money, it trickles, it trickles in all the time. So, I thought at one time about changing my attitudes about inheritance so I wouldn't pass anything on to my kids until they could pass a test about the money. They'd have to have proof that they have read the operator's guide or owner's manual before they get this big machine. What would be in the owner's manual if I decided that it was a just thing to do, giving money to them? It would be some understanding of tax law, trust law, the quantity of money that was there. The idea that it suddenly started to trickle into my back pocket. You know, I'd just turn around and its trickling in suddenly and its trickling in faster than my pocket can hold it. That's not the way to hold onto an inheritance, if you believe in the process at all. There ought to be a rite of passage. And there was none of that. So, that's why I say there would be at least that stuff. But also, I end up thinking I wouldn't want to pass it on to my kids unless I've at least reckoned with it at some point.

Here Schwartz is offering a fascinating representation of the nature of money and what is required by the way of knowledge to make sense of it, pragmatically and morally. The wealth that constitutes his inheritance is not a static or inert object; it is a dynamic "big machine" that produces a perpetual flow of money that "trickles" in and through his life and his self. He is without proper knowledge of the machine, knowledge constituted by what Schwartz call's an "owner's manual," and so the flow of money exceeds his capacity to account for it. It flows into his pocket faster than his pocket can hold it. The pocket signifies a place where he can "hold" the money—possesses it, own it, control it, and give it shape and form. Of course, as Schwartz points out, one of the most important features of the owner's manual to the money machine is knowing how much money one has. Thus, he would have his children learn the disciplinary matrix of financial accounting practices (i.e., trust law, tax law, etc.) that would enable them to know how much money they have. Although knowing how much is certainly a necessary instance of the power/knowledge of wealth as it renders visible and countable what one possesses, it is not a sufficient condition for the know-how of appropriating wealth as power and propriety. According to Schwartz, successfully owning and operating the money machine as an extension of individuality and principality requires something more: He must first "reckon" with his money. A reckoning is a deliberative calculation, a mode of rational accounting. But the accounting that Schwartz is giving notice to here is not merely quantitative; it is a qualitative moral accounting of substantive rationality, of knowing why and what for as well as how much. In this respect, Schwartz's desire to reckon with his money entails a *phronesis* of wealth and power, a quotidian practice of ethical judgment that links together his money, his choices and actions, and his moral self-identity in a coherent way. This *phronesis*, as Schwartz goes on to reveal in his narrative, is part of a larger moral framework, a territorializing machine of discourse that would coherently map the flows of fortune that the money machine produces as an embodiment of his own virtue and therefore orient him in moral and social space.

It is this quest for a stable ground of ethical judgment and moral identity, of virtue in relation to his fortune, that provides the emplotted trajectory and teleology of the "circuitous route" that Schwartz's life story
takes. His story is really a story of successive failure to find stable
ground. After inheriting money, his first reaction was to "demonstrate
my independence" by going to work for the family firm in one of their local stores. "The effort," Schwartz says, "did not go so well. I got indig-
nant with the low pay. And I thought it was outrageous that I worked so
hard for twelve hours then get five bucks or something. So I quit. Not a
prodigious beginning." Thereafter, Schwartz drifted from avocation to
avocation, place to place: He took up the bassoon, toying with the idea of
becoming a professional classical musician, but he abandoned the instrument and the career; he went to college and studied humanist psychology but dropped out before he graduated, "looking for something better
to do"; and he got involved in the human potentials movement, but that
turned out to be unfulfilling for him as well. Schwartz describes the rationale for his existential drift:

> I was looking for something more; I was looking for leverage. I laugh at the
> word now, *leverage*, but it was very important in my vocabulary at the time.
> And I found it in a place called Arcadia, a hippie commune in Vermont. My
> entire career with Arcadia was five years. A year and half of that time I was in
> Peru, doing relief and development work with the commune's organization
> that was down there. I worked. I did plumbing. I did crew work. I ran a bike
> shop for a while. My work in Guatemala was finally some leverage, and I re-
> ally grew with it. It became attractive enough that I met my wife there and
> we fell in love. We had our first child there. We stayed there for so long that I
> felt like I would die there. I would live there for that long. I just loved it there.

Although Schwartz says that he now laughs at the word *leverage*, the pursuit of leverage is an all-important theme in his narrative. What is leverage? To possess leverage is literally to have a positional advantage, a
place or locale from which one has the power to act effectively. For
Schwartz, the commune was a place where he had the power to act efficaciously in the world, not simply in terms of capacity but also in terms
of providing a coherent ethos and topos of moral identity as well. In finding leverage he also finds a stable place of self-identity and source of esteem and moral worth: Working in Guatemala brought him leverage, and
he "really grew with it." But leverage for what? What is the substantive
rationality that informs leverage as power and capacity? He describes his
own understanding of leverage:

> Arcadia had a lot to do with bringing home the concept of leverage that I
> guess had been on my mind for a while but wasn't cogent. It wasn't complete.

> We talked about saving the world there on the commune, and we had real high hopes. We were real idealistic. . . . But whatever it was, it was feeding hungry people; it was stopping having so many wars; it was getting in touch with your feelings, et cetera. So, leverage towards doing that. But it's funny. It was a mixed thing because my father had leverage. I wanted leverage like my Daddy had leverage. So it just wasn't leverage to change the world for its own sake. It was leverage because he was that. He was a big man. He was a very big man. And I always wanted to be that big man. Still do.

The notion of leverage is clearly what Taylor would call a "hypergood," a reigning concept of moral value that orients the subject in moral space in terms of location and direction. Yet it is also a complicated and contradictory one for Schwartz. At one level, leverage is simply power to "change the world" as well as one's self as part of a collective social project. At another level, leverage is the power of the sovereign individuality of masculinity, the power to make one's will and desire manifest in the world. This is the power enacted and embodied by his father as "a very big man," who Schwartz still desires to emulate. Yet Schwartz ultimately recognizes as a man of wealth that both types of leverage cannot be disentangled from his money. On the positive side of things, wealth and money as a power resource is "as pure as an individual can get about leverage. In so far as money can be effective, for me personally, it would be as leverage to change things in the world." However, there is a downside to possessing the leverage of money, which is that it becomes impossible for him to disentangle money as power from money as moral identity. The confusion between Schwartz's money and his identity forced him to leave Arcadia:

> At one point some of the trust money came through to me and I wanted to give about $250,000 to the commune. My father cautioned me about doing that, and we agreed that I would put the money aside for ten years. In the meantime, all the income from the trust was going to Arcadia and was basically keeping it afloat. . . . So we stayed there for five and half years, and by the end there were problems. My money was not something I could walk away from. It became apparent to me that I was a source of more than just my personal energies there. My identity got linked up with my money once again. I felt that I couldn't be reproached. I'd have to say something really rotten to be criticized. And I felt like I wanted some more parity with other members there. So I pulled out.

After leaving Arcadia, Schwartz continued his quest for leverage, primarily in the field of left-liberal social activism. He did several volunteer stints at various progressive social change organizations, and he became involved in the emergent field of radical philanthropy, both as an individual grant maker and as a member of several progressive philanthropic foundations.

Yet no matter what the involvement, Schwartz says his search for a coherent vocation of leverage that would morally account for his money
eludes him—and eludes other inheritors as well:

> You feel like you gotta make it in your field, your equivalent to a field. Often
> you are incompetent at making money, you weren't necessarily trained for
> it. You don't have the incentive for it. And you want to prove yourself in that
> field and you talk about leverage. Well, if you want to give that seed grant
> that turns over a major operation, that has a major effect. Not only that,
> there are some other benefits of being someone who's looking for leverage
> like this in that you can hold out. You don't have to commit yourself to
> much of anything. You don't have to face the fact that you don't deserve the
> money in the first place, and you probably ought to give it all away because
> you're looking for your best shot. Then I also know personally, vocationally,
> and in my grant-making, by being noncommittal, by holding out for just
> that right piece of leverage, I don't have to face the thing that most people
> have to face, which is if you commit yourself, you stick yourself all the way
> into a thing and you may fail at it. It may not work, and you have to face the
> fact that you're no good at something. So this way I've been able to be more
> of a dabbler. These are the side effects of the search for leverage that I've
> been on in a lot of ways. I haven't been sucked into some vocational disci-
> pline, just drawn in almost involuntarily with a passion that just overtakes
> me. Every once in a while, the passionlessness about my activities can get to
> me, and I notice that I'm doing it in a shallow manner, and so it kind of fills
> me with a concern about my prospects.

Here again Schwartz returns to the theme of the ambivalence of fortune:
On the one hand, it provides leverage; on the other hand, his inheritance
allows him to forever be a dilettante without a vocational passion. From
an individualistic standpoint, one might simply read Schwartz's story
and conclude that he really has been personally "fucked up" by his
money, that he had better get a grip on himself or just give his money
away, and that either way people without money would not be too sympathetic with his plight and would gladly take on his "burden." However, I want to argue that Schwartz's dilemma is not just the artifact of
character flaws or simply the artifact of being an inheritor as opposed to
an entrepreneur who "deserves" his wealth because he has, as Schwartz
told me, "made it in the arena where men make it—business." As I discuss in Chapter 5, there is a narrative of fortune and virtue that produces
a coherent moral identity and mode of appropriation for inheritors.
Schwartz's problem is that he cannot find a legitimating ethos of invocation and evocation in the moral economy of wealth that would enable
him to tell a compelling and seductive narrative of fortune and virtue.

Like Edward Hoffman and Nicholas Whimster, Schwartz understands that wealth can provide power or, to use his words, "leverage"—leverage to change things in the world and to change one's self in the world—as a resource of individuality and principality. But Schwartz is unable to rhetorically perform the symbolic alchemy that will transform wealth into the valorized moral identity of the sovereign individual. Quite the contrary: He is by his own account "paralyzed" by money and struggles to make moral sense of it.

Recall what Schwartz said about finding a place where he fits in the world with his money. Finding an ethical location is a question of elaborating a "model" or map of the world, a story space, where "making money" and "making sense" are compatible activities and generative of virtuous self-identity. Schwartz has thought long and hard about such models. In fact, during the course of the interview he handed me a list of a dozen or so models he has written down, none of which provide a satisfactory answer to his question, "Where do I fit in this world?" For example, in talking about his current dilemma he offers two contrasting models. On the one hand, he says,

> there is a model or paradigm that the money is somehow evil, if not evil, then venomous in some way. There is something poisonous about it. It's radioactive and it's slowly killing you. And pass it on. Liquid in, liquid out. You see what comes with inheritance is the sense like, you are a little incompetent. I mean its just weak blood. I mean you think about hemophilia and the tsar's son in Russia. All that stigma is around inherited wealth, and inherited money will upstage any other identity you've got. If you've got it and choose to be anonymous that's different. I would say that I have personally chosen not to be anonymous in a self-interested manner. I would like to be someone's case study. But I also end up thinking that I enjoy being Clark Kent Superman. I don't have the willpower in some ways to avoid revealing my true identity, and the identity is money and it keeps coming back to bite me. . . . I don't know if people want me for my money or myself. It's almost like a john who is complaining that his whore, who he has just paid, doesn't love him. You lament that they want you for their money, but you obviously made that representation to them and somehow thrive off your association with people with great leverage in the world.

A corollary to this model of money—"venomous poison" that overwhelms his identity—is what Schwartz calls "sophisticated and inescapable forms of guilt," guilt that is grounded in the belief that "you can't look logically at the world and this particular ownership right, the right of inheritance, and say that it makes sense." In contrast to inheritors, Schwartz argues, it is easier for entrepreneurs to get to a "liquid in, liquid out" attitude about it. It's a decent model. Given that there is no fairness in the world, money is pure energy. It's slightly sticky. Strange complexes attach to it. But you can actually wield it with a free hand. And that's the way it should be treated. Liquid in, liquid out; it's easy to make and it's easy to give. And I know some people who do that too. It's an excellent model. If you can live it. They have an easier time getting to it than the inheritor. It's not such a tangle. You're not stuck. It's a different ownership right. Even though some of them make it in strange ways that aren't so positive for what the world needs right now, in America, if you have made yourself, through your own labors, it is a completely different ownership right. One of the kinkiest ownership rights is that you own what your father made. It makes for great accumulations and great income disparities.

On the other hand, says Schwartz, there are models that can potentially diminish the guilt of inheritance:

Then there are models that say, "I am the wild card. I'm the one with the society's fortunate wild card." Don't waste any time feeling guilty about it. Get to work. Do good stuff. Follow your nose. Enjoy the freedom and power you got. It's a decent model, but I have problems with it. They give it to some of society's weakest potential wild cards because anybody who is raised without the get-up-and-go necessary to raise and make money is often too flabby to be given the role of the wild card because of the paralysis that comes with inherited money.

In the tension between these two models it is possible to discern why Schwartz's story is a failed spatial story of propriety and power. These two accountings of his wealth are the telos, the manifested destiny of his narrative, and it is destiny that leaves him betwixt and between, dislocated, without a place to stand in and without a path or trajectory to move through moral and social space. Schwartz's quest is to find a resonance between the interior space of his subjectivity and the external world of the social as a space of individuality and principality. He is looking for a space of engagement with world, a space within which he is autonomous and over which he is sovereign. Unfortunately for him, he is unable to find what he is looking for and, unlike Norris, cannot look upon the world from his window and lay claim to what he sees. But his failure to manifest a destiny of sovereign individuality tells us much about the way in which the empowerment of wealth is contingent on the symbolic alchemy of turning money into moral identity through rhetoric and narrativity.

First, Schwartz again foregrounds the relationship between money as flow and moral discourse as a territorializing machine that must govern it through accounting for it. The territorializing map he is seeking is what he calls "liquid in, liquid out." Within this cartographic grid of intelligibility, money flows through one's life, without its possessor getting "tangled," "stuck," or "paralyzed" by the "strange complexes" that attach to it. These "strange complexes" are the ethics of "ownership right," the moral legitimacy of appropriation. The moral legitimacy of appropriation as ownership and property, as I argue, is an artifact of *proprietas*, the proper signification of words. Schwartz cannot find *proprietas* in his models, and without the transubstantiating magic of a discourse and spatial story of propriety, he cannot claim his money and its empowerment as his own. In fact, the money owns him, so to speak. He is subservient to it, a victim of its flows. The flow of fortune through his life is corrupting and enervating—it is "venomous," "poisonous," "radioactive," and is "slowly killing" him.

Second, note the different, imbricated registers of space that he evokes in these statements. There is the register of corporeality and embodiment. His money courses through his body like the hemophiliac blood of the corrupt hereditary fortune of the doomed Romanovs, making him "weak" and "flabby." The flow of money through the figural space of his body invades the psychic space of personal identity as well. As he says, "Inherited wealth will upstage any other identity you got." He doesn't know if people want him for who is or what he has. In fact, he cannot separate the two, as his money is his identity and his identity keeps coming back to bite him. He can no more claim respect from recipients of his money than a john can claim love from his prostitute. Both are relations of power and exchange mediated by money rather than relationships of reciprocity. The corrupting flow of money through his corporeal and psychic space puts him in a perpetual state of displacement in social space. He can and should be the "wild card"—the "Clark Kent Superman" who has the leverage to move about and change the world at will. Surely, there is no better mythic personification of the sovereign individual and "better angel" of capitalism than Superman! Yet Schwartz cannot be Superman or even, in a somewhat less heroic and mythic incarnation, the "wild card." He finds himself paralyzed and generally unable to use his wealth as empowerment in the service of individuality and principality because he cannot find the Archimedean point in social space from which to leverage it without corrupting himself. In fact, Schwartz has given up the quest for leverage in terms of philanthropy and has put literal and figural distance between himself and his money:

> I kind of decided last year and made a pledge to myself to stop giving money away directly. It was a distraction. I needed to develop my identity outside it. From now on, if you want money, you go ask for my money. My

money is over there. It's got a different address than me. I'm here. That's my
money. Go talk to it. I have it in foundations, where other people make the
decisions. The part that's the leverage thing, the sense of identity that comes
from money that you long for, at some point, even though its a false sense, is
that I'll make a better decision than someone else. I have to trust myself to
make a decision, that somebody else would be as wise about it as me. It's
largely bullshit.

Finally, the proper articulation of the spatial registers of the corporeal,
the psychic, and the social are contingent on finding an ethos in moral
space. Schwartz asks the question "Where do I fit in this world?" and no
satisfactory answer is forthcoming. As such, Schwartz is lost—lost in
space. The reason is that he is unable to perform a spatial story that
maps, as power-geometry, the relationship between the flow of money in
relation to his self-identity as an appropriate embodiment of his will and
desire and territorializes the different registers of space into comfortable
and habitable places of moral identity.

When such a spatial story fails to territorialize the flow of money as an
extension of the self, wealth becomes something other than a surplus resource of empowerment; it becomes an excess source of abjection. It is excessive because it evades or transgresses the boundaries of moral accounting. It cannot be reckoned with. Further, as Judith Butler argues, the
"abject" designates "precisely those 'unlivable' and 'uninhabitable' zones
of social life which are nevertheless densely populated by those who do
not enjoy the status of subject" (1993: 3). Within the hegemonic social
imaginary of the moral economy of wealth, Schwartz doesn't enjoy the
status of subject or, at least, the magisterial status of the masculine sovereign individual of capitalism. He is, by his own accounting, "weak,"
"flabby," "incompetent," and "uncomfortable." Unlike his father, he is
not a "big man." The world of wealth is unlivable for him, and therefore
he is abject. In this respect there is more to the significance of Schwartz's
narrative for my analysis than being a failed spatial story of appropriation. As Butler argues, the abject exists in subtle relation of alterity with
the subject that is valorized in discourse and rhetorically performed in
narrative as a technology of power/knowledge:

> The exclusionary matrix by which subjects are formed thus requires the si-
> multaneous production of a domain of abject beings, those who are not yet
> "subjects," but who form the constitutive outside of the domain of the sub-
> ject. . . . This zone of inhabitability will constitute the defining limit of the
> subject's domain; it will constitute that site of dreaded identification against
> which—and by virtue of which—the domain of the subject will circumscribe
> its own claim to autonomy and to life. In this sense, then, the subject is

constituted through the force of exclusion and abjection, one which produces a constitutive outside to the subject an abjected outside, which is, after
all, "inside" the subject as its own founding repudiation. (1993: 3)

The subject seeks to exclude the abject from its territory of identity as it is
a "specter" that "threatens to expose the self-grounding assumptions of
the sexed subject" (1993: 3). At the same time, however, the subject requires the abject as *différance*, as it gives the form of the subject coherency
and the space of the subject definable and knowable boundaries. Without
the abject of the weak, the dissolute, the irrational, the chaotic, and the
"feminine," the ethical subject of masculine sovereign individuality and
its story space of fortune and virtue could not exist. Norris's story succeeds because it forms a space where the abject is securely placed "outside" the borders of his sovereign individuality. He is a virtuous master
of the flows of fortune. Schwartz's story fails because the abject infiltrates
and corrupts the borders of his corporeal, psychic, social, and moral
space. Rather than being a master of fortune, it has mastered him. The
question remains, however, as to how the story space of the narrative of
virtue emerged to define the subject of sovereign individuality and its abject other. Investigating the emergence of the narrative of fortune and
virtue is my next step.

Notes

1. Much of what follows in the next few pages is taken directly from Schervish
and Herman (1988, 1991). Paul Schervish has gone on to explore the empowerment of wealth using this conceptual framework in Schervish (1994) and
Schervish (forthcoming) in much greater detail than I have here.

2. To be fair to myself and Paul Schervish, in our original writings we did explore a third form of empowerment, what we termed "psychological empowerment," which entailed how a wealthy individual's sense of self-worth and the legitimacy of his wealth and power was dynamically formed in relation to the
other forms of empowerment. Schervish (1994, forthcoming) has gone on to elab-
orate this form of empowerment in his writings. For my part, I have found the
concept of psychological empowerment too epistemologically and ontologically
individualistic for my analytical purposes.

3. For recent overviews of different approaches to narrative analysis in the interpretive human sciences, see Denzin (1996), Hinchman and Hinchman (1997),
and Polkinghorne (1988, 1995).

4. As I note in Chapter 1, I am not suggesting that this process of narrative subjectification is uniformly successful, either in general terms or in terms of the
wealthy men I interviewed. As numerous recent studies of narrative and everyday life have argued, storying the self is a dialectical process whereby individuals
draw upon the collective narrative imaginary to creatively cast their own individual identity into sense. I have referred to the two moments of this dialectic as the

moments of invocation and evocation. As Chase (1995) and Gubrium and Holstein (1998) note, there is often a disjuncture or discontinuity between dominant narrative conventions and how they are invoked in order to evoke personal stories of identity. Gubrium and Holstein call this discontinuity "narrative slippage." They describe narrative slippage as "points of articulation among culture, lived experience, and storytelling, points at which there is considerable play or elasticity in the way shared understandings are circumstantially brought to bear on matters of interpretive concern. Cultural resources do not determine how they are used but, instead, provide material for the narrator to construct his or her own story as distinguishable from others who are similarly placed in life" (Gubrium and Holstein, 1998: 167). Although it is important to attend to the creative moment of narrativity, it also important to keep in mind that cultural narrative imaginary is constraining as well as enabling. There are epistemological and ontological limits, both in terms of the dynamics of emplotment and emplacement as well as the performative practice of storytelling, to the creativity of individuals in order for their narrative identity to be considered coherent and valid. In other words, as Maines (1993: 21) and Fisher (1987) point out, in order for a narrative to be compelling and seductive as a will to truth, it must contain both "narrative probability," or coherence, and "narrative fidelity," or believability. Both of these characteristics of narrative are circumscribed by the conventions of narrative as form and storytelling as a practice.

5. The centrality of emplotment to narrativity can be found in theories and approaches to narrative analysis across the humanities and social sciences. For example, in literary theory see Brook (1984); in historiography see White (1978, 1996) and Veyne (1984); in philosophy see Kerby (1991) and Ricouer (1984); in psychology see Bruner (1987, 1991); in anthropology see Conquergood (1993) and Feldman (1991); in sociology see Maines (1993) and Somers and Gibson (1994).

6. For an incisive critique of Taylor along these lines see Lemert (1994).

3

The Mastering of Fortune: Machiavelli, Masculinity, and the Subject of *Virtù*

I compare Fortune with one of our destructive rivers which when it is angry, turns the plains into lakes, throws down trees and buildings, takes earth from one spot, puts in another; everyone flees before the flood; everyone yields to its fury. . . . But we need not conclude therefore that when the weather is quiet, men cannot take precautions with both embankments and dikes, so that when the waters rise, either they go off by a canal or their fury is neither so wild nor so damaging.
—**Nicollò Machiavelli (1965b: 90)**

The raging stream is called
violent
But the riverbank that hems it in
No one calls violent
—*Berthold Brecht (quoted in Theweleit, 1987: 229)*

In this chapter I commence my genealogical analysis of the narrative of fortune and virtue as a technology of power/knowledge and rhetoric of moral selfhood for men of wealth. This chapter consists of three sections. In the first section, I argue that a genealogical "history of the present" that links together past and contemporary formations of the moral economy of wealth is necessitated by the presence of what I term the "Machiavellian uncanny." This uncanny, or the sense of mysteriously "strange familiarity," is manifested in the (auto-)biographical narratives of contemporary men of wealth as a repetition of the ontological categories of fortune and virtue that were engendered in the discourse of Renaissance civic humanism and Machiavellian civic republicanism. Machiavelli, I argue, lurks as a "ghost" in the shadows of the "common sense" of the moral "truth" of wealth. In the second section, I examine the discursive field which gave rise to the autonomous male individual whose secular virtue was manifested in the taming and mastering of fortune. Here I discuss the ambivalent meanings of autonomy as sovereignty, the phenomenological "centering" of the autonomous male individual through the development of linear perception, the new bourgeois subject and the cult of *virtù*, and the articulation of these three aspects of the Renaissance social imaginary with the "active" virtues of commerce and republican citizenship. In the third section, I explore Machiavelli's own conjuring of the moral characters of Founder and Citizen. I conclude that Machiavelli's civic republican discourse displaces wealth as a sign of virtue from the social imaginary of nascent capitalism. Thus, even though his narrative of fortune and virtue has a resonant and enabling affinity with life stories of the "better angels" of the present, the Machiavellian uncanny also haunts the present as an accusation of the corrupting influences of wealth upon the common good.

The Machiavellian Uncanny:
Shadows of Fortune and Virtue in a History of the Present

Machiavelli: Founder, Father, or Ghost?

In *Fortune Is a Woman*, Hannah Pitkin (1984) argues that one of the principal images of manhood in Machiavelli's political cosmology is that of The Founder, a mythically potent father figure who through his will, charisma, intelligence, and strength of character (all aspects of the quality of individuals and collectivities Machiavelli and his contemporaries summarized as *virtù*), institutes a worldly order that perdures for generations after his mortal death. To men of lesser *virtù*, he bequeaths a *principio*, a "founding principle" or institutionalized *nomos*, within which succeeding generations will live. From Machiavelli's perspective, Founders such as Moses, Romulus, Theseus of Athens, and Lycurgus of Sparta are historical foundlings. They are first causes without precedent, paternity, and (especially) maternity (Pitkin, 1984: 54). The Founder is thus an entrepreneur of history, both self-made as well as the maker of the selves of other men by founding a place upon which they can ground their identity.

We will encounter the figure of the Founder as one of the originary moral characters or ethical subjects of the narrative of fortune and virtue shortly. But before engaging with Machiavelli's narrative of worldly efficacy and power, I think it will be useful to briefly reflect on his status in the annals of political and social thought. It is perhaps the proverbial Hegelian "cunning of history" that Machiavelli, who frequently despaired over how he spent his adult life abjectly currying favor with the power elite of Rome and Florence, is now universally treated as a Founder in his own right. Within the disciplines of intellectual history and political theory, there is a unanimity of opinion concerning Machiavelli's "originality," "brilliance," and even lofty "solitude" as a thinker who, in his own words, created a "new route that had not yet been followed by anyone." Indeed, regardless of whether twentieth century interpreters of Machiavelli view him as having engendered the amoral practice of cynical realpolitik, the totalitarian cult of the state, the modern republican vision of liberty, a Jacobin vision of revolutionary nation-building, or a rational science of politics, he is accorded the revered status of a founding patriarch of almost protean proportions.[1] According to Ernst Cassirer (1946: 126), the "plain historical truth" is that "Machiavelli wrote not for Italy, nor even his own epoch, but for the world—and the world listened to him." Machiavelli, the dead Founding Father of modern politics and its rational analysis, remains very much alive in that he still speaks to his progeny with an authority that borders on the mystical.

Typical of such reverence for Machiavelli as Founding Father is the following assessment of his enduring legacy and relevance to present-day political analysis by the historian Felix Gilbert. Gilbert testifies to the experience of Machiavelli's powerful contemporary presence when he asserts that

> when we read his works we find that he still speaks to us directly, in a strangely compelling way. . . . There are passages which touch us like an electric shock. In placing politics in the stream of history, in demonstrating that every situation is unique and requires man to use all his forces to probe all the potentialities of the moment, Machiavelli has revealed—more than anyone before him or after him—that at any time, politics is choice and decision. *Tanto nomini nullum par elogium* [To such a name there is no equal epitaph]. (Gilbert, 1965: 200)[2]

However, not all those who sense the continuing pertinence of Machiavelli regard their encounters with him with such deference and devotion. In one of his last essays before he succumbed to the demons of his mind, Marxist philosopher Louis Althusser wrote:

> Even today, anyone who opens *The Prince* or the *Discourses*, texts now 350 years old, is, as it were, struck by what Freud called a strange familiarity, an *unheimlichkeit*. Without our understanding why, we find these old texts addressing us as if they were from our own day, gripping us as if, in some sense, they had been written for us, something which concerns us directly, without our exactly knowing why. (Althusser, 1988: 470)

Although both Gilbert and Althusser are testifying to the resonance of Machiavelli's thought with present-day realities, the experience means something quite different to each.

For Gilbert, Machiavelli is truly a Founder and Father in that he bequeathed to succeeding generations a singularly revelatory and perspicacious framework of political analysis. Because of Machiavelli's superior empirical observation and insight, we are able to understand the realm of modern politics with stunning clarity. The essential nature of power and politics, which Machiavelli articulated as a matter of choice and decision within the contingencies of the moment, is the same for us as it was for him. Gilbert has no doubt as to why Machiavelli remains relevant: He discerned what no one had discerned before, and, as the practices of power he saw described are still being practiced today, we are beholden to the perceptual framework of his analytical gaze.

For Althusser, however, the matter of Machiavelli's contemporary legacy is not so simple. In the quote above, Machiavelli appears to be less a guide for understanding the empirical present than a ghost who haunts it. Althusser's invocation of the Freudian notion of *unheimlichkeit* or the "uncanny" to describe Machiavelli's relation to the contemporary world suggests a presence that is more evanescent (yet insidiously pervasive) than for which the enduring calculative rationality of power politics can account. For Freud (1919), the uncanny, or Althusser's "sense of strange familiarity," is part of the analysand's compulsion to repeat and reenact past repressed experience as part of the present. The uncanny is manifested in the "constant recurrence of the same thing—the repetition of the same features, of the same vicissitudes, of the same crimes, or even the same names" (Freud, 1919: 234). Locked in the process of repetition, patients often feel that they are being pursued by a demon, a double in which is congealed the repressed, condensed, and displaced experiences of the past.

Unfortunately, Althusser does not really specify how we can understand Machiavelli's contemporary presence as a manifestation of the Freudian uncanny. Yet his image of Machiavelli as a lonely, solitary ghost, perhaps a demon, that vaguely haunts the present is richly suggestive as an analytical metaphor. If Machiavelli is a ghost who grips us "without our exactly knowing why," then the full materiality of his presence cannot be discerned in the visible and obvious (i.e., the calculative rationality of political action). Rather, it is to be located in the shadows of the visible or, more precisely, in the way Machiavelli rhetorically conjures the visibility of the ethical subject of the narrative of fortune and virtue as an artifact of power/knowledge.

It spite of its vagueness, I think Althusser's evocation of Machiavelli's uncanny and ghostly presence represents a far more appropriate and critical position from which to explore his place in the moral economy of wealth. There must a reckoning of how the ghostly presence of Machiavelli is constitutive of the shadowplay by which the contemporary language of wealth maps a world of fortune and virtue for the masculine sovereign individual of capitalism. That is to say, even though Machiavelli's presence in the rhetoric of selfhood of wealthy men is ghostly and evanescent, it has very real and material effects. If Machiavelli is a ghost, then in order to evoke his presence a ghost story must be written. Indeed, no other kind of story of difference and its effacement can be written. As Avery Gordon points out:

> The ghost is not simply a dead or missing or person, but a social figure, and investigating it can lead to a dense site where history and subjectivity make social life. . . . The way of the ghost is haunting, and haunting in a very particular way of knowing what has happened or is happening. Being haunted draws us affectively, sometimes against our will and always a bit magically, into the structure of feeling of a reality we come to experience, not as cold knowledge, but as transformative recognition. (A. Gordon, 1997: 8)

Althusser's solicitation of the transformative recognition of the ghostly uncanny in order to evoke Machiavelli's legacy is intriguing. In the course of talking to the respondents of the study, I was struck by a sense of the resonance of their life stories with Machiavelli's tale of fortune and virtue. This resonance was, in a word, "uncanny," as there was the repetition of the same features, the same vicissitudes, and sometimes even the same names. Thus, like Althusser and Freud, I am moved to ask why and how a narrative of and about power written almost five centuries ago comes to be repeated, almost obsessively and compulsively, in the rhetorical performance of the moral identity of wealthy men.

However, unlike Althusser and Freud, I do not locate the power of the Machiavellian uncanny within the structures of the unconscious. Rather, the place where I locate the shadows of the visible within which the Machiavellian narrative of fortune and virtue operates is the structure of "common sense." For Antonio Gramsci (1971), it was in the epistemological assumptions and ontological categories of the "spontaneous philosophy" of common sense that ideological hegemony exerted its most profound influence over quotidian structures of feeling, perception, and experience. From a Gramscian perspective, the repetition of the past in the present is mysteriously uncanny, not so much because it is unconscious in a psychoanalytic sense but because it is unreflective in a historical and biographical sense. Even though individuals and groups in contemporary society might explicitly use vocabularies and languages inherited from the past in order to construct their personal and collective identity in the everyday of the present, they forget that such language has a history. As Gramsci put it, common sense is the "product of the historical processes to date which has deposited in you an infinity of traces without leaving an inventory" (1971: 324). From a Gramscian perspective, therefore, the critical analysis of ideology involves a practice of memory-work whereby the conditions under which prevailing conceptions of self and society embedded in common sense emerge are recovered and interrogated.

In this task, Gramsci shares common ground with the Foucauldian project of genealogy through the construction of a "history of the present." For Foucault, genealogy seeks to provide a critical inventory of traces of ideology and discourses that constitute contemporary structures of subjectivity. Genealogy, according to Foucault, is "grey, meticulous, and patiently documentary. It operates on a field of entangled and confused parchments, on documents that have been scratched over and recopied, many times" (1977: 139). The task of the genealogist is to traverse this tangled and confused field of intertextuality, descending to historical points where the oppositions and differences that compose social identity emerge in the symbolic space of the social imaginary, then retracing their articulations back to the present. It is this methodological "dance" of multiplicity between textual inscriptions and rescriptions, past and present, descent and emergence, that can help to understand the presence of the Machiavellian uncanny in the moral economy of wealth (Pfohl, 1992: 179).

Therefore, I begin my genealogical exploration of the narrative of fortune and virtue by visiting two "better angels" of contemporary capitalism. Their narratives will serve as a point in the present, from which I will descend into the past, traversing the discursive field within which the spatial stories and story spaces of the moral characters of Founder and Citizen emerged.

Founder and Citizen: Fortune and Virtue in the (Auto-)Biographical Narratives of Two "Better Angels" of the Present

At the time he was interviewed for the study, midwestern fast-food entrepreneur Mark Dahlin was one of the wealthiest individuals in the United States. In the popular business press of the early 1980s, Dahlin's spectacular career and wealth was invoked as testimonial to the renewed capitalist vigor and entrepreneurial spirit of the Reagan era. Indeed, by his own account of his life story in our interview, Dahlin is a contemporary living embodiment of the Horatio Alger myth of the completely "self-made man."

Dahlin was born into impoverished circumstances during the Great Depression, which wrecked havoc upon his family and his childhood. His father died when Dahlin was a child; unable to cope with the burdens of being a single working parent with two children, his mother packed him and his brother off to a variety of foster homes and orphanages, where he spent his adolescent years. For Dahlin, the unfortunate circumstances of his childhood were both curse and blessing. The curse came in the form of the shame and stigma of his lowly circumstances. "I was embarrassed," Dahlin says, "about not having the things that other kids had, and not only not having the things that other kids had in the way of clothes and things like that, but also the circumstances. I was ashamed of my mother. . . . She had no perception of how to fix her hair, wear her clothes, how to act in public, and I was embarrassed of her." Yet for Dahlin this shame of poverty and family provided a blessing, a character trait that has long been configured as the central virtue of the self-made man: ambition and the will to overcome the adversity of misfortune. "Will it and it is thine," said an Algeresque, popular, rags-to-riches self-help manual from the Gilded Age: "No longer grovel as if the hand of fate was upon thee. Stand erect. Thou art a man, and thy mission is a noble one" (quoted in Wyllie, 1954: 40). For Dahlin, the masculine mission of erecting the self through entrepreneurship was engendered in the experiential crucible of, for all intents and purposes, being an orphan:

> I always seemed to have an inclination [for entrepreneurship], even in the orphanage. I can remember being a little kid, setting up a store and pretending that I was selling stuff. And when I got out of the orphanage, I found myself being very entrepreneurial. I had a lot of different things going, from raising rabbits to growing vegetables and selling them door to door, and when it snowed I would grab a shovel and broom and knock on doors. I'd go fishing and catch and clean fish and take them door to door.

According to Dahlin, this entrepreneurial spirit was given force and guidance by dreams and visions of wealth, power, and accomplishment:

> I was always a daydreamer. . . . I had a lot time to think [in the orphanage] and I daydreamed about being a teenage tycoon, just to entertain myself. And I think, in retrospect, it was probably one of the best things I could have done. It makes you think about a lot of things you wouldn't ordinarily think about because every accomplishment you come up with in your mind creates two or three more problems that you need to figure out. . . . I've always wanted the best of everything, and I think it has something to do with not having anything. I've always make a study of what is the best of everything and I make a note in my mental notebook, "Someday I want to have that." I always had a priority, I had my goals pretty well organized. I want a nice home, nice car, nice clothes. That to me was the big three. . . . I was probably a pretty good goal setter without knowing anything about goal setting. And it's been satisfying to me to see these goals come about.

In spite of the emphasis in this statement on consumption, for Dahlin the project of self-making takes place primarily in the realm of the accumulation of wealth as it is embodied in the business enterprise:

I'm different than a lot of people that are in my position financially in that most of them didn't have as little when they grew up as I did. So, first of all, I think I appreciate it more. [Second], even though I'm worth a lot of money, the business is growing, and there isn't a lot of disposable income. We're solid financially, but what profit we're making I'm plowing back in to grow the company. This is the way I'm built. That's the way I've always been. I can't imagine a company where I'm not growing and where it's not grow- ing. To me it just would not make any sense to just be a caretaker. That wouldn't be any fun.

From Dahlin's perspective, his business enterprise does not simply stand as a monument to his ability to accumulate wealth; perhaps more importantly, it operates as a potent symbolic framework and institutional site within which others can develop and pursue their own dreams of fortune. As he says:

I bought this hamburger place that was available with five hundred dollars. I realized that I might get stuck here, but I also realized the potential. I worked hard to make a lot of money and I've said to myself and others many times, "Although making a lot of money isn't enough, I want to show people that you can be successful and be honest." Because everybody I knew seemed to believe that if anyone was successful they had to be crooked to do it. And I never believed that. I don't know if I read too many Horatio Alger books or what, but I believed that it was the opposite. I be- lieved that if you provide a service, the more service you provide the more you get. And I thought that it would be great example to show people. . . . I think the free enterprise system is a great thing and I feel that I am in a good position to give a good example of that. Our company [provides an example of that] by putting hundreds of young kids in business that never thought they would do anything more than a nine-to-five job, and many of them are millionaires today. And you're seeing them blossom and they develop other people under them that are going the same route. It's like magic!

I have quoted from Dahlin's (auto-)biographical narrative at length without interpretative commentary in order to allow its trajectory and teleology as a tale of fortune and virtue to emerge. Dahlin's narrative of self-making starts with the misfortune of shame, deprivation, and adver- sity. Yet this misfortune provides Dahlin with the circumstances for culti- vating virtue. In the orphanage, he disowns, so to speak, the humiliating shame of his maternity by dreaming of greatness. Thus, the first virtue he cultivates is that of vision and ambition. Through dreams of being a "teenage tycoon," Dahlin frees himself from the limiting burdens of his unfortunate circumstances of birth. In refusing to accept his condition as his only possible future, he transforms misfortune from inescapable fate into opportunity and possibility. This virtue of vision and ambition in the service of upward social mobility entails a second virtue, that of reason and rationality. Teenage daydreams provide Dahlin with the goals that will chart his biographical trajectory. These goals are then prioritized, and the existential horizon is scrutinized for the potential means and opportunities for realizing them. This calculative rationality is given coherent form through the entrepreneurial practice of wealth accumulation. As a means to the end of wealth accumulation, entrepreneurship evinces several other virtues: diligence, hard work, honesty, the willingness to take risks for uncertain rewards, and continued investment in the business enterprise. Accordingly, Dahlin's narrative of self-making entails the confrontation with fortune as opportunity and, on the basis of an array of virtues, turning it into a fortune of wealth, power, and autonomy.

Dahlin's moral identity is inseparable from the literal and figural fortune he has virtuously created, as the processes through which his self and his company are "built" are metonymically linked: When it "grows," he "grows" and vice-versa. His wealth and business are material embodiments of his virtuous will and desire. As such, they constitute a worldly principality that is an extension of individuality. As a spatial story, Dahlin's narrative clearly articulates and aligns psychic, corporeal, social, and moral space. Within each and across all, he is sovereign. Furthermore, this sovereign principality is not only a site and sign of Dahlin's virtue; it also an institutional territory within which others can cultivate their virtue and make their own fortunes. Their stories, like his, have the potential to be "magic": mythical narratives of transcendence and transformation wherein selves are spatially manifested as the money is counted to the temporal rhythm of fortune begetting virtue begetting fortune. This spatial story, in its emplotment and emplacement, is the story of the Founder. This story has been inscribed in the social imaginary of capitalism as a monumental manifested destiny of the virtuous project of masculine self-making: *Tanto nomini nullum par elogium.*

Although Stuart Dean's (auto-)biographical narrative is not one of transcendence, it is no less magical than Dahlin's as a moral tale of fortune, virtue, and transformation. Dean is a scion and patriarch of one of wealthiest families in the Pacific Northwest. By his own reckoning, quite unlike Dahlin and David Schwartz, Dean is the inheritor and beneficiary of extraordinarily good fortune. "I feel fortunate," Dean told me, "I feel lucky. I could have been born Calcutta, India. The little eggs that turned out to be me were in the right place at the right time." Attending these fortunate circumstances of birth and geography was a fortune of money, privilege, and opportunity: "I was born with a silver or, rather, gold spoon in my mouth. My father was before me too. I guess it all stems back to my grandfather, who was successful, and my father carried on in his footsteps, and I have carried on in my father's and so far we haven't gone downhill."

From the beginning of Dean's (auto-)biographical narrative then, the emplotted teleology that will lead to a virtuous self-identity follows a very different trajectory than that of Dahlin. Through ambition and will, Dahlin had to wrest from fortune an empire he could call his own. There were no "footsteps" for Dahlin to follow that would lead him to wealth and virtue. Quite the contrary: Any path that was inscribed in Dahlin's initial circumstances of fortune could only lead to shame, humiliation, and poverty. In order for Dahlin to make himself, he had to sever his links to paternity and maternity by becoming an orphan. In contrast, Dean's narrative has no dramatic tale of the transcendence of fortune wherein he makes himself all by himself. Dean is neither orphan nor foundling; rather, he is the cherished child of fortune. As such, it is the inherited fortune of family and wealth that provides him with what Paul Schervish and I (1988) term a "career" of inherited wealth. This career consists of an array of roles and responsibilities that give form to Dean's cultivation of virtue. Dean succinctly describes his career of wealth:

> I went to public grade school here. I went to private high school here and then I went back east to D. College, graduated from there and went right into the navy. Was in the navy, served on a destroyer, came out as a lieutenant, and went into business with my father. When my father died, he was fifty-three and I was thirty-three, I then sort of took over the responsibility for seeing that the family was able to live according to the style to which they had been accustomed. If I have had a goal at all I suppose that's it. Whatever we get into I try to see that it improves the family.

Note in comparison to Dahlin's narrative the distinct lack of dramatic transformation in Dean's biographical career. There are no dreams of greatness, no triumph over adversity, and no founding of a new sovereign principality of wealth and autonomy. Indeed, there appears to be no transformation of the self through the transformation of fortune. Dean simply did what his inherited position as patriarch and steward of the family fortune required him to do. Dean's claim to virtue seems to be quite circumspect, as it is measured by the rather modest criterion of having not "gone downhill." Although the virtues of fulfilling the obligations of stewardship appear humble, as I will explore in Chapter 5, they are extremely powerful in legitimating the possession of inherited wealth as a trust. However, here I am concerned with a story of the virtuous engagement with fortune entailed by the discourse of citizenship. It is through the narrative logic of emplotment and emplacement derived from this discourse that Dean is able to articulate a moral tale in which the self is transformed through virtuous reworking of fortune, although the meaning of this transformation in his conjuring of moral identity is quite different from that of Dahlin's.

As with Dahlin, I let Dean speak for himself in order to discern the peculiar narrative logic through which fortune is transformed through virtue before commenting on its structure. According to Dean, the wise and judicious stewardship of family wealth provides the basis to cultivate and practice the virtue of philanthropic beneficence: "Being able to earn a sufficient amount of funds so that we can take some of those dollars and put them to good use in the community and make it a better place in which to live is certainly one of the activities that I have been involved in, and I suppose one of the rewards I get out of it is being able to not only to support ourselves but to generate some support for others, for certain projects we think are important."

Philanthropic beneficence thus clearly has its "rewards" as a practice and sign of virtue. The successful preservation and expansion of family wealth enables the family in general, and Dean in particular, to be good citizens in the community. Through philanthropy, funds that are accumulated privately are used to benefit the public, albeit in the form of projects that the family and its patriarch "think are important." Other projects that might equally benefit the community presumably do not get their support. But no matter what projects Dean and family support, each venture is an occasion to cultivate his distinctive virtue as a man of wealth who is also a good citizen. As he told us, one of the criteria he uses to decide which philanthropic projects he will pursue is whether or not it "allows you to make a mark":

> I don't like to get involved in things that are routine, mundane, unless they are exceptionally important. I'm excited about doing something different, you know, and once it's established then let somebody else carry on with that. . . . I headed up the campaign to raise $5 million towards working capital for the city World's Fair. We did, and that all the money was returned. It was the first fair that ever returned the money that was put up for working capital. I got tremendous satisfaction out of that. Seventy-two acres that we converted to our now City Center is a great asset, we built the Obelisk, three others of us, we were 25 percent builders of that. That stands for the city today. You know, these are the rewards that you get for doing something that is good for the community, things that are different, it's a challenge, they aren't routine and they're important. . . . I drive by and look at the Obelisk everyday I come to work you know, and I feel good about it. I walk around there on a sunny afternoon and see all the people who are so enjoying themselves and I feel good. If there was anything of lasting result that probably benefited more people in this area, that was it.

Dean's ability to make a distinctive contribution to the community is not only a source of personal "satisfaction" to him; it also provides a example of civic virtue that will hopefully inspire others. The good citizenship that philanthropic beneficence represents "makes the community a better place to live, for everybody to live. I would like to believe that some of the things I do might have encouraged other people to say, 'Well, God, if Dean can do it, you know so can I.'" Finally, according to Dean, the practice of citizenship is not only a source of "intangible benefits" that are derived from the pleasures of doing good in the community; it is also a responsibility attendant upon the possession of wealth as fortune:

> If you are in a position to create a better environment in your lifetime, if you're in a position to something about the community and you don't, I think you are missing out on a lot of reward that you should get. You're really not living up to the responsibility that you should have as someone who is healthy and wealthy, not only in terms of dollars but in terms of time to help the community be a better place to live because you were there. . . . And something I do not understand is why people who do not give of themselves are content to pay money in taxes when they could spend some of their dollars reducing the taxes they are paying by seeing to it that those dollars go to support those activities they feel are important.

As a rhetoric of moral selfhood, Dean's (auto-)biographical narrative (compared to that of Dahlin) evinces a different logic of emplotment and emplacement through which both self and fortune are transformed through virtue. As a child of fortune, Dean inherits an already existing principality of sovereign wealth and power that provides the opportunities and obligations to be virtuous. As steward of the family wealth, he is duty-bound by the obligation to keep it intact, if not to enhance it. However, this successful discharge of his responsibilities to the family principality does not constitute Dean's most important claim to a place of virtuous self-identity. The primary spatial locus of virtue for Dean is inscribed in the practice of philanthropic beneficence and citizenship. True, as Dean himself points out, the impetus to citizenship is also an obligation and responsibility inherent in the fortunate position of being "healthy and wealthy." However, the obligations of fortune as wealth present Dean with the fortuitous opportunity to "make his own mark," to make his own indelible stamp upon the principality he inherited and upon the community. Through Dean's philanthropic endeavors such as the World Fair, fortune is not only protected; it is transformed into a project of Dean's own making and is reflective of his visions of the common good.

This first transformation of fortune entails another transformation: A principality of fortune that is privately inherited and possessed is expanded into a principality in which private interest and the common-weal of the community are elided. For Dean, the boundaries of the sovereign "I" rooted in privately held wealth are redrawn to encompass the "We" of the community. The Obelisk stands as a sign, to both himself and those who play in its shadows, of his civic e-/rectitude as a man who has made a unique and enduring contribution to the public good. As such, it is a sign in material space that enacts and embodies his magisterial location in moral space. This spatial story, in structure and teleology, is the story of the Citizen. This story is also inscribed in the social imaginary of capitalism, albeit with a distinctly different moral valence, as a manifested destiny of the masculine project of virtuous self-making: *Tanto nomini nullum par elogium.*

These (auto-)biographical narratives of Dahlin and Dean, within which fortune is confronted by men and transformed through their virtue, represent the two basic forms of the rhetoric of moral selfhood articulated by men of wealth. These rhetorics conjure contrasting character masks from two distinct topoi of subjectivity in the moral economy of wealth of the present and, as such, constitute points from which I will descend to the moral economy of wealth of the past in order to explore the conditions of their emergence. In this movement of descent and emergence, I will endeavor to reveal the uncanny resonances between the moral tales of Dahlin and Dean with the moral characters of Founder and Citizen that were conjured by Machiavelli and his civic humanist predecessors in Renaissance Florence. My descent will be guided by a figure who also exists in both present and past, a figure who men of wealth act against in order to demonstrate their virtue. This is the figure of Fortuna, the goddess of chance.

Wheels of Fortune: An Encounter Between Vanna White and the Ghosts of Civic Humanism

Unheimlichkeit. Every weekday night at 7:00 P.M., Pat the bartender at Irving's Lounge in Brookline, Massachusetts, tunes all three TVs to channel 7 and turns up the volume so they can be heard above the chatter. As the announcer begins his ritual introduction, most patrons (largely retirees, employees of the local fire, police, or public works departments, house painters, and construction workers—many Vietnam Veterans and all members of the working class) turn to watch. As the camera pans the stage, the announcer excitedly invites us to "Just look at this studio filled with cash and prizes worth—$237,000!!!" The figure, which flashes on the screen as soon as it is announced, provides the cue for the patrons to join with announcer in enunciating the program's mantra: ". . . all to be won on *Wheel of Fortune!!!*" And there is Vanna White: Vanna smiles,

Vanna twirls, Vanna turns letters, revealing whether contestants have ridden fortune's wheel to consumer's paradise, where they are temporarily empowered by possessions without possessing power.

As ritual and spectacle of consumer gamesmanship, *Wheel of Fortune* bears the traces of cultural conceptions of fortune and virtue that date back to Western antiquity, though it is doubtful that the game show's participants or the viewers at Irving's remember the origins or meanings of the terms. The most prominent trace is the wheel of fortune itself, which during antiquity was an aspect of the goddess Fortuna.[3] The word *fortuna* in Latin is derived from the noun *fors*, or "luck," and the verb *ferre*, "to bring" (Flanagan, 1972: 129). The rotating wheel represents the exigencies of chance and luck and is presided over by Fortuna (she who brings fortune). To the Romans, she was the *bona dea*, the Good Goddess who smiled on human undertakings and brought fortune in the form of successful adventures, good harvests, and healthy children. According to Harry Patch (1927), she was the most popular Roman deity as well as the most enduring, her influence on intellectual life and quotidian consciousness lasting well into the Middle Ages. Of course, good fortune was not guaranteed: The Goddess was considered to be capricious and required propriation and supplication if one was to gain her favor. Accordingly, the realm of fortune was not the realm of fate, and human influence could be brought to bear upon the unpredictable.

In *Wheel of Fortune*, the power and influence of the goddess has long been forgotten. Her postmodern embodiment, Vanna White, exerts no influence over the wheel or the secret of the riddles she reveals. Smiling yet mute, she is present as an object to be visually consumed. She is nothing more than another cold star in the firmament of commodities. The wheel is spun by the contestants themselves, who attempt to influence chance by aiming for the highest dollar amount on the wheel. They then attempt to skillfully take advantage of chances offered by the wheel by correctly guessing the letters and words that compose the hidden phrase, thereby winning prizes and money. The virtue of skill is thus directed toward turning chance into possession. Indeed, it is the realm of commodities and cash that constitutes the dominant meaning of fortune within the symbolic framework of the game. The original meaning of fortune as chance and luck is subordinated to the more historically recent meaning of fortune as money and wealth. In antiquity, fortune could refer to goods and possessions, the gifts that fortune brought, as well as to chance and circumstance. However, it was not until the fifteenth century, in the cultural context of the zenith of the mercantile capitalism of Renaissance Italy, that fortune acquired the denotation of wealth (Jardine, 1996). Thus, in true post-Renaissance fashion, the goal of the game is to acquire a fortune by mastering fortune.

Lurking in the shadows of the bar, the ghosts of the civic humanists of the Quattrocento (fourteenth century) and Cinquecento (fifteenth century) observe the unfolding drama of the game and the viewers' rapt attention to it. They are fascinated and disturbed. As it is a metaphor for the arrangement and conduct of human affairs, there is much they recognize as being similar to their own cosmology and social ontology. Like their own worldview, due consideration is given to the role of *fortuna* in shaping the circumstances of and opportunities for social and individual action. Furthermore, as in their own worldview, success in worldly affairs appears to be determined by the skill of the individual in taking full advantage of the opportunities that *fortuna* has to offer.

Beyond these resemblances, however, there is a gap between fortune and virtue in the late Renaissance and that in *Wheel of Fortune*. From the perspective of civic humanists, *Wheel of Fortune* represents a pallid and atrophied conception of individuality, autonomy, and virtue. For the participants and viewers of *Wheel of Fortune*, the autonomy and self-determination promised by good fortune is strictly limited to the realm of consumption and the capacity to acquire money and goods. Such a circumscribed notion of self-determination and autonomy is, to the ghostly presences, a very impoverished one indeed. This is not to say that they do not consider money, property, and possession to be an important dimension of autonomy and self-determination. In some (though not all) quarters of later civic humanist thought, the acquisition of wealth was considered to be a sign and sustaining source of virtue.[4] However, the possession of wealth was never considered to be an end in its own right. It was only valued to the extent it enhanced the ability of individuals to independently cultivate their intellect and to contribute to the *vivere civile* (civic life) of the community. Further, the ghosts aver, not only is the acquisition of consumer goods a paltry sort of fortune; so too is the virtue that was required to produce it. In *Wheel of Fortune*, they concur, there is no true *virtù*, no real mastery of fortune. Even though it is the individual who spins the wheel, the opportunities for action are far too controlled by random probability and too predetermined in advance by powers beyond contestant control to be a realm where individuals can impose *virtù* upon *fortuna*.

Entering the shadows to join the ghostly ensemble, I concede that *Wheel of Fortune* represents a diminished inheritance of their dynamic worldview. However, I point out that it does accurately reflect the opportunity structure of advanced consumer capitalism. For all but the tiny elite of whom I write, this opportunity structure consists of many predetermined options but no real choices as to which options will be on the menu. We are incessantly encouraged to "master the possibilities" by credit card companies, but accepting the invitation only binds us tighter into relations of subordination to the requirements of work and consumption. It is precisely the desire to escape from such relations that motivates the fortune-seekers in the game show and the viewers who vicariously participate in their quest. The hope is that fortune will yield up a fortune, thereby providing the possibility of magically leaping from the realm of necessity into the realm of freedom. Indeed, in the realm of freedom engendered by the possession of wealth it is believed that the narrative of fortune and virtue, a narrative that articulates the teleological promise of sovereign individuality, can be truly lived out.

The ghosts are pleased by my explanation, taking it to mean that outside this scene of spectacle and spectatorship there are some who actually live out this narrative and therefore are exemplars of virtuous individuality. I try to explain that for me the matter is not as simple as finding the virtuous few among the many. The question is how are they made to *appear* to be virtuous as ethical subjects. What is the hegemonic power of the narrative of fortune and virtue, both as a seductive allure for those without wealth and as a phenomenological and rhetorical ordering principle for those with it?

My spectral friends are puzzled by my concern. They are intimately familiar with the philosophy and practice of rhetoric as articulated by Protagoras, Seneca, and Cicero. Accordingly, they understand quite well the importance of language in shaping and conveying meaning.[5] However, they are disturbed by the implications of what I have said. For them, rhetoric is an exchange between autonomous and centered subjects, not a process by which subjectivities are created and sustained. To shift the locus of rhetoric from intersubjective communication between speaking subjects to the discursive construction of spoken subjects represents a radical displacement of the autonomous individual they celebrated as being, to use Giovanni Pico della Mirandolla's famous words, "at the center of the world" (1948: 227). Have I not, they ask, reconstructed in the form of a prison house of language the determining power of fate, that realm of unfreedom that they tried so strenuously to displace from the social imaginary of the nascent capitalism of the Renaissance? They tell me that I do not understand or value free will, responsibility, and self-mastery. Come with us, they say, and we shall show you the true nature of the autonomous individual and glory of *virtù*. We will show the displacement of fate and the taming of the goddess of fortune. And, on the other side of the displacement of fate and the taming of fortune, they promise, is Machiavelli himself. Before I have the chance to respond that their "truths" are not self-evident, and that their language of individual virtue institutes a social regime of power/knowledge, they disappear back into the ghostly vortex of cultural memory. If I am to understand the presence of the Machiavellian uncanny in the imagination of wealth among those who have a fortune and those who desperately yearn for one, I must descend with them to the point of emergence of a discursive field within which Fortuna is tamed.

Meanwhile, back at Irving's, the game show ends with a winner. However, the pleasures of vicarious sharing in good fortune are fleeting for the viewers. Imagining a life of wealth, freedom, and power, some of them resolve to redouble their virtuous efforts at securing that realm . . . and walk down to the local convenience store and buy a lottery ticket.

Taming the Goddess:
Fate, Fortune, and the Renaissance Social Imaginary

Beware, Fortune Is a Woman

How is a goddess tamed? Machiavelli provocatively suggests the following. "Fortune is a woman," he wrote in *The Prince*. And, since she is a woman, he continued, "it is necessary in order to keep her under, to cuff and maul her. She more lets herself be overcome by men using such methods than by those who proceed coldly; therefore, always like a woman, she is the friend of young men, because they are less cautious, more spirited, and with more boldness master her" (1965c, 25: 92). Although this passage represents one of the most stark and extreme of Machiavelli's formulations of the relationship of *virtù* to *fortuna*, it is consistent with his overall perspective on the matter. Fortune is a woman in that she is capricious, crafty, tempestuous, and passionately volatile. If fortune is a woman in these ways then fortune, like "woman," is also a metaphorical incarnation of the great feminine Other of patriarchal rationalism: nature.[6] Like nature, fortune as a feminine power is fecund, giving, and pregnant with possibility; yet like nature fortune is irrational and unpredictable, given to harsh storms and violent upheavals. Fortune is a "raging torrent" that can "destroy whatever its current anywhere reaches, and adds to one place and lowers another, shifts its banks, shifts its bed and bottom, and makes the earth tremble where it passes" (Machiavelli, 1965c: 748). Fortune can therefore be a friendly ally or a dangerous adversary. Accordingly, a man must be either bold or prudent, depending on the circumstances, but always strong, emotionally disciplined, and rationally perspicacious in order to ascertain Fortune's designs, survive her vagaries, and turn the opportunities she offers into a successful result. Above all, opines Machiavelli in *The Prince*, in order to master *fortuna* the individual can only rely upon himself: "those defenses [against *fortuna*'s "storm"] alone are good, are certain, are durable, that depend on yourself and your *virtù* [abilities]" (1965c, 24: 89).

With this characterization of *fortuna*, we are very far away from the beneficent *bona dea* of Roman antiquity. Fortuna is no longer a goddess to be respected, revered, supplicated, or worshipped. Indeed, what seems to be most operative in Machiavelli's understanding of Fortuna is awe and fear: awe in the face of her inconstant power and the concomitant fear that she will overwhelm men with her floods and storms. Accordingly, men must build defenses and dams against her fearsome unpredictability and use these bulwarks as outposts from which they can tame and master fortune and what she has to offer.[7] To adumbrate what follows, the contest between *fortuna* and *virtù* is a zero-sum game where the prize is autonomy and sovereign individuality. The more that fortune is able to rage out of control, the more men are dependent and their masculinity is diminished and they become, like David Schwartz, abject. The characters of the Founder and the Citizen are truly manly men because they are able to impose their *virtù* upon *fortuna*, to bring fortune under control to create a worldly realm of autonomy, propriety, and power. As such, these characters perform the moral subject of sovereign individuality as the "virile figure of the subject-agent of history" (O'Hanlon, 1988: 207).

How is a goddess tamed? In many ways, Fortuna was already tamed by the time Machiavelli offered his strategy of expanding the realm of autonomy and sovereignty through mastering the feminine wiles of fortune with the disciplined, masculine will to power of *virtù*. This is because the principal discursive categories with which Machiavelli crafts his narrative and its characters were already circulating in the moral economy of the period. Accordingly, several important issues must be considered before I encounter Machiavelli himself. The primary issue involves exploring the meaning and nature of "autonomy," the quest for which is the primary telos and manifested destiny of the narrative of fortune and virtue.

The meaning of autonomy, in the moral economies of both Renaissance Florence and contemporary capitalism, is ambivalent in that it posits a paradoxical relationship between sovereign individuals and the communities of which they are citizens. The paradoxical nature of the meaning of autonomy, as it was discursively configured in the Florentine Renaissance, will be further elaborated in the context of three other issues. The first involves how the notion of autonomy is articulated in the context of changing understandings of *fortuna* and the emergence of the egocentric perspective. The second issue concerns how the autonomous individual ego, having been perspectively placed in the world, becomes mandated to discipline itself and dynamically impose its *virtù* upon *fortuna*. The third issue encompasses the intersection of autonomy, wealth, and civic virtue in the *vita activa* (active life) of citizenship.

The Paradoxes of Autonomy

The word *autonomy*, as Hannah Pitkin points out, is derived from two Greek words: *auto* or "self" and "own," and *nomos*, which can mean "law," "ordering principle," or "way of life" (Pitkin, 1984: 7). Autonomy, depending upon which of its etymological components one emphasizes, can refer to two distinct yet related processes. If one places the emphasis on the first component, the *auto*, then autonomy comes to mean the process by which the self makes or possesses its own laws or way of life. It is this meaning that is operative when one speaks of autonomy as *sovereignty of the self*, that is, as individual independence, freedom, self-control, or self-governance. Autonomy in this sense as well locates authority and mastery in the "self" unit, whether it be defined individually or collectively. If one emphasizes the second component, the *nomos*, then autonomy can refer to the process by which the self is created and sustained through a matrix of overarching cultural beliefs, social relations, and institutional practices. It is this nomoetic matrix that provides what Foucault would call "structures of intelligibility" that give shape to individual and collective identities for persons and people.

The first meaning of autonomy has guided most historical interpretations of the Renaissance ever since Jacob Burckhardt's classic treatise *The Civilization of the Renaissance in Italy*. In this view, one of the principal defining characteristics and contributions to Western culture of the period was the emergence of the aesthetic, moral, and political salience of the autonomous individual.[8] According to Burckhardt, the Renaissance was witness to the first flowering of the modern unique and sovereign individual who awoke from the spell-binding "charm laid upon the human personality" by the feudal order and proceeded to cultivate "his" (the male basis of this brave new individual bordered on the absolute) powers as author of the self and master of the world (Burckhardt, 1954 [1860]: 123).[9]

The problem with emphasizing this dominant meaning of autonomy, and how it was manifested in the Renaissance, is not so much that it is "untrue" as it is incomplete and teleological. It accepts the emergence of the autonomous individual as a self-evident and inherently progressive social fact rather than as a historically specific process by which a particular configuration of "autonomy" and "individuality" is discursively constructed and instituted in a range of social and spatial practices that are morally valued as being productive of autonomy and individuality. What is at stake in considering these two dimensions of autonomy is not so much the causal priority of one process or the other. Rather, it is to highlight the centrality of the historically relative nature of the social production of "individuals" and "individuality" through technologies of power/knowledge. In considering the Renaissance understanding of autonomy, it is important to remember that we are not simply speaking descriptively of the emergence of the autonomous individual who then marches, free and unencumbered, down the teleological road of Enlightenment and historical progress. To paraphrase Michael Shapiro (1988: 5), we are also speaking of a process by which individuals become "autonomized" subjects within a particular regime of power/knowledge so that particular valuations of autonomy and individuality are manifested in an imposed grid of intelligibility while other possible valuations are repressed or pushed to the margins of social desirability.

The problem of autonomy is worth dwelling upon because it is of central importance to the aims of this book. Autonomy, when it is construed as an essential component of sovereign individuality, is viewed as one of the principal rewards of wealth and is primarily manifested in temporal and spatial empowerment. Furthermore, as I argue in Chapter 2, such power requires *proprietas*, the proper signification of words that is the condition for appropriation. This requires a regime of power/knowledge that marks out and justifies such forms of autonomous individuality as being right, true, and natural. That is to say, individuals must be subjectively autonomized so to speak before they can be actively autonomous. It is thus imperative to genealogically discern how these dispositions that govern the relationship between the wealthy masculine individual and the social world were formed.

The relationship between the wealthy man as autonomous subject and the social world as space of social engagement takes on further importance when considering the language of citizenship and practice of philanthropy (which is the focal concern of Chapter 5). As with Stuart Dean, through philanthropy—and how it is rhetorically figured as a virtuous act of citizenship—many wealthy men are able to link their autonomous selves to an imagined community of others to whom they feel obligated and responsible. This relationship manifests a paradox that was expressed in John Norris's gesture to the world: He was able to make a sovereign claim of ownership over the community while claiming a subordinate relationship of fealty to it. This paradox is intrinsic to the modern notion of autonomy that emerged in the Renaissance. Autonomy, as Pitkin insightfully explains, "concerns borderlines, found or made" between individuals, between collectivities, and between individuals and the collectivities of whom they are a part (1984: 7). Autonomy concerns not only the formation of sovereign individuals but also their interrelation as members of a political community in which they participate. As such, Pitkin argues, "at every level and in every sense, the idea of autonomy is itself problematic, implying both a connection and a separation: a separation that challenges, denies, or overcomes a connection. Thus, autonomy may be conceived as either a sovereign isolation or, paradoxically, as the rightful acknowledgment of interdependence" (1984: 8).

The discourse of citizenship is a language that promises a redefinition of the autonomous individual. This redefinition is performed by the moral character of the Citizen, who embodies the moral virtue of having an enlarged awareness of how individuality and community are connected in the self. However, in the context of a society where the capacity and resources to engage in the practices of civic virtue are unequally distributed, the wealthy man as Citizen is never really able to dissolve the boundaries of the autonomous bourgeois ego; he is only able to expand those boundaries to include the community as part of his principality and extended patrimony.

Fate, Fortune, and the Centering of the Autonomous Individual

Thomas Flanagan (1972: 142–144) has argued that Machiavelli's assessment of the relationship of *virtù* to *fortuna* was rooted in the ascendancy of an "immanent" over a "transcendent" conception of the role of fate and fortune in worldly affairs that occurred during the Renaissance. The immanent notion of fortune was rooted in the cosmology of ancient Rome. As I note above, during antiquity Fortuna was considered to be a capricious yet beneficent goddess who wielded considerable influence over the course of human life. In spite of her capriciousness and unpredictability, it was believed that manly *virtù*, as manifested in courage, wisdom, strength, and self-control, could provide a counterweight to her power and increase one's chances of acquiring *bona fortunae* (the goods of fortune). As Pitkin points out, even though in the Roman imagination *virtù* was contrasted with *fortuna*, one always acted toward the dispensation of the goddess with respect (1984: 139). She could not be controlled or mastered; one could control only one's actions in regard to what she dispensed in terms of chance and circumstance. Flanagan terms this conception of fortune "immanent" because its workings were considered to structure all aspects of life. As such, no one could refuse to play fortune's game.

In the Middle Ages the realm over which the goddess held sway shifted from that of chance and unpredictability to that of fate. "Behold the wheel that Fortune grimly turns" wrote the medieval philosopher Boethius in *The Consolation of Philosophy* (quoted in Pocock, 1975: 40). For Boethius, Fortune was implacable and her turning of the wheel that determined the secular fate of "men" was inexorable. In fact, medieval representations of Fortuna show her with a very grim visage as she turns her wheel, bound to which are figures depicting all the orders of feudal society, connotating the vanity of seeking earthly goods.[10] Men's fortunes may rise and they may fall, but within the providential reason of God and his great chain of being there was naught that they could do to control or predict them. Fate, as represented by Fortuna, is the manifestation of divine providence in secular time or, to use Augustinian terms, in the *civitas terrena* (city of man). Accordingly, for Boethius all fortune was "good fortune," as it was ordained by God.[11] This notion of fortune was "transcendent," according to Flanagan, because it directed people to eschew concern with worldly strivings and turn their attention to cultivation of Christian virtue in the face of *fortuna* and the philosophical contemplation of the divine.

Although the transcendent understanding of *fortuna* exerted considerable influence within the Renaissance imagination during the Trecento (thirteenth century) and early Quattrocento (e.g., in Dante's *Inferno* and Boccaccio's *Decameron*), it was gradually displaced by a revival and transformation of the immanent conception. Both Fortuna and "man" were freed from the constraints of divine providence. She, once again, becomes a feminine power who represents the vicissitudes of chance and circumstance amenable to human intervention, and men, once again, are able to contest her wiles with *virtù*. As Machiavelli himself said in a well-known passage from *The Prince*: "Fortune may be the mistress of half our actions but . . . even she leaves the other half, or almost, under our control" (1965c, 24: 90).

This conception of an expanded arena of human action is reflected in the different tropological representations of Fortuna that emerged in the fourteenth and fifteenth centuries. Perhaps because of the centrality of maritime trade to the prosperity of mercantile capitalism, the use of aquatic metaphors to evoke the relationship between *fortuna* and *virtù* became prevalent. In a manner similar to Machiavelli's characterization of Fortuna as a raging stream, Leon Battista Alberti was fond of equating fortune with a river in which the individual must swim strongly enough to negotiate the current and reach one's goal (Cassirer, 1963: 77). According to Cassirer, the image of Fortuna and her implacable turning of her fateful wheel is replaced by that of the goddess in a sailboat, blowing the sails, while the individual steers it (Cassirer, 1963: 77). This activist imagery of individual *virtù* that is increasingly in control in relation to the stream of *fortuna* is supplemented by Alberti with the image of individuals in contest and competition with each other for the goods of fortune. For Alberti, life is a boat race upon the waters of *fortuna*: "Thus in the race and the competition for honor and glory in the life of man it seems to me very useful to provide oneself with a good ship and to give opportunity to one's powers and ability, and sweat to be first" (quoted in Burke, 1986: 194).

These new tropic figurations of *fortuna* were indicative of the increasing cultural power of the discourse of individualism, a discourse that socially inscribes the ontological primacy of the autonomous male individual.[12] "For reasons of prudence or habit," according to Ralph Ketcham (1988: 44), this discovery and celebration of the autonomous individual was couched in terms that placed with God the divine inspiration and wisdom to make such a creature. When Pico describes the relation between the human and divine in his famous *Oration on the Dignity of Man*, God tells Adam:

> Neither a fixed abode nor a form that is thine alone nor any function peculiar to thyself have we given thee . . . thou mayest have and possess what abode, what form, and what functions thou thyself shalt desire. . . . Thou, constrained by no limits, in accordance with thine own free will, in whose hand We have placed thee, shalt ordain for thyself the limits of thy nature. We have set thee at the world's center that thou mayest more easily observe whatever is in the world. We have made thee neither of heaven or of earth, neither mortal or immortal, so that with freedom of choice and with honor, as though the maker and molder of thyself, thou mayest fashion thyself in whatever shape thou shalt prefer. (1948: 225)

Accordingly, the individual is endowed the capacity, indeed the responsibility, to make of himself and the world in which he lives what he wills. Within this new discourse of individualism there is a double displacement of the divine. First, with man placed at the center of the world, God is displaced *to* the socio-ontological margins. He may have created the world and man—and may still judge men's actions—but what occurs in secular time and space is no longer a matter of divine providence. It is now preeminently a matter of human desire, will, and action. Therefore, the first displacement entails a second: The power to shape and influence worldly affairs is displaced *from* the divine to the human. Pico makes this second displacement explicit in regard to *Fortuna* in arguing that man himself has created the goddess. As such, Pico argues in *In astrologium libri*, man has mistakenly invested in her the power of destiny that resides in the individual self as *sors animae filia*, the "daughter of the soul" (quoted in Casirer, 1963: 120).

In such statements we can begin to ascertain why Erik Erikson (1962: 193) termed the Renaissance the "ego revolution *par excellance*." The source of meaning for the individual is shifted from a divinely ordained web of hierarchical social and spiritual relationships of subordination and obligation in which the individual was embedded to an array of political, economic, and intellectual institutions and practices that were considered be dynamic, secular creations of man. This shift can be described as the transition from the heteronomy to the autonomy of the individual. In the corporate order of feudal society, authority descended down from the pinnacles of sacrosanct political-economic and religious hierarchies to individuals who were completely subject to it (Ulmann, 1967). In the Renaissance, as Pitkin explains, authority and mastery became "internalized" within individuals who sought to shape their selves and their communities according to choice and design (1984: 12).

However, the "ego revolution" of the Renaissance did not consist solely of this internalization of authority. In order to exercise authority and mastery—and to be able claim that the Fortuna is really the "daughter of the soul"—the newly autonomous individual of the Renaissance had to literally *see* the world in a different way. The epistemic framework for the practice of autonomy was provided by the so-called re-discovery of linear perspective (cf. Jay, 1994). To phrase the issue another way, it is through the ocular gaze of linear perspective, an essential component of the story space of sovereign Eye/I performed by John Norris in the first chapter, that the self truly becomes autonomized.

Interestingly, it was Alberti, one of the most prominent civic humanists to extol the virtues of wealth, who first formalized the elements of linear perspective in his *De Pictura* in 1495.[13] Alberti's simple procedure of placing the eye of the perceiver behind a "window" so that it looks straight ahead to a vanishing point on the horizon generated a series of radical implications for the relationship between the self and the world. Perhaps the most fundamental of these was the creation of the perceptual framework of the autonomous ego. Autonomy, as I noted above, is about borders and boundaries, and the most fundamental of these boundaries is the perceptual boundary that is created between the self and the world. Laying the ground for the Cartesian *cogito*, linear perspective establishes the self as "an observing *subject*, a *spectator*, as against a world that becomes a *spectacle*, an object of vision" (Romanyshyn, 1989: 42). This positioning of the subject privileges the eye as the dominant sensory source of knowledge about the world. Staring out into the space of the world, where everything is on the same horizontal plane as the observer, the eye penetrates the newly established depth of the world with its vision, seeking to map, dissect, and explain it. It is through this regime of perception that men, to use Pico's words, are placed at the center of the world and God is displaced to the margins. The eye, therefore, "becomes the measure of the world's horizon" (Romanyshyn, 1989: 47). And by measuring the world, the eye charts and maps out its space as a territory to be controlled and mastered. Behind the window, the autonomous ego beholds the world and plots how to extend its dominion over it. Kathleen Kirby explains the relationship between the visual mapping of space and the formation of the autonomous individual:

The individual demonstrates a spatial format and projects a particular form of space. The individual and its corresponding form of space arose contemporaneously, with each dialectically reinforcing the other. The "individual" expresses a coherent, consistent, and rational space paired with a consistent, stable, and organized environment. Their relationship between the two is enabled by the separation: clear boundaries ensure the delimitation of inside and outside space, the order of each and the elevation of the former over the latter. This is both an expression of the new form of subjectivity and a technology of allowing (or causing) the new subjectivity to coalesce. (1995: 40)

The autonomous individual as subject, and his sovereignty over the spatial territory of the social as principality, are thus linked in the cartographic field of vision as power/knowledge.

The New Bourgeois Subject and the "Cult of Virtù"

This new perspective on the world constituted, according to Alfred von Martin, the basis for the *weltanschauung* of the new bourgeoisie of Renaissance mercantile capitalism. As he summarizes the essential difference between the perspectival regimes of feudalism and the Renaissance, the "*homo religiosus* of the Middle Ages had interpreted the world as a divine creation; the bourgeoisie of the Renaissance saw it as an object for human work and foresight; for human ordering and fashioning" (von Martin, 1963: 23–24). It is this perspective that sets up a new confrontation between *virtù* and *fortuna*, one that was radically different from the immanent conception of antiquity. Fortuna is no longer a goddess to be supplicated. She is, in fact, increasingly stripped of any mythic aura of divinity at all. As I say above, within the field of vision of linear perspective the divine is displaced and decentered. But whereas God is exiled to the margins of vision, Fortuna remains squarely within its field. She becomes part of the objectivized fabric of the perceived world as the manifestation of the irrational and unpredictable. In this perceptual framework, where the eye seeks to rationally know the world, she becomes that which is to be measured and explained. Fortuna, then, becomes the unpredictable element of a world newly constituted as an object of human goals and purposes. As the embodiment of chance and contingency, she must be anticipated and mastered to the fullest extent possible. As von Martin (1963: 19) argues, "Men ceased to believe that any thing irrational might intentionally interfere with their own systematic designs, they thought themselves able to master *fortuna* by *virtù*."

Within this understanding of *fortuna*, *virtù* comes to embody the characteristics of discipline, self-control, strength of purpose, reason, and foresight that enables men in general, and the *haute bourgeoisie* in particular, to, in Klaus Theweleit's words, "perceive and subdue the 'objective world' with increasing efficiency" (1987: 309). In order to impose *virtù* upon *fortuna*, to expand the domain of sovereign autonomy, the individual must become

> a sharply defined entity; a kernel of energy and enterprising spirit, a tough, armored ship that can be sent out to seize and order the world according to the European [centered, linear] perspective. The man puts on a coat of armor. A lengthy process of "self-distancing," "self-control," and "scrutiny" ensues—a "subduing of affect," and opposition of "interior" and "exterior," of "near" and "far." . . . The new scion of the bourgeoisie had to able to look beyond the surface of things, to plan ahead. He had to distance himself from objects, other humans, and his own emotion; to learn to wait for the right moment to act; to acquire diverse knowledge; to live in the awareness of being his father's successor. In short, he had to perceive himself as a citizen and man. (Theweleit, 1987: 311, 302)

The celebratory moral valuation of this combination of subjective discipline and reason with objective, world-transforming action constitutes what von Martin terms the "cult of *virtù*" (von Martin, 1963: 15). It is interesting that both Theweleit and Norbert Elias (1978), whose history of "civilizing" discipline enables Theweleit to draw his conclusions, neglect the Florentine cult of *virtù*. This is because it was within the cultural crucible of the moral economy of Italian mercantile capitalism that the rational, disciplined habitus of the bourgeois ego was first formed.

As von Martin and others point out, one of the intellectual virtues most valued by the Renaissance citizen was reason or *ragione*. Although *ragione* had many meanings, it preeminently referred to the ability of individuals to rationally calculate the relationship between means and ends and to prudently choose the most appropriate course of action. According to Felix Gilbert:

> *Ragione* was the instrument that enabled man to steer a straight course between illusory hopes and exaggerated fears to arrive at a correct decision. However, *ragione* was useful to man not only by guiding him on his own course of action, but also by providing the means for anticipating how others would act. At all times and places, man had responded to the same motivating forces. There was a recurrent pattern behind man's behavior that made his actions calculable. *Ragione* enabled man to deduce general rules of human behavior and apply them to the individual case under deliberation. (Gilbert, 1965: 38)

Ragione became the basis of the quotidian praxeology of substantive rationality in Renaissance mercantile capitalism. As such, it was a crucial form of power/knowledge that linked knowing and doing in everyday life and gave form to the ethical subject of the autonomous individual. The habit of calculation was applied to all spheres of social life, from politics to economics to family life. For the bourgeoisie, calculative rationality was manifested in the development of strict rules of accounting (account books were called *libri della ragione*), as well as in an obsessive emphasis on thrift or *masserizia*. Several centuries before Franklin formulated his famous dictums concerning thrift, frugality, and industry, Alberti (1967: 160) spoke glowingly of the virtue of *sancta cosa la masserizia* or "holy thrift."[14] For Alberti, the discipline of thrift was the fount of all economic virtue, and spending should be strictly calibrated according to need. Avarice consists not in having wealth per se but in using wealth to satisfy lascivious desires and, therefore, to spend without *ragione*. The "vile longings" of spendthrifts represented a surrender to irrational, "bestial pleasures" and brought financial ruin and social dishonor upon their family. The virtuous wealthy man "uses his possessions as the need arises and spends enough, but not more than enough. . . . We should not despise riches therefore, but remain lord over our desires when we live with ample possessions or in superfluity" (1967: 161).

The same rational calculation and discipline that is applied to the expenditure of money is also applied to the expenditure of time. Time is as "precious" as money. Alberti's interlocutor in *I Libri Della Famiglia*, his wealthy merchant uncle, Giannozzo, says:

> My plan therefore, is to make as good of use as possible of time, and never to waste any. I use time as much as possible on praiseworthy pursuits. I do not spend my time on base concerns. I spend no more time on anything than is needed to do it well. And to waste no part of such a precious thing, I have a rule I always follow: never to remain idle. I avoid sleep, and I do not lie down unless overcome by weariness, for it seems disgraceful to me to fall without fighting or to lie beaten—in short, like so many people, to take an attitude of defeat sooner than enter the battle. (1967: 171–172)

Alberti's metaphorical invocation of "battle" is clearly indicative of Theweleit's "armoring" of the bourgeois subject. The outward demonstration of *virtù* in the successful accomplishment of worldly goals and purposes was dependent upon the inward *virtù* of being able "to rule and control the passions of the soul" (1967: 136). Further, if inward *virtù* is manifested in the armoring of the self through thrift and industry, then outward *virtù* is manifested in bold and daring undertakings of grand designs. According to von Martin, the "typical spirit of the entrepreneur . . . expressed itself in forethought and an organizing will, fitting the means to the desired end; it denied all heedless impulse, but there was room for initiative, daring and elasticity" (1963: 49). The glory of successfully challenging *fortuna* through brave and audacious commercial enterprises is, again, underscored by Alberti in the following passage:

> You may object that profit making alone, where industry and wisdom together with zeal and industry seem to count for practically everything, is not like this. Good enough, yet I shall not retract my argument on this point for it seems to me largely answered thus: if profits in business come from our zeal, our efforts, still they will never be great if our zeal and our efforts are applied within a narrow field. From small affairs no great fortune come, however vigorously the enterprise is carried through. Profits only grow as the affairs themselves expand, and with the our industry and our labor. Great affairs bring great profits, but in these, as no one doubts, fortune is often vitally involved. In such business as our Alberti firms have traditionally done, for instance, enough wool was brought from faraway Flanders to fill all the baskets in Florence itself and in most of Tuscany. We will not trouble ourselves here to relate how many other goods were brought by at great expense, by steep and difficult mountain passes, to Florence through the efforts of our house. Did so many bales of wool by any chance travel outside the reach of fortune's hand? How many risks they ran, how many rivers and barriers they traversed, before they rested in security! Thieves, tyrants, wars, negligence, cheating on the part of middlemen, all these things did not fail to threaten them. . . . Such is the way, I think, with all great business enterprises, all merchant and trading adventures worthy of a noble and honorable family. (1967: 146–147)

I quote this passage at length because it contains key defining elements of the perspective of the new ethical masculine subject of the narrative of fortune and virtue that emerged in the Renaissance. First, it is important to note the use of the word "fortune" to describe the risks, hazards, and uncertainty of business enterprise as well as its result in terms of profits. The latter usage was an invention of the Renaissance, and the deployment of both meanings in this passage highlights a new understanding of the relationship of *virtù* to *fortuna*. *Virtù* was not simply that by which the individual successfully challenged *fortuna*; it was also that which transformed fortune into *a* fortune. To use Richard Goldthwaite's words, Alberti is celebrating the "merchant-patrician who had ventured alone into the world and wrested from it his fortune" (1968: 268).

Secondly, this "venturing" into the world is a manifestation of the ability to see and imagine spatial depth that was produced through linear perspective. One must see the world as being an infinite terrain for worldly action before one can venture into it. Indeed, it is important to emphasize the entirely spatial and topographical understanding of the nature of wealth that Alberti's statements evince. In spite of his emphasis on thrift and industry, in true mercantilist fashion there is little understanding of profit or wealth being systematically produced through the social and technical organization of labor. Wealth is produced by buying, selling, and trading, and the greater the space over which such activity occurs, the greater the profit. Therefore, the merchant displays outward *virtù* through the courageous and masterful insertion of himself into the space of exchange rather than, as will be the hallmark of the virtuous entrepreneur after Adam Smith, in the space and time of production.

Finally, the last sentence of the passage is indicative of the social purposes of wealth as understood by the bourgeoisie of the Renaissance. The most important function of wealth was to bring honor and fame to oneself and one's family. Honor did not consist directly in the possession of "goods and money" but in the "dignity" and "respect" "in the eyes of men" that active acquisition and use of wealth elicited.[15] Further, such glory did arise solely from the *virtù* of commercial deeds themselves. Just as important was the use of wealth to beneficently help others and to contribute to the cultural and political life of the community and republic. In this way, the *virtù* of the merchant-capitalist came to be valorized as part of the *vita activa*.

The "Better Angels" of Florence:
Wealth, Civic Virtue, and the Vita Activa

As Hans Baron (1955), J. Pocock (1975), and others argue, during the transition between the Trecento and the Quattrocento there occurred a fundamental shift in the Florentine language of virtue.[16] At the risk of vastly oversimplifying a complex issue, I will say that this shift essentially entailed a moral revaluation of the *vita activa* in relation to the *vita contemplativa*. The Trecento humanist proponents of the *vita contemplativa*, such as Petrarch, argued that only in a life of intellectual and spiritual contemplation could the individual cultivate wisdom and virtue. Echoing their medieval scholastic predecessors and their Stoic ancestors, Petrarch and others counseled that the path to virtue entailed withdrawal from the quotidian concerns of social life into a solitary, ascetic life of scholarship. Within the framework of the *vita contemplativa*, *virtù* consisted in a self-sufficient independence from Fortuna, her games of chance and contingency, and her worldly goods.

In contrast, a series of Petrarch's humanist successors, such as Coluccio Salutati, Leonardo Bruni, and Matteo Palmieri, expressed the view that a life of virtue was premised on practical engagement in political and economic affairs instead of stoic withdrawal. Using the classical texts of Aristotle, Cicero, and others as sources of inspiration and legitimation, they argued that the moral worth of an individual was demonstrated in social action and in vigorously participating in the life of the community.

One of the most highly exalted of the active virtues, according to this new humanist view, was civic virtue, or the virtue of citizenship. Hence, the discourse of citizenship articulated in Florence in the fifteenth and sixteenth centuries came to be known as "civic humanism."

The idea of civic virtue as rooted in the Aristotelian belief that "men" (again, the gender of the citizen in this discourse was exclusively male) were essentially *zöön politikon*, political creatures whose human potential could be realized only as active citizens among peers in the polis or political community. It was upon this Aristotelian ideal of the political man who publicly articulated and pursued his interests in association with others, and thus attempted to harmonize particularistic interests with the public good, that the civic humanists based their ideology of *vivere civile* or civic life. Essentially, *vivere civile* entailed a life devoted to civic concerns and the practice of citizenship. This meant that the community had large claims upon the individual in that it was a duty and responsibility of the citizen to participate in the affairs of the republic. Accordingly, the meaning of autonomy and *virtù* encompassed more than that of the singular individual. Autonomy now preeminently referred to that of the political community, which itself was contingent on the collective *virtù* of individuals dedicated to the res publica and to confronting the political uncertainties and instability that *fortuna* now represented. According to Pocock, within the discursive frame of civic humanism "*virtus* was now politicized; [it was] not the heroic manhood of a ruling individual, but a partnership of citizens within a polis" (1975: 78).

In the language of civic humanism, there was subtle balance between the autonomy of the male individual and his interdependence with others. The civic virtue of the citizen, in one sense, rested on his ability to be both morally and economically autonomous; he had to freely and willingly choose to practice citizenship and needed the material wherewithal to do so. Further, he could not be economically dependent upon others, for that would subordinate him to their particular interests. From the perspective of civic humanism, "the republic could persist only if all its citizens were autonomous so that they would be equally and immediately participant in the pursuit of the universal good" (Pocock, 1971: 87). Should the distribution of the ability to engage in civic activity become unequal, if some were to possess the power and authority to equate their particular interest with that of the public good, then the republic would become "corrupt." The stability of the republic and the pursuit of the universal interest of the community was contingent upon the ability of each citizen to practice civic virtue. Therefore, the virtue and autonomy of each individual in the community was dependent upon the virtue and autonomy of all.

The civic humanist position that economic independence was a prerequisite for the practice of citizenship raises the issue of the relationship of wealth and property to civic virtue. In the classical Aristotelian discourse of citizenship, it was property in the form of the household or *oikos* (which included slaves, women, and children) that enabled citizens to have the power, leisure, and opportunity to cultivate their human potential as practitioners of civic virtue. Although in this discourse the use of property to exchange and trade for profit was considered to be antithetical to the practice of citizenship, the early Quattrocento civic humanists often invoked Aristotle's position on property in order to link the active virtue of commerce with civic virtue.[17]

Commerce was portrayed as an active virtue in itself as well as the precondition for all other active virtues. Commerce is an exquisite example of that which is "practical" and "useful" and, therefore, is one of primary avenues by which the individual can live the *vita activa*. After all, argued Alberti (1967: 144), "if riches come from profits, and these through labor, diligence, and hard work, then poverty . . . will follow from the reverse of these virtues; namely, from neglect, laziness, and sloth. These are the fault neither of fortune nor of others but of oneself." Citing what was then thought to be Aristotle's *Economics*, Bruni argued that wealth gave men "the capacity to exercise their virtue . . . for riches can serve as an aid to such virtues as magnanimity and liberality since money . . . is necessary to maintain the state and safeguard our social existence" (quoted in Baron, 1988a: 230). For Bruni, wealth was not to be accumulated for its own sake but "for the sake of [civic]*virtus*, as an instrument, so to speak, for bringing *virtus* into action" (quoted in Baron, 1988a: 232).

Similarly, in his *Vita Civile*, Palmieri maintained that the virtues of charity, prudence, and temperance need the foundation of wealth because, without it, "they remain fragmentary and never attain perfection" (quoted in Baron, 1988a: 235). Without both the active experience of commerce and its material benefits, it was inconceivable that a man could devote himself to justice and the public good: "He who passes his life in solitude and is neither skilled in important matters . . . such as in the business affairs of the community will never become just and courageous." "The precondition for liberality," he continued, "is money; for justice, possessions; for courage, strength" (quoted in Baron, 1988a: 236). And, finally, to Alberti, the profits of trade, which were often considered to be "mercenary" by the public, are ultimately the sustaining source of the community for a very simple reason: A great republic needs a "great treasury," and a great treasury is "one which commands the loyalty of those who are not poor. It is a treasury to which all rich citizens faithfully and conscientiously contribute" (1967: 142).

When we consider this litany of humanist claims regarding the purposes of wealth, together with the cult of *virtù*, we can be begin to ascertain the complex interplay of the discourses of individualism, citizenship, and property that compose the rhetorical field of the moral economy of wealth and that produce the ideological linkage between wealth and virtue. At the most basic level, there is the valorization of wealth accumulation as a sign of the *virtù* of the autonomous individual. Here, virtue and *virtù* are almost identical, as the very qualities of a man of *virtù* (reason, discipline, boldness, strength) are simply more general forms of the specific virtues that the accumulation of wealth is said to evince (labor, diligence, hard work, thrift, individual initiative, etc.). Even though this moral equivalence of *virtù* and the more specifically capitalist virtues of the autonomous individual would come under harsh attack by Machiavellian proponents of civic republicanism, it perdures to this day as perhaps the most stable and common currency of exchange in the moral economy of wealth.

However, it is important to reemphasize that the heroic strivings of the autonomous individual, particularly that of the merchant-capitalist, were given a broader social context by reference to other discourses that contain other vocabularies of virtue. It is through the matrix of such interdiscursive relations that the linkage is forged between individual actions in the private sphere of virtuous wealth accumulation and the virtues relevant to the public sphere of the community. For the civic humanists, as the statements of Alberti and others indicate, two distinct vocabularies of virtue provided this link. First, there is the deployment of both classical and Christian (particularly Thomist) notions of virtue in relation to wealth. Wealth as property and possession provides the opportunity (and the challenge) for men to embody the cardinal virtues of prudence, temperance, courage, and justice as well as the biblical virtue of charity (cf. MacIntyre, 1981). Although the first three virtues are more private than public, they are character traits that are indispensable to the practice of the public virtues of charity and justice.

Of far more importance to the civic humanists was the vocabulary of virtue embedded in the Aristotelian discourse of citizenship, a vocabulary that gave "charity" and "justice" a sharply and distinctively republican meaning as they were viewed through the prism of civic virtue. Justice entailed the equality of respect, rights, and privileges among the citizens of the republic, and it would prevail when citizens equally fulfilled their obligations of service to the public good. In this context, "charity" did not primarily mean benevolence toward the poor and less fortunate of the community. Indeed, the horizon of virtuous, other-directed action in the civic humanist vision did not extend very far; it encompassed only those who were citizens, and in order to be a citizen one had to be economically independent. The Other to whom the autonomous individual was connected in an enlarged sense of self was essentially homogeneous and undifferentiated. Charity, then, meant a willingness and dutiful obligation to help others like oneself (fellow citizens) and was primarily manifested in the magnanimity and liberality of citizens in contributing to the political and cultural institutions of the community.

To civic humanists, therefore, wealth and commerce enabled men to support the republic financially and to freely and effectively participate in the management of its affairs. Magnanimous, liberal, and devoted to the public good, the merchant-capitalist of the Quattrocento civic humanist imagination was perhaps the first incarnation of George Bush's vision of the wealthy in pursuit of the "better angels."

Did this civic humanist vision, in the context of the workings of the Florentine republic during the fifteenth and early sixteenth centuries, bear some correspondence to reality, or was it simply an ideological sham? Von Martin (1967: 31–46) delivers the latter judgment upon the civic humanists, as they were (in Gramscian terms) traditional intellectuals in the employ and service of the wealthy elite. The purpose of civic humanism was simply to provide the intellectual legitimation for the de facto rule and hegemony of a tiny elite of patrician, merchant families that increasingly became an oligarchy controlled by the Medici.[18] The problem was that as the Medici consolidated their hold on power the practice of citizenship diverged from its ideal. The ethos of public service was supplanted by a cynical manipulation of public offices and the public purse for furthering the self-interest of the ruling elite of wealthy families. In essence, according to the standards of civic humanism itself, the republic had become irredeemably corrupt. Using the standard of civic virtue and its negative pole, corruption, Machiavelli would hoist the Quattrocento defenders of wealth as a community-oriented practice of the *vita activa* with their own petard.

Founders and Citizens: Machiavelli and the Narrative of Fortune and Virtue

The Logic of the Narrative of Fortune and Virtue

My long march through the issues of autonomy, wealth, and civic virtue was necessary in order to establish the meaning of the elements that compose Machiavelli's narrative of fortune and virtue. Now that the march has been completed, it is possible to see how the narrative of fortune and virtue is constructed and set into motion. The *subject* of the narrative is the masculine individual, egocentrically placed at the center of the world. The telos of the narrative, that which the subject seeks or desires to possess or achieve, is autonomy, a realm of sovereignty and freedom. This telos is also an ethos of moral identity where power and propriety converge. In narratological terms, there are two *powers* that mediate the relationship between the subject and the telos (Bal, 1984). The first power that enables the individual to secure his object is virtue, the personal qualities of the individual that allow him to prevail over the second power of the narrative, fortune, which he must master. The manner in which the subject dynamically relates virtue and fortune in pursuit of the telos enacts and embodies the emplotment and emplacement of the narrative.

Unfortunately, the attractive simplicity of this structure obscures the nuances of two of its components, the object or telos of autonomy and the power of virtue, that I discuss in the preceding section. Both autonomy and virtue have what Norman Fairclough terms an "ambivalent" signifying potential in that they can have different, though not necessarily exclusive, meanings (1991: 39). As I argue above, autonomy can be interpreted as meaning the sovereign isolation of the individual, or it can refer to the interdependence of individuals who find an enlarged awareness of self in the collective freedom of the republic. Virtue has a similarly ambivalent meaning potential. At one level, the virtue of the enterprising bourgeois subject consists entirely of *virtù*. Here virtue refers to the rational, calculative will to power by which the desires and intentions of the subject are imposed upon the world. Virtue qua *virtù* is valued as a sign of masculine potency that brings glory and honor to those who demonstrate it. At another level, however, virtue is primarily civic virtue, of which *virtù* is an important but subordinate element. The honor that one gains from exhibiting civic virtue is that of being a good and dutiful citizen.

To Machiavelli's civic humanist predecessors, within the parameters of the ideology of the *vita activa*, these ambivalences did not present a problem. There was no reason for them to prefer one meaning of autonomy over the other, or to choose *virtù* over civic virtue, as they saw the different dimensions of autonomy and virtue, as well autonomy and virtue themselves, as being connected by wealth. It was the rational and disciplined acquisition and use of wealth that represented the apotheosis of manly *virtù* and secured the autonomy and glory of the male individual (and his family). Furthermore, it was wealth that enabled men to fulfill their moral obligations to the *res publica* and to embody and practice the higher civic virtue of citizenship.

In Machiavelli's formulation of the narrative of fortune and virtue we also find the same ambivalent duality of the meanings of virtue and autonomy.[19] However, to Machiavelli, the exaltation of wealth and commerce by the Quattrocento humanists as the resource and practice that would unproblematically link *virtù* and civic virtue, and sovereign autonomy with the mutuality and interdependence of citizenship, was naive. The Quattrocento was the period of the full flowering of the Italian Renaissance in all its political, economic, and cultural dimensions, and given the prosperity and influence of Florence, the perceived harmony between wealth, virtue, and autonomy was perhaps understandable. However, by the early sixteenth century, the time Machiavelli retreated to his farm in political disgrace and exile to write his most famous works, it appeared to him and many of his contemporaries that Fortuna had turned against Florence. More importantly, from Machiavelli's perspective wealth and commerce had contributed in large measure to the decay of the virtue and autonomy of the republic and its citizens.

Externally, the autonomy of Florence and other Italian republican city-states was threatened by a series of military invasions by northern European powers, commencing with the French invasion of 1494. Internally, as I already mention, the democratic workings of the Florentine city-state were progressively corrupted by the manipulations of the Medici and their allies. Although the French invasion brought the overthrow of the Medici and the establishment of a new participatory republic (in which Machiavelli was a principal figure), by 1512 the rule of the Medici had been restored. Indeed, within a few years of Machiavelli's death in 1527 the last vestiges of republican rule had died, and Florence became a hereditary principality of the Medici. Finally, by the beginning of the sixteenth century Florence had been displaced as a leading center of textile manufacturing, finance, and commerce by northern European cities such as Antwerp and Amsterdam.[20] Although it is not clear whether this was a cause or consequence, a key feature of the decline of Florentine mercantile capitalism was an increasing propensity of the wealthy elite to shift their capital from manufacturing and trade to land and conspicuous consumption of high status luxury goods (cf. Goldthwaite, 1980; Jardine, 1996; Hale, 1994). According to Ferdinand Braudel (1972: 223), this change in the economic behavior of wealthy of Florence represented the "bankruptcy of the bourgeoisie" and marked their degeneration from a dynamic, innovative class of capitalist entrepreneurs to a rentier class of landed gentry.

With fortune so unfavorably disposed toward Florence, Machiavelli sought to discover in the glorious past of the Roman republic exemplars of virtue and autonomy that would inspire his contemporaries to recover their *virtù* and wrest control of their collective lives from the vagaries of *fortuna*. In so doing, Machiavelli isolated the different meanings of virtue and autonomy in their purest forms in the moral characters of the Founder and the Citizen that inhabit the narrative of fortune and virtue as subjects.[21] The irony of history of the narrative of fortune and virtue is this: Even though Machiavelli displaced wealth and commerce from the dramatic stage upon which the narrative of fortune and virtue would be enacted, in time its figural actors would once again be reconfigured in terms of wealth. However, this discursive reconfiguration would occur in a manner that neither Machiavelli nor the civic humanists could possibly imagine.

The Founder: Master of Fortuna and Entrepreneur of Self and History

Of the two moral characters that occupy a central place in Machiavelli's discourse, the Founder is the most pristine in content and the most easy to situate in terms of the narrative of fortune and virtue. The Founder is, quite simply, *virtù* incarnate. He is a singular and solitary fount of manly authority and power that is able to create a worldly realm of sovereignty and autonomy. The goal of the Founder is the creation and extension of his dominion in the world by imposing his *virtù* upon *fortuna*. The Founder is not simply a ruler; he is an innovator, a creator of a spatial principality that is temporally new and enduring. This principality may be a religion (as with Numa), a republic (as with Brutus), an empire (as with Alexander the Great), or a nation (as with Moses or Romulus). But whatever its nature, the dominion of the Founder is an extension of his will and character in both space and time. It is worthy of "glory in the world," as it provides a framework within which lesser men will live and cultivate their own *virtù* for generations to come (1965c, 8: 38). The Founder is thus the prototypical entrepreneur, the self-made man par excellence, and any resemblance between his configuration as a moral character and the rhetorical presentation of self offered by Dahlin may be uncanny, but it is not at all coincidental, for the peculiar form of the narrative of fortune and virtue inscribed in the moral character of the Founder provides the template from which contemporary entrepreneurs such as Dahlin craft their moral identity. *Tanto nomini nullum par elogium.*

The narrative trajectory of the Founder's quest for glory and greatness is set up by Machiavelli as a direct contest between his solitary *virtù* and the vagaries of *fortuna*. Indeed, this contest begins at the very birth of the Founder, as the goddess has seen fit to place him in adverse circumstances as an infant. The Founders begin their lives as orphans, like Moses abandoned in the bulrushes or Romulus left to suckle at the teat of a wolf, severed from any connection to the paternal and (especially) maternal source from which they issued. In a clear prefiguration of the Horatio Alger myth, Machiavelli remarks in the "Life of Castruccio" that "all, or the larger part, of those in this world have done very great things, and who have been excellent men of their era, have in their birth been humble and obscure, or at least been beyond all measure afflicted by Fortune. All of them have been exposed to wild beasts or have had fathers so humble, being ashamed of them, they have made themselves sons of Jove or of some other god" (1965d: 533).

Accordingly, the glory and *virtù* of the Founder consists, in part, of a biographical trajectory that begins with the unfortunate circumstances of lowly birth. As such, the Founder is truly a self-made man, as he owes the greatness he aspires to and achieves to nobody but himself. Even so, given the fact that it was Fortuna herself who conferred upon the Founders the lowly origins from which they would ascend, it is clear that they owe her something. Machiavelli does indeed acknowledge this debt. However, this debt is limited simply to the chance and opportunity for the Founders to demonstrate their *virtù*. He argues in the sixth chapter of *The Prince*:

> It will not appear that they owed anything to fortune except opportunity, which gave them matter into which to introduce whatever form they thought good; without the opportunity their *virtù* would have been wasted and without *virtù* the opportunity would have been in vain. It was necessary then that Moses should find the people of Israel slaves in Egypt and oppressed by the Egyptians, so that they were disposed to follow him in order to escape from servitude. It was necessary that Romulus should take no root in Alba and be exposed at this birth, in order that he be king of Rome and founder of that nation. It was necessary that Cyrus find the Persians ill content with the rule of the Medes, and the Medes soft and effeminate through long peace. Theseus could not have displayed his *virtù* if he had not found the Athenians dispersed. (1965c, 6: 31)

The relationship between *fortuna* and *virtù* that is embodied in the Founder is clear. In order to achieve greatness, the Founder must have the opportunity. However, his glory and *virtù* consist in taking that opportunity, which is a situation of pure chance and contingency, and intervening so as to impose form and order upon it. Without the abilities and power that inhere in the personal qualities of the Founder, whatever opportunities that lay before him would never be transformed from the realm of the possible to that of the actual.

The confrontation between the Founder and *fortuna* as contingent opportunity makes clear the specific personal characteristics that constitute his *virtù*. At one level, the *virtù* of the Founder is a pure and unadulterated will to power. As an innovator, he steps into a situation and violently imposes a new order upon it without regard for what has come before his intervention. The violent nature of the act of founding is underscored by Machiavelli in *The Discourses* when he says that "with violence, they enter into the countries of others, kill the inhabitants, seize their property, set up a new kingdom, and change the name of the country as did Moses, and those people who took possession of the Roman

Empire" (1965b, II, 8: 345). For Machiavelli, such acts of violence are far from regrettable. On the contrary, the very violence of the Founder and his overthrow of the prevailing order of things is the hallmark of his creative glory.

However, the *virtù* of the Founder does not consist solely of the infliction of his will upon the world. In order to institute a new order, the Founder must be able to ascertain the designs of Fortuna and act according to strategic intention in order to take advantage of what she has given him. That is, in addition to power, the Founder must have the vision to prefiguratively imagine what is to be achieved. Although their "opportunities enabled them to prosper," argues Machiavelli, it was their "surpassing abilities [that] enabled them to recognize their opportunities. As a result, their countries were exalted and became very prosperous" (1965c, 6: 32). Here, prefiguring the foundational virtue of John Norris's "success," the *virtù* of the Founder consists primarily of insight. He sees his chance to mold something of his own design, not some inert or physical thing, but something human, some community or social endeavor. Moreover, he has the imagination and intelligence to see what can be done, to see what is invisible to others, and strength of purpose enough to do it. Accordingly, the *virtù* of the Founder is demonstrated in his ability to have foresight or, in Pocock's words, to "discern what time was bringing and what strategies were required to cope with it" (1975: 177).

Once the Founder recognizes the opportunity that fortune has brought and imagined what could be achieved, it remains for him to choose the appropriate course of action for instituting his vision. For Machiavelli, the question of strategically relating means to ends revolves primarily around a single choice: whether to be prudent and cautious or bold and audacious. There are times, Machiavelli concedes, where it might be more advantageous to be cautious and bide one's time in order to ascertain the dispensation of the goddess more clearly. However, for Machiavelli, discretion and prudence is not often the better part of valor or *virtù*. Offering yet another image of Fortune as a woman, in the poem "Dell'occasione" (On opportunity) Machiavelli describes opportunity as a frisky and elusive young lass whose hair falls over her face so she is hard to recognize and bald in back so she is hard to grab. Not only is opportunity hard to recognize and seize, but she passes by only once, and those who temporize will be left her sad companion, *pentitenzia* or "regret" (Flanagan, 1972: 147). Accordingly, the wiser course of action is to act boldly when opportunity presents itself, or, as Machiavelli himself says, quoting Boccaccio, "it is better to act and repent than not to act and repent" (quoted in Pitkin, 1984: 22). Moreover, not only can caution lead one to miss opportunity; to bide one's time is also to place one's fate in the hands of *fortuna*. Such a strategy is, in the long run, a recipe for disaster, as

Fortuna will inevitable turn against those who do not master her. Therefore, "he who depends least on Fortune sustains himself the longest"
(1965c, 16: 25).

There are, of course, those who are truly indebted to fortune in that
they were born into positions of power. It is possible for men who inherit
such a position to be men of great *virtù*. Their task, however, is a difficult
one, and they must be men of extraordinary abilities so as to reduce their
dependence on *fortuna*: Such men, like Cesare Borgia, are of "so great
virtù that [they] can promptly take steps to preserve what *fortuna* has
thrown into [their] lap, and lay after becoming a prince those foundations which others lay in anticipation of it" (1965c, 7: 35). That is, they
must be able to impose their own distinctive and innovative stamp upon
the domain that they have been given. Unfortunately, such men are rare.
Those who are so indebted to good fortune tend to be "made drunk" by it,

> assigning all their prosperity to an ability which they have not displayed at
> any time. As a result, they become hateful and unbearable to all around
> them. From this situation, then, issues some sudden change in their lot, and
> why they look it in the face, they fall at once into the other defect and be-
> come despicable and abject. Consequently, princes of this sort, when in ad-
> versity, think more about running away than about defending themselves,
> since having used good fortune badly, they are unprepared for any defense.
> (1965b, III, 31: 498)

There are clear resonances between Machiavelli's assessment of inheritors of good fortune and David Schwartz's narrative of abjection. But
even when inheritors are able to avoid this fate and are able to impose
their *virtù* upon *fortuna*, they can never attain the status of Founders, of
truly self-made men. Historical entrepreneurship, the ability to impose a
new form upon the tabula rasa of time and contingency, is a virtue that
inheritors can never truly claim as their own. Moreover, it is a standard
against which they are forever condemned to measure themselves. As
Machiavelli describes the incomparable virtue of entrepreneurship and
the mastery of fortune, the *virtù* of a Founder will

> make him appear ancient, and render him more swiftly more secure and
> more established if he were established from old. For a new prince is always
> more observed in his actions than a hereditary one, and when these are seen
> to be virtuous he wins men over far more and they become more bound to
> him than to ancient blood. For men are more taken by things present than by
> things past, and when they find themselves well off in the present, they en-
> joy it and ask no more; they will then undertake to defend him, so long as he
> does not fail of himself in other respects. And so he will have the double
> glory of having founded a new principate and adorned and strengthened it

with good laws, good arms, and good examples; as he will have the double
shame who was born a prince and has lost it. (1965c, 24: 89)

This statement takes us to the very heart of the legitimating power of the
narrative of fortune and virtue that the moral character of the Founder
enacts. In the context of the discourse of individualism that emerged during the Renaissance, the Founder is a towering figure precisely because
he embodies the fulfillment of the teleology of sovereign individuality
promised by God to Adam in Pico's *Oration*. Indeed, as the master of fortune and entrepreneur of history he assumes the mantle of a secular deity: He who creates Himself by creating a world of His own design.

Pitkin correctly notes such a figure can only be mythical, as no man really creates himself (1984: 79). But it is the mythological nature of the
Founder that constitutes his allure and seduction as a moral character. As
R. Barthes explains its workings, "Myth is constituted by the loss of the
historical quality of things; in it things lose the memory of their fabrica-
tion" (1972: 129). I would modify this to say that in the myth of the
Founder we are presented with a *particular* memory of the history of fab-
rication of things that is specific to the moral economy of capitalism. In
this memory, the social dimensions of the production of wealth are displaced from the story. All that we remember is a history of wealth that
begins and ends with heroic efforts of intrepid individuals. Thus, the
Founder is conjured by a narrative where both origin and telos, and all
points between the two, is the manifested destiny of individual prowess
and will. Within the frame of this narrative, no other memory is possible—not unless we work hard, very hard, to conjure another narrative.
Of course, there is another narrative apart from that of the Founder that
would eventually enable men of inherited wealth, such as Dean, to claim
a virtuous moral identity. This is the narrative of the Citizen.

The Citizen: Wealth, Corruption, and the Problem of Civic Virtue

It has often been said of Machiavelli that he had no understanding of the
relationship between economics and politics. The seeming absence of any
detailed consideration of the role of economics in the establishment and
maintenance of republics prompted his twentieth-century Marxist interlocutor, Antonio Gramsci, to state that "it might be queried whether
Machiavelli really had any economic theories. One will have to see
whether Machiavelli's essentially political language can be translated
into economic terms, and to which economic system it can be reduced"
(1971: 143). Gramsci would find no satisfactory answer to his question,
primarily because it was not the right question to pose in regard to
Machiavelli. As a Marxist, Gramsci was trying to discern in Machiavelli a

discourse of the "economic" that was analogous to his own. Gramsci's hope was that in Machiavelli's social ontology there would be embedded concepts that pointed to an understanding of the economic as an abstract representation of a system of production, exchange, and consumption. Unfortunately, Gramsci was looking for what could not possibly be found, as such an understanding would not begin to be developed until the latter half of the seventeenth century (cf. Tribe, 1981). As such, Gramsci's attempt to find an economic discourse and system to which Machiavelli's political thought can be "reduced" actually obscures rather reveals the economic dimension of Machiavelli's thought, because within the framework of Machiavelli's discourse the "economic" is entirely subordinated to and configured in terms of the political. Within this framework, wealth and property were seen essentially as static things taking the form of land or treasure rather than as fluid constituents and products of a dynamic system of production and circulation. Furthermore, wealth and commerce figure in Machiavelli's analysis of the political primarily in terms of their effects on the capacity of a republic and its citizens to virtuously preserve their autonomy and freedom. And, for Machiavelli, these effects were primarily negative.

Although it would be an exaggeration to say that Machiavelli blamed the wealthy elite entirely for the declining fortunes of Florence (his most caustic criticisms were directed at the Papacy and the Catholic Church), it is clear that he thought wealth and commerce had sapped the citizens of the republic of their *virtù* and their civic virtue. On a personal level, Machiavelli had little interest in or respect for commercial activity. He often expressed his contempt for Florence as a city run by and for *uomini nutricati nella mercanzia*, or petty shopkeepers, and proudly described himself as a man "who could not reason about the production of silk or wool, or about gains and losses, but that it was his lot to reason about politics" (Gilbert, 1965: 176). Indeed, in true Aristotelian fashion, politics was the real vocation of the manly man, and to the extent that commerce distracted men from their proper telos as *zöön politikon*, it was to be guarded against.

As Gilbert (1965) points out, wealth took on the character of an original sin for Machiavelli, as it was the source of all that would rob a republic and its citizenry of *virtù* and civic virtue. The foundation of Machiavelli's analysis of the deleterious effects of wealth is his belief that the pursuit of wealth encouraged men to put their own self-interest before that of the republic. The power of wealth and property in commanding the allegiance of the individual is so great, he argues in *The Prince*, that "men forget more easily the loss of their father or brothers than the loss of their patrimony" of wealth and property (1965c, 17: 65). It is this overriding concern with the preservation of self-interest as configured by the desire for wealth, to the detriment of the common good, that was the source of "corruption" in the body politic.

This corruption took a number of different forms. First, inequality of wealth lead to the rise of political factions that were primarily devoted to struggling over the distribution of *ricchezza* or "riches." Such a struggle over the distribution of wealth and property took place between the patricians and plebeians in Rome after Gracchi's reintroduction of the Agrarian Laws and ultimately, according to Machiavelli, lead to the downfall of the republic (1965c, I, 37). Second, inequality of wealth produced a situation where the wealthy could buy the services of the poor, thus diverting them from service to the republic, and the poor would be left with no choice but to become clients of the rich. Accordingly, inequality of wealth violated the cardinal rule of the civic republican ideal, which was that citizens had to be economically autonomous in order to practice civic virtue. Finally, and most importantly in light of Machiavelli's celebration of the masculine power of *virtù*, he noted with disdain and horror that in republics where the citizenry had become wealthy the city had also "become effeminate and a prey to her neighbors" (1965b, I, 19: 290).

To Machiavelli, no graver sign of corruption and abjection could be imagined than a citizenry that was *effiminato*, and wealth and commerce contributed to this sad state of affairs in two ways. First, the desire for wealth itself was effeminate in that it signified a surrender and enslavement to the inconstant passions of greed, avarice, and envy. Remember that the manly man of *virtù* is rational and disciplined and thus stands in marked contrast to the irrational and capricious feminine Other of Fortuna. Accordingly, for a man to devote himself to seeking a fortune is to court, emulate, and eventually embody the disordered irrationality and undisciplined desire that Fortune herself represented.[22] Of course, as I discuss above, such a contrast between the rational will of *virtù* and the excessive passions of avarice was central to Alberti's depiction of the manly merchant capitalist. However, whereas Alberti argued that the ability of the wealthy man to resist the temptations of luxury was a clear litmus test of his *virtù*, Machiavelli held a less sanguine view of such abilities. Machiavelli had a rather pessimistic view of human nature and argued that men, left to their own devices, would naturally pursue their own self-interest and indulge their desires. As he argues in *The Discourses*, "It must needs be taken for granted that all men are wicked and that they will always give vent to the malignity that is in their minds when opportunity offers. . . . Men never do good unless necessity drives them to it; but when they are too free to choose and can do just as they please, confusion and disorder become everywhere rampant" (1965b, I, 3: 210). From Machiavelli's perspective, therefore, when wealth and commerce occupy a central place in social life, the natural tendencies of men toward selfishness and effeminate indiscipline would only be reinforced. When a republic grows prosperous, he argued, its citizens grow indolent and decadent and become more interested in the sybaritic pleasures of luxury than in the glory and honor of the republic.

Given the manifold negative effects of wealth, opines Machiavelli in *The Discourses*, it is better to keep the republic rich and the citizenry poor. A republic that is more wealthy than any of its citizens can command the allegiance of even the most self-interested of men, as only the republic can provide the material rewards he seeks. Conversely, it is necessary to "keep the citizens poor, so that their wealth and lack of *virtù* will never corrupt themselves or corrupt others" (1965b, III, 26: 469).

Who, then, is this moral character of the Citizen and in what does his virtue and autonomy inhere? The moral essence of the Citizen resides in a quality of *bontà*, or goodness, that is best expressed by the motto *ne supurbemente dominare ne umilmente servire* (neither arrogantly to dominate nor humble to serve) (1965b, I, 58: 314). When the Citizen acts in accordance with this maxim, he will embody and practice civic virtue as defined by the characteristics of friendship, mutuality and concord, and devotion to the public good. As these characteristics suggest, to say that the ideal Citizen is neither arrogantly domineering nor humbly servile is to prescribe a particular mode by which the individual perceives and relates to others in a community. As Pitkin notes, whereas *virtù* in its purest form entails a relationship of mastery between the self and an objectivized world, civic virtue entails a relationship of interdependence and reciprocity between the self and other subjects (1984: 81). Therefore, it is through the practice of citizenship that the locus of personal identity shifts from the singular sovereignty of the autonomous individual—the subject who says "I"—to the larger community—a collective subject that says "We."

At the root of this transformation of self-identity through the practice of citizenship is friendship, a mode of social consciousness and interaction that Machiavelli evoked in the *Art of War* by calling for citizens "to love one another" (1965a, I: 570). As with many other aspects of the discourse of citizenship, the conception of friendship that is embodied in the figure of the Citizen is Aristotelian in origin. For Aristotle, friendship was the intersubjective bond that held a community together and insured that it operated according to the principles of justice.[23] In this sense, friendship entails more than a feeling of love, affection, or goodwill toward one's fellow citizens (though these sentiments are important); it also entails a recognition of communality, of a shared membership in a joint venture that is the sustenance of social life.

Accordingly, friendship also entails mutuality and what Aristotle called *homonia* or "concord." Mutuality refers to the recognition of other members of the community not as superior or inferior to oneself but as equals and peers. Furthermore, mutuality also requires a recognition and respect for differences among one's fellow citizens. This dimension of friendship was particularly important to Machiavelli. In spite of his perspective on the dangers to the republican way of life posed by economic inequality, he was by no means a proponent of a radically egalitarian, classless society. He assumed that any republic would be stratified according to social status, political rank, and, to a certain extent, wealth. The problem for Machiavelli was not wealth per se but rather an overriding concern among citizens with wealth's accumulation through commerce. He believed that each social class had a distinctive perspective on the community and particular configuration of needs, ambitions, and desires. What was important to Machiavelli was not so much that there should be absolute equality between all citizens but that there be a mutuality of respect and regard for the needs and interests of different classes. This mutuality is the basis for concord, that is, the recognition of and concern for these different interests when citizens come together to publicly decide how to pursue these interests.

For Machiavelli, concord was manifested in the open and honest articulation and pursuit of different interests in the political arena. For this reason one of the defining characteristics of the Citizen was "to decline faction" (1965a, I: 570). Political factions, which bedeviled the Florentine republic throughout its history, were inimical to the well-being of the republic not only because they hardened and institutionalized divisions in the community but also because factions were so obsessed with pursuing their own particular interests that they often worked surreptitiously to impose their will upon the rest of the public.[24] Without open dialogue and discussion of the divergent interests and desires of different citizens, there could be no hope of arriving at a policy that took into account the interest of each when developing a policy that was in the interest of all.

From Machiavelli's perspective, it was necessary for the Citizen to be prepared to "give thought to private and public interest together" in deliberation with fellow citizens (1965b, II, 2: 333). In this way, the heterogeneity of interests, needs, and desires that exist in a community are openly expressed and brought into conflict. Out of this conflict the Citizen becomes aware of the different needs of others as well as his communality with them. It is also out of this conflict that specific interests of individuals are modified and redefined in terms of the public good. In the process, the very meaning of self is transformed: One is no longer an isolated, sovereign individual responsible only to oneself; one is now a member of a community with shared interests in which one has a personal stake and to which one is obligated to help sustain and preserve.

The boundaries of identity have been redrawn: He who says "I" is now also able to say "We."

For Stuart Dean, the elision of the sovereignty of the "I" with the community of the "We" allows him to claim the virtue of citizenship. Like Machiavelli's Citizen, Dean takes advantage of the opportune circumstances that fortune has bestowed upon him and uses them to virtuously insert himself in the public sphere in the name of the common good. In Dean's moral tale of fortune and virtue, the private interests of wealth and family are harmoniously linked to the wider interests of the community. Clearly, however, the uncanny resonances between Dean's (auto-) biographical narrative and Machiavelli's figure of the Citizen only go so far. However exemplary Dean's acts of citizenship might appear to Machiavelli, from the latter's perspective they would be tainted by the risk of corruption entailed by the former's grounding in the accumulation of wealth. In order for the discourse of citizenship to provide an efficacious language for the conjuring of virtuous moral identity among men of wealth, a place would have to be created where the flows of fortune as money would enhance rather than corrupt civic virtue. Within the terms of Machiavelli's civic republican discourse, no such place is to be found, as he effectively *displaced* the accumulation of wealth from the territory of virtue. How, then, is it possible to render intelligible in discursive terms Dean's conjuring of himself as good citizen? A partial answer to this problem is located in a symbolic and material spatial territory of social practice that Machiavelli thought to the fount of vice and corruption: the marketplace of commerce. Within this territory of the market, a new moral character is to be found who is able to unite the flows of money with cultivation of virtue. This character represents a profound remapping of the narrative of fortune and virtue as a spatial story. This is the moral character of *homo mercator*, or Market Man, and I now turn to his conjuring in the discourse of the Scottish Enlightenment.

Notes

1. On the history of different interpretations of Machiavelli's legacy of "originality" see Berlin (1980), Cassirer (1946), and Harriman (1995).

2. Thanks to Sandra Joshel for the Latin translation.

3. The word *fortuna* is used in two ways in this chapter. When capitalized as Fortuna it refers to the goddess of chance; when it is not capitalized, fortuna refers to chance, contingency, and opportunity.

4. I am referring here to humanists such as Leonardo Bruni, Matteo Palmieri, and Leon Battista Alberti who were pivotal in changing the humanist perspective on wealth. In the Trecento (thirteenth century), as exemplified by the writings of Francesco Petrarca, the prevailing humanist view held that a truly moral and

virtuous life required poverty. As I discuss below, in the Quattrocento (fourteenth century), Bruni, Palmieri, and Alberti articulated the position that an active life of virtue could not be lived without a good measure of worldly possessions and riches. See Hans Baron (1988a).

5. On the complex relationship of civic humanism to the classical tradition of rhetoric, see Jerrold Siegel (1968) and Pocock (1975).

6. On the figuring of "woman" and the feminine as nature in rationalist thought, see Lloyd (1984).

7. The logic of equivalence—"Women, floods, fear; men, dams, mastery"—represents a structure of desire that is, as Klaus Theweleit argues, at the core of the capitalist social imaginary that the bourgeois ego inhabits. In its extreme form, such a structure of desire gives rise to the fascist imagination, an imagination that seeks, *über alles*, to obliterate difference for fear of having its pure, uncontaminated self overwhelmed by the "floods" of communism, inferior races, and female sexuality. I raise this point not to suggest that either Machiavelli, or the manner in which the narrative of fortune and virtue animates his work, is prototypically or intrinsically fascist. Rather, it is to suggest that the language of the narrative of fortune and virtue, like the language of fascism, is excessively masculine. Both employ a vocabulary of power that sees power as the embodied instrument of individuals (or collectivities) that is wielded to cut a swath of dominion through space and time according to will, intention, and desire. As languages, they are symbolic spaces in which it is extraordinarily difficult for women to enter in anything other than a subordinate, controlled, and, ultimately, dehumanized way. See Theweleit (1987, esp. pt. 2). As Lorraine Code (1991: 120) has argued, "A set of traits that are discursively, ideologically constitutive of masculinity cannot simply shift or expand to incorporate women and retain their referential and evaluative scope. Women who seek inclusion will at best achieve the status of aliens, immigrants, whose presence is tolerated not on their own terms, but on the native's terms."

8. In a famous passage, Jacob Burckhardt (1954 [1860]: 70), describes this emergence as follows: "In the Middle Ages both sides of human consciousness—that which was turned within and turned without—lay dreaming or half awake beneath a common veil. The veil was woven of faith, illusion, and childish prepossession, through which the world and history were seen clad in strange hues. Man was conscious of himself only as a member of a race, people, party, family or corporation—only through some general category. In Italy this veil first melted into air; an *objective* treatment and consideration of the state and of all things of this world became possible. The *subjective* side at the same time asserted itself with corresponding emphasis; man became a spiritual *individual*, and recognized himself as such."

9. It should be noted that throughout this chapter I use the word "man" and its concomitant masculine pronouns to denote the subjects of the narrative of fortune and virtue and its constituent discourses. As Kelly-Gadol (1977: 139) has argued, "There was no Renaissance for women—at least, not during the Renaissance." Accordingly, it is important not to erase this fact by substituting gender-neutral nouns and pronouns for "man" when it was, in fact, almost always men to whom the word referred.

10. See Patch (1927), plates 1 and 2.

11. According to Pocock (1975: 39), with this equation of all that occurs in secular time as "good fortune," "fortune is swallowed up in the twin concepts of Providence and Fate. Providence is that perfection in which God sees to (or, to human intellects, foresees) all circumstantial things; Fate is the perfection of the pattern in which he decrees and perceives them." See also Parel's (1992: 64–65) discussion of Fate, Providence, and Fortune in Machiavelli and his contemporaries.

12. It is important to note, however, that in the Renaissance we do not yet see the full-blown conception of the sovereign individual, whose autonomy is rooted in the confluence of property and personality, that emerged in the seventeenth and eighteenth centuries. The ego that inhabited the social imaginary of the time was not yet inextricably tied to property, motivated by self-interest, and governed by the rules and relations of market exchange. This linkage between individuality and property, selfhood and money, will be explored in Chapter 4 in the context of the Scottish Enlightenment.

13. My discussion of Alberti's articulation of linear perspective and its phenomenological implication is a gloss on Robert Romanyshyn's discussion of the same (1989: 32–47). For a discussion of its social repercussions, and its repercussions for social and cultural theory, see Jay (1994).

14. It is interesting to note that there was a major (and acrimonious) debate between Werner Sombart and Max Weber over the significance of the Renaissance bourgeoisie, Alberti in particular, to the development of the "spirit of capitalism." For Sombart (1967 [1913]: 103–104), Renaissance Florence was the "cradle" of the "respectable citizen" who was animated by the middle-class "virtues" that constituted, in a clear reference to Weber, "what today is called the capitalist spirit." He argued that Alberti's book on the family represented "a perfect picture of Benjamin Franklin, the incarnation of the spirit of respectable citizenship." Weber, who used Franklin as his ideal type of the embodied, ascetic, capitalist spirit of accumulation, vehemently disagreed. Referring to the discursive formation of the "Protestant ethic," he argued that "such a powerful, unconsciously refined organization for the production of capitalist individuals has never existed in any other church or religion, and in comparison what the Renaissance did for capitalism shrinks into insignificance" (1966: 270).

15. In this regard, the overt display of wealth was a key part of the lifeworld of the Florentine wealthy. This display, as Alberti's pronouncements on thrift would indicate, did not consist in conspicuous consumption. Rather, it was organized primarily around the patronage of the arts, support of the humanist intellectuals, and the construction of private and public buildings that would stand as monuments to the *virtù* and civic virtue of the wealthy merchants and their families. It was absolutely imperative to the acquisition of honor and glory that the builder of such monuments be ostentatiously identified. It was common for the Florentine bourgeoisie to inscribe the familial coat of arms and their names, as well its cost, into the artifact. For example, according to Burke (1988: 222), the claim that "the marble alone cost 4000 florins" was inscribed on a tabernacle commissioned by Piero de Medici. For a detailed historical analysis of the impact of the architectural display of wealth on social space of fifteenth and sixteenth century Florence, see Goldthwaite (1980).

16. The so-called Baron thesis, which states that this shift was a consequence of the threat posed to the liberty of republican Florence by the Duchy of Milan, has been criticized by many historians, especially Jerrold Seigel (1965). Although it may seem strange for a sociologist to say this, I am not particularly interested in the sociohistorical causes of this shift. Rather, I am interested in the change to the moral economy of wealth this shift in language entails and its consequences for discursive configuration of the virtue of the autonomous individual.

17. In addition to Aristotle's work, Xenophon's *Oeconomicus* was an important classical source of arguments for the virtues of wealth and commerce. This is particularly true of Alberti, whose dialogical method of articulating economic values was directly borrowed from Xenophon. See Baron (1988b).

18. On this relationship of civic humanism as ideology to the hegemony of the merchant elite see Hale (1977: 18–19), Gilbert (1965: 25–26), and Rubenstein (1990).

19. I should point out that I am well aware of the injunction of many Machiavelli scholars that one should not equate "virtue" with Machiavelli's concept of *virtù*. According to Parel, in Machiavelli's thought *"virtù* has no affinity with moral virtue" (1992: 86). Although this is true if one thinks of virtue in a religious sense (i.e., the cardinal virtue of Christianity) or in philosophical sense (i.e., Aristotle's virtues), it is not true to think of virtue as the qualities of character action that are aimed at achieving what Taylor (1989) called "hypergoods." There is most definitely a conception of the hypergood in Machiavelli, and this is the public good of the state. Virtue for Machiavelli, then, are those moral dispositions and abilities that produce the public good, and *virtù* is a fundament of civic virtue. For an elaboration of this perspective, see Mansfield (1996).

20. On the decline of Florentine capitalism see Braudel (1979: 390–393), Burke (1986: 390–393), and Lachman and Peterson (1990).

21. I have borrowed the Founder and Citizen as names for these moral characters from Pitkin.

22. This equation of the pursuit of wealth with the effeminate was at the core of the civic republican moral critique of the proponents of the emergent commercial society, such as Bernard Mandeville and Adam Smith, in the eighteenth century. I will discuss this critique and the Scottish Enlightenment's response to it in the next chapter.

23. Aristotle's discussion of friendship and its relationship to the community of the polis is found in Books 8 and 11 of the *Nicomachean Ethics*. My discussion of the Aristotelian notions of friendship and concord draws heavily upon the analysis of Oldfield (1991: 20–24) and Wood and Wood (1978: 69–73).

24. The destructiveness of faction is the principal theme of Machiavelli's *Florentine Histories*, wherein he compares and contrasts the internal class conflicts of the Roman republic with those of the Florentine republic. Machiavelli argued that it was the superior institutionalization of conflict and its concordant resolution that was the strength of Rome in comparison to Florence: "The enmities that at the outset existed in Rome were ended by debating, those in Florence by fighting and intrigue; those in Rome were terminated by law, those in Florence by the exile and death of many citizens" (1965f, VII, 2: 1331).

4

How Much Is Enough?
Counting and Accounting for Money
in the Market as Moral Space

Wealth, as Mr. Hobbes says, is power. But the person who either acquires, or succeeds to a great fortune, does not necessarily acquire or succeed to any political power, either civil or military. His fortune may, perhaps afford him the means of acquiring both, but the mere possession of that fortune does not necessarily convey to him either. The power which that possession immediately and directly conveys him to him is the power of purchasing; a certain command over all the labor, over all the produce which is then in the market. His fortune is greater or less, precisely in proportion to the extent of this power.

—Adam Smith, (1976a: I.5.35)[1]

Capitalism brought with it a comprehensive deterritorialization; in the course of its evolution, it dissolved every previous order and code (religious, scientific, philosophical), altering their functions and rendering them obsolete. It opened up new worlds, made new areas accessible, created new avenues for the deployment of human bodies, thoughts, and feelings, even for escaping from the existing order. Like every dominant force that wishes to remain dominant, [capitalism] took up the task of blocking new possibilities, obscuring their existence, chaining them up, redirecting streams [of desire] for their own benefit, "codifying" them in a way that served dominant interests, yet allowed subject peoples to retain the illusion of new found freedom. . . . The new overlords, interested in the flowing of desire, at least insofar as it might bolster the flow of currency, looked then to the possibility of encoding. Streams of desire were encoded as streams of money. How quickly did America as the land of limitless opportunity become synonymous with the unlimited chance of making money! The sad thing wasn't so much that the slogan "From dishwasher to company boss" was ideological or untrue, as the fact that desire had been reduced to that narrow ambition.

—Klaus Theweleit (1987: 270–271)

In this chapter I examine the emergence of a distinctively new figural actor in the moral economy of wealth, *homo mercator* or "market man." This moral character, I argue, is conjured through a reconfiguration of the narrative of fortune and virtue in which flows of money are united with the public good under the sign of "self-interest" within the material and symbolic space of the market. In this reconfigured spatial story, a new calculus and praxeology of substantive rationality emerges through which money and wealth can be fully represented and accounted for as signs of virtue. This chapter contains three sections. In the first section, I discuss how *homo mercator* performs and enacts a distinctive narrative of power and propriety with respect to the accumulation of wealth, in contrast to that elaborated by the Renaissance civic humanists. In the second section, I explore how *homo mercator* and the moral territory of the marketplace were conjured in the discourse of Scottish Enlightenment figures such as David Hume and Adam Smith. Here, I discuss the neo-Machiavellian critique of the new "commercial society" of eighteenth-century Britain and how this critique was countered by Hume and Smith through the development of a new language of secular virtue based on the concepts of "desire," "interest," and the "progress of opulence." In the third section I examine how this language of virtue is articulated by contemporary men of the market. Here I confront the moral dilemma entailed in the instrumental rationality of the accumulation of wealth and power, a dilemma that is manifested in the question as to how much money and wealth is enough for one to possess and pursue as a morally sensible goal. This dilemma, I argue, is resolved through a rhetorical construction of moral selfhood that is based on four discrete virtues of the marketplace: justice, enterprise, extension of the territory of the market, and benevolence. These virtues, derived from the discourse of the Scottish Enlightenment, provide a potent form of power/knowledge, of knowhow and can-do-ness, for making moral sense out of the seemingly amoral activity of wealth accumulation.

Money, Property, and Identity: Tracking the Subject of Sovereign Individuality from Florence to Edinburgh

The Power/Knowledge of Wealth and the Failure of Civic Humanism

In Chapter 3, my primary concern was the discursive formation of the sovereign masculine subject of the narrative of fortune and virtue and its emergence in the social imaginary of Florentine mercantile capitalism. In my analysis of Machiavelli and his civic humanist predecessors, I located two moral characters that provide different performances of the narrative of fortune and virtue: the Founder and the Citizen. These contrasting figures represent a basic antinomy between valorized sources of moral identity that resides at the core of the moral economy of wealth.

The moral character of the Founder represents the apotheosis of the global and autonomous masculine self, the atomistic individual who is able to make himself through rational, methodical, and disciplined action while carving out a sovereign space of mastery and control. The locus of the moral identity of the Founder is in the heroic instrumental objectification and mastery of feminine disorder of *fortuna*. In contrast to the solitary *virtù* of the Founder, the figural character of the Citizen finds his moral identity in a vocation of civic virtue that links the self to others through a devotion to the public good and a responsibility to the community.[2]

These two characters represent the polarities of a discursive axis of secular virtue, an agonistic vector of force, around which the moral valuation of wealth and wealthy men cohere. Indeed, the very essence of George Bush's rhetorical invocation of the "better angels" is to unite the subject of power, the sovereign individual, with the civic virtue of the citizen under the sign of wealth. Accordingly, to reframe the aims of this project in light of the analysis in the preceding chapter, the central unifying theme of my genealogy is the tracing of how this tension between the sovereign individuality of wealthy men and their moral obligation to others is discursively configured and rhetorically effaced at different moments in the history of the moral economy of wealth. More specifically, the question I seek to answer is how the securing of sovereign principality through the accumulation of wealth is conceived as being naturally linked with, if not a necessary prerequisite for, the practice of pursuing the public good.

In Chapter 3, we encountered one such conception in Machiavelli's civic humanist predecessors such as Alberti and Bruni. In Quattrocento civic humanist discourse, the moral valorization of the wealthy man occurred along two dimensions. First, it was argued that the accumulation of wealth through commerce is a prime example of the *vita activa*, a life of active engagement in worldly affairs that was fruitful of honor and glory. Second, it was argued that the active life of commerce provides the material and experiential basis upon which the wealthy individual can fulfill his moral obligation to the community as citizen. In this way, the sovereign self of *virtù* is rendered compatible with virtue of responsibility to others in the community.

In Foucauldian terms, the civic humanist disquisitions on the virtues of the Florentine merchant-capitalists represent the first modern historical attempt at formulating a coherent "governmentality" of wealth. For the later Foucault, the concept of "governmentality" was key to his explorations of technologies of the self and power/knowledge deployed in the formation of the ethical subject (Foucault, 1991). *Governmentality* refers literally to the mentality of governance or, more specifically, to the substantive rationality of morally valorized social practices developed to shape and form the ethical conduct of the subject in everyday life.[3] However, as a coherent governmental technology that positively grounded the moral identity of the subject of sovereign individuality, the civic humanist discourse on wealth and the wealthy man was inherently unstable. In essence, this instability is manifested in the fact that whereas the subject that is articulated through their discourse is distinctively bourgeois, in that its *virtù* comes to be recoded in terms of the qualities necessary to be run a successful commercial enterprise and accumulate wealth, it is not quite yet a modern "capitalist" subject. This is because the languages that were deployed in order to place the accumulation of wealth in a moral frame, and thus define it as being constitutive or representative of virtue, do not give full expression to commercial activity as being virtuous *in and of itself*.[4] The languages used to configure the virtue of wealth accumulation were principally derived from two distinctively noncapitalist ethics that were, to use Charles Taylor's (1989: 212–213) characterization, the "honor ethic" of *virtù* and the "citizen ethic" of civic virtue.

This instability of civic humanist discourse is an important point because it underscores what Mikhail Bakhtin (1981) terms the "heteroglossia," or the often conflicting diversity of the discourses and languages, that characterizes the moral economy of wealth and the ethical subject of sovereign individuality. The civic humanist ideologists of wealth tried to valorize the merchant capitalist by interpreting his quotidian activity of accumulation and commerce through a moral grid derived from conceptions of virtue that were either fundamentally ambivalent or hostile to this activity. As key components of the narrative of fortune and virtue as a spatial story, both the honor ethic (and its embodiment in the Founder) and the citizen ethic (and its embodiment in the Citizen) ultimately viewed the insertion of the self into public space, either through heroic deeds and the pursuit of glory or devotion to the polis, as more exalted forms of life than the mere acquisition of wealth. Within the moral frame of reference of these ethical discourses, the quotidian activity of making money was, at best, considered to be banal and ordinary and thus lacking honor. At worst, commercial activity was perceived as being corrosive of heroic manliness and allegiance to the public good. Working within the gravitational moral field of these discourses, the civic humanists could only render the acquisition of wealth through commerce *compatible* with these other secular virtues, instead of establishing the ontic and moral primacy of commerce as the foundation of a distinctively different technology of the self. It is the essentially derivative nature of the civic humanist defense of wealth that enabled Machiavelli and subsequent generations of civic republicans to rhetorically sever the link between commercial activity, on the one hand, and the virtues of honor and citizenship on the other.

"Possessive Individualism" and the Moral Character of Homo Mercator

Keeping in mind this failure of Renaissance imaginations to anchor the subject of sovereign individuality within its own distinctive moral field, I now turn my attention to the Scottish Enlightenment.[5] The work of Adam Smith, David Hume, and others, through a critical engagement with the civic republican tradition, effected a profound transformation in the moral economy of wealth. The result of this transformation is the emergence of new figural character, a fully capitalist subject who we shall call, following Hannah Arendt (1958), *homo mercator* or Market Man. In this character, and the manner in which he enacts the narrative of fortune and virtue, is congealed the manifold changes in the cultural understanding of the relationship between wealth, sovereign individuality, and the public good that the Scottish Enlightenment engendered.

Perhaps the most fundamental characteristic of Market Man is the spatial location of his moral identity: the terrain upon which he enacts the drama of fortune and virtue shifts from the realm of politics to that of "civil society." For the thinkers of the Scottish Enlightenment, the sphere of civil society is dominated by the relations of the market economy. Reversing the emphasis of the classical Aristotelian and civic republican tradition, for which the socius of the polis was privileged as the arena of freedom and personal fulfillment to the exclusion of the economic, Hume, Smith, and Adam Ferguson argued that it was through the relations of interdependence and independence generated by market exchange and the division of labor that individuals develop and fulfill their needs.[6] "Every man," Smith (1976a: I.4.26) inveighed in *The Wealth of Nations*, "thus lives by exchanging, or becomes in some measure a merchant." Accordingly, in the discourse of the Scottish historical school, and its filiate political economy, "man" is no longer *zöön politikon* but *homo mercator*.

This shift of the ontic and moral grounding of the individual from the civic to the civil, to paraphrase John Pocock (1982: 242), entailed significant consequences for understanding the relationship between wealth, property, and subjectivity as well as the relationship between private virtue and the public good. In civic republican discourse, wealth, primarily in the form of landed property and the *oikos*, was valued to the extent that it provided the foundation for the citizen to find and develop his self-identity in the intimate relationship with fellow male citizens in the polis. In contrast, the identity of Market Man is formed and developed through his relationship with strangers in the market, a relationship that is mediated by things in the form of money and commodities. He is guided in daily life, not by any overarching conception of the public good, but primarily by the pursuit of his individual well-being. The moral character of Market Man is first and foremost, as Foucault (1991) has argued, a subject of *interest*, and it is through the accumulation and exchange of mobile forms of property and wealth, principally money, that his interests are expressed, old needs met, and new desires generated.[7]

In fact, it is the desire for material wealth, as "desire" is newly conceived in relationship to need and scarcity, that is posited to be the essential characteristic of human nature that propels individuals along their own paths of self-improvement and society down the road of "progress" and "civilization." Instead of the story space of the polis, within which individuals manifested their destiny of sovereignty by struggling against the corrupting influences of *fortuna*, there is the emplotment of limitless desire and historical progress that is emplaced in the space of the market and civil society. Beyond that, it is argued that the self-interested desire of the individual for the "augmentation of fortune" and the "betterment of his condition" has the result of enhancing the material well-being of all in commercial society (Smith, 1976a: II.3.363). This putative correspondence between self-interest and social improvement is not a result of the design or intention of Market Man. Rather, this fortuitous convergence of private interest and social benefit is the unintended consequence of the providential order of market society that is encapsulated in Smith's famous invocation of the "invisible hand."

Figural characters, I argue in Chapter 1, are the representational masks that are worn by moral philosophies and social ideologies. From the perspective of much neo-Marxist ideology critique, if there is one moral philosophy or discourse that is fully embodied in the moral character of *homo mercator*, it is what has come to be known as "possessive individualism." According to C. B. MacPherson (1962), possessive individualism first emerged in the seventeenth century in the writings of Thomas Hobbes and John Locke and furnished the fundamental assumptions about human nature, property, and society that suffused the liberal social theories of the eighteenth century in general and the political economy of Scottish Enlightenment in particular. Indeed, it is in the characteristics projected onto Market Man by possessive individualism that reveals him to be a fully capitalist subject of sovereign individuality. "The possessive quality" of seventeenth- and eighteenth-century individualism, argues MacPherson,

> is found in its conception of the individual as essentially the proprietor of his own person and capacities, owing nothing to society as a whole. The individual was seen neither as a moral whole, nor part of a larger social whole, but as an owner of himself. Their relationship of ownership, having become for more and more men the critically important relationship determining their actual freedom and the actual prospect of realizing their potentialities, was read back into the nature of the individual. The individual, it was thought, is free in as much as he is proprietor of his persons and capacities. The main essence is freedom from dependence on the wills of others, and freedom is the function of possession. Society becomes a lot of free individuals related to each other as proprietors of their own capacities and of what they have acquired by their exercise. Society consists of relations of

exchange between proprietors. Political society becomes a calculated device for the protection of this property and the maintenance of an orderly relation of exchange. (1962: 3)

As I argue in Chapter 3, the sovereign individual of *virtù* consisted primarily in his autonomy, freedom of will and action, and his capacity to transform his environment in a rational and disciplined way according to intent and design. In the discourse of possessive individualism, and its embodiment in Market Man, these characteristics of sovereign individuality become linked to the possession of property. In terms of freedom and autonomy, Market Man is what he possesses as a form of property (including his own person), and it is through the augmentation of his possession through exchange in the marketplace that he enhances and expands his sovereignty. The capacity of the individual selves to "realize their potentialities" in terms of their needs, talents, and desires thus becomes positively correlated with the ownership of property.

Possessive individualism is certainly one of the dominant discourses that gives shape and substance to the figure of Market Man and his emplotment and emplacement within the narrative of fortune and virtue. However, when looking at how the elements of possessive individualism were appropriated and employed by the Scottish Enlightenment, and how they comprise a basic vocabulary of identity and motive among modern men of the market, it is important not to accept its ontological presuppositions too readily. The most fundamental ontological presupposition of possessive individualism, at least as it is articulated by MacPherson and others (cf. Abercrombie, Turner, and Hill, 1986; Bellah et al., 1985), is that the individual is prior to society.[8] If the possessive individual is seen as "owing nothing to society as a whole," then society exists only insofar as individuals as proprietors find it in their interest to participate in exchange relations. In essence, the ontological grounding of possessive individualism displaces any *deontological* understanding of Market Man as a moral character or of the modern men of the market I will discuss shortly. MacPherson's rendering of possessive individualism obscures the fact that there is a "moral whole" to which Market Man is a part, and that would be the market itself. As one entrepreneur told us, "It is amazing the amount of morality that is determined by economics." That is to say, it is the discourse of the market itself, as originally formulated in the Scottish Enlightenment, that provides a language of moral obligation that enables Market Man to construct and affirm his identity as a virtuous individual within a reconfigured narrative of fortune and virtue.

Conjuring *Homo Mercator:*
Money, Virtue, and Commercial Society

The Dread of Money:
Neo-Machiavellianism and the Critique of Commercial Society

"Money," writes anthropologist Paul Bohannan, "is one of the shatter-
ingly simplifying ideas of all time, and like any other new and compelling idea, it creates its own revolution" (quoted in Parry and Bloch,
1989: 13). During the latter half of the seventeenth century, and especially
after the so-called Glorious Revolution of 1688, a revolution of money
swept England as it entered the world of mercantilism as a trading
power. This revolution of money was primarily manifested in the emergence of new forms of mobile and liquid property such as stock, credit,
and debt, upon which a new class of merchants, financiers, and specula-
tors rose to political prominence and economic power.[9] The expansion of
trade and the development of new forms of property produced profound
changes in the quotidian life of British society, as an unprecedented material prosperity of "opulence" and "luxury" ushered in what has been
called the first "Consumer Society" (McKendrick et al., 1985). Eager to
publicly display their new prosperity and identity as men of money, merchants, "stock-jobbers," financiers, and the new gentry became inveterate
consumers of fashion and household goods, setting into motion a dynamic cycle of competitive social emulation and conspicuous consumption.[10] In the crucible of this new spatial territory and practices of mobile
property, commerce, and consumption, a new social subject was conjured
and engendered. This was the enterprising subject of self-interest who,
motivated by an insatiable desire for what Smith called the "augmentation of fortune" in the form of things he did not have, relentlessly pursued the means through which his desires might be realized: money.

From the perspective of the inheritors of Machiavelli's civic republican
legacy in late-seventeenth- and early-eighteenth-century Britain, this
new revolutionary culture of money portended a social disaster of apocalyptic proportions. To the neo-Machiavellians such as Andrew Fletcher,
John Brown, John Trenchard, Thomas Gordon, and Lord Bolingbroke, the
spread of luxury and commercial values brought with it the dreaded social and political disorder of corruption.[11] In *Discourse on Government with
Relations to Militias* (1698), a document that is typical of the civic republican jeremiads against the new money culture of accumulation and consumption of the time, Fletcher argues:

> By this means [commerce and trade] the Luxury of Asia and America was
> added to the Ancients'; and all Ages, and all Countries concurred to sink Eu-
> rope into an Abyss of Pleasures; that were rendered more expensive by a

perpetual Change in the Fashions in Clothes, Equipage, and Furniture of Houses. These things brought a total Alteration to the way of living upon which all government depends. 'Tis true, Knowledge being mightily increased, and a great curiosity and nicety in every thing introduced, Men imagined themselves to be gainers on all points, by changing from their frugal and martial way of living, which I must confess had some mixture of Rudeness and Ignorance in it, tho not inseparable from it. But at the same time they did not consider the unspeakable evils that are altogether inseparable from an expensive way of living. (quoted in Sekora, 1977: 78)

As with Machiavelli, the standard by which these latter day civic republicans measured the corruption of the new commercial society was the commonwealth of the freeholding, independent, and austere citizen who was skilled in the martial virtues and devoted to the public good. The moral identity of the citizen was rooted in the real property of land that provided him with the autonomy and leisure to contemplate and pursue the common interest in concert with fellow citizens. In contrast, the new commercial man of the eighteenth century was seen as too absorbed in the daily activity of trade, speculation, and finance, too involved with competitive accumulation and conspicuous consumption, and thus too concerned with his own self-interest, to be able to display any form of civic virtue at all. "The Spirit of Commerce," argued Brown in *Estimate of the Manners and Morals of the Times* (1757), "begats a kind of unregulated Selfishness" (quoted in Sekora, 1977: 93). This selfishness, according to Lord Bolingbroke, represented the highest form of moral turpitude, as the new men of money were "debased from their love of liberty, from zeal for the honor of their country, and from a desire for honest fame to an abject submission, to a rapacious eagerness after wealth, that may sate their avarice, and exceed the profusion of their luxury" (1965: 8). Casting a wary eye back, as Machiavellians always did, to the example of Rome, Trenchard and Gordon argued that it was the spread of luxury and commercial values that brought about that society's downfall. With the spread of wealth and opulence among the citizenry of the empire, they wrote in *Cato's Letters* (1720), "private regards extinguished that of love of liberty, that zeal and warmth, which their ancestors had shown for the interests of the public; luxury and pride became fashionable . . . and having before sold everything else, at last they sold their country" (quoted in Horne, 1978: 55). And, they prophesied, as Rome went, so too would England.

Whereas the citizen-patriot led a life of simplicity and frugality, the new commercial man immersed himself in the epicurean pleasures of commodities, refining his tastes and sensibilities according the shifting currents of fashion. As Fletcher recognized, in comparison to the sophisticated manners and tastes of the men of the market, the ideal citizen may be "Rude" and "ignorant," but at least he was not "a gainer." To be a "gainer" meant to devote oneself to the acquisition of money and possessions and to measure one's worth and identity by how much one had gained. However, as the quote from Bolingbroke intimates, what men gain in money and material possessions, they lose in virtue, rationality, and discipline. To be a "gainer" is to be a man who is irrational, who lives in "abject submission" to his "rapacious eagerness" and "avarice" for wealth, as well as to his "profuse" and "excessive" desire and appetites for luxury. Of course, from the Machiavellian point of view, a man who is a slave to the passions, who lives a life of undisciplined excess and pleasure, is no longer a man at all. He has become effeminate, as he surrendered to the disordered irrationality that the feminine represented. Indeed, in the language of the civic republicans of the period, Luxury, Money, and Credit join Fortuna in the pantheon of female goddesses of instability who threaten to drain from men their masculine *virtù* (Pocock, 1985: 114).[12]

This fear of the feminine disorder of irrationality, personified in the forms of luxury, money, and credit, essentially reflected an existential dread of the profound deterritorialization of desire and power that the emergent commercial society entailed. The market, with its specialized division of labor and new forms of mobile property, posed a threat to the civic republican ideal of selfhood and autonomy. The flow of social energy and desire that was deemed to be constitutive of civic virtue and moral identity originated in landed property and was channeled through the political institutions and practices of the polis, republic, or commonwealth. The autonomy and moral identity of the citizen was grounded in the tangible reality of land, which was the source and sustenance of his civic virtue. It was, as Pocock (1985: 110) argues, landed property that provided the citizen with the unspecialized leisure and opportunity to develop his self and personality with other citizens in the management of the affairs of the commonwealth. The institutional order and practices that produced and sustained the subjectivity and moral identity of the citizen were thus premised upon fixed stability of property and the direct and intimate relationship between men that it supported. As property, the land of the citizen was not fungible, for to buy, sell, or trade his property would be tantamount to buying, selling, or trading his virtue. To exchange the property that enabled one to be virtuous for money, of course, represented the highest form of corruption that a civic republican could imagine.

In contrast, the new territorializing institutions and practices of the market—and the subjectivity and moral identity they produced—were seen to be inherently unstable and irrational. The identity of the man of the market was considered to be as chaotic as the social relationships he engaged in and as evanescent as the forms of property he accumulated and exchanged. The subjectivity of the new commercial man was seen by the civic republicans as being deformed and atrophied by his quotidian life in the marketplace. The merchant, the financier, and the manufacturer occupied specialized places in an occupational division of labor, and their relationships to other men were mediated by commodities and money. Accordingly, his perception and understanding of the needs and interests of others, and the public good in general, were obscured by the processes of exchange. Moreover, everything the new commercial man owned, and thus everything he was in terms of social identity, could be exchanged on the market and dissolved into the universal equivalent of money. The citizen was considered to be self-possessed because of the mastery over his personal and public life his landed property conferred upon him. By comparison, the man of the market was seen as being possessed by the commodities and money around which his everyday life was constructed. What disturbed the civic republicans most about the fluid and mobile property of the men of the market was that its value, and thus the worth of the individual who owned and traded it, was dependent on the fluctuating currents of subjective opinion in the marketplace. The price of goods, the rate of return on stock and government bonds, interest rates on capital, even the value of money itself, was contingent upon seemingly irrational currents of the subjective estimation of others in the marketplace. Accordingly, the property upon which the new commercial man based his identity was seen to be transient, imaginary, and fantastically disreal. Pocock summarizes the existential fear and loathing the civic republicans felt toward the market and its denizens:

> Once property was seen to have a symbolic value, expressed in coin or credit, the foundations of personality themselves appeared to be imaginary or at best consensual: the individual could exist, even in his own sight, only at the fluctuating value imposed upon him by his fellows, and these evaluations, though constant and public, were too irrationally performed to be seen as acts of political decision or virtue. . . . The landed man . . . was permitted the leisure and the autonomy to consider what was to other's good as well as his own; but the individual engaged in exchange could only discern particular values—that of the commodity which was his, that of the commodity for which he exchanged it. His activity did not oblige or even permit him to contemplate the universal good as he acted upon it, and he consequently continued to lack classical rationality. It followed that he was not a master of himself, and that in the last analysis he must be thought of as activated by nonrational forces. (1975: 464)

In sum, in the discourse of Scottish and English civic republicanism, the men of the new money culture were rendered as being corrupt and effeminate creatures of passion. Such men were subject to the fantasies and fictions of the marketplace of commodities and money and congenitally unable to perceive, let alone pursue, any notion of the public good that transcended their own narrow self-interest. This representation of commercial man is quite different from the image of *homo mercator*, the rational, virtuous, and disciplined enterprising self who, in steadfastly pursuing his own self-interest, contributes to the public good. Just how this new moral character was discursively constructed, and how the reterritorialization of desire and power that he embodied was conjured, constitutes perhaps the most important nodal point in my genealogy of the moral economy of wealth and the narrative of fortune and virtue.

Passion, Desire, and the Enterprising "Subject of Interest"

In constructing this new moral character and their defense of emergent commercial society, Hume, Smith, and other figures of the Scottish Enlightenment wielded a double-edged rhetorical sword against the civic republican condemnation of the market. The leading edge of this sword was honed and sharpened by the imbricated concepts of concepts of passion, interest, and desire, the trailing edge by a materialist conception of historical progress. Their notions of passion, interest, and desire became the foundation for a new dynamic model of selfhood and autonomy that was united to the acquisition of wealth and commodities. In turn, this dynamic model of selfhood, based on the insatiable desire for material gain, would be extrapolated by the Scottish Enlightenment into a logic of the progressive historical development of civil society. On the basis of this vision of the intertwined progressive development of the individual and society, the civic republican ideal of the citizen would be consigned to the proverbial ash can of history, and *homo mercator* would take his place as the new avatar of secular virtue.

At the core of the Scottish Enlightenment's discourse of the market is the assertion that all men are essentially, to use Foucault's (1991) term, "subjects of interest." "Every man's interests are peculiar to himself," Hume argued in the *Enquiries*, "and the aversions and desires that result from them, cannot be supposed to affect others in a like degree" (1975: 228). It is this assertion of the irreducible peculiarity of the individual's interests that constitutes the ultimate ontological grounding of the sovereign individuality of Market Man, as those interests cannot be exchanged, transferred, or surrendered. Unlike the mobile forms of property with which Market Man interacts, his interests are inalienable and uniquely his own. As a subject of interest, therefore, *homo mercator* is essentially a unique configuration of individual desires, preferences, and choices. An individual's unique, "interested affections," and the actions they animate, are "original facts and realities, compleat in themselves" (Hume, 1973: II.III.3.459). As such, interests are purely private and subjective, intrinsic to the personality of the individual, and cannot be explained by any prior moral or social causal principle. Moreover, Hume maintained, these interests are rooted in passion, sentiment, and feeling that cannot be subordinated to reason. In distinct contrast to the classical rationality of civic republicanism, where the very essence of *virtù* is the ability of men to conquer passion by reason, for Hume, "reason is and ought only to be a slave of the passions" (1973: II.III.3.462).

At first glance, Hume's position that reason should be a slave to the passions would not seem to be a very promising basis upon which to build a moral character that is enterprising, disciplined, and virtuous. However, Hume's point was not that men in society should blindly and irrationally follow their passions wherever they might lead but rather that reason could only be expected to give shape and direction to passions as opposed to combating or conquering them. The passions were the source of all social energy, volition, and productivity. "Everything in the world," Hume averred, "is purchased by labor; and our passions are the only causes of labor" (1955b: 11). Reason was only important as an instrumental medium of cathexis and communication whereby the passions were oriented toward objects and other people in the social world. That is to say, reason was useful only insofar as it could enable the individual to discern the objects and relations toward which the passions would be directed and to calculate the means of social actions that would satisfy the desires and interests the passions engendered. So the most important question, from Hume's perspective, concerned the role reason could play in channeling, that is, *territorializing*, the passions in socially beneficial and productive ways. In other words, under what regime of governmentality could the potentially anarchic and passionate subject of interest be configured into an enterprising subject that labors to purchase "everything in the world"?

As Albert Hirschman (1977) and Victor Hope (1989) have shown, Hume's arguments concerning passion and reason were part of a vibrant debate concerning how best to govern and control the passions that dominated political and social discourse in the seventeenth and eighteenth centuries. Hume, Smith, and their precursor in the school of Scottish moral philosophy, Francis Hutcheson, shared a common ground with Montesquieu and other continental social philosophers in making a conceptual distinction between passions that were "violent," "unsocial," and destructive and those that were "calm," "social," and constructive. Violent passions, for example, included hatred, envy, greed, and sexual lust.

The category of calm passions included sentiments such as friendship, sympathy, and benevolence. All agreed that the passions, as the fount of social energy, could not be eliminated from the conduct of human affairs. Accordingly, the "calm" passions had to be encouraged and cultivated so as to counterbalance and ameliorate the effects of the violent passions. In what Hirschman notes was one of the most profound moral revaluations in the history of Western culture, the passion that was encoded as the one that would assure the judicious conduct of the individual in everyday life, and render a society orderly and governable, was the desire for material gain. For centuries, Western moralists, whether they be Stoic, Christian, or civic republican, had fulminated against avarice and the desire for money and material gain as a primary source of personal ruin and social evil. Yet in the eighteenth century, primarily through the discourse of the Scottish Enlightenment and the territory of the market and commercial society it conjured, this desire was elevated to the status of a universal categorical imperative of human nature from which a multitude of positive social benefits would flow.

The assertion that the desire for material gain is a universal and intrinsic feature of human nature is stated with characteristic bluntness by Hume in his essay "Of Avarice." "Avarice, or the desire for gain, is a universal passion which operates at all times, in all places, and upon all persons" (1963: 563). Similarly, in *Treatise*, he argued that "the love of gain" and "the avidity . . . of acquiring goods and possessions for ourselves and our nearest friends, is insatiable, perpetual and universal. . . . There is scarce anyone, who is not actuated by it" (1973: III.II.3.543). For Hume, the prevalence of this passion rendered the civic republican ideal of the austere soldier-citizen a misguided and foolish pipe dream. The "passion for the public good," and its concomitant willingness "to undergo the greatest hardship for the sake of the public," were far too weak and "disinterested" to motivate men into socially beneficial activity. Therefore, it is "requisite to govern men by other passions, and animate them with the spirit of avarice and industry, art and luxury" (1955a: 13).

Such an assertion was naturally scandalous to the civic moralists of his day, for whom avarice was an unmitigated vice. However, in making his case for the passion of avarice and the desire for gain, Hume was careful to sever its connotative links to passions and behaviors that the critics of the new commercial society automatically associated with being a "gainer." In particular, Hume maintained that, in the context of commercial society, the passion of avarice was quite different from the passion of "the insatiable lust after pleasure" that led to profuse and immoderate expenditure and the enervation of mind, body, and soul (Hume, 1955b: 53). In fact, argued Hume, it was the "infallible consequence" of the market to channel the passion of avarice away from profusion and pleasure and toward frugality and industrious labor that constituted one of the primary social benefits of commercial society:

> Deprive a man of all business and serious occupation, he runs restless form one amusement to another; and the weight and oppression, which feels from idleness, is so great, that he forgets the ruin which must follow him from his immoderate expenditure. . . . But if the employment you give him is lucrative, especially if the profit be attached to every particular exertion of industry, he has gain so often in his eye, that he acquires, by degrees a passion for it, and knows no such pleasure as seeing the daily encrease of his fortune. And this is the reason why trade increases frugality, and why, among merchants, there is the same overplus of misers above prodigals as, among possessors of the land, there is the contrary. . . . [Commerce] encreases frugality, by giving occupation to men, and employing them in the arts of gain, which soon engage their affection and remove all relish for pleasure and expence. It is an infallible consequence of all industrious professions to begat frugality, and make the love of gain prevail over the love of pleasure. (Hume, 1955b: 53)

In this passage we can see the image of *homo mercator* as a rational, disciplined, and enterprising subject of interest beginning to emerge. To Hume, as well as to Smith, the love of gain is a "calm" passion because it evinces a rational calculation of means to ends and reflects a concern with long-term future good rather than the gratification of immediate desires (Miller, 1981: 47). The end of commercial activity, profit, is directly correlated with and produced by the means of "every particular exertion of industry." Accordingly, with "gain in his eye," the man of the market is steadfast, methodical, and single-minded in his quest to see a "daily increase in his fortune." As Hirschman (1977: 56–66) points out, this constancy and predictability with which commercial man was seen to pursue material gain led Hume and others to maintain that commercial activity was a source of social stability. Montesquieu, for example, characterized the everyday market activity of *homo mercator* as *doux* (or soft, sweet, gentle, and calm). *Le doux commerce* and the calm desire for material gain were contrasted with the violent passions of glory and honor that motivated the aristocracy and invariably led to the ruinous destruction of war. Accordingly, commerce was represented as an innocent and innocuous activity that, even though it was not an "honorable" activity, was far more benign in social consequence and thus far more preferable than the aristocratic pursuit of military glory.

However, what is more interesting about this passage than its depiction of avarice as a calm passion and commerce as a harmless activity is its apparent celebration of the tautological instrumental rationality of capital accumulation. There appears to be nothing in *homo mercator*'s "eye" other than gain, no other purpose to frugality and industry than the production of a daily increase in his fortune. Accordingly, one might wonder, along with Smith, "to what purpose is all the toil and bustle" of Market Man's exertions; "what is the end of the pursuit of wealth?" (Smith, 1976b: I.iii.2.1.50). The issue of instrumental rationality brings to the fore the conception of selfhood and autonomy that is inherent in the moral character of *homo mercator.*

Echoing Hume, Smith grounds the selfhood of *homo mercator* in the difference between the violent passions of immediate self-gratification and expenditure and the calm passions of gain and frugality:

> It can seldom happen, indeed, that the circumstances of a great nation can be much affected either by the prodigality or misconduct of individuals; the profusion or impudence of some, being always more than compensated for the frugality and good conduct of others. With regard to profusion, the principle that prompts to expence, is the passion for present enjoyment; which, though sometimes violent and very difficult to be restrained, is in general only momentary and occasional. But the principle which prompts to save, is the desire for bettering our condition, a desire which, though generally calm and dispassionate, comes with us from the womb till we go into the grave. In the whole interval which separates those two moments, there is scarce perhaps a single instant in which any man is so perfectly and completely satisfied with his situation, as to be without any wish of alteration or improvement of any kind. An augmentation of fortune is the means by which the better part of men propose and wish to better their condition. It is the means most vulgar and the most obvious; and the most likely way of augmenting their fortune, is to save and accumulate some part of what they acquire, either regularly and annually, or upon some extraordinary occasions. Though the principle of expence, therefore, prevails in almost all men upon some occasions, and in some men upon almost all occasions, yet in the greater part of men, taking the whole course of their life at an average, the principle of frugality seems not only to predominate, but to predominate very greatly. (Smith 1976a: II.5.362–363)

For Smith, then, it was the very structure of the market, the interdependency of men in exchange relations, that systematically encouraged them to privilege thrift over luxurious indulgence in the ceaseless quest for a better condition. More specifically, in the discourse of the market as articulated by the Scottish Enlightenment, there are several specific characteristics of *homo mercator* that comprise his virtues as a moral character. For Smith, what enabled men in the marketplace to discipline themselves in the face of the corrupting temptations of money and luxury were the virtues of justice, prudence, and self-command. These individual virtues, which kept men in the market fair and frugal, were the basis for the unintended social benefits of what Smith termed the "progress of opulence." It is in this particular feature of the Scottish Enlightenment's discourse of commercial society that the argument concerning the "invisible hand" of the marketplace is grounded.

That argument, which fundamentally transformed the very understanding of virtuous behavior, remains to this day one of the most potent and profound legitimating arguments for capitalism. As MacIntyre (1981) and Ross Poole (1991) have argued, from the Pre-Socratics through Augustine and Aquinas to the civic republicans, a man could act virtuously only to the extent that he consciously did so. If virtue, however defined, was a mode of acting in everyday life that produced happiness, then one had to intentionally act virtuously so as to produce the desired state of happiness. The good Christian, for example, consciously cultivated a life of pious spirituality. By the same token, as I explore in great detail in Chapter 3, the good citizen had to quite intentionally subordinate his private self-interest to the public good. In distinct contrast to this traditional notion of virtue where consequence is linked by intention to action, the founding of a subject of interest who primarily pursued his own private desires established the rhetorical basis for severing the link between action and outcome. Indeed, for Smith, the unintended social benefits of the individual desire to better one's condition were far greater than if *homo mercator* had consciously intended to produce them. Yet what for Smith were the providential workings of a commercial society with an advanced division labor has become for modern men of the market the very raison d'etre of their accumulative activity.

In order to see how the Scottish Enlightenment's discourse of the market, and the virtues of *homo mercator* as moral character, find a central place in the rhetoric of selfhood of contemporary men of the market, it is necessary to pay another visit to the "better angels" of the present. In visiting these "better angels," several issues will come to the fore. The first concerns instrumental logic of wealth accumulation, which Max Weber (1958) identified as the prime example of the soulless rationalization of modern capitalist society. The issue here is whether one can find in the language of the market an ethical grounding for the ceaseless activity of accumulation, the only goal of which seems to be itself. Second, I argue that in order to address this issue, it is important to consider, once again, the particular mode of sovereignty, power, and autonomy that wealth provides. Employing Simmel's insights into the unique nature of money as medium of self-expression and Deleuze and Guattari's analysis of the "territorializing" impulses of capitalism, I suggest that the power of wealth must be understood in terms of the symbolic and material mapping of the liquidity and flows of desires in capitalist society. As wealthy men are empowered agents, their desires flow through the social field on the basis of liquid and malleable forms of property and capital. This capacity to use money as a fluid medium for the expression and materialization of desire characterizes the wealthy as uniquely empowered subjects in capitalist society. Finally, I contend that in the particular manner in which this flowing of individual desire through different spheres of activity is expressed by men of the market—that is, as being productive not only of themselves but of the social good—it is possible to discern how power and propriety is embedded in the language in the marketplace and embodied in the moral character of *homo mercator*.

A Visitation with the "Better Angels" of the Market: Money, Liquidity, and Desire

Capitalism and the Conundrum of Instrumental Reason

In his conclusion to *The Protestant Ethic and Spirit of Capitalism*, Weber articulates one of the most scathing moral critiques of modern capitalism this side of Marx's *Capital*. Lamenting the loss of the concern with religious salvation that provided an overarching substantive rationality to the accumulative activity of the early Protestant entrepreneur, Weber argued that the Market Man of modern capitalism operated according to a logic of instrumental reason that was perverse in the extreme:

> Since asceticism undertook to remodel the world and to work out its ideals in the world, material goods have gained an increasing and finally an inexorable power over the lives of men as at no previous period in history. Today the spirit of religious asceticism-whether finally, who knows?-has escaped from the cage. But victorious capitalism, since it rests on mechanical foundations, needs its support no longer. The rosy blush of its laughing heir, the Enlightenment, seems also to be irretrievably fading, and the idea of duty in one's calling prowls about in our lives like dead religious beliefs. Where the fulfillment of the calling cannot be directly related to the highest spiritual and cultural values, or when, on the other hand, it need not be felt simply as economic compulsion, the individual generally abandons the attempt to justify it at all. In the field of its highest development, in the United States, the pursuit of wealth, stripped of its religious and ethical meaning, tends to be associated with purely mundane passions, which actually give it the character of sport. (1958: 181–182)

For Weber, the irony of the capitalist spirit is that the rational and disciplined pursuit of wealth, once it has been institutionalized as a categorical imperative of a market economy, has lost any substantive connection with a telos beyond itself. The pursuit of wealth had once constituted an emplotment toward a moral goal—spiritual salvation; but now the end was accumulation itself. The logic of capitalist accumulation entails, in deconstructive terms, a continual displacement or deferral of ends. The end of entrepreneurial activity is the production of profit, yet profit is continually reinvested back into the accumulation process so as to produce more profit. According to this logic, wealth and profit is an "end" in only the most temporally fleeting sense, for in reality it is merely a means to itself. As Ross Poole describes the nature of this logic, the entrepreneurial pursuit of wealth is a "rational activity which is directed towards an end, but where the end is always a means towards a further end of exactly the same kind. In so far as individuals have ends of this kind, they must have desires which are never satisfied and which are, in a certain sense, unsatisfiable" (1991: 32). Thus deprived of a telos of ethical or spiritual fulfillment, Weber's Market Man is caught in an endless spiral of desire, the "successful" pursuit of which can only be measured in the quantitative terms of money. If the game has no end beyond the means itself, then the only standard to judge one's success is the quantity of means possessed. Within the "iron cage" of modern capitalism, wealth ceases to mean or signify anything beyond itself.

Or so it would seem. There is, however, one social force that wealth, and the logic of instrumental rationality that guides its production, does indeed signify other than itself (or rather signifies within itself): power. Remember, this is precisely what Edward Hoffman said was the essential meaning of money and wealth. Money, as Georg Simmel pointed out, was more than a medium of exchange; it was a medium of self-expression and empowerment. Unique among all forms of property, it was infinitely fluid, malleable, and yielding to the purposes of its owner:

> [Money] adjusts with equal ease to every form and every purpose that will wishes to imprint it with. Money itself complies equally to every directive with regard to the object [purchased], the extent of expenditure, the speed of spending or retaining. In this manner money grants to the self the most complete freedom to express itself in an object. . . . All that money is and has to offer is given without reservation to the human will and is completely absorbed by the will. (1978: 325)

Liquid wealth in the form of money, for both Weber and Simmel, represented the apotheosis of instrumental reason in capitalist society. In a monetized market economy, where human purposes and goals are deemed to be satisfiable by commodities, and where all commodities have a price, money is the ultimate means, as it can be applied to all conceivable ends. Because of its infinite utility as a means to an end, money tends to dominate modern capitalism as the most valued end in and of itself. This dominance of means over ends constituted, for Simmel, the "tragedy" of modern capitalist culture, for "the domination of the means has taken possession not only of specific ends, but of the very center of ends, of the point where all purposes converge and from which they originate as final purposes" (1978: 483). This centrality of money to the constitution of individual and social purposes in capitalist society is, as Poole argues, equivalent to the pursuit of power for itself: "To pursue ends which are means to further ends, is to pursue, not ends as such, but the capacity to pursue ends; it is thus identical with the pursuit of power for its own sake" (1991: 39). And, as Poole notes, when power stands supreme as an end in and of itself, it needs no justification outside of itself.

For Weber, the "laughing heir" of religious asceticism, the Enlightenment, paved the way for the triumph of instrumental reason. By postulating the existence of a providential order of the natural harmony of interests, as exemplified in Smith's invisible hand, the Enlightenment detached the virtues of accumulation from any substantive grounding in religious ethics.[13] By secularizing asceticism under the name of the rational pursuit of self-interest, the Enlightenment rendered it unnecessary to link this behavior to anything greater than the self itself. Weber, I think, is correct about this up to a point. For most modern men of the market, there is no reference to a religiously grounded teleology that would furnish an ethical justification for their pursuit of wealth. Moreover, the logic of instrumental rationality, which is in essence a logic of power, is manifestly present in their language. However, neither the presence of instrumental rationality nor the absence of such a religious justification in Market Man's vocabulary of motives does not necessarily mean, as Weber contends, that he "generally abandons the attempt to justify [the accumulation of wealth] at all." The accumulation of wealth may indeed be considered to be a game without end, but it is certainly not without moral purpose or ethical justification for men of the market.

Consider, for example, the case of Robert Collins, a middle-aged, East Coast entrepreneur who made his wealth in advertising. At first glance he would seem to conform to Weber's pessimistic assessment of the mentality of the modern entrepreneur as being motivated in his accumulative activity by the "mundane" passion of sporting success. Money-making, says Collins, "is for keeping score . . . to me its about sports, to play basketball, or baseball. It's competitive. And that's what it is in anything." Similarly, Dick Balbus, a West Coast film producer and entertainment industry entrepreneur, reflected upon the nature of money as a score-keeping measure of success by saying that money is a "benchmark . . . it's like a report card. At the end of the day, if you've gone through your course work and understood your material, the grade is just a reflection of what you understood." If taken at face value, such statements would indicate that these men are truly locked in the mobius loop of instrumental rationality.

Indeed, as Balbus emphasizes, it is not the money itself as an end that is important but rather "the process of making the money." And this process, in his (auto-)biographical narrative and vocabulary of motive, is seemingly without a specific telos. Succinctly summarizing the emplotted trajectory of his business career, he says:

> I think even though there weren't any specific goals as to how far to achieve, I thought that, somewhere in the back of my mind the sky's the limit.... From a career standpoint, I tend to manage my life with intermediate goals. If we are doing 10 million, then I'll want to do 50 million dollars. [And] now that I've built companies that can do 100 million dollars three times, I have this burning desire to build a company that does a billion.

Marx's famous statement of the categorical imperative of capitalism comes to mind here: "Accumulate, accumulate! That is the Moses and the Prophets" (1973: 742). Given Balbus's rhetoric of selfhood, it would certainly seem that the prophet who commands and configures his desire is the neverending accumulation of wealth. Moreover, Balbus's "burning desire" is one that can never be fulfilled; there is always more business to do, more money to be made. As I argue above, it is this desire without limits that represents both the energizing dynamic of capitalism and the triumph of instrumental reason. Within the framework of instrumental reason, therefore, the only answer to the question of how much is enough is that there is never enough. The only possible accounting is that which simply counts the quantity of what one has made rather than one that provides a moral reckoning. But the issue here is whether one can find in the language of the men of the market a sense of moral purpose and ethical justification to this ceaseless accumulative activity. In order to explore this issue, it is necessary to look briefly, once again, at the correlate of wealth and money within the logic of instrumental rationality—power— and how it is constitutive of the sovereign individuality of Market Man. On the basis of this understanding of the relationship between wealth and power, it is possible to examine how these entrepreneurs are able to account for the empowerment of wealth and money and @-'prō-prē-āt it as a sign of their magisterial moral identity.

For Marx, the essence of the relation among wealth, money and power was quite simple: "The power which each individual exercises over the activity of others or over the social wealth exists in him as the owner of ... *money*. The individual carries his social power, as well as his bond with society, in his pocket" (1976: 157). And, in terms very similar to that of Marx, as I discuss in Chapter 2, the empowerment of wealth is revealed to be just as simple in the language of the men of the market themselves: Wealth is the capacity to command and mobilize labor, commodities, and other resources to pursue self-interested goals and desires. However, as Balbus evinces in the following statement, the accumulation of wealth as quantity of means is inseparable from the qualitative evaluation of its purposes:

> I would say selfishly that [money gives you] the personal pleasures of life. You want to buy something, take a personal vacation, that's still the most important . . . from a personal standpoint, [our wealth] means that we can go out and do anything we want to do. Second, since I'm still in business it gives me the ability to continue to be an influential business man. [It enables] me to use it for corporate and business purposes, to continue to build net worth, not so much for me but for the company. Ultimately, it becomes mine anyway but in the meantime keeping it invested in the company so it can grow. And, thirdly, [it enables me] to share with people, those without money, for charitable purposes that I decide are important.

This statement is fascinating on two counts. First, it offers a rich, albeit brief, illustration of Simmel's analysis of the fluid and malleable nature of money as a medium of power. Second, it shows how substantively rational qualitative earmarking gives the fluidity of money shape, form, and direction. For Balbus, money can be formed and channeled into an array of purposes—consumptive, accumulative, and philanthropic. The characteristic that is common to all these activities is that the money is given direction by his desires and interests; it bears the imprint of his will. On the basis of the liquidity of money, his desires are able to flow through and into different spheres of sovereignty where he is able to exercise efficacious power. For Deleuze and Guattari (1983), the flowing of self-directed desire along the streams of money is indicative of *territorializing* practices of capitalism, the channeling of desire and social energy toward goals and purposes that contribute toward its reproduction.[14] At a very basic and mundane level, the confluence of desire and money into each of these spheres is reproductive of his own position of power and the institutional structure of capitalism: His consumption contributes to the circulation of commodities; his business investment contributes to the production of commodities; and, as I argue below, his philanthropic beneficence is meant to bring those who are abject within the moral space of the market—"those without money"—into the flows of money and desire that he so skillfully negotiates. Everything that flows out of him in terms of desire and money returns, so to speak, valorized in the form of money capital, psychic capital, and symbolic capital. Money capital, obviously, is returned in the form of the enhanced "net worth" of his company. Psychic capital is returned in terms of a psychological confidence that his needs, desires, and pleasures can be pursued at will, that he "can go out and do anything" he wants to do. Finally, symbolic capital is returned in the recognition (by both himself and society) that he has performed his moral obligations to himself, his family, his company, and "those without." As such, his property and power is rendered as being @-'prō-prē-@t. It is the composition of this symbolic capital, and how it represents actions that have been encoded as being virtuous, that brings us to the heart of the character of *homo mercator*.

From Justice to Benevolence: The Symbolic Capital of Market Man

Symbolic capital, as I argue in Chapter 1, is what is produced, circulated, and accumulated in the moral economy of wealth. Symbolic capital signifies moral legitimacy and ethical rectitude, prestige and social honor, and it is accrued by enacting communally shared definitions of virtue (Bourdieu, 1991). For the men of the market, the virtues that they themselves present as embodying and providing the ethical justification for their power and wealth, fall into two broad categories: those that pertain to the actual acquisition of wealth and those that pertain to the social implications of wealth accumulation. And it is here that one can see quite clearly how private virtues of sovereign individuality are linked to the public virtues of social benefit in the figure of Market Man. This array of virtues, and their symbolic power as a medium of ethical justification, is articulated by Balbus in response to the question whether he feels any regret or guilt about being wealthy:

> No, I used to, once in a while when we started to get comfortable in life and we started spending for the things we always dreamed of like a Mercedes Benz and the country club and fur coats and the like, then we had a tinge of guilt. When I used to leave work in the middle of the day and go out to play golf with my "rich friends" at the country club and everyone else is back working their fannies off, I used to have this guilt feeling. But once you get comfortable with the fact that you're not a bad person, that you haven't stolen this money or ripped anybody off, that you've worked hard for this money, and that you are still contributing towards everybody else's chance to make money, then personally I got over the guilt quite easily. . . . The biggest charity I contribute to today is helping make this company grow. I'll affect more people and make a better quality of life for, [pause] wow, now you've got me thinking all these grandiose thoughts, for America by staying right here and contributing my time and money to this company which will someday [be worth] a hundred million dollars when I cash out. And then I can make wonderful philanthropic thoughts with that kind of money.

What is interesting is the serried, quasihierarchical arrangement of the virtues of Market Man as a coherent logic of substantive rationality.

These virtues are revealed to be fourfold in nature, with the first two pertaining to the acquisition of wealth and the second two regarding its social consequences. The first virtue has to do with the propriety of his conduct of wealth accumulation in regard to the basic rules and laws of private property. The second virtue is derived from the fact that his wealth flows from his own individual productive labor. The third virtue designates his accumulative activity as being productive of the social good. The fourth and final virtue encompasses his utilization of wealth for philanthropic purposes. By examining each of these virtues more carefully, we can begin to see the peculiar logic of legitimation that is embedded in the language of marketplace as moral space.

Virtue #1: Market Man is "Just."   Balbus's first and most basic level of ethical justification of wealth is that he is not a "bad" or evil person because he "didn't steal this money." As he elaborated elsewhere in the interview, this means that he didn't violate the property rights of others, he honored his contracts and agreements, he vied fairly with his competitors in the marketplace, and he treated his customers well and his employees with respect. This virtue is what Hume and Smith called the "negative" virtue of justice and consists in rules and laws of property and propriety that prohibit men in market society from doing harm to others. Justice was a negative virtue because, at a minimum, it required the virtuous person to "sit still and do nothing" by simply refraining from violating the rights of others (Smith, 1976b: II.1.9.82).[15] Yet of all the virtues identified by Hume and Smith as being constitutive of the morality of Market Man, this one was the most important to commercial society, as it prevented it from degenerating into a Hobbessian war of each against all. More importantly, such rules of propriety are institutionalized through civil government as laws of property that "maintain the rich in the possession of their wealth against the violence and rapacity of the poor, and by that means preserve that useful inequality in the fortunes of mankind which naturally arises from various degrees of capacity, industry and diligence in the different individuals" (Smith, 1978a: vi.19.338).[16]

For a few of the entrepreneurs in our sample, the rhetorical invocation of this virtue of "justice" was enough to eliminate any feelings of guilt they might have and legitimate their wealth. Hayden Hiller, a Boston computer entrepreneur, was quite vehement about this point and its implications for linking his sovereign individuality with social responsibility. "Why the hell should I feel guilty?" he firmly stated,

> I don't see anything I should feel guilty about. Guilt implies that I've done something wrong or illegal, which are things that I haven't done. . . . [So] I

feel no moral obligation. I'm not the one who has a problem with having made some money, and I think I lot of people who give have a problem with the fact that they have a lot of money. And this is a way of assuaging their guilt. . . . I don't feel that way, so I'm unsympathetic to the idea that I have a moral or social obligation to do anything. If this is what I hear from people, I'll say "No, I don't care, I'm sure." I'll do what I want to do, when I want to do it. If I do something it's because of what I'm interested in and not what someone tells me I have to do.

In spite of his bluntness, Hiller is not at all unusual among wealthy men in saying that philanthropic behavior is an expression of self-interest and power. Yet most, like Balbus, do offer a more nuanced discourse of the moral legitimacy that grounds their power.

Virtue #2: The "Prudence" and "Self-Command" of Market Man. The second virtue that provides the ethical grounding of wealth as it pertains to its accumulation is perhaps the most ideologically powerful in contemporary American capitalist culture. It also articulates what inheritor David Schwartz called the "ownership right" of wealth accumulation by entrepreneurs, against which he measured and defined his own abjection. This virtue is expressed quite simply by Balbus as having "worked hard for the money." Wealth and financial success are the direct result of individual labor, and in accordance with the notion of property rights first articulated by the Lockean natural jurisprudence tradition and absorbed by the Scottish Enlightenment, the mixing of one's labor with capital entitles one to ownership and control over wealth and the privileges it entails.

This notion that wealth is the direct result of individual labor, which is somewhat modestly invoked by Balbus, is stated with considerably more brashness by Andrew Nash, a New York real estate mogul: "Everything I have earned, everything I own today, everything I am today. I've earned myself." These words, the reader may recognize, can be traced to the rhetoric of the Founder, the original self-made man. As such, they are freighted with all kinds of connotations concerning the manner in which Market Man enacts the narrative of fortune and virtue. The virtues associated with self-making through accumulation that are articulated by Balbus, Nash, and other entrepreneurs are none other than the qualities of Machiavellian *virtù* and Protestant worldly asceticism, which Smith transposed to the marketplace and rendered as the virtues of "prudence" and "self-command": thrift, frugality, deferred gratification, the plowing of profit back into business, and disciplined labor dedicated to building an enterprise. Of course, such qualities enable men of the market to turn fortune, in terms chance and contingency, into a fortune in terms of wealth. For Market Man, fortune is completely secularized, part of the dynamics of the marketplace. Fortune and virtue become firmly united under the sign of the rational accumulation of wealth; as Smith argues, for Market Man "the road to virtue and that to fortune are . . . very nearly the same" (Smith, 1976b: I.iii.3.5).

The virtues of just conduct and disciplined individual labor directed toward the rational accumulation of wealth provide the first level of ethical justification for Balbus's, and *homo mercator*'s, claim to their realm of sovereign individuality and power. In this regard, as I mention above, this articulation of the moral grounding of the accumulative activity of Market Man is essentially a restatement of the natural jurisprudence principle of *suum cique*, "to each his own," which is also the essence of possessive individualism.[17] According to this principle, *cique* is distributed *suum* according to an individual's accumulative prowess. As Balbus himself explains, capitalism "is certainly not a system [that is] meant to be egalitarian. It's meant to distribute wealth from a personal contribution standpoint. I don't believe that everybody should make the same amount of money, everybody should make a different amount of money depending upon their own ambitions and capabilities." However, this rhetorical strategy of legitimating one's wealth and power by underscoring the personal labor (and putting under erasure the labor of others) that went into its acquisition is not so different from the one we encountered in Chapter 3 in the writings of Leon Alberti and the other Quattrocento civic humanists. The true innovation of Smith and Scottish Enlightenment in providing a language for grounding the moral justification of the private accumulation of wealth lay not so much in their account of its production by virtuous, enterprising individuals. Rather, it lay in how such accumulation entailed positive social consequences. For Smith, the path of virtue was not only the path to fortune for the successfully prosperous Market Man alone; it was the path to fortune, in a number of ways, for all who live in commercial society as a whole.

Virtue #3: Market Man Expands the Territory of the Market and Makes Other Market Men. For Balbus, it is first and foremost through his accumulative activity itself that he is able to link his sovereign individuality with a sense of having contributed to the community and the public good. As he said above, his business is the "biggest" and most important "charity" to which he personally contributes. By investing his time and money into his enterprise, he makes a far bigger contribution to the "quality of life for America" than he would if he simply gave his money away by providing jobs, income, and desired goods and services. The unequal distribution of wealth and property that is intrinsic to the market, a distribution that is based on the "personal contribution standpoint" of virtuous labor, provides the incentives for individuals to invest and innovate. By constantly seeking the best return on their labor, time, and money, those involved in the enterprise of accumulating wealth set into motion a dynamic cycle of economic growth, the benefits of which extend to all in society. This logic of legitimation is none other than the invisible hand theorem developed by Smith, that is, by striving to accumulate wealth for himself, the entrepreneur provides opportunity for others to fulfill their needs. As Balbus notes elsewhere in the interview:

> Underlying the market system is free enterprise capitalism, we all invest savings to make companies grow and leave them unregulated as much as possible as they don't hurt the citizens they come in contact with. And there are people who are trusted with that responsibility who are going to cause the system to be inefficient. But that's the way it is and fortunately, most people who have that responsibility are going to be efficient because they are taking care of their own needs and in the process take care of others.

Balbus's argument that there is a natural and harmonious convergence between capitalists "taking care of their own needs" and "taking care of the needs of others" in the process of accumulation expresses the essential meaning of the new mode of socioeconomic citizenship that was ushered in by the Scottish Enlightenment. The accumulation of wealth becomes, in and of itself, a profound act of citizenship and responsibility to others in the community. But there is more going on here than the simple argument that by unintended consequences Market Man furthers the interest of the community by pursuing his own. There is also an expression of how the moral identity of Balbus, and Market Man in general, is based upon a particular governmentality that defines desired forms of selfhood, the "others" in the community, and their "needs."

I argue in Chapter 3 that during the Citizen's process of participating in collectively managing the affairs the republic the boundaries of identity shift for the Citizen as his self-interest becomes redefined in light of communal definitions of the public good. That is, the "I" of sovereign autonomous individuality is redefined and transformed by the "We" of the community. Because the primary spatial practice through which his sovereign individuality is linked to the public good is his act of accumulation, there is no so such transformation of the self and self-identity for Market Man. In fact, something quite different happens; rather than a process by which the self is redefined in terms of relations of difference and otherness in the community, the act of accumulation is a process for the production of selves that are just like that of Market Man. If the virtues of justice and hard work ethically ground the process by which Market Man produces himself through accumulation, it is the means by which Market Man produces others that grounds the social benefits of the accumulation process.

The understanding of "others" in the social imagination of Market Man is inscribed in the very concept and logic of power he evinces. The conception of power that animates market society privileges the wealthy as the fullest subjects that money literally can buy. In a capitalist society, where the territorialization of desire is constricted so as to channel and encode needs and desires in terms of what is available in the marketplace, the meanings of selfhood, autonomy, and citizenship are defined in terms of an individual's capacity to satisfy needs and pursue desires in the market. That is, selfhood and autonomy are positively correlated with the possession of money and wealth. In the discourse of the market, there are no structural antagonisms between rich and poor, no relationship of domination and exploitation between social classes; there is simply a vertical continuum of power and identity. This continuum is anchored on the top by those with wealth and money and on the bottom by, to use Balbus's terms, "those without money." It is this category of "those without money"—those who are defined not by who they concretely and positively are but by their lack of what the wealthy possess in superfluity—who constitute the differential alterity of "otherness" within the representational system of the market. In other words, they have the status of abject, for whom the market has no place or location of valorized ethical or moral habitation. Accordingly, the moral obligation that Market Man meets by his act of accumulation, the most important social benefit that the private accumulation of wealth produces, is to produce others in his own image.

Consider the language with which Balbus describes the positive social benefits of his accumulation. For Balbus, at the most abstract level, the primary benefit of his accumulation is that he is "contributing to everyone else's opportunity to make money." More specifically, he views his business as an institution that creates "good citizens," that is, individuals whose autonomy consists in their ability to labor, work, and add their flows of money and desire to the market. "I think we provide a very stable environment to make good family people," he says. "Even if they don't have a family, they are good social citizens to the community because they get up every morning, stand up on their own two legs (or pay taxes on their house) and come to work." For Adam Smith, this production of individuals who are able to economically autoambulate in and through the social space of the market constituted one of the primary ways in which commercial society represented historical progress in comparison with previous modes of subsistence. "Nothing," he argued, "tends to corrupt and enervate and debase the mind as dependency, and nothing gives noble and generous notions of probity as freedom and independency. Commerce is the one great preventative of this custom" (Smith, 1978a: VI.8.333). Note here Smith's reversal of the relation between commerce and corruption in comparison with the discourse of civic republicanism. For the Machiavellians, it was commerce that was the fount of corruption and abjection; for Smith, it was commerce itself that prevented it.

Accordingly, the most compelling moral virtue that *homo mercator* evinces in the know-how and can-do-ness of his quotidian business practices is, in a Foucauldian sense, the disciplinary creation and forming of the "other" into subjects that aspire to the selfhood and autonomy on offer by the market. This belief in moral obligations that are simultaneously constituted and met by the act of accumulation is stated with exquisite clarity and forthrightness by Troy MacDonnell, chief executive of a midwestern insurance company. Echoing and amplifying Smith's assertions concerning the freedom and independence created by the market, McDonnell argues:

> I think you do a hell of a lot of charity when you create a good business enterprise. That's the best damn charity you can do for anybody. Let 'em earn for themselves. Teach 'em that they can earn money rather then being dependent. . . . It is far more important in our society to create the ability to make money than it is to retain money. I want to create the ability and the desire to make money. Wealth has an absolute responsibility to create jobs, create a better environment for people to do things for themselves, to feel better about themselves. I am sure of the need to take care of the indigent, but that's a hard task. I'd rather we spent more time in creating them so they have a good image of themselves. And to be something, [to say] "I own part of this, I am something."

The moral structure and interpretive economy of the market, with its privileged notions of what constitutes selfhood and autonomy, are revealed in the rhetorical equivalences and oppositions of MacDonnell's statement. There is a stark opposition drawn between two distinct modes of mobilizing wealth in capitalist society. On one side of the opposition, there is what MacDonnell terms "charity," or the voluntary redistribution of surplus. This is opposed to the reinvestment of wealth in order to "create a good business enterprise." Each of these modes of mobilizing wealth is viewed as producing different types of socioeconomic citizens. That is to say, they are conceived as being different technologies of subjection and governmentalities of guiding conduct in everyday life.

"Charity" is directed toward the "indigent," who are by definition needy, impoverished, and lacking. They are, to use Balbus's characterization, "those without." In a word, they are abject. The fundamental social problem of the abjected indigent, a problem that calls forth and structures the moral obligation of Market Men like MacDonnell and Balbus, does not consist solely or even primarily in the fact that "those without" are without because they lack money capital. Rather, MacDonnell's discourse states and implies that "those without" are impoverished in their presence and identity as socioeconomic citizens primarily because they lack psychic and symbolic capital. Psychically, the indigent are deemed to be deficient in that they are lacking in purpose, direction, initiative, responsibility, and self-esteem. This psychic deficit entails a symbolic deficit. Lacking in the requisite qualities that constitute the morally valued characteristics of selfhood and autonomy in the market, they gaze into the mirror of capitalist society and find that they don't, as MacDonnell says, "have a good image of themselves." Charity is a flawed and perhaps ultimately even a pernicious mode of mobilizing wealth because, although it may meet the short-term, material needs of the indigent in terms of money, it does not address psychic and symbolic deficits. Charity severs the link between virtuous individual labor and monetary reward and thus produces an empty, enervated, and corrupt subjectivity of dependence.

The "good image" that is mirrored back to "those without" and reflects their lack is, of course, the image of Market Man himself. In contrast to the atrophied, diminished, and enervated selves that compose the amorphous social body of "those without," Market Man is a sharply defined kernel of individual energy that is, above all, an enterprising self. Disciplined, goal-directed, independent, and self-reliant, the enterprising self displays initiative, boldness, and vigor in the quest for self-improvement.[18] The enterprising self is an entrepreneur of the self, thoroughly involved in and motivated by the project of self-making. However, this project of autonomous, independent self-making is wholly defined in terms of the market. The desire structure that is evinced by Market Man as an enterprising subject is not simply the desire for self-improvement per se. Rather, the ability of and desire for self-improvement is, to use MacDonnell's words, synonymous with the "ability and the desire to make money." Accordingly, the primary social field in which the virtues of the enterprising self can be cultivated and inculcated is within the commercial enterprise. By drawing "those without" into the disciplinary matrix of the market and commercial enterprises, they are "created" anew as good socioeconomic citizens, as subjects of self-interest who work to better their condition. They learn how to "earn for themselves," to "do for themselves," and on the basis of these money-making virtues they are allocated the psychic and symbolic rewards of being able to "feel better about themselves" and to have "a good image of themselves." Moreover, if they are truly taught to be enterprising selves, if they learn well the lessons of desire for money, then perhaps at the end of their labors they will be able to claim the fullness of sovereign identity that comes with the ownership of wealth and property and say "I own part of this, I am something." In the market, identity and property are united under the sign of *suum cique*, and the primary moral obligation of Market Man is to provide the opportunity so that each will be able to claim his own.

Virtue #4: Market Man Is Benevolent. Although the creation of enterprising subjects of self-interest who develop their identity on the basis of their desire and ability to make money constitutes the primary social benefit of the private accumulation of wealth, and thus represents the most exalted moral obligation of Market Man, it is by no means the only one. In spite of MacDonnell's criticism of "charity," there is still an important place for what Smith would call the virtue of "benevolence" in Market Man's moral vocabulary. For Smith, the private accumulation of wealth not only has the unintended yet positive consequence of providing the population of commercial society with the opportunity to "better one's condition"; it also provides the material wherewithal to those who are successful in grasping this opportunity to help those who are not. It is the "generosity" of the productively virtuous, he says, "that relieves us by their assistance when the schemes fail that have been laid for the attaining of [the] necessities and conveniences of life" (Smith, 1978a: VI.20.338).

Accordingly, for Balbus, MacDonnell, and other men of the market it is the fact that their accumulative activity enables them to engage in philanthropic activity that provides the fourth and final level of ethical justification of their wealth. After all, reasons MacDonnell, to who but the wealthy is society going to turn in order to undertake projects for the public good that would otherwise go undone because of lack of money? "When you have to do some good in the world, you don't go to the paupers. You've got to have wealth to do some good. You know, to take on any sort of project, you've got to have some wealth. So you've got to permit people to make wealth. If you want to do a new YMCA project, you don't go to the people that need the YMCA most to do it." Similarly for Balbus, philanthropy as a social practice of redistributing wealth is only possible on the basis of its prior accumulation. As he says above, with the $100 million that will accrue to him when he finally sells his company, Balbus will have the opportunity and capacity to both "think wonderful philanthropic thoughts" and act upon them. Without his devotion to his accumulative activity, such thoughts would either not be possible or would simply be idle ruminations on how one could be beneficent and generous, if one only had the money.

However, in terms of the language and moral identity of Market Man, more important than the simple fact that accumulation of wealth enables one to be benevolent is the manner in which philanthropic activity is conceived in relation to the market. Essentially, philanthropy is a residual category of wealth allocation that is of secondary social importance to the investment of wealth in business enterprises. As we have just seen, from the perspective of market men like Balbus and MacDonnell, it is through the incorporation of "those without" into the structure and logic of the market that society can best provide for their needs and create productive enterprising subjects. "I truly believe in philanthropy and philanthropic causes," Balbus averred, "but I would rather see most of the capital in America be used for enterprise purposes because that's going to make a better society than if it used for pure philanthropic causes. [You can't] have a charitable redistribution of excess wealth that's needed to provide growth in America and personal initiative. Personal initiative does have to happen, otherwise there won't be any growth."

Remember, central to the ethical justification of the market and its instrumental rationality is the argument that the dynamism of the market rests on the differential allocation of material rewards on the basis of individual labor. This "useful inequality of fortune," as Smith would say, calls forth the best effort of enterprising individuals and spurs economic growth. Growth, in turns, expands the territorializing frontiers of the market, bringing ever more people into its flows of desire and money.

There are, however, a number of people who remain obdurately resistant to the market's project of transforming them into enterprising subjects of interest. For Balbus, there is a particular threshold or "breakthrough level" inherent in the market, above which individuals are both able to and responsible for developing their talents and capacities and, accordingly, are justly rewarded according to their virtuous efforts. As Balbus says, the market may have "inefficiencies" as far as including such people within its structure of desire and opportunity. By "inefficiencies" Balbus means the problems of the market in either extending the opportunity for social mobility to "those without" or in providing them with the talent and capacity to take advantage of such opportunities. When asked to explain *why* the market was inefficient in this regard, why there were many who were not able to reach this "breakthrough level," Balbus was, quite literally, speechless. "I'm not really answering your question," he temporized. "I guess what I really . . . I really can't verbalize all the inefficiencies of our system. But I know they are there."

Balbus's inarticulateness on this point is not, I think, an attempt to be dissembling or evasive on his part. Rather, Balbus's inability to specify the reasons for the "inefficiencies" of the market is because the discourse of the market *in and of itself* does not provide him with the vocabulary to do so. Within the terms of its discourse, there is no way of conceiving of "those without" as being a product of market forces or of the accumulative activity of the wealthy themselves. Whatever the reasons, the lack of capacities or opportunities among "those without" could not be attributed to the logic of the market itself or the structural inequities in wealth and power it entails. This would undermine the moral logic that ethically grounds Market Man's accumulative activity, as it is the context of the market itself that renders it just, virtuous, and integral to the public good. If the market is an ongoing drama of fortune and virtue, where the virtuous produce and accumulate a fortune, then "those without" can only be understood as those who have failed to perform according to the script. Within the symbolic world that is conjured by the language of the market, this failure of performance of "those without" must be attributed to factors extrinsic to the structure and workings of the market itself. That is to say, the "inefficiencies" of the market system do not consist of factors internal to the market that serve to *exclude* people from its rewards and benefits but of external factors that prevent their *inclusion*. The reasons given for their failure in the discourse of the market vary, ranging from government interference in what Smith called the "natural system of liberty" of the market, to inadequate schooling and "pathological" family structures, to welfare dependency and the simple lack of individual initiative and virtue. But "whatever the reason," argues Balbus, they are embodied in the souls and psyche of "those without" as an inability to "perform in the mainstream effort" of the market. Accordingly, it is upon the bodies of "those without" that philanthropy must work and "take care of," seeking to remediate them in such a manner so that they can be included within the performative drama of the market. Accordingly, the language of virtue that is embedded in the market displaces the responsibility for the persistent existence of "those without" away from the territorializing structure of money, power, and desire that re/produces Market Man and onto those lacking in fortune themselves.

In spite of the fact that benevolence is, for *homo mercator*, merely a residual category of wealth distribution, there are many men of wealth for whom philanthropy is a vocation and moral duty that it is every bit as important as the accumulation of wealth. However, in order to understand the conceptions of self, other, and community that inform and shape the language of philanthropy among wealthy men, it is necessary to move beyond the discursive categories of the Scottish Enlightenment that gave birth to *homo mercator*. In Chapter 5 I will explore another rhetorical terrain, or topos, that encodes and territorializes flows of money and desire within the social field. This is the topos of philanthropy, and within this terrain it is possible to locate the "better angels" that George Bush imagined shining brightly in his "thousand points of light." These angels are the moral characters of Steward-Citizen and

Steward-Entrepreneur who were engendered in the nineteenth-century American discourses of philanthropic beneficence.

Notes

1. In order to conform to scholarly conventions regarding citation of this work, references will include book and chapter numbers as well as page numbers of the particular edition. Thus, this reference refers to Book I, Chapter 5, p. 35, of the 1976 University of Chicago edition of *The Wealth of Nations*.

2. It should be remembered, however, that civic virtue contains a healthy measure of manly *virtù*. The Citizen, at least in his Machiavellian configuration, must be austere and disciplined in order to combat the chaos, decay, and corruption, principally represented by wealth and dependency, with which *fortuna* threatened to deluge the republic.

3. For Foucault, governmentality refers to *la conduite de la conduite* or "the conduct of conduct." Governmentality is a form of know-how and can-do-ness, its aim being to shape or guide the conduct of people, whether individually or collectively. Like all forms of discourse, governmentality is both nominal and practical: It embodies a particular coding and articulation of social reality and, on this basis, furnishes a particular program toward social reality that is manifested in a morally valued mode of being and acting in the world. For a discussion of Foucault's concept of governmentality in relationship to his larger project of genealogy see Gordon (1987, 1991), Ransom (1997), and Rose (1996).

4. This is not to suggest that the lack of a language of virtue that is intrinsic to the production and accumulation of wealth is the sole reason for the failure of the civic humanists to provide an enduring moral grounding for the new social subject they helped engender. There were, of course, other limitations intrinsic to the Renaissance episteme, such as the cyclical understanding of secular time and history and the static understanding of wealth (as I discuss in Chapter 3), that precluded the discursive articulation of a fully capitalist subject. See Donald Lowe's (1983: 11–12) discussion of the limitations of the protocapitalist perspectival regime of Renaissance mercantile bourgeoisie.

5. As a coherent intellectual movement, the Scottish Enlightenment in generally considered to span the period from 1740 to 1790. In addition to Smith and Hume, the principal figures of the Scottish Enlightenment were Adam Ferguson, John Millar, and William Robertson. Although each wrote on a variety of subjects, their salience in the history of ideas is generally seen to be present in three main areas: the moral philosophy of human nature (Hume, Smith), the conjectural history of political and civil society (Smith, Millar, Ferguson, and Robertson), and political economy (Hume, Millar, and, of course, Smith). The literature on the Scottish Enlightenment is vast, but for comprehensive overviews of its intellectual components as well as the social and cultural context see Camic (1983) and Chitnis (1976). For an analysis of the discursive field of the Scottish Enlightenment that departs from the usual intellectual history of the "five great men" see Dwyer (1987).

6. For an exhaustive discussion of the concept of civil society from Aristotle to the present—which inexplicably only briefly discusses the Scottish Enlightenment—see Cohen and Arato (1992).

7. Unfortunately, most of Foucault's analysis of the Scottish Enlightenment, which he undertook as part of his investigations into the liberal mode of governmentality and which he presented as lectures at the College de France in the late 1970s, is almost entirely unpublished. Only one of these lectures, "On Governmentality," is available in English and can be found in Burchell et al. (1991). This volume contains two articles that discuss Foucault's analysis of governmentality in general, and the Scottish Enlightenment in particular, in some detail. See Burchell (1991) and Gordon (1991).

8. It is often assumed by contemporary scholars and pundits, most of whom have never cracked the spine of works such as *The Wealth of Nations*, that Smith and other members of the Scottish Enlightenment foreground the ontic primacy of the individual. However central this presupposition may have been to the seventeenth-century individualism of Hobbes and Locke, it is most decidedly not a feature of the social thought of Scottish Enlightenment. As Adam Ferguson argued, "Mankind are to be taken in groups, as they have always subsisted. The history of the individual is but a detail of the sentiments and thoughts he has entertained in the view of his species: and every experiment relative to this subject should be made with entire societies, not with single men" (1986: 2).

9. The introduction and spread of these new forms and representations of property were part of what has been called the "Financial Revolution" of the late seventeenth century. This revolution consisted primarily of two institutional innovations. The first was the establishment of joint stock companies that sold and traded shares in both manufacturing and trading ventures. The second was the establishment of the Bank of England in 1694, which, in order to finance the numerous mercantile wars of the period, began to sell government securities and brought into being the brave new world of public credit and debt. See J. Appleby (1978) and Dickson (1967). For a fascinating, if idiosyncratic, examination of the Financial Revolution and its implications for understanding money as a form of social representation and medium of empowerment for the rising bourgeoisie, see Caffentzis (1989).

10. See also Xenos (1989), discussing the consumer revolution and its relation to theories of social emulation put forward by Hume and Smith.

11. To call these people "neo-Machiavellians" is slightly misleading, as their theoretical and discursive links to Machiavelli are indirect at best. Machiavellian civic republicanism, with its emphasis on landed property and popular militias as the basis of civic virtue and citizenship, was translated and applied to the English context after the civil war by James Harrington in *The Commonwealth of Oceana* (1656). Harrington, and not Machiavelli directly, provided the English and Scottish civic republicans with their rhetoric and language. In fact, Trenchard, Gordon, Davenant, and Fletcher explicitly laid claim to Harrington's political patrimony and were known, accordingly, as the "New Commonwealthmen." The links to Machiavelli of men like Bolingbroke and Brown, who emerged in the generation of political figures subsequent to the New Commonwealthmen, are even more attenuated. However, all spoke from within the broadly Machiavellian paradigm of civic virtue. See Raab (1964), Robbins (1955), and, of course, Pocock (1975) for detailed textual and historical analysis of the diverse strains of civic republicanism in England and Scotland.

12. The personification of new forms of mobile property as capricious and fickle females who can dominate the imaginations and lives of men is exemplified by

the following passage from one of many of Daniel Defoe's magazine articles published during the early-eighteenth-century English debate on money and credit. "Money," he wrote, "has a younger sister . . . Her Name in our Language is call'd CREDIT. . . . 'Tis a strange thing to think, how absolute this Lady is; how despotickly she governs all our Actions: If you court her, you lose her, or must buy her at unreasonable Rates; and if you do, she is always jealous of you, and Suspicious; and if you don't discharge her to a Title of your Agreement, she is gone, and perhaps may never come again as long as you live; and if she does, 'tis with long Entreaty and abundance of Difficulty." Quoted in Pocock (1975: 452–453). Interestingly, Defoe provided the capitalist social imaginary with one of its most powerful myths of masculine mastery and autonomous self-making in the figure of Robinson Crusoe.

13. This analysis is articulated more explicitly in the *General Economic History* than it is in the *Protestant Ethic*. See Max Weber (1961: 270).

14. Here I am being very liberal in my appropriation of the concept of territorialization. Deleuze and Guattari deploy the term in relation to a different concept of desire than the one I use. For Deleuze and Guattari, desire is not a lack, absence, or yearning that can be fulfilled by the acquisition of something. Rather, desire is free-floating energy that is positive and productive and flows across the social field, pooling and congealing into configurations of social relations and institutions, then disintegrating and flowing on in search of new stations and configurations. This process of the coagulation and dissolution of "desiring-forms" is what they refer to as reterritorialization and deterritorialization. Capitalism deterritorialized desire by dissolving the kinship systems, communities, class relations of feudal society, and the way they were "encoded" by philosophy and religion. It reterritorialized desire by rechanelling it into new institutions of economy, state, and family that were geared toward the production of commodities and surplus value while "recoding" them in terms of the positive values of freedom, individualism, property, and the nuclear family.

15. In order to conform to scholarly conventions regarding citation of this work, references will include book, section, paragraph, and page numbers of the particular edition. Thus, this reference refers to Book 2, Section 2, Chapter 1, Paragraph 9, p. 82 of the 1976 Liberty Press edition of Adam Smith, *The Theory of Moral Sentiments*. As Smith argues in this passage, echoing Hume's treatment of justice in *The Treatise on Human Nature*, "Mere justice is, upon most occasions, but a negative virtue, and hinders us from hurting our neighbor. The man who barely abstains from violating either the person, or the estate, or the reputation of his neighbors, has surely very little positive merit. He fulfills, however, all the rules of what is properly called justice."

16. In order to conform to scholarly conventions regarding citation of this work, references will include volume, section, and page numbers of the particular edition. Thus, this reference refers to Volume 6, Section 19, p. 338 of the 1978 Oxford University Press edition of Adam Smith, *Lectures on Jurisprudence, Report of 1762–1763*, edited by R. L. Meek, D. D. Raphael, and P. G. Stein. The second work, *Lectures on Jurisprudence, Report of 1766*, was edited by R. L. Meek, D. D. Raphael, and P. G. Stein and published in London by Oxford University Press in 1978 and will be similarly cited.

17. On the history of this principle in the discourse of natural jurisprudence and its pre-Lockean antecedents see Pocock (1985), Skinner (1978), and Tuck (1980).

18. The notion of an entrepreneurial or enterprising self has gained considerable currency in the discourse of conservatives in the United States and Great Britain during the 1980s and 1990s as part of a largely successful attempt to discredit the welfare state and government efforts at regulating and constraining the market. For analyses of how this moral character has been deployed in conservative rhetoric, particularly in Britain, see du Gay (1991) and Rose (1992).

5

Stewards, Citizens, and Entrepreneurs: Discourses of Philanthropy as Manly Vocation

Benevolence, Beneficence, and Beyond: Crossing the Atlantic to the Topos of Philanthropy

The "Story" of the "Better Angels" Thus Far

Rhetoric, as I argue in Chapter 1, is a practice of power/knowledge through which symbolic topoi in the social imaginary are conjured and sustained. These topoi are places of "common sense" and shared meaning, mappings of moral and social space, within which social groups locate and perform their moral identity. In exploring different topoi in the moral economy of wealth, I have attempted to analyze two moments in this rhetorical conjuring of place and identity through narrative: the *invocative* and *evocative*. I have further argued that a fruitful way of understanding the linkage between the moral economies of present and past, between the rhetorical moments of evocation and invocation, is through the examination of the moral characters with particular topoi that perform the narrative of fortune and virtue as spatial story.

In Chapter 3, my aim was to examine the emergence of the narrative of fortune and virtue in Florentine mercantile capitalism as a rhetoric of masculine selfhood, as well as how this narrative was embodied and enacted by the moral characters of the Founder and the Citizen. The *topos*, or story space, these moral characters inhabited was primarily the realm of politics. This realm was materially and symbolically territorialized through the spatial practices of the founding of states, the building of empires, and the managing and defending of republics. Accordingly, the masculine qualities of both *virtù* and civic virtue were discursively configured as attributes with which men, either individually (as was the case with the Founder) or collectively (as with the case with the Citizen) dominated the feminine wiles of *fortuna* so as to preserve and extend political autonomy and power. As I endeavored to demonstrate, the emplotment and emplacement of the narrative of fortune and virtue performed by these characters is clearly invoked in the (auto-)biographies of contemporary masculine "better angels" such as Mark Dahlin and Stuart Dean.

However, this provides a partial understanding of the place of virtue wealthy men evoke, for I argue that the locations and trajectories of virtue the honor and civic ethics mapped upon the territory of the political were unable to fully accommodate commerce as a vocation. The accumulation of wealth was ultimately viewed as being dangerously corrosive of manly virtue and a capitulation to the seductive power of fortune. If *fortuna* was a raging stream of chance and contingency that had to be controlled by men of *virtù* and civic virtue, then wealth as fortune represented a stream of uncontrolled desire and corruption that would inundate and overwhelm masculine autonomy and the territory of the political within which such autonomy was located. Thus, if the integrity of the boundaries of the autonomous masculine self and the republic were to be maintained, they would have to be armored and defended to resist and turn away the flows of fortune as temporal chaos and the flows of fortune as money and wealth.

With these considerations in mind I shifted my analysis to the Scottish Enlightenment. In Chapter 4, I investigated a second topos, that of the marketplace, inhabited by a new moral character, *homo mercator* or Market Man. Following G. Deleuze and F. Guattari (1983), I argue that the Smithian discourse of the marketplace represented a "reterritorialization" of the social dynamics of selfhood, autonomy, and power as well as a concomitant recoding of virtue. Autonomy and power came to be defined in terms of the accumulation of goods and commodities through social relations of exchange, relations that were facilitated and mediated by the fluid medium of money. Within this new territory of the market, money and wealth were no longer sources of corruption and vice but rather the embodiment of masculine power and virtuous propriety.

However, the Scottish Enlightenment's discourse of the marketplace go only so far in helping understand the place of virtuous self-identity rhetorically evoked by contemporary men of the market. Specifically, the Smithian rendering of the relationship between wealth and benevolence cannot fully account for the central importance of beneficence and philanthropy as categories of virtue that are constitutive of the "better angels" in the contemporary moral economy of capitalism. For Smith, "benevolence" is basically a *residual* concept in two senses of the term. First, even though benevolence is undeniably an important facet of *homo mercator*, it is not intrinsically necessary to his activity in the marketplace or to the stability of commercial society as a whole. Benevolence for Smith was a human sentiment derived from empathy that could be expressed independently of one's wealth or rank in society. Although wealth certainly enhanced a man's capacity to act upon feelings of benevolence toward others, neither good will nor charity was articulated as being the special responsibility or prerogative of the commercially successful. Furthermore, within the moral geography of the market mapped by Smith, benevolence is a residual category in a second, perhaps more fundamental sense in terms of understanding the "better angels" of the present.

The sentiment of benevolence was the phenomenological foundation for beneficence as a social practice of charity. Yet the social practice of beneficence was conceived as being ancillary to and derivative of *homo mercator*'s commercial activity. Through his everyday activity as a "gainer," to employ Hume's term, this moral character accumulated wealth and made his primary productive contribution to society. Though charitable beneficence may feed the hungry and give succor to needy, it was a purely distributive activity that unlike commerce did not have any "positivity" in the Foucauldian sense. That is to say, within the terms of the discourse of the market beneficence was not productive of the material and symbolic space of the market or its inhabitants. One might say that benevolence and charity were an "excess" moral sentiment and a social practice, as they could not be accounted for by the discourse of the market. Accordingly, in order to understand how George Bush, John Norris, Stuart Dean, and their peers are able to evoke a place in the social imaginary where wealth and virtue are mutually constitutive and they as "better angels" take flight, there is one final place of invocation and evocation, one final articulation of the emplotment and emplacement of the narrative of fortune and virtue that I must examine. This is the topos of "philanthropy" as it emerged in nineteenth-century America and is evoked in the rhetoric of virtuous selfhood of contemporary men of wealth.

The "Luxury of Doing Good" and the "Proper Administration of Wealth": The Moral Characters of the Topos of Philanthropy

What is this topos of philanthropy? What are the discourses that chart the domain of this territory and mark its boundaries? What is the moral character that inhabits this territory and is emplotted and emplaced by its constituent discourses? In this chapter I argue that nineteenth-century discourses of philanthropy conjured and mapped a new material space of social engagement for wealthy men and a new practice of directing flows of money and capital that went far beyond those entailed by traditional notions of paternalistic benevolence and charitable beneficence. Although the new rhetoric of philanthropy deployed older languages of charity, stewardship, noblesse oblige, and citizenship in constructing this topos, it created a fundamentally new moral identity for the wealthy man in industrial capitalist society.[1] This moral identity was based upon a construction of philanthropy as a *productive* rather than primarily *distributive* use of wealth, through which men of wealth were bound by duty and empowered by responsibility to imprint their vision of culture and the "public good" upon the community.

This distinction between distributive and productive deployment of wealth marks the fundamental difference between charity and philanthropy. In brief, charity as a practice of wealth distribution seeks to address and fulfill the extant needs of its recipient(s). As a productive practice of "wealth administration," as Carnegie characterized it, the goal of philanthropy is to transform the very life situation, and thus the needs, of its beneficiaries. Accordingly, the discourses I examine in this chapter represent an interpellating hail that calls upon men of wealth to insert themselves into the social space of the "community" through philanthropy as a *vocation*. Furthermore, I argue that this vocation of philanthropy is conceived as being as vitally important to social stability and progress as is the creation of wealth itself.

In exploring the topos of philanthropy and its constituent discourses, we will encounter two moral characters that inhabit its territory: the Steward-Citizen and the Steward-Entrepreneur. Both moral characters can be understood as specie of the genus *philanthropist* in that both embody the idea that philanthropy is a productive as opposed to a distributive use of wealth. As their names indicate, both moral characters share a common genealogical grounding in the discourse of stewardship. Through this discourse, men of wealth were hailed as "trustees" of fortune and community and, as such, are duty-bound and obligated to administer the former trust on behalf of the latter. As stewards, wealthy men are represented as being responsible for the social, economic, and cultural improvement of their communities. Consequently, philanthropy becomes a spatial practice that binds wealthy men and their communities in a hierarchical relationship of power and influence in which the public good is essentially a private trust.

Although these moral characters share a common identity as stewards, they are located somewhat differently within the territory of philanthropy because of their embodiment of divergent discourses of virtue that serve to position them differently in relationship to fortune, to their social class, and to their community. The virtue of the Steward-Citizen is primarily configured through the discourse of citizenship, that of the Steward-Entrepreneur by the discourses of autonomous individualism and entrepreneurship. To the Steward-Citizen, the virtue attendant upon fortune is less a function of its making than its productive deployment in service of the community. The fortune of wealth provides an ethos of grace, so to speak, within which wealthy men can cultivate the virtues of citizenship and public service that become the source and sign of their moral identity. Moreover, the responsibility of stewardship is a collective one, one that is passed down from generation to generation of men in the wealthy elite. To the Steward-Entrepreneur, the virtue of wealth accumulation is very much foregrounded in his moral identity. His fortune is a product of his individual capabilities as innovator and entrepreneur, a set of virtues that is recapitulated in the vocation of philanthropy. Consequently, his stewardship is individualized, an expression of his own particular interests, talents, and priorities rather than primarily a collective class responsibility.

The outlines of these two related yet distinct moral characters, and the manner in which they engage in philanthropy as a vocation and perform the duties of stewardship, are exemplified in the pronouncements by two nineteenth-century men of wealth: the Boston Brahmin, Samuel Atkins Eliot, and the robber baron/philanthropist par excellence Andrew Carnegie. In order to frame my genealogical analysis, through which I link the invocative and evocative moments in the (auto-)biographical narratives of contemporary philanthropists, it is important to have a basic understanding of these real-life moral characters and the historical conditions under which they emerged in the nineteenth century.

In an 1845 polemic entitled "The Private and Public Charities of Boston," Eliot argued that philanthropy was the very raison d'etre as well as moral justification for wealth accumulation. Waxing eloquent on the generosity of his fellow Brahmins, Eliot wrote:

> Wealth combined with liberality, comfort extended through the whole community, a desire to improve physically and intellectually, a general disposition to order, industry and sobriety, and a prevailing reverence for the institutions, means and objects of religion, unite to render Boston an agreeable residence to the well-disposed, and an agreeable subject of contemplation to the philanthropist. . . . A large portion of the [charitable] sums stated have, no doubt, arisen from the gathered mites of the generous poor, but another large portion has also been received from the generous rich; and if a man be rich without being generous he can certainly find many cities that would be more agreeable places of residence to him. So far as has hitherto appeared, the influence of the rich has been exerted, in this country, only for beneficent purposes; and it is time that the uncharitable constructions put upon their conduct should be abandoned. . . . So long as the money is freely spent in support of the church, the school, the college, the hospital and the asylum, for memorials of the departed good and great, for the sustenance of the poor, and the comfort of the prisoner, there is little fear of its being greatly misapplied in luxurious extravagance, wanton waste, or vicious indulgence. If we are greedy of gain, it is not to hoard it with the passion of the miser,

but to procure to ourselves the advantages which cannot be obtained without it—the cultivation, the improvement, the luxury of doing good, which
are the stimulus, the means, and the reward of virtue. (Eliot, 1845: 140,
158–159)

Specifying philanthropy as a use of wealth that was morally superior to
the corruption of "luxurious extravagance" and penurious frugality, Eliot
argues that if the wealthy appeared to be "greedy of gain" it was only because of a sincere desire to "procure to ourselves the advantages" that
only wealth can bring. Such advantages are not primarily power and
prestige but the "luxury of doing good," a luxury that is the "stimulus,
the means, and the reward of virtue." Thus, in the terms of Eliot's
rhetoric, the philanthropic use of wealth was encoded as a calling and
a duty, the performance of which was an undeniable and indelible sign
of virtue.

Eliot's disquisition on Boston as a place within which "wealth combined with liberality," and thus had no equal as "an agreeable subject of
contemplation to the philanthropist," was published in the *North American Review*. The *Review*, one of the preeminent periodicals among the
reading public of the period, was also a "virtual house organ" of the
Brahmins during the nineteenth century (Story, 1980: 181). It was essentially a medium of expression for the organic intellectuals of the capitalist
elite and provided a public forum in which they could express and exchange views on the pressing issues of the day. As many historians of the
Boston ruling class of the period have noted, the *Review* played a critically important part in articulating the ideological positions that would
form the basis of that class's moral identity and hegemony (cf. Baltzell,
1979; Hall, 1982; Jaher, 1982). Eliot's article appeared when the political,
economic, and cultural authority of the Brahmins was under attack. Having lost political power at the national, state, and local levels, the Brahmins found their positions of authority in other key social institutions
called into question.

For critics of the Brahmins, their control over Harvard, the Lowell Institute, the Athenaeum and a host of other prominent Boston institutions
was a classic example of the naked corruption of civic virtue. In essence,
critics argued that the Brahmins were utilizing public money and public
institutions for private interests and goals. From Eliot's perspective, such
charges of corruption against the Brahmin elite were "uncharitable constructions put upon their conduct." After all, he reasoned, the United
States was a democratic republic with no hereditary aristocracy. In "so far
as hitherto appeared," he argued, "the influence of the rich has only been
used for beneficent purposes." In order to prove his point Eliot listed
page upon page of benefactions made to Boston and other Massachusetts

communities. Although Eliot admitted that a "large portion" of the gifts had come from the "gathered mites of the generous poor," a more significant and important portion had come "from the generous rich." However, Eliot's rhetorical goal involved more than the simple enumeration of the monetary beneficence of Boston's "generous rich." At stake for Eliot was the articulation of a place of moral identity where wealth was joined with virtue so as to reaffirm, for the Brahmins as well as for the public at large, faith in their capacity and duty to lead. The good fortune of the Brahmins entailed an obligation and an opportunity to be virtuous, and in order to be virtuous they would have to act collectively as responsible stewards and civic-minded citizens.

Forty-odd years after Eliot's missive to the good citizens of Boston, Andrew Carnegie's famous article entitled "Wealth" was published in the pages of the very same *North American Review*. By that time, the *Review* was no longer primarily a parochial "house organ" of the Brahmins. In 1878, its editors and funders, good Brahmins all, decided to move its base of operations to New York as part of an effort to spread the reach of their institutions and ideology, and thus integrate the power of local elites, on a national basis (Hall, 1982).[2] Accordingly, like Eliot's piece, Carnegie's subsequently retitled essay on "Gospel of Wealth" can been seen as a call to philanthropic arms addressed to the capitalist class, though this time at a national level.[3]

> The problem of our age is the proper administration of wealth, that the rites of brotherhood may still bind together the rich and poor in harmonious relationship. . . . The contrast between the palace of the millionaire and the cottage of the laborer with us today measures the change which has come with civilization. This change, however, is not to be deplored, but welcomed as highly beneficial. It is well, nay, essential for the progress of the race that the houses of some should be the homes for all that is highest and best in literature and the arts, and for all the refinements of civilization rather than none should be so. Much better this irregularity than universal squalor. Without wealth there can be no Maecenas. . . . The question then arises—and if the foregoing is correct, it is the only question with which we have to deal— what is the proper mode of administering wealth after the laws upon which civilization is founded have thrown it into the hands of the few? And it is of this great question that I believe I offer the true solution. . . . This, then, is held to be the duty of the man of wealth: . . . to consider all surplus revenues which come to him simply as trust funds, which he is called upon to administer, and strictly as a matter of duty to administer in the matter in which in his judgment, is best calculated to produce the most beneficial results for the community—the man of wealth thus becoming a mere trustee and agent for his poorer brethren, bringing to their service his superior wisdom, experience and ability to administer, doing for them better than they would or could do for themselves. (Carnegie, 1992 [1889]: 1, 5, 9–10)

As with Eliot's polemic, Carnegie's appeared at a time of increasing social and economic crisis as well as public resentment and suspicion of the
rich.[4] However, the crisis of hegemony that the capitalist elite faced at the
end of the nineteenth century was national rather than local.[5] The extrava-
gant excesses of the Gilded Age were reaching a crescendo, as was the
concomitant immisseration of the urban working class and poor. For example, in 1886 two events symbolized the vastly different material conditions of everyday life for rich and poor. William K. Vanderbilt commenced
construction on Marble House, the first of the famous Newport, Rhode Island, mansions that would eventually cost $11 million. The same month
that Vanderbilt commissioned renown architect Richard Hunt to build
this "summer cottage" as a present to his wife, Alva, workers at the Mc-
Cormick Reaper Works outside Chicago went out on strike for an eight-
hour workday and a minimum wage of $2 per day.[6] The strike produced
one of the bloodiest episodes in American labor history, the Haymarket
riots, in which more than one hundred people were killed.

According to Carnegie in an article written before "Gospel of Wealth," the
Haymarket riots were the "mad work of foreign anarchists" who were justi-
fiably and "remorselessly shot down" as a legitimate expression of "public
sentiment" (1965 [1886]: 118). Yet for Carnegie the strike and the ensuing riots were also a profound tragedy that could have been avoided. The class
conflict that Haymarket represented was not, according to Carnegie, the result of the vast disparity in wealth exemplified by the contrast between the
whims of the Vanderbilts and the dire necessity of the McCormick workers.
After all, as Carnegie argued in the opening paragraph of "Gospel of
Wealth," the "contrast between the palace of the millionaire and the cottage
of the laborer" was an inevitable outcome of the "laws" of capitalism as well
as a measure of the "progress" of "civilization." Rather, the increasingly violent conflict between capital and labor, which would be visited upon
Carnegie's own house in the form of the bitter Homestead strike of 1892, was
the result of miscommunication and misunderstanding. The "intelligent
workman," argued Carnegie elsewhere, "knows that labor without his
brother capital is helpless." Unfortunately, the workman is prevented from
having a "truer conception" of the corporatist interdependence and fraternal
solidarity of capital and labor by the "blatant ignorant man, who regards
capital as the natural enemy of labor" and thus "does so much to embitter relations between employer and employed" (1965a [1886]: 98–99).

However, the animosity between capital and labor was not simply the
result of "false consciousness" spread by the "ignorant demagogue."
Such demagoguery could only flourish in a situation where the quotidian spatial and moral distance between capitalist and worker was vast
and deep. "The price we pay" for the material abundance produced by
industrial capitalism and its advanced division of labor, Carnegie argues
in "Gospel," is

no doubt great. We assemble thousands of operatives in the factory, and in the mine, of whom the employer can know little or nothing, and to whom he is little better than myth. All intercourse between them is at an end. Rigid castes are formed, and, as usual, mutual ignorance breeds mutual distrust. Each caste is without sympathy with the other, and ready to credit anything disparaging in regard to it. . . . Human society loses homogeneity. (1992 [1889]: 2–3)

In "Gospel," Carnegie asserts that he was in possession of the "true solution" to problems of industrial capitalism and the crisis of corporate hegemony. "What," asked Carnegie, "is the proper administration of wealth after the laws upon which civilization is founded have thrown it into the hands of a few?" As I explore in detail below, the answer was a restatement and an innovative expansion of Eliot's articulation of philanthropy as a virtuous vocation of wealth. The wealthy man could do his part in bridging the yawning gap between capital and labor through the "proper administration of wealth." It was the "duty of the man of wealth" to consider himself a "mere trustee" of the "surplus revenues" that had been "thrown" into his hands as a result of the Social Darwinist "laws" of competition and accumulation, laws that justly rewarded his entrepreneurial virtue. Having proved his mettle in the marketplace, Carnegie's Steward-Entrepreneur was licensed and commanded to act as "trustee" and "agent" for his "poorer brethren." As trustee, the man of wealth was obligated not only to give his wealth away but also to give his gifts the stamp of his "superior wisdom" so that they were "calculated to produce the most beneficial effects for the community." By redirecting the flow of "surplus" capital back into the "community," and giving such flows a form that embodied his own "judgment" and "experience," the man of wealth would be enacting a "rite of brotherhood," a rite that would "bind together rich and poor in harmonious relationship." On the basis of his philanthropic beneficence, the man of wealth would insert himself productively and positively into the everyday lives of his "poorer brethren" and would, presumably, take on a corporeal or material presence that would dissolve the harmful myths born of social distance.

Of course, neither Eliot's discourse of the Steward-Citizen nor Carnegie's discourse of the Steward-Entrepreneur offered a "true" solution for demythologizing the identity and power of the wealthy or for the problems stemming from an inequality of wealth and fortune. To the contrary: Both moral characters embodied potent new mythologies in Roland Barthes's (1973) sense of myths as systems of signification. These myths offered "true" solutions to the crisis of capitalist hegemony in terms of providing a moral identity and virtuous vocation for men of wealth as a form of the know-how and can-do-ness of power/knowledge.

More precisely, moral characters and their constitutive discourses constructed a grid of intelligibility that mapped social space as a topos where fortune, virtue, and moral identity were united through the philanthropic flows of money that coursed through the community. This particular will to truth, as with the will to truth in general, is also a will to power.

I would argue that this connection between discourses of philanthropy as a will to both truth and power is highlighted in Marcel Mauss's analysis of the *potlatch* in *The Gift* (1967). He writes:

> *The Obligation to Give.* This is the essence of *potlatch.* A chief can keep his authority in his tribe, village and family, and maintain his position with the chiefs inside and outside his nation, only if he can prove that he is favorably regarded by the spirits, that he possesses fortune and that he is possessed by it. The only way to demonstrate his fortune is by expending it to the humiliation of others, by putting them "in the shadow of his name." Kwakitul and Haida noblemen have the same notion of "face" as the Chinese mandarin or officer. It is said of one of the great mythical chiefs who gave no feast that he had a "rotten face." The expression is more apt than it is even in China; for to lose one's face is to lose one's spirit, the dancing mask, the right to incarnate a spirit and wear an emblem or a totem. It is the veritable *persona* which is it at stake. . . . To give is to show one's superiority, to show that one is something more and higher, that one is *magister.* To accept without returning or repaying more is to face subordination, to become a client and subservient, to be *minister.* (Mauss, 1967: 37–38, 72)

As Mauss says, the essence of philanthropy, as with the *potlatch,* is "the obligation to give." This obligation, in both cases, gets played out in the social arena as a will to truth and a will to power. The will to truth consists in the desire to construct a moral identity wherein the wealthy man demonstrates to self and others that "he possesses fortune and is possessed by it." Fortune and identity become one as a unity of possession and "persona" is forged through the virtue of the expenditure of excess or surplus wealth. To put it another way, through the expenditure of wealth in the *potlatch,* as in philanthropy, excess becomes a surplus that can be accounted for in moral terms as a sign of symbolic worth and value. For Mauss, as Julian Pefanis (1991) astutely observes, the social importance of the gift was primarily phenomenological and intersubjective rather than structurally functional (as most anthropologists have interpreted his analysis). The gift operated in archaic societies as "a mediator of inter-human relationships that was governed by a desire for recognition and mastery . . . [the gift] is the form of things charged with personality, of persons as possessions" (Pefanis, 1991: 30).

Of course, there is a vast difference, as Georges Bataille (1988) argues in his revolutionary reworking of Mauss's analysis, between the annihilation of wealth entailed by the *potlatch* when the Kwakitul chieftain throws his coppers into the sea and the permanent institutionalization of wealth embodied in such architectural memorializations to capitalist beneficence as the Carnegie Law Library on the campus of Drake University. The former practice festively destroys wealth in celebration of the energy of life that according to Bataille is expenditure itself, whereas the latter soberly recirculates it in perpetuity.[7] Nonetheless, Mauss's *potlatch* and Carnegie's philanthropy entail a will to truth and power in that both seek to demonstrate that the possessor of wealth "incarnates" a virtuous spirit, is able to wear the "dancing mask" of beneficence, and therefore does not present a "rotten face" to the community. Moreover, both practices seek to bind giver and recipient in a relation of power, for to expend wealth is to "show one's superiority." Whether wealth is wasted or deployed philanthropically, both practices suture the wealthy giver and the community together so that the former, to use Mauss's characterization, is *magister* whereas the latter is *minister*.

Accordingly, in this chapter I explore how philanthropy is the performance of a will to truth that unites wealth and virtue and of a will to power that binds giver and recipient together so that the latter is positioned in the former's "shadow of his name." In the next section, I examine the emergence of the moral character of the Steward-Citizen in the discourse of philanthropy articulated by the Brahmin elite of nineteenth-century Boston. In the section thereafter, I explore the emergence of the moral character of the Steward-Entrepreneur in the figure and discourse of Andrew Carnegie. As I argue, these moral characters, and the languages through which their identity is spoken, are not merely dead and forgotten artifacts of a glorious past of Brahmin hegemony or triumphalist Social Darwinism. To the contrary, the language of the Steward-Citizen and the Steward-Entrepreneur is alive and well, and by visiting two "better angels" of the present I seek to show how this language constitutes a nominating discourse of philanthropic virtue that casts a penumbra between the angels in flight and those on the ground below.

The Grace of Wealth and the Duty of Fortune: Brahmin Boston and the Philanthropic Vocation of the Steward-Citizen

"Rich, Well-Born, and Virtuous": *True Brahmins at the "Gateway to Heaven"*

If one proceeds northwest out of Harvard Square on Mount Auburn Street along the Charles River toward Belmont and Watertown, one will come upon what used to be known among Brahmins as the "Gateway to

Heaven"—Mount Auburn Cemetery. For generations of Brahmins, Mount Auburn was the ultimate or (if one was truly faithful) the penultimate place of grace. Within the brick walls of the cemetery and among its terraced gardens and ornate sepultures, the hum and noise of the city of humanity is stilled, and the vicissitudes of secular time seemingly come to rest. For the Brahmins, Mount Auburn was as close to the eternal peace and quiet of God's heaven as any earthly piece of landscape could come. Indeed, as Cleveland Amory humorously notes in his polite satire of Brahmin morays, *The Proper Bostonians,* one First Family matriarch was so moved by the tranquil beauty of Mount Auburn that she wrote an epic poem about it. This poem, apparently an apocryphal element of Brahmin legend, as it was never published, reportedly suggested that the cemetery's history was coterminous with the deity's divine plan and timetable for the birth and salvation of humanity itself. According to Amory, the poem set out "to tell the story of the cemetery in three phases: Mount Auburn As It Was on the Day of Creation, Mount Auburn As It Is, and Mount Auburn As It Shall Be on the Day of Resurrection" (1947: 257). As an earthly analog to the *nunc stans* (eternal now) of heaven, in the poetic imagination of Proper Bostonians, Mount Auburn was a fitting place for Brahmins to be laid to rest.

Even for those Brahmins whose faith in the eternal verities of the cemetery was not quite so abundant, Mount Auburn was still a most desirable spot for interment. As one Boston financier wrote to a friend in 1848, "I always persuaded myself that when H. is old enough for College you will take a place here and besides a little patch of Mount Auburn for yourself and your's in the neighborhood of ours. . . . The thought of an everlasting home for one's dust in a beautiful spot near to one's friends presents the dark future with rather a pleasing aspect" (quoted in Story, 1980: 113). Thus, in the face of a possibly "dark future" in the hereafter, the prospect of having one's Brahmin bones turn to dust within the peaceful grounds was a "pleasing" palliative for the uncertainties regarding one's ultimate eschatological destination.

However, in addition to the salience of Mount Auburn in the Brahmin imagination of death as either the portal to heaven or simply a nice place to be laid to rest, the cemetery had a more important function as an institutional and symbolic topos to Brahmins whose most pressing concerns were decidedly on the mortal side of heaven. According to Joseph Story (1980: 16–20, 160–167), Mount Auburn was one of the key elements of an intricate network of educational, charitable, financial, and industrial institutions that produced and sustained the hegemony of the Brahmin elite. Along with the Lowell Institute, the Athenaeum, the Academy of Arts and Sciences, the Natural History and Historical Societies, and the Horticultural Society (which governed its operations), Mount Auburn

Cemetery was part of what Story terms the "cultural complex" of Brahmin institutions. Membership in these organizations was highly selective. Thus, having a plot at Mount Auburn, like having a degree from Harvard, a seat at the Academy of Arts and Sciences, or a share in the Athenaeum, was a sign of one's prestige, status, and proper place as a "true" Brahmin.

What, then, did it mean in nineteenth-century Boston to be a "true" Brahmin, and how did Mount Auburn cemetery figure in the construction of this truth? In a memorial eulogy delivered at Mount Auburn to one of the most prominent Brahmin leaders of the mid-nineteenth century, Josiah Quincy, John Lothrop Motley offered a definition of "the Brahmin" that was as eloquent as it was concise. A Brahmin, inveighed Motley, is a "gentleman" who is "rich, well-born, and virtuous" (quoted in Story, 1980: 196). For all of its stark simplicity, Motley's definition involves a nuanced rhetorical logic and narrative trajectory that emplaces and emplots the Brahmin as an ethical subject of sovereign individuality within the symbolic and material landscape of Mount Auburn.

A man who was in possession of just one of these characteristics was not a "true" Brahmin, who had to evince or embody all three. Clearly, wealth was a necessary requirement for belonging to the elite, but it was in no way sufficient. As one of the primary mercantile, manufacturing, and financial centers of the nation, particularly before the Gilded Age, Boston was home to many parvenu entrepreneurs and businessmen. Yet most, for all their wealth, would never become recognized by Proper Boston as "true" Brahmins, as they would not have possessed what Oliver Wendell Holmes Sr. called "character." To be "well-born" was certainly a step in the right direction, but the connotative meaning of the term extended beyond the mere inheritance of wealth or even of a First Family name such as Eliot, Quincy, or Lowell. To be well-born also meant to be well-bred, and breeding entailed more than the quality of one's gene pool. To be well-bred meant that one passed, as did Josiah Quincy and all subsequent generations of Quincys, through a series of institutions that inculcated the core values of the Brahmin elite.

This institutional matrix, which encompassed educational institutions such as Harvard, financial institutions such as the Massachusetts Hospital Life Insurance Company, or charitable institutions such as McLean Asylum, constituted a disciplinary technology of selfhood through which Holmes's vaunted Brahmin "character" was produced. According to Ralph Waldo Emerson, "character" was defined as "moral order through the medium of individual nature" (quoted in Sussman, 1984: 274). Given this definition, the Brahmin understanding of character clearly embodies the dual meanings of ethos I discuss in Chapter 2. In a narrow sense, *ethos* or ethics refers to the conduct and character of autonomous individuals;

in the broader Heideggerian sense, *ethos* refers to a "dwelling place" or location within a larger collective moral geography. Through character, the inner qualities and outward behavior of autonomous individuals is harmonized with the moral order of the community. And character as embodied in the masculine virtues of self-command, rationality, prudence, stewardship, and citizenship was the fundament of Brahmin ideology upon which the practice of virtue in commerce and philanthropy was built.

The rhetorical logic of Motley's "true" Brahmin discourse can be summarized as follows. Wealth is a fluid or liquid resource of empowerment that courses through market society. In the case of the Brahmins, wealth as a fluid medium of power became territorialized in a dense network of social institutions that guided its flow through the community. Wealth was a necessary requirement in sustaining these institutions and in providing the individual Brahmin with means to enter and pass through them. Passage through these institutions represented a biographical trajectory and teleology of becoming a "true" Brahmin through the disciplinary formation of "character." Finally, these character traits were to be evinced in the Brahmin's virtuous conduct of everyday life and thus comprised a mode of governmentality. Here, however, I am less concerned with the specific socializing processes of these institutions through which character was formed than I am with how character was represented in discourse as product of territorialized wealth and productive fount of virtue. And at Mount Auburn cemetery, the earthly telos of the unfolding truth of Brahmin ideology, one is presented with the signs of Brahmin virtue making it possible to begin to understand the moral character of the Steward-Citizen.

Mount Auburn was a crucial part of the disciplinary institutional matrix through which the "true" Brahmin was produced, although its functions were clearly different from a university, a banking house, or an insane asylum. In addition to its obvious function as a place of burial for the dead, the cemetery was intentionally constructed as a place of retreat and reflection for the living. Beginning in the 1830s, the cemetery became, according to Story (1980: 113), a "fashionable promenade" for Cantabridgians in general and members of the nearby Harvard community in particular. The core belief of nineteenth-century New England Romanticism in the soul-transforming and character-building powers of the landscape of nature, which would find its most influential expression in Transcendentalism, was quite salient in the minds of the directors of the Horticultural Society who oversaw the management of the cemetery. Cemetery directors, such as Harvard professor Jacob Bigelow, envisioned Mount Auburn as a place where the good citizens of Boston and Cambridge, patrician and plebeian alike, could enhance the vitality of their bodies and souls by spending leisure time among the arbors and botanical gardens of its pristine landscape (Linden-Ward, 1989). But as a material space that was landscaped according to design and intention, Mount Auburn was more than a garden spot within which the living walked amid the tranquil beauty of nature. It was also a symbolic topos, a story space of emplotment and emplacement, wherein the moral identity of the Brahmin Steward-Citizen is literally given form through its inscription in the sepultural monuments of the dead. These monuments were intended to testify to the character and virtue of those in whose honor and memory they were erected, thus signifying to the living the enduring meaning of the "true" Brahmin.

Although the name "Mount Auburn" implies a rather grand or majestic topographical presence, the "Mount" itself is actually a gently sloping hill that sits atop the northern banks of the Charles River between Cambridge to the east and Belmont to the west. In spite of its undramatic quality as a geographical feature of the landscape, the hill is rich in signs and stories that evoke its meaning as symbolic topos. At the crest of the Mount, near Washington Tower, the signs of "true" Brahmin moral identity are many, but none is more indicative of Mount Auburn as topos than the gravesite of one Abraham W. Fuller. Fuller's resting place and monumental testament to his life as a Brahmin lies just to the eastern side of the hillcrest. There, inscribed upon a white marble obelisk about fifteen feet tall, is Fuller's epitaph. It reads:

> Abraham W. Fuller. Born in Princeton, Massachusetts 28 March 1781. Died in Boston 6 April 1847. In early life a merchant, enterprising, honest, successful; satisfied with accumulation, impelled by a manly desire of literary and intellectual pursuits, he became a member of the legal profession 25 May 1812. Distinguished by activity and force of intellect, correct in judgment, ingenious, cheerful, furnished with good learning, a welcome companion; in faith and practice a benevolent Christian; in spirit and action a beneficent citizen of the community.

The triumvirate of qualities that constitute true Brahmin identity—wealth, character, and virtue—are clearly present in the epitaph. However, most intriguing is the manner in which the qualities are arranged as parts of a teleologically ordered biographical narrative of fortune and virtue. The trajectory of Fuller's life as a Brahmin begins with the acquisition of wealth. In this segment of Fuller's biography, he is depicted as evincing the key virtues of the Smithian *homo mercator*: He is "enterprising," "honest," and therefore "successful" in the marketplace; mercantile virtue is rewarded by monetary fortune. Yet the "augmentation of fortune," to use Smith's phrase, represents only the first part of Fuller's narrative of becoming a "true" Brahmin. Around the age of thirty, Fuller finds that he is "satisfied with accumulation." The acquisition of wealth for the "true" Brahmin, as Samuel Eliot argues above, is never an end in itself. Rather, wealth provides an earthly, existential state of grace in the form of the "luxury of doing good," and as such fortune becomes the "stimulus, means, and reward" of virtues that are quite different from those that aid in the accumulation of wealth. Accordingly, having acquired enough wealth to secure his station, he is "impelled by manly desire" to develop his intellectual talents and capacities in other worldly vocations. So impelled, he becomes a lawyer.

This transition from merchant to attorney in Fuller's posthumous representation of self is so important that the very date upon which he entered the bar is prominently featured in the inscription. To those telling the tale of Fuller's life, the date carries as much significance as the dates of Fuller's birth and death. Indeed, this passage from merchant to lawyer can be interpreted as a moral and social metamorphosis that is enabled by his entrance into the graceful state of wealth and driven by a "manly desire" to reshape his character. In this regard, Fuller's choice of the legal profession as an occupation suiting his "manly desires" richly illustrates the relationship among wealth, character, and virtue that is central to Brahmin ideology and its figural embodiment in the Steward-Citizen. For Brahmin men of the nineteenth century, according to E. Digby Baltzell (1979: 336–352), law was considered to be a "gentlemanly" profession, that is, a profession suited for men of wealth and means whose material well-being was relatively assured. As a gentlemanly profession, its practitioners were supposedly motivated primarily by an interest in law as an intellectual enterprise and not as a means of accumulating wealth.[8] Law, like other gentlemanly professions such as medicine, the professorate, or the ministry, was a worldly vocation and secular calling through which wealthy men formed and cultivated their inner "character." From the inscription, it appears as though Fuller was as successful in the gentlemanly cultivation of character as he was in the mercantile pursuit of riches. He was, according to the narrative, an industrious lawyer who was prudently wise, intelligent, and ingeniously creative. He was also broadly educated and refined, cheerful in disposition, and thus a worthy and "welcome companion" for other gentlemen of his kind.

Finally, ascribing these quintessential hallmarks of good Brahmin character to Fuller frames the narrative telos of his epitaph: the virtuous insertion of the autonomous individual self into the social space of the community. Possessing wealth and character, Fuller is able to externalize his inner faith and personal qualities into a social practice of benevolence as a Christian and beneficence as a citizen. With wealth and character united to virtue, Abraham Fuller's story is now complete. The visitor to his monument reads the tale and, hopefully, is interpellated into a privileged subject position from which its meaning and import are properly understood: Abraham W. Fuller did not simply walk the earth as a good man; rather, he walked it as *true* Brahmin. The obelisk itself provides an architectural exclamation point to the end of the story as well as a signpost to the path of Fuller's spirit in the afterlife. Having lived the life of the true Brahmin, Fuller has ascended through the Gateway to Heaven, a "better angel" of Boston. It is so written.

Such "writing" of true Brahmin identity through Fuller's epitaph is a prime example of de Certeau's (1984) "scriptural economy" of discourse that I discuss in Chapter 1. That is to say, through the narrative construction of Fuller's biography his "life" becomes inscribed with the ideology of Brahmin character and virtue and is thus intended to be recognized by the visitor who reads it as being a testament to its moral and social truth. However, what is occurring in the topos of the Mount of Mount Auburn is more than the immediate circuit of representational exchange between discourse and the subjects it speaks that produces the *vraisemblance*, or the "reality effect" of discourse. Another circuit of exchange in the scriptural economy of Abraham W. Fuller is constituted by the presence of another obelisk, about ten feet away, that is the architectural double of the first.

This obelisk is a monument to the life of Fuller's brother, Henry. Inscribed upon it is a similar narrative of "true" Brahmin identity.

> Henry H. Fuller. Born in Princeton, Mass 1 July A.D. 1790. Died 15 September 1852. Was graduated at Harvard University 1811. Became a member of the Suffolk Bar 19 September 1815. Was married to Mary Buckminster Stone 24 August 1826.
> Accomplished and accurate as a scholar; Learned and skillful as a lawyer; Public spirited and useful as a citizen; Courteous to all men;
> A reverent lover of the past, Yet zealous for new forms of truth;
> A devout believer in the Christian Religion, And a constant supporter of its institutions.
> This monument erected by will of his wife, Less a witness to his mental gifts,
> Than as a tribute to his fidelity and affection, As a husband and father

However, we are not "witness" to these final qualities, nor are we to Mary Fuller or Henry Fuller's family. The family is nowhere to be found, and her epitaph, which contains no narrative, is on the opposite side of the obelisk, facing away from the hill and Washington Tower. Indeed, in attempting to find her inscription one risks falling down the hill. Apparently, her presence was an afterthought at the time and quite tenuous in the present. Indeed, the very doubling of the obelisks constructs a circuit of representation that enacts a metaphysics of presence and self-same sovereignty that resists this intrusion of the feminine, the domestic, and the private into the domain of the masculine, the civic, and the public.

This is because the second obelisk had another function in addition to being a monument to the life of Fuller the younger: to extend both Fullers' testament to true Brahmin identity beyond their small spot in the Gateway to Heaven. As a matched pair, the obelisks are meant to be looked at together, and in order to do so the beholder must move back toward Washington Tower (and away from Mary's epitaph) to a viewing position where the eye is equidistant from both monuments. Stepping back to view the obelisks simultaneously, one arrives at the vantage point of the visual perspectival triangle of linear perception. As I discuss in Chapters 1 and 3, the emergence of linear perspective during the Renaissance is central to the moral economy of wealth, as it provides the phenomenological foundation for the mapping and insertion of the autonomous male individual into the newly conceived space of the social. Through the gaze of linear perspective, the social world becomes a terrain to be possessed through both vision and action. This is a perfect example of what Doreen Massey (1993) calls the "power-geometry" of cartography that articulates space, place, and identity. As with John Norris's gesture to the world, the Fuller obelisks enact a similar power-geometry of visual as well as rhetorical possession, of setting into motion the symbolic circuit of exchange between the individual of wealth and the territory through which his wealth flows. Now, with the help of the dead Fuller brothers, we can better understand how the living Norris is able to claim sovereignty over that which he sees from the Capital City Club.

The Fullers' claim to true Brahmin identity is constructed on the basis of the narratives of epitaphs. Moreover, these narratives are spatial stories that map material space as a place of moral identity. The *vraisemblance* of the moral truth of Brahmin identity is enhanced by its inscription upon that which lies within the field of vision created by assuming the perspectival position between the two obelisks. What one sees framed by the obelisks is the good city of Boston (and Cambridge) and the array of institutions that served to create and sustain Brahmin hegemony and testify to the legitimacy of their moral authority and cultural leadership: Harvard University, the Massachusetts General Hospital complex, the Athenaeum, the downtown financial district, and the Unitarian Church on Boylston Street. Thus, the biographies of Abraham W. Fuller and Henry H. Fuller become resonant affirmations of the beneficence of these institutions and are inscribed upon the built environment of Boston so that the symbolic topos of true Brahmin identity is mapped upon the material territory of cityscape. Positioned by the narrative teleology of Fullers' epitaphs and the physical placement of the obelisks,

Boston becomes for the spectator atop Mount Auburn, as Samuel Eliot argues, "an agreeable subject of contemplation," for it is a virtuous place where "wealth is combined with liberality." Emplacement becomes emplotment and literally constitutes a monumental story space that performs the know-how and can-do-ness of the Fullers as true Brahmins.

Finally, the double circuit of symbolic exchange that is constituted by the obelisks and the epitaph does not simply produce a metonymic relation of identity and equivalency between the character of the Fullers, the philanthropic institutions of the Brahmins, and the liberality of both through which "comfort extended through the whole community" (Eliot) of Boston and its environs. The suturing relation of unity between the Fullers and their city that is forged through the power-geometry of perception is hierarchical as well as inclusionary. The site of Mount Auburn Cemetery affords the man of wealth (either as living flesh or ghostly memory) a spatial vantage point of sight from which he can look *down* upon the community in order to claim it as possession. Yet what constitutes the moral "truth" of this hierarchical gaze of possession as a power that is right, true, and natural are the discourses of stewardship and citizenship with which the gaze is articulated.[9]

These discourses configure the Steward-Citizen not simply as a man of wealth but as man whose "wealth and liberality" puts him in a position of paternalistic authority with respect to the community. As Mauss would put it, on the basis of this double circuit of representation the man of wealth becomes *magister*. In a word, both discourse and gaze provide a magisterial symbolic topos in which Fuller and the community of Boston are bound together in a relationship of "trust." Emplotment becomes emplacement. In executing their duties and calling as trustees, rendered in epitaphs as "Benevolent Christians" and "Beneficent Citizens," the Fullers are able to claim their identity as true Brahmins and "get their wings" as "better angels."

The Problematic of the "Trustee": Articulating the "Corpus" of Wealth Through the Steward-Citizen

In a manner befitting the company of angels, we will pretend that we too have wings, and although we will not ascend to the heavens with Magisters Fuller, we will fly to our next destination. Taking to the air above Mount Auburn, we head across the Charles River and toward Boston Harbor. As we venture east and look down upon the cityscape, the signs of more than two centuries of Brahmin beneficence are many and impressive. Looking north along the line of Massachusetts Avenue as it bisects Cambridge, we see the first and most famous gift of the Brahmins to the eternal pursuit of *veritas*, Harvard University. Moving our focus in a slow arc from north to northeast across the Charles River estuary, we behold the Academy of Arts and Sciences, the Boston Athenaeum, the Museum of Science, and the Massachusetts General Hospital complex. As we approach the Boston side of the Charles, we shift our gaze south, look beyond the elegant row houses and apartments of Back Bay, and see the Brigham and Women's Hospital, the Isabella Stewart Gardner Museum, the Museum of Fine Arts, and Boston Symphony Hall. Although each was founded under a different set of historical circumstances with different specific purposes in the minds of the Brahmins who created them, they share the communality of the ideal of "true" Brahminism being given "institutional flesh," as Paul DiMaggio has described the Museum of Fine Arts and the Boston Symphony Orchestra (DiMaggio, 1986: 209).

DiMaggio's use of a corporeal metaphor to describe the spatialized performance and territorialization of the beneficent impulses of the Brahmins is interesting because it (unwittingly) evokes the figural rhetoric of the body that suffuses the discourse of the Steward-Citizen. From John Winthrop's sermon-command to Puritan compatriots aboard the *Arabella* to follow "A Modell of Christian Charity," to Henry Lee Higginson's appeal to Brahmin brethren to fund a symphony orchestra that would impose a hegemonic, high-culture harmony upon the noise and din of the "grotesque" low culture of Boston's ethnic working classes, the community has been rhetorically rendered as a corporeal territory that the rich and well-born were to virtuously discipline and manage. This metaphorical figuring of the community as body has deep roots in the emergence of political economy that becomes articulated with the discourses of stewardship and citizenship in the ideal of true Brahminism in the nineteenth century. As Foucault (1991) and Dean (1991) argue, the emergence of a political economy of government based upon a conception of the market was a mutation of a political *oeconomic* conception of the territory over which the sovereign holds sway as a household. The relationship between the sovereign and the inhabitants of his territory was patriarchal in nature; they were seen as the corpus, the material, bodily substance of his household, to be "wisely governed as a family . . . for the common welfare of all" (Foucault, 1991: 92). Within the corpus of the household, sovereign and subjects were bound together by interdependent relations of service and obligation. Similarly, within the discourse of the Steward-Citizen, the community is rendered as a patriarchally ordered and managed corporeal household that is held together and wisely governed through philanthropic beneficence.

In order to better understand community as corpus and the position of Steward-Citizen within, as well as to orient our flight toward terminus, consider Nelson Aldrich's reflections on what he terms the "extended patrimony" of the "old money" elites of Philadelphia, New York, "but above all Boston" (1988: 60). A *patrimony* is a legacy or inheritance that is passed down from generation to generation, and being an inheritor of old money himself, Aldrich speaks about the import of this legacy with sacral awe and reverence. The extended patrimony of old money, according to Aldrich, is more than a family name, wealth, property, a legacied admission to Groton and Harvard, a membership in the Somerset Club, or a position at an elite law firm or banking house. Although these items can be essential to the lives of inheritors, they are given a coherent structure and meaning by being part of a spatial zone of engagement within which the privately held wealth and power of old money is extended outward into the community so that they become bound together. Aldrich (1988: 59–60) describes the phenomenological dynamics of the extended patrimony:

> [The] extended patrimony radiates outward from a nuclear private property to more remote relationships with public property, or, as policy analysts might put it, from private goods to public ones. The good in question could begin with something quite insignificant: an island off the coast of Maine, for example, handed down in metaphorical (or actual) trust from generation to generation in the same family. But from there it is a short leap of the imagination to the operations of the Maine Coast Heritage Trust, a state environmental group, where the beneficiary suddenly finds himself contemplating a rather different notion of property than "his" island evoked, a broader notion of trust, and a more comprehensive notion of posterity.

This evocation of the extended patrimony, within which the sovereignty of the privately held trust is extended to encompass the public sphere and its future history, is couched in almost mystical terms.[10] Bequeathed an "insignificant" island as part of his legacy, perhaps one such as the Bush family compound off Kennebunkport, Maine, the inheritor "suddenly" experiences a profound epiphany born of the symbolic alchemy of metonymic transubstantiation: The corpus or material substance of his inheritance becomes identified with a "rather different notion of property," the body of the community and its future that the inheritor holds, shapes and molds as "posterity." However, this process of eliding the private and the public through what Aldrich calls the "radiant pulse of imagination" (1988: 60) of old money becomes less mystical if understood as an example of what Deleuze and Guattari term "territorialization." As I discuss in Chapter 4, territorialization involves the encoding and structuring of flows of desire. In this case, desire is encoded in terms of the temporal ordering of the "trust." The trust is handed down from forbears and is a source of private power and public authority. As such, the trust is a state of grace, as it provides a symbolic framing and institutional framework for the enactment of the virtue of civic responsibility in the present. If the duties and obligations entailed by the trust are discharged properly, the name and deeds of the inheritor will be inscribed in the trust as it is bequeathed to the future as posterity. It is within this interpretive framework of the trust that Harvard, the Museum of Fine Arts, the Athenaeum, and so on can be understood as monuments to the Brahmins' extended patrimony.

This notion of the trust is central to understanding the figure of the Steward-Citizen, as it is through the position of the "trustee"—one who manages the trust and its corpus—that the virtues of this moral character are enacted. Yet in order to analyze the rhetorical and symbolic meaning of the trust as corpus and how it is constitutive of the "better angels" of Boston and their institutions, it is necessary to foreground the material nature of its substance. Aldrich, in spite of his mystical reveries, understands that the essential material substance of trusts is money. Furthermore, like Deleuze and Guattari, Aldrich understands that in capitalist society desire flows through the fluid medium of money, and it is through this medium that desire is territorialized. Without money, there can be no extended patrimony, no magical transubstantiation of the corpus of the private into the corpus of the public through acts of beneficence.

Indeed, the logic and language of this transubstantiation is embedded in the legal definition and structuring of the trust. The "material base" of the trust, as Aldrich calls it, that is passed down to inheritors is the trust fund (1988: 59). The trust fund is an array of property, assets, and cash that provides income for the beneficiary. The core of the trust fund is the principal, which is wealth or capital that produces income for heirs. In the terminology of testamentary and trust law, which has its origins in nineteenth-century Massachusetts, the principal is called the "corpus" (Marcus, 1992: 62).[11] This corpus, quite literally, is the material embodiment of the will of the testator or founder of a family fortune in that it constrains as well as empowers heirs. There is an almost sacred quality to the principal; as many inheritors said in their interviews, the cardinal rule of trust funds is that the principal "is not to be touched," because it is the source of income for the current generation and the wealth that will be passed on to future ones. As Marcus (1992: 25) points out, the capital of the trust is "collective" in that it belongs to and sutures together members of a wealthy dynastic family within and across generations. Accordingly, the legal structuring of the principal of the trust (basically, as impervious to any financial designs by heirs contrary to the will of the founder), as well as its symbolic meaning (as an inviolable sacred bond between generations that is to be respected and revered), comprises the first step in the discursive logic of transubstantiation inscribed in the notion of trust. That is to say, the principal as corpus becomes constitutive of and identified with the filial body of the extended family. This step in the process of creating the extended patrimony of the trust in turn becomes the basis for the second step, which is to extend the body of family wealth to include the body of the community.

However, the corpus is not a passively inert teat from which successive generations of inheritors draw financial succor and sustenance. As Stuart Dean, one of the "better angels" I discuss in Chapter 3, stated quite clearly, in order for the family trust to perpetuate itself and for a legacy to be passed down from generation to generation, the principal must be actively put to work in order to produce more money.[12] In other words, it must flow and be territorialized in the form of business enterprises and investments that in turn provide the money that will flow through the community as philanthropic gifts and be territorialized in institutions that such gifts found and sustain. As G. Marcus (1992) and P. Hall (1982) explore in great detail, nineteenth-century Brahmins invented and perfected the legal and institutional mechanisms through which the corpus of the trust would be monetarily fruitful and temporally enduring. Although the organizational innovations of the Brahmins that engendered the modern form of trust were many, none were more significant or profound than the establishment of the Massachusetts Hospital Life Insurance Company.

Founded between 1818 and 1823 by a consortium of investors who represented almost all of the prominent industrial and mercantile Brahmin families, the company's ostensible purpose was charitable: profits from sale of life insurance annuities were to be shared with its namesake, the Massachusetts General Hospital (White, 1955: 9). Yet its primary function was most definitely not philanthropic. Indeed, John Lowell, a chief architect and shareholder of the company, told fellow Brahmin Samuel Appleton, "It [the company] is *eminently* the Savings bank of the wealthy . . . the best institution on earth" (quoted in Dalzell, 1987: 54). Of course, then as now, the wealthy do not "save"; they invest and thereby enhance their wealth by circulating their money through the market.

Although scholars have described the money-making and circulating operations of the Massachusetts Hospital Life Insurance Company in mind-numbing detail (cf. esp. White, 1955), no description is more compelling and insightful that of Aldrich himself. Using a metaphor that is deeply resonant with Deleuze and Guattari's notion of "desiring-machines" that structure flows of desire, Aldrich calls the company (and other trust and investment companies modeled after it) a "Newtonian machine of money production, money entrustment and investment, and money expenditure, a circulatory machine whose movement was supposed to be cared for by heirs and assigns forever. . . . Money flowed . . . but it was the physics of this system, *how* it flowed, that was significant"

(1988: 61). To recall George Bush's words in his speech about the "better angels" of capitalism, there is a "magic" to this machine, the magic of transubstantiating the corpus of privately held wealth into public power through the machine of the trust.

According to Aldrich, the money machine of the Brahmins consisted of several distinct yet interdependent circuits through which money flowed. The first circuit, of course, was structured around the "money production" apparatus of Brahmin-owned mercantile and industrial enterprises, the most important of which were the new textile mills in the company towns organized by and named after the Lowells and the Lawrences. Such enterprises, and the productive labor of the new American industrial working class within them, were the fount of nineteenth-century Brahmin wealth. Money then flowed through a second circuit, within which family fortunes were formed into trusts, their corpuses being circulated in the money market as investment capital. In this circuit, money was primarily invested back into Brahmin enterprises in textiles, railroads, or real estate (Jaher, 1982: 52–53). Yet also within this circuit money flowed from the market, albeit "in carefully stipulated amounts," to the trusts' beneficiaries as a capitalized, existential state of grace within which it was "unnecessary for them to send themselves into any market at all" (Aldrich, 1988: 62). Finally, as Aldrich notes, there was "another beat and pulse" in the system, a third circuit that "sent assets and imaginations out towards the public" (Aldrich, 1988: 62). This was the circuit of philanthropic expenditure:

> It was the declared purpose of the patrician founders of this system, and the practice of their inheritors, that some part of the family's income and savings should go the care and maintenance of the welfare and cultural institutions of Boston. The very name of the "savings bank for the wealthy" points to one such institution, the Massachusetts General Hospital. Harvard College, and later its professional schools, was another. And as the nineteenth century went on, there would be more and more of them: the Symphony, the Museum of Fine Arts, the Trustees of the Reservations and so forth—though never so many as to tax the prudence or unduly swell the ranks of the patriciate. (Aldrich, 1988: 62)

Aldrich's invocation of the Smithian virtue of "prudence" in characterizing the Brahmin perspective that framed the philanthropic flowing of "assets and imaginations" through their money machine brings us closer to our destination—and to a rendezvous with a contemporary "better angel" of Boston. At the coordinating center of the different circuits of money that comprise the material corpus of the extended patrimony was (and still is) were trust companies like Massachusetts Life. The company's management of the corpus, whether in the form of investment capital, family trust funds, or philanthropic endowments and eleemosynary funds, was to be governed by the standard of prudence, another enduring Brahmin contribution to trusts law. The Prudent Man Rule (also known as the Massachusetts Rule) emerged in an 1830 lawsuit between Harvard and the trustee of a family trust (the college being one of its beneficiaries); the new standard imagined an ideal trustee who would engage in the "safe and discreet investment" of the corpus of a trust (Hall, 1982: 119). Uncannily echoing Smith's mediations in *The Theory of Moral Sentiments* on how *homo mercator* cultivates the virtue of prudence by taking the perspective of the "Impartial Spectator," the court said that the ideal trustee should guide his management of the trust by observing "how men of prudence, discretion and intelligence manage their own affairs" (quoted in Marcus, 1992: 64).

As L. Friedman (1964), G. Marcus (1992: 64–70), and P. Hall (1982: 119–122) argue, this simple rule had profound consequences for the internal organization and structural cohesion of the Brahmins in particular and the American capitalist class in general. One consequence is especially pertinent for understanding the moral character of the Steward-Citizen. The Prudent Man Rule legally enshrined the autonomy and independence of the trustee not only from the beneficiaries of a trust but also from public control or interference. Moreover, the only source of guidance as to what was prudent, judicious, and wise in structuring flows of money would be the internal standards and behavior of the men of the Brahmin elite. After all, as Friedman (1964: 554) notes, the rule "presupposes a certain class of trustees: men of business ability, whose social and economic position allows them to easily observe how their peers manage large estates for themselves or others." In other words, by fashioning a new legal standard the Brahmins conferred upon themselves—and themselves alone—the power and authority to use their wealth for whatever purposes, private or public, that *they* deemed to be "prudent." Accordingly, on the basis of trusteeship as technology of power/knowledge and mode of governmentality the Brahmins would be able to stand as guardians of the public good and enact their vision of the true Brahmin ideal.

More specifically, the "ideal trustee" became, in Stuart Hall's (1986) sense of the term, a site of "articulation" that was central to the practice of Brahmin beneficence and the formation of their cultural hegemony in Boston. For Hall, *articulation* refers to two social processes that are crucial to the creation and maintenance of a social group's hegemony. The first process is "linking" or "connecting"; the second is "speaking" or "enunciating." The juridical establishment of the autonomous trustee provided the Brahmins foremost a set of institutional positions, from which they could control and manage flows of capital through the circuits of their own money machine. In structural and organizational terms, they were able to create an intricate network of interlocking directorships and trusteeships that articulated or linked together positions of power in mercantile and industrial enterprises, banking houses, investment firms, and trust management firms with those in philanthropic, educational, cultural, and welfare institutions.

However, for my purposes, the more significant consequence of the trusteeship is that it enabled, and continues to enable, men of inherited wealth to articulate or speak their moral identity as Steward-Citizens. More specifically, the structural position of the trustee as one who manages a trust on behalf of others functions, to borrow a term from Elspeth Probyn (1993:13), as a "problematic of the self." Building upon Althusser's (1970) concept of the theoretical *problematique* as an epistemological framework of knowing, Probyn argues that the conjuncture of the discursive and ontological dimensions of experience provides the conditions of possibility for "speaking the self." I would argue that the position of the trustee offers such a conjuncture for men of inherited wealth. It provides them with an existential site or location for the practice of beneficence through which they speak or enunciate their identity as virtuous men. In this regard, the position of the trustee is a site of articulation in two further senses. First, it is a site of a discursive practice of articulation where the rhetorical moments of invocation and evocation, whereby the fortune of a trust inherited is linked with the virtue of a trust enacted, are conjoined in the process of crafting moral identity. Second, through this rhetorical conjuring of the self as a benevolent steward and beneficent citizen, the man of inherited wealth is able to articulate or speak the language of transubstantiation whereby the body of his trust becomes articulated or linked with the body of the commonweal.

Now we are ready to end our flight and meet our contemporary "better angel" of Boston. Crossing into the airspace of downtown Boston, we begin our descent over the glittering golden dome of the Massachusetts State House. It was there, in the early part of the nineteenth century, that the Brahmin-controlled legislature gave the courts equity jurisdiction over the disposition of trusts. Indeed, the same courts that promulgated the Prudent Man Rule and engendered the modern form of the trust lay just ahead, on Court Street, as we make our final descent to our destination, State Street—and the heart of the financial district of Boston. Here, at 70 State Street, the Massachusetts Hospital Life Insurance Company opened its offices in 1823. The company no longer exists in form or function, as it did when it was "eminently the Savings Bank for the wealthy" in the nineteenth century. It now operates as the Massachusetts General

Life Insurance Company, and although the members of its board of directors are predominantly Brahmin in lineage, it no longer functions as the primary trust institution of Boston's wealthy. Newer investment and trust management firms were founded in the late nineteenth and early twentieth centuries. These firms, such as Kidder, Peabody and Company, the Wellington Management Trust, Thorndike, Doran, Paine and Lewis, and the Boston Safe Deposit and Trust Company, continue to dominate the trust business in the United States and to this day are predominantly directed and managed by Brahmin descendants. Their offices are also here on State Street; walking into one such office, we meet a modern-day Brahmin trustee, through whom the Steward-Citizen speaks and is spoken.

Fortune, Virtue, and Trusteeship in Modern Boston

The "Long Run": The Extended Patrimony of the Lowells. In discussing the differences in the management of family wealth between the upper classes of Boston and Philadelphia, E. Digby Baltzell (1979) argues that the true Brahmin ideal is alive and well on State Street. Using the metaphor of a footrace to describe the longevity of Brahmin wealth and prominence in banking and finance, Baltzell (208–209) writes:

> Egalitarian and individualistic cultures of great social and economic mobility tend to be hundred yard cultures; hierarchical and communal cultures are more likely to emulate the style of the long distance runner. Similarly, democracies foster the making of fabulous fortunes; aristocracies, the preservation of more modest ones. . . . Bostonians tend to be long-distance runners whereas hundred yard dash cut flowers are more characteristic of Philadelphia.[13] And so it has been with wealth and the preservation thereof. . . . Today, though hundred yard speculators flock to Wall Street, the long distance runners entrust their fortunes to the money mangers of Boston. . . . A. Lawrence Lowell once expressed concern that nobody in his family was still engaged in money-making. He need not have. For scions of early Colonial Families are now doing well as money-managers: names like Paul Cabot, Richard Saltonstall, John P. Chase, Augustus Loring, John Lowell, and Nick Thorndike still grace the chief executive offices of the city's leading financial institutions. Boston's values have nowhere been better expressed than when a member of Thorndike, Doran, Paine and Lewis told the [Boston] Globe: "Divorced from Wall Street and the herd, we are thought to have an independent point of view. People think "here's a group that can sit back and reflect."

The "Boston values" to which Baltzell refers are those embodied in the trustee—the wise, judicious, and prudent management of the corpus of family wealth so that it preserves the power and prestige of "aristocratic" families over the multigenerational course of the "long distance run." However, Baltzell's admiration for the money managers of State Street is not limited to prudent investment practices. Speaking, for example, of the many civic contributions of George Ticknor, Harvard professor and one of the original stockholders and directors in the Massachusetts Hospital Life Insurance Company, Baltzell opines that nineteenth-century Brahmin Boston was "the one place where wealth and the knowledge of how to use it are apt to coincide" (1979: 42).

Thus for Baltzell, the Brahmins were sterling examples of the virtuous know-how and can-do-ness of wealth as power/knowledge. He is therefore deeply gratified to conclude, upon examining the lengthy business and philanthropic résumé of a contemporary State Street trustee, one John Lowell, that "money-making and civic responsibility still mark the breed" in Boston (1979: 209). In fact, the very same John Lowell confirmed for Baltzell the enduring presence of the Brahmin ideal of "character"; he is the "better angel" of Boston who will articulate for us the moral "truth" of the Steward-Citizen.

I am tempted to say that as a Lowell this person needs no introduction. Yet John Lowell's very name serves as introduction, and it is impossible to evade his identification.[14] The family name is a synecdoche of his extended patrimony of a fortune consisting of a literal and figural trust that serves as a condition of possibility for him to articulate a virtuous moral identity. Therefore, a brief historical introduction to Lowell's (auto-)biographical moral tale is necessary to understand how he embodies the problematic of the trustee inscribed in the figure of the Steward-Citizen.

The history of the Lowell family is coterminous with the history of the formation and ascendance of Brahmin economic and cultural hegemony in Boston itself. It is also extremely long and complex. Accordingly, this synopsis is meant to elucidate the composition of the corpus, both material and symbolic, of the trust bequeathed to John Lowell.[15] As Lowell says in his interview, "We've [the Lowells] been around a long time"—and indeed they have. The first Lowells emigrated to the Massachusetts Bay Colony in 1638 and quickly became prominent members of the three institutional elites—ministers, merchants, magistrates—that composed what was called the Standing Order of colonial New England (Hall, 1982: 21). Prominent and respectable in colonial and federalist-era New England, the Lowells became wealthy and powerful thanks to the textile industry. Francis Cabot Lowell, along with his cousin, Patrick Tracy Jackson, founded the Boston Manufacturing Company in Waltham in 1814; it was the first textile factory and modern industrial corporation in the United States. In 1833, after Francis Cabot Lowell's death, Jackson started the Merrimac Manufacturing Company in a rural settlement along the Merrimac River that would become Lowell, Massachusetts.

The Lowells and the Jacksons, along with other prominent Brahmin families, then formed a business consortium, the Boston Associates, which dominated the textile industry throughout the nineteenth century. As R. Dalzell (1987) explores in great detail, the Boston Associates created and set into motion the great Brahmin money-making and circulation machine described by Aldrich. In addition to the Massachusetts Hospital Life Insurance Company, the Boston Associates created a series of other financial institutions, such as the Provident Institution for Savings, the Suffolk regional bank system, and the investment houses of Lee, Higginson and Co. and the Old Colony Trust Co. These institutions kept the money flowing through the circuits of the money machine, forming the labor of slaves (who picked the cotton) and of New England farm girls (who turned it into cloth in the Lowell mills) into an enduring corpus of wealth, of which our John Lowell was ultimately a beneficiary.

However, the wealth that John Lowell inherited in trust is far less significant in the construction of his moral identity than is the position of trusteeship that was bequeathed to him. Like other Brahmin families, the Lowells were centrally involved in the funding and management of all the philanthropic institutions that gave shape to the aristocracy's hegemony during the nineteenth century. There is, perhaps, no better example of the Brahmin notion of trust than the Lowell Institute. At the core of the trust is, of course, the corpus of money. In his will, John Lowell Jr. (the son of textile entrepreneur Francis Cabot Lowell) bequeathed $250,000 to found the Lowell Institute in 1836. Although small by contemporary standards, this bequest was the second largest in the history of the United States at the time.[16] This endowment was sent flowing through the circuits of the Brahmin money machine, and it continues to circulate to this day. Prudently managed and invested by successive generations of trustees and Brahmin brethren on State Street, its value at the time of the interview exceeded $13 million, with annual interest of approximately $600,000. The corpus constitutes, according to John Lowell, "a tidy piece of change."

Although that description may seem woefully inappropriate, it is standard rhetorical understatement characteristic of the language of inheritors of wealth in general and the moral identity of the Brahmins in particular. Foregrounding the magnitude of one's wealth, whether it be held individually or in trust, is not only impolite; more importantly, doing so violates the moral grounding of Brahmin power by privileging possession over purpose, means over ends. The ordering and territorialization of the corpus makes the "piece of change" "tidy," and consequently a site and sign of virtue, is more important than the sheer size of the fortune itself. And the Lowell Institute corpus gets its territorializing order from the beneficent desires of the founder articulated in his will and inscribed in the structure of the trust instrument.

The transubstantiative logic of the trust as extended patrimony is evident in the terms of John Lowell Jr.'s will: In framing the mission of the Lowell Institute, he explicitly linked disposition of the private corpus with the future body of the community. The purpose of the endowment, Lowell wrote, was to enhance the "prosperity of my native land, New England" (quoted in Greenslet, 1946: 197). Lowell's vision of prosperity was indicative of the Brahmin ideal of character in that it had less to do with the satisfaction of material wants and desires than with the cultivation of virtue, both spiritual and civic. Such prosperity "depended, first on the moral qualities and second on the intelligence and information of its inhabitants" (quoted in Greenslet, 1946: 197). These two conditions of prosperity where in turn dependent upon the "truth of those moral and religious precepts, with which alone men can be secure of their happiness in this world and that to come" (quoted in Weeks, 1966: 42). To this end of disseminating truth to the inhabitants of Boston, the Lowell Institute was to support vocational and moral education programs for the working class as well as to stage free lectures to the educated public, meaning the upper and middle classes, on a variety of topics ranging from science to literature. Although couched in the lofty terms of secular and spiritual virtue, the mission was to aggressively insert the presence and influence of Brahmin religious, cultural, and social values in Boston civil society.[17]

In spite of its obvious public function as one of the dominant cultural institutions in New England, control over the Lowell Institute and its functions was to remain the private property of the Lowell family and, indirectly, their fellow Brahmins. John Lowell Jr.'s will stipulated that management would be the prerogative of a sole trustee, who was to be a male member of the Lowell family. Each trustee was empowered to personally select his successor so as to keep control within the family. This trustee, in turn, was subject to the oversight of the board of trustees of the Athenaeum, themselves members of other prominent Brahmin clans. In spite of the "visitation" oversight of the Athenaeum, the Lowell Institute and its trustee constitute a unique example of the Brahmin notion of trusteeship as legal institution and discursive logic (Story, 1980: 16). The Lowell Institute is one of a handful of U.S. charitable trusts using the governance structure of a single trustee, which is handed down to lineal descendants of a family. As John Lowell told us in his interview, the Lowell Institute was given legal sanction by the Massachusetts legislature and the courts to concentrate public cultural authority in the hands of a lone family representative on the basis of the principle of *corporation solus,* which recognizes the individual trustee as a corporate entity. This legal identification of individual as corporation sets up the figurative logic of transubstantiation that comprises the extended patrimony within which John Lowell's moral identity as Steward-Citizen is located.

"Pulling the Weight of Wealth": Fortune, Virtue, and the Discourse of Stewardship. The individual as trustee is a position through which the myriad meanings of the trust as corpus flow and merge. The initial corpus of the monetary endowment is territorialized in the form of a charitable trust that as a corporate body is the institutional embodiment of the will of the founder. As the trustee is identified as the corporate body in and of himself, he is also the embodiment of the will of the founder. Each successive trustee is bound to the terms of the trust, enacting the will of the founder through the generations. As John Lowell says, as the sole trustee of the Lowell Institute he is "working under the will of this gentleman [John Lowell Jr.]," which has provided him with his "marching orders." In this manner, the patrimony of the founder is extended through time as his corpus is transformed into a filial collective or corporate identity that links each trustee to his forbears in carrying out the duties and obligations attendant to his position. Finally, in fulfilling the duty of trusteeship through the practice of beneficence, the corpus of the founder and family are articulated with the corpus of the broader community.

On the basis of the position of trustee, and the nuanced discursive logic inscribed in it as a problematic of the self, the latter-day John Lowell articulates his moral identity. In fact, it is hard to find a better example of a man who speaks from and through the position of trustee as a site of spatial practice. Indeed, Lowell spoke to us in the office of one of the smaller, yet exclusive and prestigious, personal trust banking management firms on State Street, where he is a managing partner. Thus, in addition to being the sole trustee of the Lowell Institute, he holds in trust the corpuses of many family fortunes. The management of trusts has been Lowell's sole career occupation and, as a vocation, has been a source of deep satisfaction for him. He told us that the fiduciary management of trusts is "fascinating" and a "wonderful business to be in." The basis of his satisfaction can be located in the position of trusteeship as a site for the enactment of virtue. He is able to coordinate and control the flows of capital through the magical territorializing machine that links wealth accumulation and philanthropy, private virtue with the public good. As a spatial zone of engagement, the trustee position has enabled Lowell, by his own account, to act virtuously in three ways. First, the trust business has enabled him to accumulate wealth far beyond that which he inherited. Second, from his base of operations on State Street, he is able to enact the quintessential Brahmin virtue of trusteeship—the prudent investment and management of capital—by being on the board of directors of a dozen or so other leading Brahmin banking houses and trust companies (including the successor to the Massachusetts General Hospital Life Insurance Company). Finally, he has been able to articulate himself with a truly impressive array of philanthropic institutions through the giving of money and time. He is on the board of trustees of well more than thirty organizations, ranging from universities and hospitals to public television stations and museums. For Lowell, "all of this [his philanthropic involvements] goes along with the trust business, getting to manage so much property." Accordingly, Lowell would probably accept with great pride Baltzell's characterization of him as a sign that "money-making and civic responsibility still mark the breed in Boston."

However, this synopsis of Lowell's vocation does not get us very far in understanding the complex relationship of fortune and virtue that is inscribed in the position of trusteeship as a problematic of the self and embodied in the figure of the Steward-Citizen. This complexity is apparent at the very beginning of Lowell's (auto-)biographical narrative, when he presents himself as having an ambivalent relation to the fortune he inherited. Here I am referring to Lowell's fortune in a double sense, as his inheritance consisted of money as well as the vocational position of trusteeship. In terms of the latter, Lowell not only inherited the sole trusteeship of the Lowell Institute; he was also provided with an executive position within one of the most prestigious trust companies on State Street, which has been run by family members and other Brahmin clans for several generations. This position, as Lowell himself indicates, provided him the financial resources and institutional networks to engage in philanthropy. Yet in spite of the obvious fact of fortune in his life, Lowell initially speaks in a way that seemingly vitiates its importance in his sense of self-identity.

For example, when asked about the size of his inheritance, Lowell responded, "Well I really haven't inherited [much]. I tell you specifically, I think I inherited $100,000 which, as inherited wealth goes, isn't very much. No, it's [his wealth] mainly what I've been able to make." From the outset of his moral tale, then, Lowell wants to claim for himself the virtue of self-making in the market that is generally the hallmark of the discourse of *homo mercator*. Indeed, Lowell explains the existence of the wealthy as a class as ultimately being a function of the virtues of entrepreneurship. In a revealing reflection on the relationship between fortune and virtue, Lowell argues that "there are wealthy people because somewhere along the line somebody was motivated to work a little harder than the next guy. Either work a little harder or a little smarter, invented something, had the greater initiative, and so he was able to accumulate a little more than next guy."

It is likely that if he were asked about the source of his family wealth, Lowell would reflect upon the mercantile, industrial, and financial enterprises of Francis Cabot Lowell and the Boston Associates and make the same argument. That is to say, the virtuous practices that render the possession of wealth legitimate are to be located in its making. But within this legitimating argument, where will a man who has inherited a fortune to ground his moral identity? One answer was given by Lowell himself: He has taken monetary inheritance and increased it through his own labor in the business world. However, this argument only partially "works" as a rhetoric of selfhood, as it cannot morally account for the profound presence of the extended patrimony of the trust in the lives of inheritors as an spatial zone of engagement. Indeed, Lowell seemingly evades the task of making a moral argument for the legitimacy of extended patrimonies by offering a pointed critique of inherited wealth and its perpetuation in the form of trusts and other tax shelters: "Now, then, a lot of the wealth that has been passed down through families has been squandered. From shirt-sleeve to shirt-sleeve in three generations. There is a lot of that, and I think that it is a disgrace, really. These tax breaks that allow wealth to be passed on are a disgrace because I don't think wealth should be allowed to perpetuate itself. I think we should all earn it ourselves." Considering the fact that Lowell was himself a beneficiary of a trust fund, and that he is a prominent figure in the State Street banking and trust community, this is a surprising, unexpected statement. Indeed, the person who conducted the interview was so taken aback that he asked Lowell if he had really heard the comment correctly. The ensuing exchange between Lowell and the interviewer indicates the primary locus of virtue within the rhetoric of selfhood of the Steward-Citizen:

Interviewer: Oh, I thought you just said that it was a disgrace that [wealth] could be passed on.

Lowell: I think it's a disgrace that, that [pause] yeah, that people who have a lot of wealth don't pull their weight in society.

Interviewer: They don't?

Lowell: I think it's a disgrace that a lot of people who have wealth don't.

Interviewer: They don't? What would be pulling their weight?

Lowell: Well, I think they should be using their talents for their fellow man rather than running around on their yachts and so forth.

Interviewer: Well, you certainly have a different perspective on that, don't you?

Lowell: I do, I do. And yet I am rock bound Republican! [He laughs.]

In his novel *The Book of the Laughter and Forgetting*, Milan Kundera says that the act of laughter is a practice of forgetting, of effervescently shaking off and transcending the binds that tie one to an often unhappy existence in the everyday. Of course, Kundera knows that ecstatic cleansing of memory, both biographical and historical, is temporary; one always comes back to earth, although hopefully in a slightly different place. For Freud and the psychoanalytic tradition, jokes and laughter are never a matter of forgetting; what is laughed off is not erased but displaced somewhere else in the configuration of one's unconscious desire and conscious subjectivity. Lowell's laughter at the end of the exchange marks a profound displacement of the site of virtue, and consequently a shift in the grounding of his moral identity, in his rhetoric of selfhood. In the passage about the perpetuation of wealth, Lowell argues that the inheritance of a trust fund is a "disgrace." In other words, the extended patrimony of inherited wealth is a place *without* grace and honor and, therefore, a site where virtue is impossible. In these terms, the trust might be understood as a "weight" that pulls the inheritor down to a place of vice and corruption where wealth is squandered. Better to earn wealth in the present, Lowell seems to be saying in this statement, than to be subject to the dead weight of the past. However, when asked to clarify the meaning of his first statement, Lowell seems to realize the rhetorical bind he has created for himself as inheritor and trustee. He cannot evade the "weight" of his own extended patrimony and therefore creates a new rhetorical location from which to articulate the relationship of fortune and virtue. The site of virtue is displaced from the manner in which the "weight" of fortune as wealth is acquired to its disposition and movement in society. From Lowell's perspective, the unvirtuous wealthy are those who "don't pull their weight in society." In order to virtuously pull the weight of wealth, according to Lowell, the wealthy must use "their talents for their fellow man rather than running around on their yachts." With this invocation of the use of one's "talents" to distinguish the virtuous wealthy from the unvirtuous, Lowell has begun to evoke his moral identity as a trustee through the discourse of stewardship.

The biblical Parable of the Talents (Matt. 25:14–30) has long been understood as being one of the key scriptural foundations upon which the Puritan doctrine of stewardship, as well as the Puritan ethic of productive worldly asceticism, was erected. In brief, the parable tells of a man who entrusts his property in the monetary form of "talents" to three of his servants before departing on a journey. The "master" distributes the talents to his servants on the basis of their "ability." In the parable, the ability of the servants is revealed in their capacity to make the master's talents multiply by "putting his money to work" by investing it with bankers. Two of the servants were able to double the money entrusted to them through interest. The third, being of a fearful and idle disposition, buried his one talent in the ground and, naturally, only had one talent to show the master when the latter returned to "settle accounts" with his servants. Having come up woefully short in the master's account ledger, the third servant is vilified as being "wicked and lazy." The parable ends with the master pronouncing a harsh judgment upon the servant: "Take the talent from him and give it to the one who has ten. For everyone who has will be given more, and he will have an abundance. Whoever does not have, even what he has will be taken from him. And throw that worthless servant outside, into the darkness, where there will be weeping and gnashing of teeth" (Matt. 25:28–30).[18] For this unfortunate servant, or those who follow his perfidious example, there will clearly be no laughter or forgetting. Of course, one might aver that laughter was never one of the human propensities that the sober asceticism of the Puritans sought to encourage anyway. However, there is something in this parable, and the way in which it was rearticulated as a part of the Puritan discourse of stewardship, that enables Lowell to laugh and thus locate a source of virtue in trust.

In order to render Lowell's displacement of the site of virtue intelligible, I want to briefly explore how the Parable of the Talents fits generally into the discourse of stewardship that Lowell invokes. This parable was given two distinct yet related interpretations as a guide to virtuous behavior in everyday life within the discourse of stewardship as articulated by English Puritans, such as William Perkins, and New England Puritans, such as Cotton Mather. The first interpretation used the parable as a commandment to disciplined labor and worldly asceticism. The second interpretation deployed the parable as a commandment to "do good" through the practice of beneficence. As E. Morgan (1966), R. H. Tawney (1938), S. Innes (1995), and, of course, Weber (1958) have argued, both interpretations have a common ground in the doctrine of the divinely ordained yet earthly enacted vocation or "calling."

According to Perkins's famous treatise on callings, all individuals are assigned a vocation or calling by God. This vocation or calling, Perkins argued, "is a certaine condition or kind of life; that is, a certaine manner of leading our lives in this world" (1966: 6). Each calling entailed a certain set of duties and obligations that was specific to that vocation. To paraphrase Perkins (1966: 36), the calling of a king is to rule his subjects; the calling of the subject is to obey his magisterial sovereign; the calling of the minister is to preach the Gospel; the calling of "master of the family" is to patriarchally govern his household; and so on. As each individual was assigned by God to a particular vocation, so was he given a particular set of "talents" or abilities as a gift, by God, to fulfill the duties of his calling. Talents are gifts from God that the individual holds in trust as a steward for the glorification of God. Virtuous behavior in the performance of one's calling is exemplified by making the best of one's talents by enacting "the duties of his calling with diligence" (1966: 42). At this juncture in Perkins's treatise the Parable of the Talents is invoked to give initial form to what is now known as the Protestant Work Ethic:

> Wee must take heede of two damnable sinnes that are contrary to this diligence. The first is idlenesse, whereby; the duties of our callings, and the occasions for glorifying God, are neglected or omitted. The second is slouthfulnes, whereby they are performed slackly and carelesly. God in the Parable of the hus-bandman, cals them that are idle into his vineyard, saying, *Why stand ye idle all the day? Mat. 20.6.* And the servant that had one talent, is called an evill servant, because he was slouthfull in the use of it : for it is said, *Thou evill servant and slouthful, Mat. 25.26.* Now the idle and slouthful person is a sea of corruption. (1966: 42–43)

For Weber, this doctrine of the calling, along with the Calvinist ideas of election and predestination, formed the core of a coherent *lebensführung*, or an ethical mode of conduct in everyday life, through which one glorified God on the basis of disciplined labor as a duty and obligation. *Lebensführung*, as Weber argued, had an "elective affinity" with the rational practices of investment and accumulation of the modern capitalist enterprise. Accordingly, the doctrine of the calling was seen as giving moral sanction to the disciplined pursuit of wealth through business activity. Of course, the pursuit of wealth and riches was not to be an end in itself. Perkins and other Puritan ministers condemned the luxury of the idle rich as much as they did the slothful poor. The "richer sort" who "spend a great part of their increase upon hawkes, buls, beares, dogs, or riotously mispend the same in sporting or gaming" are as lost in the "sea of corruption" as the poor man who buried his talent (1966: 47). "Men are honored with their riches," Perkins wrote, only to the extent that they "Honor God with thy riches" (1966: 47). And to honor God meant to forsake current enjoyment of wealth for productive investment, contributing to the Church, and giving generously to the community:

> We learne by this, that miserable and damnable estate of those that being enriched with great livings and revenewes, do spend their daies in eating and drinking, in sports and pastimes, not imploying themselves in service for Church or Common-wealth. It may be haply thought, that such gentlemen have happy lives; but it is farre otherwise: considering every one rich or poore, man or woman, is bound to have personall calling, in which they must perform some duties for the common good, according to the measure of gifts that God hath bestowed upon them. (1966: 53)

At this point the second interpretation of the parable, a commandment to public-minded beneficence, begins to emerge. This particular meaning of talents within the discourse of stewardship runs deep in the collective memory of the Boston patriciate, going back to the first generations of the Massachusetts Bay Colony. Although the call to charitable beneficence was a common theme among the sermons of the Puritan ministry in early New England, one of its foremost interlocutors was Cotton Mather (cf. Stout, 1986). Like Perkins, Mather maintains that "idle gentleman and idle beggars are the pests of the commonwealth" (Mather, 1966: 107). However, the idle rich will much have more sin and impiety to account for in the final reckoning of the Judgment than the idle poor, because they have not made virtuous use of the talents bestowed upon them by God. For Mather, the concept of "talents" is a metaphor for money as well as individual capacity and ability.[19]

Yet what gives these connotations of "talents" their positive moral valence in Mather's discourse of stewardship is a third metaphorical meaning of talent—as the opportunity to "do good" in the world as a calling:

> Our *opportunities to do good* are our TALENTS. An awful account must be rendered unto great GOD, concerning the use of the TALENTS, wherewith He entrusted us, in these precious opportunities. We do not *use* our *opportunities*, many times because we do not *know* what they are; and many times the reason why do not *know*, is because we do not *think*. Our *opportunities to do good*, lie by unregarded and unimproved, and so 'tis but a mean account that can be given of them. We *read* of a thing, which we *deride* as often as we behold: *there is, that maketh himself poor, and yet has great riches*. It is a thing too frequently exemplified, in our *opportunities to do good*, which are some of our most valuable *riches*. Many a man seems to reckon himself destitute of those *talents*; as if there where nothing for him to do; he pretends he is not in any condition to *do* any *good*. Alas! *poor man; what can he do?* My friend, *think* again; *think* often. *Inquire* what your opportunities are. (Mather, 1966: 31–32)

For Mather, the notion of talents as the opportunity to do good structures the other meanings of talents into a coherent governmentality of virtuous conduct. Talents are the earthly embodiment of the grace of God in the form of the opportunity to do good; it is this grace that is a man's true fortune and riches. However, of those to whom God has given much in terms of talents as material riches, and thus material capacity to do good, much is expected. Such talents must be invested and circulated through the community in the form of good, charitable works, otherwise they will remain "unregarded and unimproved." Where the rich do not actively contribute to the community by investing their talents in its material and moral well-being, they are, like the servant in the parable, burying their talents and will suffer the same fate. Directly addressing the rich merchants of New England in *Bonafacius*, Mather sermonizes:

> Charge them that are rich in this world, that they *do good*, that they be rich in good works, ready to distribute, willing to communicate, with which God, who *gives power to get wealth*, has favored and obliged and enriched them. . . . Whoever buries his talent, breaks a sacred trust, and cozens those that stand in need on't. Sirs, you cannot but acknowledge, that it is the Sovereign GOD, to whom thou art but a *steward*, who has bestowed upon you, the *riches*, which distinguish you. . . . It is also a thing, whereof 'tis be hoped, you are not unapprehensive, that the *riches* in your possession are some of the *talents*, whereof you must give an account unto the Glorious LORD, who has betrusted you therewithal: and that you will *give up your account with grief, and not with joy*, if it must be found that *all* your estates have been laid out, only to gratify the appetites of the *flesh*, and *little* or *nothing* of them consecrated unto the service of *God*, and of His Kingdom in the world. . . . That fault of not employing one's parts for the public, one calls, "a great sacrilege in the Temple of the God of Nature." It was a sad age when *Tacitus* tells, *Inertia fuit sapientia* [inactivity was wisdom]. (Mather, 1966: 107–108, 119)

In Mather's discourse of stewardship, wealth can be seen as the earthly embodiment of the extended patrimony of God. Wealth is a fortune, an array of talents consisting of money, capacity, and opportunity that the rich man holds in trust. As a trustee, the rich man is obliged by duty and responsibility to enact the will of the Holy Father as Holy Founder, by turning opportunities to do good into beneficent result. The public sphere of church and commonwealth is therefore a divinely ordained territory of worldly activity, within which the talents of the wealthy are to be productively invested and circulated. Come Judgment Day, God the Divine Accountant will audit the earthly use of wealth to ascertain whether his designated trustees were prudent and virtuous or profligate and corrupt.

Interestingly, Weber and many contemporary defenders of his thesis gloss over this dimension of the Protestant ethic of the calling as *lebensführung*, emphasizing its elective affinity to the accumulation of wealth while neglecting the call to beneficence (cf. Marshall, 1982; Poggi, 1983; Taylor, 1990). Yet Lowell, as an inheritor and trustee, is invoking this second meaning of the parable. In spite of what he said about having earned most of his wealth himself, like Stuart Dean, Lowell does not primarily configure his desire or virtue in terms of the values of the marketplace. In the very same statement where Lowell claims the virtue of accumulation, he goes on to deemphasize this virtue in the construction of his moral identity: "Well, I don't aspire to great wealth, quite frankly, and if I did have more money I'd give it away because that's what I want do." Here beneficence is described as a yearning and desire, a will to do good. However, in making sense of Lowell's rhetoric of selfhood, keep in mind that his desire cannot be separated from the duty and obligation incumbent upon his position as trustee. For Lowell, the trust he inherited as his fortune are his "talents":

> I am a fortunate person. We [Lowell and his wife] have been blessed with a marvelous life and we want to share it. We have never aspired to great wealth because, well, this is going to sound kind of silly, but it's my Christian belief that I was put on this earth to be useful to other people. And once I've taken care of my life and my family then my efforts are going to be for other people. . . . My goal has been to do the best with my talents because God knows there is a lot of deserving causes and people around the world.

Therefore, when Lowell speaks of "using his talents," it is in the sense of fulfilling the obligations of an inherited fortune that he holds in trust as a steward. This statement demonstrates the way in which the discourse of stewardship ideologically interpellates Lowell as a virtuous wealthy subject. The interpellation involves Lowell recognizing himself as being "fortunate," a possessor of wealth and the resources of life beyond what is necessary to support himself and family. In recognizing that he and his family are fortunate, Lowell is positioned in the social imaginary in relation to those who are less fortunate in society. His fortune is a state of grace, "a marvelous life," the bounty of which must be shared as a duty and obligation to those who are less fortunate. It is this successful fulfillment of the duties attendant upon fortune as a state of grace that enables Lowell to locate a place from which he can articulate a virtuous self-identity.

As a wealthy man who holds his fortune as a matter of trust, the steward has an obligation to contribute more than others less favorably endowed. In point of fact, the moral superiority that answering the call of stewardship provides for wealthy men like Lowell in relation to other wealthy people is extremely salient in the legitimation of power and privilege. Part and parcel of the imaginary social world conjured by the discourse of stewardship is a distinction between not only those who are fortunate and those who are not but also those who are *responsibly* fortunate and those who are not. The necessity of assuming the mantle of stewardship as a matter of personal salvation and social responsibility by the wealthy man is underscored by Lowell in his very pointed critique of fellow class members who seem to be solely devoted to the accumulation and consumption of wealth: "I think [having wealth] puts a hell of a burden on somebody. If you have a lot of money, what does the Bible say? How difficult it is for a man to get into heaven through the eye of a needle? It's true. And, I must say, I look around at some of my wealthy friends and I see how they spend their money and how unhappy they are and I don't want any part of their kind of life. I really don't."

Whatever anxieties Lowell may have about the burden fortune places on the eternal disposition of his soul, like the Fuller brothers obelisked atop Mount Auburn Cemetery, he has faith that the Gateway to Heaven will be opened by fulfilling his duties and obligations as steward. However, also like the Fullers, Lowell's moral identity as a "true" Brahmin is only partially conjured through the discourse of stewardship. As a trustee, Lowell not only understands himself as steward; he also understands himself as "citizen."

The "First-Rate Citizen": Disinterested Rationality and the Discourse of Citizenship. As the name *Steward-Citizen* implies, the discourses of stewardship and citizenship that cohere in this moral character are tightly linked and therefore often hard to separate in Lowell's rhetoric of selfhood. In providing the trustee with a problematic for speaking the self, these discourses are imbricated and mutually reinforcing. As such, in Bakhtinian terms, the articulation of these discourses in the problematic of the trustee represents an example of "heteroglossia," or the dynamic confluence of different languages that creates new subjects and objects of knowledge in the social field (Bakhtin, 1981: 106). However, each discourse has a distinctive moral vocabulary and language that conjure slightly different places in the social imaginary from which to conjure the virtues of philanthropic beneficence. Accordingly, the heteroglossia entailed in their articulation can produce a tension between their distinctive moral valences. In the case of Lowell as Steward-Citizen, this tension is embodied in an effacement and displacement of wealth within the rhetorical construction of his virtue as citizen that ultimately fails.

As I argue above, the discourse of stewardship orients the wealthy male inheritor toward his extended patrimony as a fortune that he holds in trust. The inheritance of the trust entails the duty and obligation to do good, the fulfillment of which is a sign of virtue. In deconstructive terms, as I argue in Chapter 1, the positivity or efficaciousness of this sign of virtue is rendered discursively and rhetorically possible on the basis of alterity or "otherness." That is to say, the self-same "presence" of virtue in the life of the trustee, and thus his moral identity as being virtuous, is always-already constituted by a relationship of difference. In terms of Lowell's rhetoric of selfhood, the presence of his virtue as steward that is inscribed in his moral tale is based upon two relationships of differential otherness: the difference between the "fortunate" and the "unfortunate"; and the difference between the fortunate who are responsible and the fortunate who are irresponsible. Accordingly, in the discourse of stewardship there is an explicit foregrounding of differences based upon wealth and privilege in conjuring a place and practice of virtue. The trustee as steward is "interested" in beneficence as a vocational enactment of virtue because he is duty-bound and obligated to it by the fact of his wealth. Through this enactment of virtue, the steward articulates the private corpus of the inherited trust with "deserving causes" of the unfortunate in the public sphere.

Like the discourse of stewardship, the discourse of citizenship also provides the trustee with a language for articulating the private with the public. However, in the discourse of citizenship, the differential terms of alterity and otherness that establish the presence of virtue tend to efface the interest of the trustee as a man of wealth in the practice of philanthropic beneficence and of acting for the public good. The terms that enable Lowell to construct himself as a virtuous citizen are evident in the following statement:

> I think a man has a real responsibility to the community in which he lives, a real one. And, as I have said, in addition to all my other involvements I've been member of the school committee and I've been moderator now for twenty-four years, so that's the way I've tried to fulfill that responsibility. I can't see these people who go to work and then come home and shut the door and don't do anything in their community.

Note here that the discursive categories of difference and alterity that establish the virtue of citizenship have no explicit relationship to wealth. The social world is not imagined to consist either of the fortunate and the unfortunate, or the fortunate who are responsible and those who are not. Rather, the moral geography of the public sphere as a territory for the spatial practice of citizenship consists simply of "men" and the community in which they live. This is in keeping with the civic republican concept of citizenship that I explore in Chapter 3. In the civic republican discourse of citizenship, to be a "citizen" is to be a member of a larger political community and civil society wherein all are equal and endowed with a certain set of rights and responsibilities. The cultivation of civic virtue entails a practice through which men collectively contemplate and act upon the public good. Civic virtue, therefore, requires that a man set aside or subordinate his particular private interests of property, family, and commerce in order to pursue the public interest of commonweal. Through this subordination of the particular to the universal, the sovereign "I" of the self becomes redefined in terms of the "We" of the community. It is this differential alterity between the private sphere and the public sphere, between self-interest and the *disinterested* pursuit of the common good, that conjures a place for what Lowell elsewhere in his interview terms the "first-rate citizen."

The notion of the first-rate citizen provides Lowell with a personally compelling standard of civic virtue. To be a citizen of the first rank means that one contributes to the well-being of the wider community to which one has a "real responsibility." By devoting a significant portion of his time and money to the betterment of the community to which a man is "responsible," he demonstrates a superior virtue than the rest of the citizenry, whether the citizens be wealthy or not. The unvirtuous are those whose zone of social engagement remains tightly circumscribed by the private spheres of the marketplace and the domestic hearth. Or, to paraphrase Lowell, the "other" that confirms the presence of virtue of the public-minded citizen are those who come home from work and shut the door.

The discourse of citizenship provides a second set of terms that configure the virtues of the first-rate citizen. There is more to the virtuous insertion of the man as citizen into the public space of the community than simply walking out the door and shouldering his responsibility to the community. As I argue in Chapter 3, according to Machiavelli and the civic republicans the public sphere was a site of virtue and *virtù* only to the extent that it was a province of *ragione* (reason). Reason, or the ability to choose among competing ends and to rationally calculate the means best suited to achieve them, was seen as being central to creating an understanding of the common good. Through reason, men would be able to "transcend" their particular self-interest in order pursue the public interest. Further, through reason, men would be able to counteract the chaotic vagaries of *fortuna* in the form of political and social instability.

The self-perceived capacity, indeed necessity, of the Brahmins to bring order and rationality to the chaos of nineteenth-century Boston grounded their claims to civic virtue. Brahmins, such as Amos A. Lawrence, framed their mission of beneficent citizenship in almost apocalyptic terms. "Save us and our money from the mobs!" exclaimed Lawrence (quoted in Jaher, 1982: 64). The salvation of Brahmin power and privilege was to be found in the creation of a network of privately controlled cultural, educational, and welfare institutions that would "elevate and educate" the "mob." Otherwise, Lawrence wrote to Daniel Webster in 1835, "they will change our system of government in fifty years" (quoted in Dalzell, 1987: 145). For the Brahmins, rationality was part and parcel of their "character," and, as such, it was their capacity to serve as disinterested citizens that would impose social stability, harmony, and "civilization" upon the anarchic and irrational masses of Boston. This *differential alterity* between disinterested rationality and its "other"—the chaos of self-interested irrationality—further inscribes the presence of virtue in the "first-rate citizen."

Unlike his Brahmin forbears, John Lowell does not locate his obligations to the community within the context of impending social apocalypse. However, the language of disinterested rationality is very much foregrounded in the manner in which he describes the modus operandi of his philanthropic and civic engagements as trustee—and thus in his moral identity as first-rate citizen. Throughout his interview, he speaks of the duties of trusteeship in instrumentally rational terms. For example, as trustee of the Lowell Institute, Lowell says that his guiding principle in making decisions as to what to fund is to "stretch the philanthropic dollar as far as we possibly can." By this he means that it is the obligation of the trustee to

> leverage the Institute's funds for the benefit of, we'll say, the Museum of Fine Arts, the Museum of Science, the Aquarium, the Constitution Museum, the Kennedy Library, and so on. We want to help their programs. Since these are free public lectures that are held on their premises, they attract a lot of people who will hopefully support those institutions. . . . I think you want to kill two birds with one stone, really. In providing free lectures I am obviously doing everything that is required of me under the terms of the original will. But I also want to benefit the museums and other cultural institutions around town, social agencies around town, by using this money as seed money that can attract other funds. You're accomplishing a lot more [this way] than if you're just going off on your own, so to speak.

There are two important aspects of Lowell's philosophy and practice as beneficent citizen to note here. First, in this statement there is a clear evocation of the extended patrimony as a trust that links past and present, private and public. Working "under the terms of the original will" he inherited from the past, Lowell "leverages" private funds in order to create the most public benefit he can in the present. Second, the workings of the extended patrimony are described in the technically neutral terms of rationality and efficiency. That is, the extrusion of the trust into the public sphere is a matter of getting the most "bang," so to speak, for the philanthropic buck.

The same dispassionate rationality and efficiency that Lowell evinces in his role as trustee of the Lowell Institute is recapitulated in his other philanthropic involvements. When asked what personal contributions aside from money he imparts to the many institutions for which is trustee, Lowell remarks that "I like to think that I bring a certain amount of common sense to the deliberations." And for Lowell, "common sense" is the wise and sagacious practice of making sense of the common interest through prudence and the principles of philanthropic efficiency. This "common sense" of disinterested rationality, according to Lowell, is a virtuous trait of all trustees who are first-rate citizens. Indeed, according to Lowell, fellow trustees on the board of the Boston Foundation set the standard of civic virtue for the rest of Boston's philanthropic community:

> The community takes its lead from the permanent charity of the fund of the Boston Foundation. The capital of the Foundation is a hundred and thirty million and they [the trustees and staff] just give away the income on the principal. . . . And they know what they are doing. They have their finger on the pulse of who needs what, and they will concentrate on those areas they feel are important. Like the inner city and trying to improve the school system. . . . They also contribute to capital drives for hospitals and museums and the symphony, and they are the kinds of things that really improve the quality of life in the city. [They are all] first-rate citizens.

Embedded in this statement is a tension between the private power of trustees to make public policy and the principle of disinterested rationality they profess. As first-rate citizens, the trustees of the Boston Foundation are exceedingly rational. "They know what they are doing," Lowell says, and knowing what they are doing entails the capacity to keep "their finger on the pulse of who needs what," then concentrating resources in that area of social necessity. This rational capacity of relating means to ends produces the beneficent result of improving the "quality of life in the community." However, this efficient instrumental rationality is, in Weberian terms, also inherently "value-rational." After all, the trustees themselves, by having their finger on the pulse of need, determine what needs are deemed worthy of attention on the basis of "what they feel is important." Clearly, then, in spite of disinterested rationality, the trustee as first-rate citizen has interests. But are these interests private, reflecting the particular values of trustee as a man of wealth, or are these interests "truly" public, reflective of the common good of the community?

For Lowell—and this is the only possible answer for him—the interests are public. When asked whether he or his fellow trustees pursue a self-interested "political agenda" in their philanthropic endeavors, Lowell emphatically denies it:

> I think [political bias] would be unfair characterization of the Boston Foundation. I really think so. You ought to have a look at the board of directors of the Boston Foundation. I don't think those folks are seeking any power for themselves. I think they are doing it altruistically. . . . [They] are not approaching who gets what from a political or power point of view. And, you know, as far as I'm concerned, the Lowell Institute doesn't need any power. It's not looking for any publicity. As I told you, I am just trying to stretch

those funds are far as I can for the benefit of those institutions around town that I think are very, very worthwhile institutions. I have my ground rules that were set forth in 1836 under this fellow's will, and they are damn good ground rules. And they really don't need to be changed.

This statement is a fitting end to our visit with Lowell as a "better angel" of Boston: It is a fascinating example of the rhetorical process through which his moral identity as trustee is produced. Here, Lowell is invoking, as well as forging, an articulating link between the discourses of citizenship and stewardship. Echoing Samuel Eliot's denunciation of the "uncharitable constructions" put upon the Brahmins' philanthropy, Lowell argues that any intimation that he or his fellow trustees are corrupt in a Machiavellian sense is an "unfair characterization." As virtuous trustees, they do not seek power or pursue their self-interest. They are, in fact, "altruistic," evincing the supreme civic virtue of *dis-owning* the interests of the sovereign self in favor of the public interest of the "other" of the community: The "I" becomes "We" in the practice of first-rate citizenship.

The Machiavellian uncanny is clearly at work here in the conjuring of the moral identity of Lowell as Steward-Citizen, but in a profoundly ironic way. As I argue in Chapter 3, there is no place for private possession or accumulation of wealth as fluid resource of territorializing power within Machiavelli's civic republican discourse. Fortune as wealth was a source of corruption and, as such, was effectively displaced from the terrain within which civic virtue was to be cultivated and practiced. In Lowell's language of civic virtue, as well as in that of his Brahmin predecessors, wealth is also displaced, but in a radically different way. Territorialized in an existential state of grace and materialized in the position of trusteeship, wealth provides the freedom and capacity to contemplate the public good. That is to say, freed from the constraints of having to pursue material self-interest in order to survive, the wealthy man as trustee is also free to become a disinterested and altruistic servant of the public good. Wealth provides, as Samuel Eliot argued, the "luxury of doing good." The Brahmin appropriation of the discourse of citizenship, therefore, displaces wealth from its ontic grounding of the moral identity of the Citizen in a paradoxical way. Wealth, as a source of power and freedom, is the fundament of civic virtue, as it provides the resources and occasions for the practice of citizenship. Already possessed of wealth and power in private sphere, the wealthy man "needs" or desires neither in the public sphere and is therefore able to "transcend" self-interest and pursue the common interest through disinterested rationality. Thus, through the language and practice of civic virtue, the wealthy man is able to represent himself, not *as* a man of wealth, but simply as a first-rate citizen who fulfills his duties and obligations to the community.

However, that which is rhetorically displaced or effaced is never forgotten or erased. And in Lowell's own rhetoric of selfhood, the displacement of wealth that is effected through his invocation of the discourse of citizenship is fleeting and temporary. At the very moment Lowell foregrounds the disinterested nature of his civic virtue as trustee of the Lowell Institute (by saying that neither he nor the Institute "needs" power or publicity), his private power as steward is also highlighted. The disinterested rationality of trying to "stretch those funds" is guided by and grounded in the clearly interested value-rationality of what Lowell thinks are "very, very worthwhile institutions." Moreover, Lowell's capacity to guide flows of philanthropic resources through the Boston community according to his standards of worth is itself structured by the "ground rules" of the trust he inherited as an extended patrimony. These ground rules, which render the public good the trust and responsibility of those with privately held wealth, are, according to Lowell, "damn good ground rules" that "don't need to be changed." Accordingly, in its articulation within the discourse of stewardship, the effacement of wealth that is effected through the discourse of citizenship is unstable and ultimately vitiated. After all, the ability of men of wealth such as Lowell to be first-rate citizens is founded upon the fact of fortune that is embodied in money as well as in institutional positions of power and authority that are passed down from generation to generation. And this fact of fortune, in the moral identity of the Steward-Citizen, cannot be rhetorically disowned unless it is materially disowned. However, if this *were* the case, Lowell would not be able to stand as a contemporary embodiment of the true Brahmin ideal: steward, citizen, a "better angel" of Boston.

An Empire of Beneficence: Andrew Carnegie and the Philanthropic Vocation of the Steward-Entrepreneur

The Face in the Penny: From Dunfermline to Des Moines via Kirkcaldy

During the summer of 1993 I went looking for Adam Smith and found Andrew Carnegie. My wife, Heidi, and I were motoring across Scotland from one engagement with real ales and clotted cream to another. We had planned our itinerary so that we would pass through the birthplace of Adam Smith, Kirkcaldy, on our way to Edinburgh. At the time, I was having some trouble working through some of the issues regarding the Scottish Enlightenment, and, for inchoate yet compelling reasons, I felt that a visit to the place where Smith lived most of his life would give me the inspirational insight that I so desperately needed to finish my analysis. The Scots, as one of the first peoples subjected to the imperial designs of the English, have a keen sense of their distinctive history and are anxious to publicly display it. Since Smith was one the most influential Scots in modernity, I reasoned that I would find significant signs of his legacy in Kirkcaldy.

The day we went to Kirkcaldy was exceptionally bright and clear for the season, and as we ventured south along the coastal road from St. Andrews to our destination, the sun glinted off the calm waters of the Firth of Forth like a warm promise. My spirits elevated by the weather, I was confident that I would find whatever it was of Smith for which I yearned. The sign on the road into town was encouraging: "Kirkcaldy, Population 45,781; BIRTHPLACE OF ADAM SMITH." Beyond this affirmation, we had no concrete idea of what we were looking for or where to look for it. Consequently, we parked in the city center and started to walk around, asking questions. "We are on the trail of Adam Smith!" we announced proudly to those we accosted on the street. "Is there a memorial, museum, or any such place we can find him?" The responses were all kindly but extremely frustrating. The good citizens of Kirkcaldy took great pride in the fact that this town was the birthplace of Smith, but none seemed to know if there was a particular site or location where his spirit, life, or work was memorialized. "Let's see," one woman told us, "there is an Adam Smith Street, but I don't think there is anything there." "Adam Smith!" another passer-by responded. "One of our most famous sons. Why are you looking for him? Oh, well, I don't think there is anything like that. There is an Adam Smith Theatre, but I really don't think it has anything to do with him. But you might have a look." Although our enthusiasm for the search was dampened by such vague responses, we marched off with the hope that someone at the theater might have a more satisfying answer. Our hopes were soon dashed as we promptly got lost in the labyrinthine streets of an old residential district.

By this point, we had spent the better part an hour wandering around Kirkcaldy, and Heidi, who was anxious to get back on the road so we might reach Edinburgh at a reasonable hour, was growing visibly impatient with our fruitless adventure. I, on the other hand, took on the manic determination that is often derived from an impending collapse of hope. I felt cursed by the cruel machinations of the gods of academe, who were leading me down a road to nowhere simply for the sport of it. I also found myself amid a profound experience of an uncanny repetition of the narrative of fortune and virtue. Kirkcaldy, I thought to myself, was a chaotic site of chance and contingency. After all, the sign on the road into town had promised the opportunity to find Adam Smith. Was I fated not to find him? Or did I need to demonstrate the will, discipline, reason—in a word, *virtù*—that would turn fortune as opportunity into desired result? The ghost of another Scot, Andrew Carnegie, was also present in my mind as I remembered his conclusion to his essay, "How to Win Fortune": "The fault, dear Brutus, is not in our stars, but in our selves, that we are its underlings" (Carnegie, 1933 [1902]: 101). We pressed on.

Walking back in the general direction of the city center, we literally stumbled upon two men who careened out of a pub into our path. Clearly, these gentlemen had been drinking their lunch and were in high spirits. Perhaps, I thought, they possessed the preternatural insight often born of beer, and so I asked them whether *they* knew where Adam Smith was located. "Yes!" came the answer from one of them. "Why, he's a good a friend of mine! We'll take you there." Heidi and I were obviously discomfited by the gentleman's inebriated claim of friendship with old Adam, but having no better idea of where to go, we followed in their erratic footsteps. Sure enough, the drunken pair led us to the first clear marking of the presence of Adam Smith since we came to town—the Adam Smith Theatre! Before we could ask where exactly Smith was, the two lumbered away toward their next (we presumed) drinking destination and shouted back at us, "Don't worry, he's there! You'll find him!" Apparently, if Adam was a friend of these gentlemen, he was a most fickle one, because, aside from the sign outside the theater that bore his name, there were no traces of him. No marker, no memorial, no plaque, no nothing. If this be a another cruel joke of the academic gods, I thought, then I am ready to consign myself to their designs of fate. In a final act of desperation, we turned to a groundskeeper and plied him with the question that now mocked us in its futility: "Where's Adam Smith?" "Well," he replied, pointing to a Victorian-era building across the street, "if he's anywhere, he's over there at the Kirkcaldy Museum." "At last!" I thought. "I am redeemed! My perseverance is about to reap virtuous rewards. It is a just world after all."

Justice, as Smith argued in the *Theory of Moral Sentiments*, is the "pillar" that holds up the entire "edifice" of commercial society. Unfortunately, Smith left no room in his sober theory of morality for irony, as the just rewards I had expected were ironic indeed. Walking into the museum with renewed spirit and hope, we headed directly to the information desk, where I announced to the person behind the counter that I was on Adam Smith's trail. She smiled sympathetically, as if others on a similar quest had been there before me, and said, "Your search does end here, but, unfortunately, Adam Smith didn't leave much of a trail to follow. He had all of his worldly possessions burned to ashes upon his death. All that's left is in a display case upstairs." Sure enough, tucked away in the corner of the second floor was a small display case that contained all that was left of Adam Smith: some period engravings of him and his mother and his mother's house, where Smith lived most of life (the house had also been consumed by flames); a cameo silhouette of Smith's visage; a pipe, a set of quill pens, and a sterling silver ink shell; some leather-bound centennial editions of *The Theory* and the *Wealth of Nations*; a single page from the original handwritten manuscript of *Wealth* that had been saved from the sacrificial flames; and a bottle of Scotch whiskey that had been distilled to celebrate the bicentennial of Smith's death.

A profound feeling of disappointment settled upon me. This was not what I had hoped for, as these artifacts conveyed no insight into Smith or his work. They were simply dead objects that had no meaning apart from a life that had ceased to be some two centuries before. As I surveyed Smith's meager material legacy, I felt a strong desire to break the glass of the display case and drink as much of the bottle of Scotch whiskey as I could before being seized by the guards. The fault, dear Brutus, lies in not being as drunk as men who lead us to this barren spot! And then I realized how appropriately ironic my quest and its paltry results were.

To Adam Smith the political economist and moral philosopher of commercial society, *homo mercator* was a man who mastered fortune by mastering flows of money and, in so doing, stoked the engines of society's "progress of opulence." But to Adam Smith the Stoic, the ceaseless drive for accumulation that was the vocation of *homo mercator* was ultimately meaningless. "To what purpose is all the toil and bustle of this world?" Smith conjectured in *The Theory of Moral Sentiments*. "What is the end of avarice and ambition, of the pursuit of wealth, power, and preheminence?" (Smith, 1976b, I.iii.2.1: 50). Wealth and power may bring to *homo mercator* the approval of his fellow men in the market, and they may provide him a certain ease of life, but they do not bring him happiness. The artifacts of wealth and greatness, argued Smith, were socially useful "deceptions" because they "rouse and keep in motion the industry of mankind." But beyond this, they were utterly without spiritual reward. To the wealthy and/or great man who is approaching death, Smith speculated that

> the pleasure of the vain and empty distinctions of greatness disappear. To one in this situation, they are no longer capable of recommending those toilsome pursuits that had formerly engaged him. In his heart he curses ambition, and vainly regrets the ease and indolence of youth, pleasures which are fled forever, and which he foolishly sacrificed for what, when he has got it, can afford him no real satisfaction. In this miserable aspect does greatness appear to every man when reduced by either spleen or disease to observe with attention his own situation, and to consider what it is that is really wanting to his happiness. Power and riches appear then to be what they are, enormous and operose machines contrived to produce a few trifling conveniences to the body. . . . They are immense fabrics, which it requires the labour of a life to raise, which threaten every moment to overwhelm the person that dwells in them, and which while they stand, though they may save

him from smaller inconveniences, can protect him from none of the severer inclemencies of the season. They keep off the summer shower but not the winter storm, but leave him as always as much, and sometimes more exposed than before, to anxiety, to fear, to sorrow; to diseases, to danger, and to death. (1976b, IV.i.8: 182–183)

It was appropriate, then, that Adam Smith should have all of his worldly possessions reduced to ash. To Smith, they were of no account in reckoning the inner worth of a man in this life or the next. Accordingly, I should have expected nothing else. But as I stood there reflecting on all of this, I saw another object in the display case that doubled the irony of the scene. There, on a side shelf, was a copper penny with Smith's face on it. The coin had been minted in 1976 to celebrate the bicentennial of the publication of the *Wealth of Nations*. I speculated that for Smith his will and intention to leave nothing behind was his last effort at exercising the Stoic virtue of self-command, of not being seduced by the spiritual ephemeralities of greatness and ambition. The irony of the scene, therefore, consisted in the fact that Smith was not remembered for his Stoic virtue but for his conjuring of *homo mercator*, a moral character who found meaning in and through the territorializing power of the universal equivalent of money. Here, Smith was memorialized precisely in way that to him would have seemed a "vain and empty distinction": a face on a penny, foolishly circulating in perpetuity in the moral economy of wealth in an arrogant attempt at temporal immortality.

The face of Andrew Carnegie, Smith's fellow Scot from County Fife, is also emblazoned on a penny. However, unlike that of Smith, the minting of Carnegie's visage was intentional on his part and therefore not at all ironic. Moreover, in a manner befitting the accumulative prowess of Carnegie as *homo mercator*, the minting of these pennies was prolific. In almost all of Carnegie's philanthropic bequests, whether they be "small" and simple in purpose, such as a community library, a city park, and a university building, or large and multifaceted, such as the Carnegie-Mellon University, the Carnegie Endowment for Peace, and the Carnegie Corporation, there is somewhere a copper plaque in the shape of a penny, with a silhouette of his face extruding from it. These pennies bear no words, simply an image: Carnegie's image, the image of the Steward-Entrepreneur.

Like Norris's gesture to the world and the Fuller obelisk-epitaphs atop Mount Auburn Cemetery, the Carnegie penny is a sign that inscribes the moral "truth" of wealth within the social imaginary of capitalism. This truth is produced through a spatial story, a particular version of the narrative of fortune and virtue, in which flows of money are territorialized as flows of philanthropic beneficence. What moral geography, and emplacement and emplotment therein, does this penny represent? How is it representative of the narrative of fortune and virtue that is enacted by and embodied in the moral character of the Steward-Entrepreneur?

My analysis of the story of the Steward-Entrepreneur, his conjuring by Andrew Carnegie and his invocation in the (auto-)biographical narrative of a contemporary "better angel" of capitalism, begins where Carnegie's own life and *Autobiography* begins: the Scottish town of Dunfermline. Dunfermline is located on a hilltop approximately twenty miles west of Kirkcaldy, overlooking the Firth of Forth. Like many old industrial towns of the Scottish Lowlands, it is gray, decaying, and depressing. In Carnegie's youth, Dunfermline was a center of damask weaving, manufacturing, and trade. Carnegie's father was a relatively prosperous damask weaver until the introduction of steam-driven looms in the 1840s. Thereafter, the fortunes of Dunfermline and the Carnegie family declined precipitously, prompting Carnegie's emigration to the United States in 1848, when he was thirteen. In addition to being a site where the forces of industrial capitalism wrecked havoc upon the lives of damask weavers, Dunfermline was also a hotbed of Chartist and Republican radicalism. According to Carnegie's *Autobiography*, Dunfermline was the "most radical town in the Kingdom," and his family's intense involvement in the Chartist movement instilled in him a desire "to have slain king, duke, or lord and considered their deaths a service to the state and thus a heroic act" (Carnegie, 1986 [1920]: 9–10). As a boy, Carnegie says, he "developed into a violent young Republican radical whose motto was 'death to privilege'" (1986 [1920]: 11). As Carnegie repeatedly emphasizes in his autobiography, he never forsook his youthful republican lust for the death of aristocratic privilege, and later he had this very motto inscribed on the Carnegie coat of arms (Wall, 1970: 2). Indeed, for Carnegie, the Chartist dream of the rights of all individuals to citizenship, sovereignty, and autonomy irrespective of class instilled in him the desire for the project of entrepreneurial self-making and was therefore fully compatible with the Social Darwinist defense of capitalism he would embrace in later years. Reflecting upon the influences of Dunfermline's economic, social, and political environment upon the ambitions of a boy, Carnegie states that "where one is born is very important, for different surroundings and traditions appeal to and stimulate different latent tendencies in a child. . . . These touch him and set fire to the latent spark within, making him something different and beyond what, less happily born, he would have become" (1986 [1920]: 6–7).

For Carnegie, then, Dunfermline constituted his initial dispensation of fortune, the original crucible of circumstance in which his entrepreneurial ambitions for transcendence and transformation were first forged. Carnegie never forgot his fortunate roots, and in 1903, after he accumulated what he considered to be the legitimate privilege of entrepreneurial wealth and power, he returned to Dunfermline to remake the fortune of the town and its inhabitants through the philanthropic dispensation of a fortune. In 1903, Carnegie established the Carnegie Dunfermline Trust with an endowment of $4 million in United States Steel bonds. With a stroke of Carnegie's pen upon the deed that chartered the trust, Dunfermline became the community with the largest private endowment in the world and the site of the most ambitious experiment in the private philanthropic funding and organization of social reform ever attempted at the time (cf. Wall, 1970: 849–855). Today, the preamble of the deed that established the trust is inscribed upon a bronze plaque that is affixed to a granite obelisk. The obelisk sits in the center of Pittencrieff, an aristocratic estate that was once the residence of the Laird of Pittencrieff. Carnegie bought the estate from its then laird in 1900 and converted its mansion and gardens into a public park. He thus made good on his motto to bring death to the privilege of the aristocracy, albeit in a small way. This park would become the jewel in the crown of beneficence that Carnegie soon bestowed upon the people of Dunfermline. The obelisk's inscription:

> I, Andrew Carnegie of New York . . . in pursuance of a duty which I have long felt incumbent on me and which I have so far already endeavored to discharge, viz.—to distribute in my lifetime the surplus wealth which I possess in such a manner as shall best advance the well-being and happiness of the greatest number of beneficiaries; and being desirous of testing by experiment the advantages which a community may derive by having placed at its disposal . . . funds dedicated to the purpose of providing the means of introducing into the daily lives of the masses, such privileges and enjoyments as are under present circumstances considered beyond their reach, but which if brought within their reach are calculated to carry into their homes sweetness and light. (quoted in Wall, 1970: 849)

Centered just below the inscription, serving as punctuating telos to the deed bestowing "sweetness and light" upon the good citizens of Dunfermline, is an Andrew Carnegie penny.

The institutional forms through which "sweetness and light" were to be bestowed upon the "masses" were many, varied, and impressive. In the first ten years of the trust's operations, under the distant yet watchful eye of Carnegie, it funded swimming pools, a gymnasium, a free medical and dental clinic for the children of the town, the College of Hygiene, a free school of music, a school of horticulture, a vocational college for women, and free concerts, lectures, and theatrical productions for the town's citizens (Wall, 1970: 854). And, of course, there was a library.

In "Gospel of Wealth," Carnegie argues that libraries were one of the finest philanthropic forms (second only to universities) that the surplus of the wealthy man could take. For Carnegie, libraries were a supremely "noble" gift, as they provided a site of learning where the enterprising virtues of self-improvement could be cultivated. Libraries provided opportunities for the "aspiring" "poor boys" to transform themselves and transcend the circumstances of their poverty. As such, the giving of libraries was a most productive way of territorializing streams of money into flows of philanthropic beneficence. By giving his wealth the institutional form of a library, Carnegie argued, "the wise administrator of his surplus has poured a fertilizing stream upon soil that was ready to receive it and return a hundred fold" (Carnegie, 1992 [1889]: 18); as Carnegie wrote elsewhere, "awakening the latent desire" for upward social mobility "lay inert in the hearts of our fellow citizens of the industrial hive" (quoted in Wall, 1970: 817). From Carnegie's perspective, therefore, libraries were not a gift of charity; they were an *investment* in the "progress of the race" that evinced the wise prudence of the wealthy man as steward in industrial capitalist society (Carnegie, 1992 [1889]: 18).

By investing in the knowledge of those who wanted "to help themselves," the wealthy man was enacting a duty to foster social progress by providing the means through which he could "begin to gently lead people upward" (quoted in Wall, 1970: 817). For Carnegie, manly individual social mobility and the social progress it engendered were the secular analog to the Ascension. Through the cultivation of the virtues of the enterprising subject of interest, the individual would be able to create himself all by himself in the marketplace, thereby enacting the metamorphosis from poor boy to wealthy man that Carnegie saw his own biography representing.[20] Libraries were thus a source of wisdom and knowledge through which the ambitious and virtuous could leave the darkness of the "industrial hive" and ascend to the bright heights of sovereign individuality as "better angels" of capitalism. Accordingly, for Carnegie there was no finer source of "sweetness and light" than a library. In fact, Carnegie was so convinced of the importance of libraries as heliocentric resources of enlightened individual transformation and social change in capitalist society that he decreed "there should be placed over the entrance of the Libraries I build a representation of the rays of a rising sun, and above, 'LET THERE BE LIGHT'" (Quoted in Wall, 1970: 819).[21]

During his career as a philanthropist, Carnegie gave funds to establish approximately 2,500 institutions of bibliothecal light in the United States and Great Britain (Wall, 1970: 828). The very first was in Dunfermline; one of the very last was the Carnegie Law Library at Drake University in Des Moines, Iowa, where I am currently employed as a professor. Although part of a vast Carnegie-funded program of library building, the Carnegie Law Library at Drake is somewhat unique. In spite of Carnegie's explicit statement in "Gospel of Wealth" that universities represented the "first best use" of the surplus funds the wealthy man held in trust, as biographer Joseph Wall (1970: 864) puts it, Carnegie was "curiously indifferent" to giving money to institutions of higher education throughout most of his philanthropic career.[22] Quite understandably, given his beneficent stature as a philanthropist of epic proportions, Carnegie was continually importuned by a horde of university presidents and trustees to direct his flows of surplus wealth their way. The vast majority of requests for the endowment of schools of law, medicine, and science, professorships, methods of teaching, and even libraries fell futilely upon Carnegie's uninterested ears.[23] Thus, the presence of the Carnegie Building on the campus of Drake University represents an interesting story that along with the its counterpart in Dunfermline will help us to understand the story of the Steward-Entrepreneur that is inscribed in the face on the penny.

In 1905, Carnegie established what was perhaps his most innovative institutional territory of philanthropic beneficence, a territory in which a good many of the readers of this book can claim a stake: the Carnegie Teachers Pension Fund, now known as TIAA/CREF.[24] At the time of the fund's endowment, very few private colleges and universities provided retirement pensions for teachers. This had a deleterious impact on the quality of teaching at these institutions, not to mention upon the lives of the teachers themselves. Colleges were forced to keep older professors on salary well beyond their productive years, and, faced with the prospect of living out their retirement years in probable penury, otherwise capable and interested individuals were disinclined to go into the teaching profession. Under the influence of Henry S. Pritchett, president of the Massachusetts Institute of Technology, Carnegie came to believe that the creation of a national pension fund for college teachers was the one area where he could make a unique and enduring contribution of "sweetness and light" to the field of higher education in the United States. In what John Rockefeller termed the "business of benevolence," some of Carnegie's Gilded Age brethren, such as Leland Stanford and Rockefeller himself, had created entire universities ex nihilo. Many others, of course, had made significant benefactions in the forms of schools, departments, scholarships, endowments, buildings, and so on to already existing institutions. But none had ever attempted, let alone conceived of, something on so broad or ambitious a scale. Unlike most of the other requests for money that were pitched to him by university administrators, Pritchett's idea of a college teachers' pension fund appealed to Carnegie's entrepreneurial *weltanschauung*. As with his introduction to the United States of the Bessemer process of converting iron into steel, Carnegie reasoned that this organizational innovation would radically transform the process and product of private higher education. That is to say, entrepreneurial *virtù* would be brought to bear upon the disordered field of higher education, creating a new institutional order of enlightened progress.

Carnegie's notion of enlightenment and progress, as well as stewardship, was irredeemably secular. That being the case, Carnegie decreed that no private college or university with denominational religious ties could be admitted to his new institutional order of higher education.[25] Accordingly, if a university wanted to apply for membership in the fund, it would have to sever all formal sectarian ties. This stipulation, which lead to the rejection of membership applications from schools such as Northwestern and Brown, sparked a national uproar (cf. Wall, 1970: 872–879). So great was the turmoil that Pres. Theodore Roosevelt felt compelled to personally try to convince Carnegie to drop the condition. However, Carnegie insisted on nonsectarianism and enlisted the aid of several college presidents who were on the fund's board of trustees to convince recalcitrant institutions to conform. One of these individuals was Hill McClelland Bell, president of Drake University.

Bell was one of only two college presidents from west of the Mississippi River who were asked to join the fund's board of trustees. However, in order for Bell to accept this prestigious position, as well as for the university to join the fund, Drake would have to sever its ties to the Church of Christ. Bell saw to it that Drake did so in short order. Carnegie and Pritchett were so impressed by Bell's alacrity in transforming Drake into a nonsectarian institution—and by Bell's capacity for convincing reluctant college trustees of the benefits of such a change—that they asked him to spread the gospel of nonsectarianism across the Midwest (Ritchey, 1956: 118–124). Apparently Bell was successful in his mission, for he managed to secure from Carnegie what so many other university presidents were unable to do: funds to build a library. Today, although the Carnegie Building of Drake University no longer serves as a library for the printed word, it still functions as a heliocentric resource, dispensing light and wisdom through electronic audio and visual media and the material wherewithal to purchase that media through the office of student financial aid. Moreover, on the wall above the front desk in the financial aid office, one can see the sign that marks Andrew Carnegie as the beneficent source of the building's heliocentric power: a four-foot bronze penny stamped with Carnegie's profile. In shape and design, the image matches that which serves as a punctuation point to the bronzed facsimile of Carnegie Dunfermline Trust deed that sits in Pittencrieff Park.

These pennies operate rhetorically as figural synedoches of the narrative of fortune and virtue through which the moral truth of the Steward-Entrepreneur is conjured. The pennies, of course, represent the universal

equivalent of money, the fluid medium through which power is territorialized in capitalist society. As such, the pennies are coins of the realm of
sovereignty. Moreover, the pennies represent two realms through which
money flows and is territorialized: the realm of the market and wealth
accumulation and the realm of philanthropy. These two realms are
tightly linked in the moral character of the Steward-Entrepreneur, as
the virtues he demonstrates in creating the first realm are recapitulated in
the making of the second. As with Carnegie's issuing into the turmoil
and ferment of industrializing Dunfermline, this moral character comes
into a world of contingency, chance, and opportunity that the social flux
of capitalist society represents. Through manly *virtù* and the entrepreneurial virtues of the enterprising subject of interest, he transforms the
fortune of circumstance into a fortune of wealth and power or into, to use
Carnegie's words, an "empire of business."

In creating an empire or principality of his own design in the marketplace, the Steward-Entrepreneur embodies the project of virtuous self-
making that is the hallmark of the Founder and *homo mercator*. Yet what
distinguishes this moral character from his ancestors in the moral economy
of wealth is his articulation with and through the discourse and vocation
of stewardship. The fortune—or "surplus wealth," as Carnegie termed it—
that is virtuously accumulated in the market becomes a "trust," a source of
duty and obligation to "advance the well-being and happiness of the greatest number of beneficiaries." Thus, the fortune of the Steward-Entrepreneur represents a further set of opportunities beyond the marketplace to
cultivate and practice the virtues of philanthropic beneficence. However,
unlike the Steward-Citizen, the trust through which the public is articulated with the private is uniquely his own. Inheriting no position of
trusteeship as part of an extended patrimony, and thus bound by no
"marching orders" from the past, the Steward-Entrepreneur is free to create a new empire of philanthropy in the present. The institutions of this
empire are entrepreneurial innovations, such as the Carnegie Dunfermline
Trust or the Carnegie Teachers Pension Fund, that are "calculated" to create a new, temporally enduring order for others to live within. As such,
these innovations are a reshaping of fortune in the name of social and historical progress. The Steward-Entrepreneur's empire of philanthropy bears
the virtuous imprint of his will and his will alone, a will that is literally
stamped upon the penny in the form of his face.

The penny can therefore be interpreted as the capitalist equivalent of
Marcel Mauss's "dancing mask" that is donned by the Kwakitul gift-
giver. By territorializing flows of surplus wealth in the form of beneficent
philanthropic innovations of his own design, the Steward-Entrepreneur
enacts the moral "truth" that "to give is to show one's superiority, to

show that one is something more and higher, that one is *magister"* (Mauss, 1967: 72). This moral tale, inscribed in the penny, demonstrates to the beholder that the face of the man upon it is, as Mauss argues, honorable and virtuous rather than "rotten." The flow of wealth is narratively structured to become the fold of virtuous identity. And therein lies the answer of Andrew Carnegie the Steward-Entrepreneur to the question of Adam Smith the Stoic. Smith wondered whether there was any spiritual purpose to the pursuit of wealth and greatness, concluded that there was none, and reduced his worldly possessions to ash. In creating a worldly empire of beneficence, Carnegie articulated a vocation of virtue that would render Smith's question moot, at least for Carnegie and the Steward-Entrepreneur. Those entrepreneurial men of wealth who enact the duties of stewardship attendant upon the creation and possession of surplus wealth, Carnegie argued in *The Empire of Business*, comprise a "celestial class" of men, among whom

> selfish considerations are subordinated in the select brotherhood of the best, the service to be done for others being the first consideration. The reward of wealth or fame is unsought, for these [men] have learned and know full well that virtue is its own and the only exceedingly great reward; and once this is enjoyed, all other rewards are not worth seeking. As wealth and fame are dethroned; and there stands enthroned the highest standard of all—your own approval flowing from a discharge of duty as you see it, fearing no consequences, seeking no reward. (1933 [1902]: 125)

The Steward-Entrepreneur thus seemingly stands as a solitary source and self-referential sign of capitalist virtue as the deontological grounding of his moral identity is constituted by the self-made empires of business and philanthropy: Having created and given away a fortune, he needs no approval but his own. However, there is no such thing as a self-referential sign, as the meaning of any sign is made discursively possible on the basis of differential alterity. That is to say, the presence of virtue in the moral identity of the Steward-Entrepreneur, like all the other moral characters I have examined, is constituted through a relationship of difference. As Mauss notes, the whole point of the dancing mask that incarnates the virtuous spirit of beneficence is to demonstrate magisterial superiority. Yet there cannot be those who are *magister* without those who are *minister*. In spite of Carnegie's claims of virtuous self-referentiality, there is a relationship of differential alterity implicit in his discourse. The presence of Carnegie's "celestial class" of men can only be understood with reference to those who remain on the ground below, gazing upward in awe at these luminescent "better angels."

However, in order to understand the differential alterity that enables Carnegie to conjure the celestial status of the Steward-Entrepreneur, and his earthly inscription within the face on the penny, it is necessary to examine how his virtues are invoked in the rhetoric of selfhood by one final "better angel" of the present.

Minting the Coins of the Realms: Entrepreneurship and the "Empires" of Business and Philanthropy

Upon first examination, the (auto-)biographical narrative of computer entrepreneur and high-tech venture capitalist Jean Pierre Bey would not appear to be a very appropriate place in which to find the invocation and evocation of Carnegie's discourse of the Steward-Entrepreneur. As a left-wing Social Democrat committed to the cause of social justice and equality, Bey has been an anathema to many of his fellow members in the capitalist class. During the 1980s, when many Reagan-era conservatives appropriated Carnegie as an iconographic hero and employed a barely revised version of Gilded Age Social Darwinism as legitimating ideology for their social and economic policies, Bey was derisively called "The Liberal of Silicon Valley" in the pages of several national business publications. Bey's liberalism and passionate commitment to progressive social change seemed to be in direct conflict with his vocation and success as an entrepreneurial capitalist. Accordingly, from the perspective of the avatars of untrammeled free enterprise, Bey appeared to be an illogical and irrational eccentric. Yet like many of the Reaganite conservatives who sported Adam Smith neckties as a sign of intellectual and political piety but never bothered to read the man's work, those who would contrast the sound capitalist beliefs of Carnegie to the misguided and dangerous liberalism of Bey have little understanding of either.[26] That is because—in spite of some of the obvious differences in social philosophy and political ideology between Carnegie and Bey as individuals (viz. Carnegie's Social Darwinism would not accord with many of Bey's social democratic principles)—the resonances between Carnegie's discourse of the Steward-Entrepreneur and Bey's rhetoric of moral selfhood are deep and profound.

Carnegie's Steward-Entrepreneur and Bey's moral identity are conjured from within the same topos in the social imaginary of capitalism. Within this topos, several discursive formations converge to produce a particular language of moral selfhood. The discursive formations that gave rise to the heroic autonomous individualism of the Founder, the enterprising virtues of *homo mercator*, and the virtuous trusteeship of the Steward, are all present here. However, what gives the Steward-Entrepreneur, and Bey's (auto-)biographical narrative, their distinctive valence and positivity is the manner in which these discursive formations are articulated with one another to produce a coherent spatial story of virtuous sovereignty that maps the realms of wealth accumulation and philanthropic beneficence as the territory and locus of moral identity. The emplotment and emplacement of this narrative logic consists of three central components that mark the trajectory and teleology of virtue and sovereignty: the entrepreneurial making of self and principality in the marketplace; the recognition of the duties of stewardship as a function of social progress; and the entrepreneurial creation of new and innovative philanthropic institutions as an enactment of this duty. Each of these components contains particular configurations of the relationship of fortune and virtue, as well as discursive categories of differential alterity, that enable the rhetorical conjuring of the moral identity of the Steward-Entrepreneur.

"A Constitutional Dislike of Compromises": The Entrepreneurial Making of an Empire of Business. The first phase of the narrative logic through which Bey's moral identity as Steward-Entrepreneur is produced is relatively simple and straightforward. In fact, we have seen many of its features before in the (auto-)biographical narratives of the "better angels" we have already met in analyzing the moral characters of the Founder and *homo mercator*. These characters, the reader may recall, embody the virtues that are deemed to be the requisites for transforming the fortune of contingency into a fortune of wealth. As with Mark Dahlin, the fast-food entrepreneur from Chapter 3, Bey's quest for a fortune of wealth begins with youthful dreams of greatness, ambition, and self-transformation. However, Bey's trajectory of virtuous self-making through the making of a fortune is guided by a very different value-rationality than that of Dahlin. For Dahlin, the quest for the sovereign power of wealth was guided by an overwhelming desire to efface the unfortunate circumstances of his impoverished upbringing. For Bey, who was a relatively fortunate child of the professional middle class, the making of a fortune was guided by a broader desire to contribute to social change. According to Bey, as an engineering student in college he "had the vague yet distinct idea that some day I would like to start a company." However, a sermon marking the death of Martin Luther King Jr. provided the impetus to set his entrepreneurial ambitions in motion:

[The sermon] drove home to the point that he was only a few years older than I at the time of death, and if I was really serious about making some major contribution to social change in this country, which has in fact been my life-long ambition, I better do something about it. So I literally sat down and looked at the various paths open to me and concluded that the direct route of trying to contribute in some areas of social progress and make a

major impact was not as feasible for me as the indirect route of starting a
company and hopefully accumulating enough wealth and influence
through that process. . . . I was out to make a fortune.

For Bey, then, his goal of making a "major contribution to social change"
furnishes the narrative teleology of his project of entrepreneurial self-
making. He enters the marketplace with the expressed intention "to
make a fortune," and in order to make a fortune, the entrepreneur must
be able to master the flows of fortune as chance and opportunity. That is
to say, he must impose his *virtù* upon *fortuna* through discipline, rationality, and foresight in order to found a principality or empire of business.
For Andrew Carnegie, the *virtù* of the entrepreneur in mastering the
chaotic flows of fortune was the fount of all his other virtues through
which a fortune is produced. In an uncanny invocation of the Machiavellian metaphor of fortune as a waterborne tempest that the man of *virtù*
must brave, Carnegie argues:

> For a man to be in business, he must be at least part owner in the enterprise
> which he manages and to which he gives attention, and chiefly dependent
> for his revenues not upon salary but upon its profits. The business man pure
> and simple plunges into and tosses upon the waves of human affairs with-
> out a life preserver in the shape of a salary; he risks all . . . [he] has been
> thrown into the sea, but he does not need any life preserver or to be coddled
> as he will swim; he was not born to be drowned, and you will see him breast
> waves year after year until he is at the head of a great business. (1933 [1902]:
> 160, 164)

Here, the entrepreneur is rendered as evincing the heroic independence
and individualism of the Founder. The entrepreneur's success is dependent primarily upon his own solitary ability to manage an enterprise and
master the raging sea of fortune. Architect of his own destiny, the entrepreneur imposes his will upon the chance and contingency of marketplace and constructs a "great business" he can call his own. In a similar
vein, Bey describes his many entrepreneurial endeavors as being fueled
by his "constitutional dislike of compromises," compromises that one
does not often have to make if one owns and controls an empire of business. Thus, the manly *virtù* of the entrepreneur is inscribed deep in his
character as a quest for sovereign autonomy and independence in the
business world.

One of the central virtues of the entrepreneur is his perspicacious ability to discern opportunities and rationally transform such opportunities
into beneficial result. As Jeffrey Decker points out, one of the central
tropes of *fortuna* in late-nineteenth-century narratives of the self-made

man, such as those of Carnegie and the popular Horatio Alger "rags to riches" stories, is what he terms "moral luck." Moral luck, argues Decker (1997: xxviii), is a "secular version of divine grace" that is bestowed upon the individual in the form of opportunities for upward social mobility and the acquisition of wealth. However, moral luck is not bestowed upon everybody—only the always-already virtuous, that is, those who possess the inner character and virtues requisite for self-making in the market-place.[27] To use Decker's terms, this particular narrative of fortune and virtue is the story of "moral luck and market pluck" (1997: 2). In terms of the argument being made here, this means that the heroic courage of the entrepreneur as Founder must be tempered by the prudence and self-command of the enterprising *homo mercator*. Those who "would sail the uncertain seas of business," Carnegie argued, must not only be brave; they must also possess "all the best traits of human nature": "soberness," "enterprise," and "judgment" (1933 [1902]: 100, 162). The seizing of opportunity, and its transformation into a fortune, requires the methodical discipline of calculative rationality. If a fortune of wealth is the initial end of enterprise, and opportunity the potentiality of fortune, then the sober judgment of prudent rationality must be brought to bear in order to determine which opportunities are the most propitious and which means are best able to exploit them. This requires foresight, planning, and an awareness of the capacities and limitations of one's own resources.

In describing his path to fortune, Bey quite clearly conveys the conjoining of the heroic and the prudent that is inscribed within the figure of the entrepreneur. "I am and always have been a maverick," Bey told us. "I felt I could see more clearly than others the frontiers of technology and that was clearly the best opportunity. That's where successful companies are built in short time out of nothing, to exploit a major opportunity that I knew better than others." However, Bey's bold perspicacity as a "maverick" was disciplined by the calculative rationality of efficiently and effectively relating means to ends. Not only did he possess the virtue of opportune insight into the "frontiers of technology"; he also possessed a "realistic" understanding of his own talents and capacities and how to prudently utilize them as resources in producing a fortune. According to Bey, he went into the field of high-technology because

> one, I was trained in and liked engineering and was aware of the opportunities it could afford; two, I had some exposure to business and business management; and three, I guess I was very ambitious and at the same time had a realistic view of my own limitations. . . . So, I looked at all the possibilities I could think of, considered many product ideas, with the help of some consultants. I didn't have any top management experience and so I actually propositioned a former boss of mine to become president of the company. I was supervised by him.

However, Bey's desire for entrepreneurial sovereignty and his "constitutional dislike of compromises" ultimately compelled him to leave the company he helped to found. At his first company, Bey says that he was forced to make a series of compromises regarding personnel policy, research and development, stock options, and management structure that were not in accordance his understanding of the virtues of enterprise. From Bey's perspective, the point of the business enterprise is not simply to make a profit but to make a contribution to the betterment of society: "To me business and high-technology are an opportunity to create wealth and to create something of value." At this point in Bey's rhetoric of self, the social benefits produced in commercial society by the enterprising *homo mercator* are being invoked. Carnegie, as well, argued that in pursuing a fortune the entrepreneur "is producing untold wealth to the community, and the profit he reaps for himself is but a drop in the bucket compared to that he has showers upon wealth and nation" (1933 [1902]: 111). Accordingly, argued Carnegie, the entrepreneur is

> the toiling bee laying up the honey in the industrial hive, which all the inmates of that hive, the community, will certainly enjoy. The bees of the hive do not destroy the honey-making bees but the drones. It would be a great mistake for the community to shoot the millionaires, for they are the bees that make the most honey, and contribute most to the hive after gorging themselves full. . . . Under our present conditions, the millionaire who toils on is the cheapest article which the community secures at the price it pays for him, namely, his shelter, clothing, and food. (1933 [1902]: 115–116)

Although Bey would probably disagree with Carnegie's metaphorical hyperbole regarding the entrepreneur as "toiling bee," he would certainly agree that the entrepreneurial making of a fortune can and should entail a profound contribution to the well-being of society. For Bey, the founding of a new enterprise entailed the creation of a new institutional order that embodied his particular vision of "value."

According to Bey, the "value" of his enterprise consists of three distinctive social contributions. First, the products of the firm represent a positive social contribution, as the company is "a world leader in what I consider socially a very productive field, which is the use of computerized systems in creating engineering drawings, which in turn leads to better, more competitive and more useful products." Second, in concordance with the socially oriented virtues of *homo mercator*, Bey expands the territory of the market and creates new, enterprising subjects of interest through employment. However, Bey is not content with simply providing employees with a job and paycheck. For Bey, his company must be "people-oriented" as well as "successful" and "innovative." Thus, the third and most important social value that Bey's enterprise creates is in the form of a corporatist structure of work relations within the company. The firm's work environment is shaped so as to "influence my people's lives in a positive manner, individually and collectively." Bey's desire to influence the lives of "his" employees is manifested in policies promoting employment security, employee participation in decisionmaking, and enhanced worker loyalty and commitment through profit-sharing. According to Bey, such policies are meant to foster a progressive understanding of the mutual interests and interdependence of the entrepreneur and his employees. Because of these policies, Bey says, the "people who work in the company feel it is their company rather than a 'we-they' feeling, which is a very unfortunate thing." For Andrew Carnegie, as I argue at the beginning of this chapter, it was precisely what Bey terms the "we-they" feeling of labor-capital conflict that was at the core of the hegemonic crisis of late-nineteenth-century industrial capitalism. Accordingly, Carnegie argued that the creation of harmonious structure of corporatist interdependence within the industrial enterprise was absolutely central to the virtuous vocation of the Steward-Entrepreneur. Through corporatist practices such as joint consultation and profit-sharing, "workers are to become part owners in the enterprises and share their fortunes. This sense of ownership would make [the worker] more of a man as he regards himself, and hence more of a citizen as regards the commonwealth" (1965a [1886]: 110–111). Thus, for both Carnegie and Bey, the empire of business is a beneficent as well as profitable one; in seeking to secure a fortune, the entrepreneur contributes to social progress by creating a new corporatist territory of fortune in the form of opportunities for others to make themselves fuller subjects.

Given my extended discussions of the moral identity of the Founder and *homo mercator*, the foregoing discussion of the accumulative virtues of the Steward-Entrepreneur may seem redundant. However, it is important to have a fresh understanding of these virtues, as they are the fundament upon which this moral character's virtues as a philanthropist are built. The array of virtues that I have examined here, the heroic *virtù* of mastering fortune, the perspicacious discernment of moral luck as opportunity, the prudent calculative rationality of the enterprising subject in the marketplace, and the social benefits of enterprise itself, form a coherent discursive logic through which the entrepreneur produces a self and a fortune. Implicit in this logic are relationships of differential alterity that give the moral identity of the Steward-Entrepreneur his positivity within the moral geography of the market. The "others" that affirm the virtue of this moral character are simply those who lack the qualities requisite for producing a fortune that he embodies: the unambitious, the meek, and the temporizing; the imprudent, the irrational, and the short-sighted;

and the "drones" who create neither wealth nor value. The fortune that is produced through the virtues of the entrepreneur is the coin of this sovereign realm, an empire of business through which money flows and is institutionally territorialized.

However, for both Carnegie and Bey, it is not enough to mint this coin of the realm and, so to speak, put it in one's pocket as the just reward of virtue. The entrepreneurial accumulation of wealth is but the initial chapter, albeit a necessary one, in the virtuous vocation of wealth. The fortune that is produced in the marketplace provides the capacity as well as the duty to virtuously insert the sovereign self of the entrepreneur into the social space of the community through the creation and mapping of an empire of philanthropy. For enterprising men of wealth to be truly "celestial," and claim their rightful status as "better angels" of capitalism, they must be stewards as well as entrepreneurs.

"Master" and "Servant": Discipline, Duty, and Stewardship.   Money, as I argue time and again, is a fluid and malleable resource through which power, desire, and identity are territorialized. However, in order for money to be considered a legitimate medium of power, its flows must be structured and encoded in a particular way so that it is recognized as a sign of the virtue of its possessor. That is to say, the flow of money must be made congruent with the moral identity of the wealthy man through the narrative of fortune and virtue. Throughout the history of the moral economy of wealth I explore here, the confluence of money and identity has been seen as fraught with danger. Flows of money can corrupt a man's moral identity in the form of greed, avarice, luxury, spiritual turpitude, and civic irresponsibility. Money, like Fortuna herself, can inundate and drown a man with its flows. To those who possess, in Carnegie's terms, "surplus wealth," the danger is particularly acute, for the seductive temptations of fortune are greater. Therefore, not only must the entrepreneur master fortune in making a fortune; he must also discipline and master the fortune that he has made. The man of wealth, argued Carnegie, "should always be master. He should keep money in the position of useful servant. He must never let it master . . . him" (Carnegie, 1933 [1902]: 80).

How is the entrepreneur to discipline his money and bend it to his will? For both Carnegie and Bey, the discourse of stewardship provides a disciplinary technology of self and power through which flows of money are virtuously territorialized into flows of philanthropic beneficence. However, the notion of "stewardship" invoked by Carnegie and evoked by Bey is somewhat different from that deployed in the rhetoric of the Brahmins and John Lowell. This distinctive understanding of stewardship and the trust that it entails has significant consequences for the enactment of the philanthropic vocation of the Steward-Entrepreneur.

According to Bey, the potential power and problems of money become a source of concern for individuals when they become "financially secure." For Bey, as for all the wealthy individuals we interviewed, financial security provides a dual set of freedoms. Wealth provides freedom from, to use Bey's word's, "any significant worry" about the fulfillment of material need. This freedom from material necessity enables the wealthy to be free to pursue their desires and choose among alternative realms of worldly involvement. As Bey told us, being financially secure puts him "in the position which I very much wanted to be in," that is, to be free to use money as a territorializing resource of power. However, as both Carnegie and Bey argue, the freedom to choose entails the responsibility to *wisely* choose appropriate uses of wealth in society. Those who make the wise choice are virtuous "better angels"; those who do not make the wise choice are something considerably less.

Given the nature of money as a fluid resource in capitalist society, Bey is on the mark when he describes the moment a man chooses how to territorialize his money: "He goes liquid." Liquidity occurs when the "paper assets" that the entrepreneur owns in his empire of business become "real assets," which can then be directed toward a variety of ends outside of his business. From Bey's perspective, the liquidity of surplus wealth presents wealthy men with three distinct choices for utilizing it:

> Essentially there are those who see their wealth as something to be displayed, which becomes consumption, others have something they want to pass down to their family or progeny, and there are yet others who say, "Okay, now that I've got it, what can I accomplish with it?" This takes the form of philanthropy of one form or another, either extremely unimaginative or conservative, or, like myself, not necessarily along uncontroversial lines.

For Bey, the third choice is the wise and correct choice, and, as he tells us, it is the one he made:

> The idea of spending large sums of money on personal luxury and for conspicuous consumption is attractive to neither to myself, nor, fortunately, to my wife. So my lifestyle is relatively modest. It is more affluent than it was fifteen years ago, which we like, but not dramatically so, which we also like. . . . We spend what we want to spend, but with a prejudice towards being modestly frugal. For instance, this year I bought a new [Volkswagen] Scirocco. I have never considered borrowing, let alone buying, say either a Mercedes or another extremely expensive car. . . . So we give about three and half million dollars per year to the Bey Foundation and in addition, I

probably gave away an additional million dollars, and probably spent for
personal life something in excess of one hundred thousand dollars. That's a
very steep ratio, and we're very happy to have it that way. [Thus] nine-
tenths of our money has been spent on what I still call philanthropic activities, but basically our contribution to social change and social progress.

For Bey and his family, the world of liquidity and financial security is a
world of freedom and choice. He can choose among multiple modes of
utilizing and territorializing his wealth, and each reflects his will, intention, and desire. Thus, the choices that Bey has made have been "happy"
ones, ones that he "likes." However, implicit in Bey's rendering of the
choices attendant upon wealth and financial security is a standard not
only of personal satisfaction born of freedom but also of moral virtue
born of fulfilling duty and responsibility. The wealthy, as Bey says, have
three basic choices: they can spend it on themselves; they can sequester
their wealth in order to pass it on as inheritance; or they can engage in
philanthropic beneficence. In Bey's rhetoric of self, the third choice is revealed almost as an epiphany in the form of a question that the virtuous
man of wealth must ponder and answer: "Now that I got it, what can I
accomplish with it?" In spite of its brevity and simplicity, Bey's question
represents a complex evocation of the particular relationship between
fortune and virtue that is the basis for articulating the distinctive philanthropic vocation of the Steward-Entrepreneur.

Bey's question can be interpreted as an interpellating ideological hail.
In asking himself the question Now that I got it, what can I accomplish
with it? the wealthy man is being interpellated into a particular subject
position located at the interstices of vectors of fortune and virtue. "It" is a
fortune that the wealthy man acquires in the "now" of the present. For
Bey as entrepreneur, not only does he *possess* a fortune in the present; "it"
is a fortune that he has virtuously *created* in the present. Thus, the subject
position conjured by the interpellating question is that of the sovereign
self who owns and can control a fortune he has created by himself in the
marketplace. Further, the fortune that he has created in the present also
represents a new dispensation of fortune in terms of opportunity and
possibility in the present: Now that he has a fortune of his own making,
he can use this fortune as means for further "accomplishment." The
question thus represents a *calling* to virtuously accomplish something in
present with one's fortune. Implicit in this question-as-calling is a rendering not only of fortune as opportunity but also of fortune as responsibility. Accomplishment is not simply a matter of choice; it is also a matter of
duty and discipline, of giving shape to the flows of fortune in the form
of philanthropic beneficence. And the rendering of fortune as both
opportunity and responsibility in the present that must be virtuously

acted upon in the present constitutes the unique philanthropic vocation of the Steward-Entrepreneur.

It is important to note that Bey never uses the terms *trust* or *stewardship* during his interview. Nonetheless, I would argue that his formulation of the calling of philanthropy is made rhetorically possible by the discourse of stewardship. Further, I would argue that it is the discourse of stewardship that renders the calling to accomplishment a matter of duty as well as opportunity. However, the specific meaning that fortune as opportunity and responsibility has for the Steward-Entrepreneur, as well the philanthropic vocation that is premised upon this meaning, is quite different from that of the Steward-Citizen and thus constitutes a different problematic of self. As I argue in the preceding section, the discourse of stewardship constructs wealth as an array of talents, capacities, and opportunities to do good that is conferred upon the wealthy man by God. It is the duty of the steward to invest and circulate his talents in the community. In the rhetoric of selfhood of men such as John Lowell, his "talents" take the form of an inherited trust that is his fortune. As one who is favored by the inheritance of a fortune, the Steward-Citizen is obligated to act on behalf of the unfortunate, thereby virtuously distinguishing himself from those who are irresponsibly fortunate. Fortune is a gift, a state of grace, that must be used beneficently for the public good.

In "Gospel of Wealth," Carnegie also argues that the fortune or "surplus wealth" that "flows" into the hands of the entrepreneur should be considered a "sacred trust" of which he is "steward." Carnegie's notion of stewardship thus shares much in common with the Christian doctrine of stewardship. As with Perkins and Mather, Carnegie maintains that the possession of a fortune entails a duty and responsibility to do good in the world by productively investing and circulating surplus wealth in the community. According to Carnegie, the responsibilities of stewardship required the wealthy man to use his surplus in a disciplined and correct way so as to resist falling, to use Perkin's words, into a "sea of corruption." However, it is the manner in which Carnegie deploys stewardship as disciplinary discourse that would give virtuous shape to flows of money that distinguishes his philanthropic vocation from that derived from the Christian understanding of stewardship.

The distinctive interpretation that Carnegie makes of the doctrine of stewardship is best exemplified in his essay "Wealth and Its Uses." In this essay, Carnegie poses the following question: "Assuming that surplus flows into the hands of but a few men, what is their duty? How is the struggle for dollars to be lifted from the sordid atmosphere surrounding business and made into a noble career?" (1933 [1902]: 118). The noble use of money, Carnegie answers, is a function of the wealthy man carrying out his duty as steward. But how is this duty to be recognized? What are the specific practices through which it can be enacted? In a manner echoing Bey, Carnegie argues that the liquidity of surplus presented the wealthy man with several choices as to how to use it: He can spend it on himself; he can "hoard" it in a miserly fashion; he can pass it on to his children as an inheritance; he can bequeath his wealth for public purposes upon his death; or can he can use wealth philanthropically during his lifetime.

The use of wealth for purposes of consumption, conspicuous or otherwise, presented little problem for Carnegie. Consumption for enjoyment may not be the most noble use of wealth, yet it was relatively innocuous and inconsequential, as a man of truly great wealth could not possibly consume most of his surplus. As far as the second disposition of wealth is concerned—miserly hoarding—Carnegie was much less sanguine. Thrift and frugality, in concord with the doctrine of stewardship, was a "civilized virtue." However, the hoarding of wealth was a perversion of this virtue, as the miser become mastered by the money rather than mastering it. Furthermore, should a man persist in this perversion to his dying day, he would reap the bitter fruit of dishonor: "The man who dies possessed of millions of securities which are held simply for the interest they produce, that he might add to his hoard of miserable dollars . . . who dies possessed of millions of available wealth which was free and in his hands ready to be distributed will die disgraced" (1933 [1902]: 120–121). The distribution of wealth to a man's heirs was hardly more palatable to Carnegie. To bequeath anything more than a modest inheritance was to invite the corruption of one's children, for "there is nothing so enervating, nothing so deadly in it effects upon the qualities of which lead to highest achievement, moral or intellectual, as hereditary wealth" (1933 [1902]: 105). The fourth possible use of surplus wealth—giving it away as part of one's will upon death—was "less injurious to the community" than giving to it one's heirs yet utterly devoid of virtue: "There is no grace, and there can be no blessing, in giving what cannot be withheld. It is no gift, because it is not cheerfully given, but only granted at the stern summons of death" (1933 [1902]: 105). Thus, according to Carnegie, the only noble use of surplus is

> that it be regarded as a scared trust to be administered by its possessor, into whose hands it flows, for the highest good of the people. Man does not live by bread alone, and five or ten cents a day more revenue scattered over thousands would produce little or no good. [However], accumulated into a great fund and expended, it establishes something that will last for generations. . . . It will educate the brain, the spiritual part of man. It furnishes a ladder upon which the aspiring poor may climb; and there is no use whatsoever gentlemen, trying to help those who do not help themselves. You cannot push anyone up the ladder unless he is willing to climb a little himself.

When you stop boosting, he falls, to his injury. . . . By administering surplus wealth during life great wealth may become a blessing to the community, and the occupation of the business man may be elevated so as to rank with any profession. In this way, he may take rank with even the physician, looking after and trying to not to cure, but to prevent, the ills of humanity. To those of you who are compelled or desire to follow a business life and to accumulate wealth, I commend this idea. (1933 [1902]: 120–121)

It is important to note just whom Carnegie is hailing with his doctrine of stewardship. It is not the inheritor of a fortune and a state of grace but the "businessman" who entrepreneurially created a fortune. Just as a businessman has created his own fortune, so too must he create his own place of grace in the world. A man who dies without "administering surplus wealth during life" is bereft of grace because he has violated a "sacred trust." But to whom or what is the entrepreneur as steward bound by the duty attendant upon possessing the trust? The Steward-Entrepreneur's trust is a product of his own individual accumulative virtues and therefore, quite unlike that of the Steward-Citizen, is not a gift from God or the fortunate circumstances of inheritance. Accordingly, the duties and obligations of the Steward-Entrepreneur are not to God, family, extended patrimony, or even to the less fortunate; they are to himself and to history. Specifically, the duty of the entrepreneur as steward is to intervene in history, foster social mobility, and to shape social progress according to his own will, design, and intention. His calling is not simply to help the poor and the community at large but to transform the very fabric of their fortune, as his duty is nothing less than to "prevent the ills of humanity." He must territorialize wealth into a "great fund" that when expended "will establish something that lasts for generations." Just as he created an empire of business, so too must the Steward-Entrepreneur create an empire of philanthropy.

"Progress in My Lifetime": Entrepreneurial Innovation and the Empire of Philanthropy.   At the core of Carnegie's distinctive rendering of the philanthropic vocation of the Steward-Entrepreneur is the post-Enlightenment idea of historical progress and social change. According to Christopher Lasch (1991), the post-Enlightenment understanding of historical progress entailed a secularization of salvation and virtue. From the perspective of Enlightenment and post-Enlightenment figures such as Adam Smith and Karl Marx, the organization of society was seen as being malleable and subject to the design and intervention of human reason. To the extent that social institutions could be shaped according to secular ideas of well-being and happiness, Lasch argues, they became earthly sites of virtue that constituted the "true and only heaven." It is

the belief in both the capacity and the duty of the entrepreneur to use his surplus wealth in order to contribute to the rational remaking of society in the name of social and historical progress that for Carnegie constitutes the basis of his philanthropic vocation as steward. From Carnegie's perspective, then, the Steward-Entrepreneur is not only a "trustee and agent" for "his poorer brethren," as he argued in "Gospel of Wealth"; he is primarily the "trustee and agent" of the "true and only heaven" of historical progress. It is this particular notion of trusteeship, and the virtuous enactment thereof, that constitutes the emplotted teleology of the narrative of fortune and virtue of both Jean Pierre Bey and the Steward-Entrepreneur.

Being an agent through which heaven on earth is created is an awesome responsibility, and, according to Carnegie, the enactment of this trusteeship requires that men of wealth sternly discipline the flows of philanthropic beneficence that they send out to the community. The proper philanthropic territorialization of surplus wealth requires the same mastery of fortune that the entrepreneur evinced in his making of a fortune. That is to say, in practicing his philanthropic vocation, the Steward-Entrepreneur must resist possible temptation and corruption through heroic and innovative entrepreneurial *virtù* as well as through the enterprising virtues of prudence and rationality. As Carnegie argues in "Gospel":

> It is ever to be remembered that the chief obstacle which the philanthropist meets in his effort to do real and permanent good in this world is the practice of indiscriminate giving; and the duty of the millionaire is to cease giving to objects that are not clearly seen as being deserving. He must remember Mr. Rice's belief, that nine hundred and fifty of every thousand dollars bestowed upon so-called charity had better be thrown into the sea. As far as my experience of the wealthy is concerned, it is unnecessary to urge them to give of their superabundance so-called. Greater good for the race is to be achieved by inducing them to cease impulsive and injurious giving. As a rule, the sins of the millionaires in this respect are not those of omission, but of commission because they do not take time to think, and chiefly because it is much easier to give than refuse. . . . The miser millionaire who hoards his wealth does less injury to society than the careless millionaire who squanders his unwisely, even if he does so under the mantle of sacred charity. . . . The rich man [must] know that the best means of benefiting the community is to place within its reach ladders upon which the aspiring can rise—free libraries, parks, and the means of recreation, by which men are helped in body and mind; works of art, certain to give pleasure and improve the public taste; and public institutions of various kinds, which will improve the general condition of the people; in this manner returning their surplus wealth to the mass of their fellows in the forms best calculated to do the lasting good. . . . There is but one right mode of using enormous fortunes-namely, that possessors from

time to time during their own lives should administer these as to promote the permanent good of the communities from which they are gathered. (1992 [1889]: 14–15, 11)

It is possible to discern in Carnegie's argument several key discursive categories of differential alterity that serve to construct the virtuous moral identity and philanthropic vocation of the Steward-Entrepreneur. Each of these categories of alterity revolves around the disciplining of the desire to do good as well as of the monetary flows of philanthropic beneficence. The first relationship of difference entails a contrast between rational "philanthropy" and irrational "charity." The man of wealth who indiscriminately gives his money away without reason and perspicacity, even if in the name of "sacred charity," violates the terms of his trust and demonstrates a pernicious lack of mastery over fortune. As such, his giving is a waste, akin to throwing his money "into the sea," and he is thus more corrupt than those who hoard their wealth for themselves. Indeed, for Carnegie, the problem of productively territorializing surplus wealth lies not in encouraging wealthy men to be generous but in teaching them to discipline their beneficent desires. The "sins of the millionaires" stems not from stinginess but from irrational "impulsive giving."

This contrast between rational and irrational giving, as embedded in the distinction between philanthropy and charity, sets up two further relations of differential alterity. The proper territorialization of surplus wealth requires that the philanthropist have an acute understanding of his status as an agent of historical progress and his unique relationship to secular time. The surplus wealth that is the corpus of the Steward-Entrepreneur's trust, and thus the coin of the realm of beneficence, is a product of accumulative virtue of the entrepreneur in the present to which the philanthropist gives form in order to shape the future. The duty of the Steward-Entrepreneur is to rationally reflect and decide upon which institutional forms are "best calculated" to "do real and permanent good in this world." Accordingly, the obligation of the wealthy man is not to distribute his wealth charitably in order to meet the extant needs of the poor or the community at large; rather, it is to invest his wealth philanthropically in order to transform those needs through the establishment of innovative institutions. Such institutions provide "ladders" of social mobility for the "aspiring," tutor "public taste," enhance "body and mind," and "improve the general condition of the people." For Carnegie, as a function of the stewardship of history and social progress, the vocation of philanthropy entails the entrepreneurial creation of a temporally enduring spatial territory of "sweetness and light" within which members of the community from which fortunes "are gathered" can cultivate the virtues of self-improvement. Finally, this duty and responsibility to history in terms of shaping the future is such that it is also the responsibility of wealthy man to do his shaping in the present. The Steward-Entrepreneur cannot wait until his death to engage in his vocation of philanthropy. As a man who has imposed his will upon fortune in order to create an empire of business, he must also impose his will upon the disordered chaos of the community and civil society through the creation of an empire of philanthropy. As Barry Karl points out with reference to the entrepreneurial innovation of the Carnegie Teacher's Pension Fund, as a philanthropist Carnegie was not only responding to "a need for change" but also instituting "a direction it should follow" (Karl, 1992: 42). Therefore, the trust incumbent upon the entrepreneurial creation of wealth entails that it be "administered" during a wealthy man's own lifetime so that it bears the virtuous imprint of his reason, will, and foresight in the present. To use Charles Taylor's (1989) term, this philanthropic intervention in the space of civil society is the "hypergood" or overarching moral value that provides the telos for the Steward-Entrepreneur.

These discursive categories and relationships of differential alterity, which Carnegie employed in order to conjure the philanthropic vocation of the Steward-Entrepreneur, are also central to Jean Pierre Bey's construction of his moral identity in his (auto-)biographical narrative. That is to say, his philanthropic beneficence represents a rational, innovative, and enduring contribution to historical progress and social change that is given shape and form during his lifetime. By Bey's own account, in order to produce the philanthropic "accomplishments" with his wealth that he felt called upon to do, he had to subject it to the same rational discipline that was required to make it. The financial security that came with "going liquid" put Bey "in the position, which I very much wanted to be in, [of] being able to devote very large sums of money to areas which I consider important in our society." However, the opportunity to territorialize his wealth philanthropically also presented Bey with the "problem" and challenge of doing so wisely. "I'm an engineer and I'm a planner," he told us, and "when the problem arose of having large discretionary amounts of money, I had made a few ad hoc decisions. But I had to develop a rational scheme. I did."

For Bey, then, the rationalization of his giving entailed developing a "three-tier" scheme of philanthropic priorities: a tertiary tier consisting of small gifts made on ad hoc basis simply as contributions to a wide array of causes; a secondary tier consisting of "major" gifts, ranging from $10,000 to several hundred thousand dollars, that are given regularly to a select number of beneficiaries; and a primary tier that consists of Bey's $40 million endowment of the foundation, dedicated to the "empowerment" of "elders" in American society, that bears his name. It is important to note this scheme entails more than a rational ordering of distribution; it also reflects a desire and intent to bring to Bey's philanthropic activities the same entrepreneurial *virtù* and enterprising virtue that he demonstrated in accumulating his wealth. Indeed, according to Bey, philanthropy can and should operate according to principles of the marketplace. "I believe in competition," he said,

> In fact, I dislike communists and extreme conservatives probably for the same reason, because I'm against all forms of monopoly and therefore believe in the role of competition. . . . I believe that private philanthropy is the perfect example of competition. There you can try to have imaginative, innovative goals and plans which would take years if you told them to get the government to try them out and if they work out well, then government will follow in their footsteps and not vice-versa. So, I see that private philanthropy has somewhat the same role that the innovative, high-technology venture capital–funded sector has had in the economy.

Accordingly, for Bey, his "success" in his philanthropic vocation is to be measured by the same criteria of virtue that he applies to his business activity, that is, whether or not he is able to make an enduring and innovative institutional contribution of "value" to historical progress and social change. As he said in a passage quoted in the preceding section, philanthropy can either be "unimaginative" and "conservative" or it can be "innovative" and "controversial." Philanthropic endeavors of the latter sort, according to Bey, are the mark of the philanthropist who virtuously carries the obligations of his trusteeship. Of course, the desire to further the cause of social change through the creation of new philanthropic institutions must be tempered by prudence, substantive rationality, and discipline. The entrepreneur as philanthropist must ascertain which opportunities for philanthropic investment are the most propitious and which means are best suited to produce the desired result. Reflecting upon his philanthropic attempts at intervening in history so as to create "a juster, more participative, fairer world," Bey said that he is

> trying to work pragmatically towards specific aspects of that, in part, because I realize there's far more than any one person can do. I accept that fact and don't try to do everything. And so I select a manageable number of things in which I have a significant understanding of them, work on that subset and don't worry about the fact that I can't work on other things. . . . It seemed to be that for the scale I wanted to do [a foundation] was the best way to do it. Because if you want to be effective, you have to concentrate your efforts. In the case of elders, I wanted something in which progress, significant progress, could occur in my lifetime. . . . We are committed to changing the role and status of elders in our society to a more participative

one. So really, we aren't concerned with ameliorating a particular situation or a particular location. We are funding empowerment, really.

Here, Bey is invoking the virtuous rationality of Carnegie's Steward-Entrepreneur who "returns . . . surplus wealth to [the] mass of fellows best calculated to do them lasting good." Bey disciplines his flows of philanthropic beneficence in an exceedingly rational and discriminating manner. His resources are "concentrated" in an institutional form—a foundation committed to a specific goal reflecting Bey's desires and priorities—that is designed to have the most effect in contributing to social change. Moreover, this institutional form was selected according to perhaps a more important criteria than that of rational efficiency: creating "progress" in Bey's own lifetime. Bey's foundation is therefore designed to take a fortune that was made in the present and fashion it into a new territory of opportunity and "empowerment" for beneficiaries in the present and for generations to come. In this manner, Bey presents himself as virtuously fulfilling the duties and obligations of the Steward-Entrepreneur. His (auto-)biographical moral tale is thus complete.

Even though our story is complete, the telling of Bey's tale of virtuous moral identity does not cease with the end of the interview. By founding new institutional orders of wealth production and philanthropic beneficence that bear the imprint of his will, desire, and name, Bey has inscribed his tale within enduring monuments to his virtue. Although no pennies bearing his image are to be found in his domains, the coins of the realms of both business and philanthropy have indeed been minted and, bearing the signs of his virtuous story, will be circulated in perpetuity in the moral economy of wealth. For his part, Carnegie (I imagine) would listen to Bey's tale of fortune and virtue and comment that he was indeed a man who successfully carried out the duties of the "sacred trust" possessed by the Steward-Entrepreneur. Founder, _homo mercator_, philanthropist, "better angel," the "celestial class" of the Steward-Entrepreneur will be remembered forever by those of us on earth as long as we know how to read the signs of his virtue. Carnegie's purpose in conjuring this moral character was to ensure that we do. To this end, Carnegie was successful, for within the moral economy of contemporary capitalism there is no greater regard than that given to men who have entrepreneurially minted coins of the realm in business and philanthropy. _Tanto nomini nullum par elogium._

Notes

1. It is important to note here that the discourses of philanthropy that emerged in the nineteenth century were not exclusively concerned with the construction of

a virtuous identity for wealthy men. Both the antebellum and postbellum periods witnessed the emergence of specifically feminine discourses and rhetorics of philanthropy that were centrally important in constructing a moral identity and quotidian vocational practice for middle-class and upper-class women. These discourses, which until the Progressive Era were all expressions of what Lori Ginzberg (1991) has termed the "ideology of benevolent femininity," were crucial in enabling women to move beyond the private sphere of domesticity and into the public sphere of civic action. Although, as Ginzberg argues, this discourse of benevolent femininity and its concomitant philanthropic practices did not directly challenge or overturn patriarchal notions of female virtue at the time, they were salient in constructing various social and political movements (e.g., abolition, temperance, etc.) that were the basis for the first wave of autonomous feminism in the late nineteenth and early twentieth centuries. For a history of the role of women in American philanthropy, also see the work of Kathleen McCarthy (1982, 1991).

2. It is important to note that the *Review* was not the only print medium for the discursive articulation of Brahmin ideology. As Jaher (1982: 60–61, 83–87) explores in some detail, one of the primary ideological differences concerning the correct vocation of wealth that divided the Brahmin intelligentsia, particularly in the immediate antebellum and postbellum periods, was between an older, more conservative faction and a younger, more radical one. The members of the former faction, such as Samuel Eliot, George Ticknor, and Edward Everett, were directly involved in the management of the businesses and charitable enterprises of the Brahmins and were thus primarily concerned with developing an effective moral discourse for the practices of entrepreneurship and stewardship. The younger faction, which included Charles Eliot Norton, Oliver Wendell Holmes, and James Russell Lowell, were more aloof from the quotidian concerns of business and charity and were more concerned with the use of wealth to cultivate a genteel life of letters. This conflict was manifested in the contrast and competition between the *North American Review* and *Atlantic Monthly*. The latter periodical, which was founded in 1857 and continues publishing to this day, was the intellectual home to Brahmins like Holmes who expressed a more ambivalent stance toward the realm of business and wealth accumulation. Whereas the *Review*, in Gramscian terms, remained organically tied to the concerns of the ruling business elite, the *Atlantic* gradually assumed the neutrally aloof stance of the traditional intelligentsia, focusing its attention on the arts and letters and becoming the premier American journal of the high culture literati in the second half of the nineteenth century. See also Baltzell (1979, esp. 281–305) for an account of the contrasting political and ideological positioning of the two publications as well as their different constituencies.

3. The idea of titularly conferring an aura of theological revelation upon Carnegie's discourse of philanthropy was that of W. T. Stead, editor of the British magazine *Pall Mall Gazette*, which published the article under its current title in 1890. For a full account of the circumstances and controversy surrounding the publication of the article both in the United States and the United Kingdom, see Joseph Wall's (1970) epic-length biography, especially pages 806–815.

4. During the nineteenth century, American society underwent immense socioeconomic change. In 1800, some 80 percent of the white male labor force was

made up of self-employed farmers or independent artisans. By 1896, some 80 percent of the labor force had become proletarianized wage laborers. America had been transformed from a relatively homogeneous and egalitarian society of small producers to one that was dominated by huge industrial trusts, polarized into hostile classes of capital and labor; some 40 percent of nation's wealth was concentrated in the hands of less than 1 percent of the population. The figures on the wage-labor composition of the American work force in the nineteenth century are drawn from Gutman (1979: 55) and Edwards (1985: 141). The distribution of wealth figures are from Pessen (1973: 32–35) and Phillips (1991: 8–23, 241). It is important to point out that in characterizing the distribution of wealth in the early nineteenth century as "relatively egalitarian," I am not affirming the Tocquevillian representation of the Jeffersonian-Jacksonian era as the "Age of the Common Man," where "fortunes are scanty" and "equality of conditions" prevailed (Tocqueville, 1981: Book 2, 445). As Pessen (1973: 35–45) points out, depending upon the city (i.e., Boston, New York, Philadelphia, etc.), some 25–40 percent of wealth was concentrated in the hands of the local urban elite (5 percent of the population). However, compared to the enormously skewed distribution of wealth that was produced during the Gilded Age, the nationwide wealth distribution of the early 1800s among the white male population *was* relatively egalitarian.

5. My analysis of Carnegie's "Gospel" and other writings as symptomatic of a crisis of hegemony has been aided by the work of historian Alan Munslow (1988, 1993). Motivated by a similar concern with the politics of language, Munslow seeks to situate Carnegie's "discourse of the entrepreneur" as part of a larger attempt at reconstructing capitalist hegemony on the basis of a "reemplotment" of the American narrative of secular social progress from one based upon a teleology of economic "self-sufficiency" of independent producers to a teleology of corporatist interdependence. At this level, Muslow's analysis is quite interesting and compelling. However, his work is marred by a mechanical application of Hayden White's typology of tropes to Carnegie's writings.

6. The cost figure for Marble House is cited in Vanderbilt (1989: 144); the wage demands of the McCormick Workers are cited in Montgomery (1979). The mansions of the Gilded Age robber barons had a great deal of symbolic value in the moral economy of the period. They were, quite literally, monumental signifiers of social status that elicited, depending on one's perspective, awe and reverence for their owner's wealth or scorn and derision for their selfish greed and moral turpitude. The propriety of "the Big House," as historian Edward Kirkland termed the phenomenon, was a subject of much public debate during the period, so much so that is was a central topic in an influential report of the U.S. Senate on labor-management relations in 1885 (cf. Kirkland, 1956: 29–49). It was the controversy surrounding such mansions that Carnegie alluded to in his reference in the opening paragraph of "Gospel of Wealth": the "palace of the millionaire and the cottage of the laborer."

7. As I have invoked Bataille's name here to evoke my own analysis of the "gift" in the discourse of capitalist philanthropy, I should point out that he would probably not agree with my appropriation of Mauss's analysis of the gift in archaic societies. According to Bataille, Mauss had misinterpreted his own evidence as to the symbolic meaning and social effect of the ritual of the *potlatch*. For

Mauss, as I note above, the ritual destruction of wealth was productive of a social and psychic hierarchy of power and subordination. In contrast, Bataille argued that the *potlatch* was important because it was supremely *unproductive*. For Bataille, the *potlatch* was a paradigmatic practice of what he termed a "general economy" of *dépense*, or "expenditure," whereby the social surplus of a society is "wasted" or destroyed. The significance of the *potlatch* for Bataille was that it represented a sacrificial elimination of the social surplus, the *la part maudite* or "accursed share," thereby avoiding the accumulation of wealth and the concomitant formation of class divisions. Consequently, for Bataille, modern productivist societies (whether of the capitalist or socialist variety) operated according to a "restricted economy" whereby the social surplus was reinvested into yet more material production. For Bataille, the sober ascetiscm and rational calculation of *homo mercator* represented a restricted or diminished form of social and spiritual existence. Bound to the necessity of producing and possessing more without a collective festival of *dépense* and destruction, modern economic man was doomed to pursue the chimera of sovereign selfhood that obscured the "truth" of wealth. For Bataille, this truth was that the source and sustenance of life energy was the ecstatic and exuberant transgression of limits where the boundaries of self were dissolved in the sacrifice of wealth.

8. This is not to imply that being a Brahmin attorney did not have its pecuniary benefits. On the contrary, next to merchants, lawyers like Fuller accounted for the largest proportion of wealthy Bostonians during the antebellum period (Jaher, 1982: 65). However, as financially lucrative as the practice of law was for many Proper Bostonians, it was considered to be unseemly and gentlemanly for the true Brahmin to enter the bar solely to make money.

9. I am using *articulation* here in Stuart Hall's (1986) sense of the term as connoting both a process of "linking" or connecting as well as a process of speaking. I discuss Hall's concept of articulation in more detail below.

10. My discussion of trusts in this chapter relies heavily on George Marcus, *Lives in Trust: The Fortunes of Dynastic Families in Late Twentieth Century America* (1992). He agrees with Aldrich that the family trust can have a "mystical" presence and meaning to inheritors. Marcus argues that the family trust operates as a "Durkheimian collective representation" that imposes a symbolic framework of social and moral identity from which inheritors often find it difficult to separate their own personal identity (17, 174–179]. In an interesting use of the Freudian concept of *unheimlichkeit*, or the "uncanny," Marcus argues that inheritors often must work through an anxiety-wrought contradiction between the ideology of autonomous individualism and the dynastic identity of the Founders that is insinuated into their lives by the social form of the trust. Paul Schervish and I also found this difficult process of identity formation to be quite salient among the inheritors we interviewed for *The Study on Wealth and Philanthropy* (1988: 73–100). Indeed, it is this very conjuncture between the moral identity inscribed in the will of the Founder and the inheritor's effort at constructing a moral identity that he can claim as his own that I explore in this chapter in the peculiar linking of fortune and virtue embodied in the Steward-Citizen. However, I disagree with Marcus's characterization of the "dynastic uncanny," as embodied in the literal and figural form of the trust, as being "mystical." In my view, the trust is a "mythical"

rather than a "mystical" presence in the lives of male inheritors in the sense that it entails a symbolic and rhetorical topos that inheritors use to make sense of their fortune and locate a virtuous zone of social engagement in the practice of philanthropic beneficence.

11. Marcus (1992: 60–70), as well as Hall (1982: 95–124), provide excellent and useful summaries of the development of testamentary and trust law, focusing in particular on its role in forming and consolidating the power of Brahmin families. For a more detailed analysis of testamentary jurisprudence, see Friedman (1964) and Shammas, Salmon, and Dahlin (1987).

12. It is important to note that family trusts, with the exception of those that are for charitable and educational purposes, cannot perpetuate themselves indefinitely. In addition to the prudent man rule (which I discuss below), the Brahmin-controlled Massachusetts court system also made an enduring contribution to trust and testamentary law in the form of the rule against perpetuities. This rule, also known as the century rule, limited the lifespan of noncharitable trusts to about a century (Hall, 1982: 119). Thus, as Marcus explores in great detail (1992: 85–103), the gradual dissolution of wealthy dynastic families over four generations is built into the very legal structure of trust.

13. *Cut flower* is a term used by Baltzell to describe upper-class individuals of "great talent and temporary (one-generation) leadership who leave no family line of any distinction" (1979: 30).

14. Obviously, by using Lowell's real name I am transgressing the sociological research norm of keeping the identity of interview subjects anonymous. However, I am doing so with his permission. The reasons for using Lowell's real name, and why I think Lowell assented to being identified, are quite pertinent to understanding the symbolic power of extended patrimony of "trusts" as collective representation. For my part, when it came to writing this section on the Steward-Citizen, I found it impossible to disentangle the moral identity that Lowell articulates through his position of trusteeship from his "real" identity. Who Lowell "is" as a better angel of capitalism is impossible to separate from the specific collective identity and history of the extended patrimony that he inherited and works within on a daily basis. For his part, too, Lowell explicitly recognizes the salience of the position of trusteeship inherited as a Lowell to craft a virtuous self-identity. Whatever his unique personal contributions to the extended patrimony of his trust, he is doing so in the name of the family and not simply himself.

15. Histories of the Lowell family, individual members, and their business, cultural, and philanthropic endeavors are almost legion (the HOLLIS online catalog system of the Harvard University Libraries lists close to 500 entries under the subject heading "Lowell Family"). The most comprehensive history, though now quite dated, is Greenslet (1946). Weeks (1966) also provides a detailed history of Lowell family philanthropy, focusing on the complex of cultural institutions clustered around the Athenaeum and the Lowell Institute. However, my understanding of the Lowell extended patrimony is primarily gleaned from more general sources such as Dalzell (1987), Hall (1982), Jaher (1980), and Story (1980).

16. The largest philanthropic bequest at the time was Stephen Girard's multiple gifts to the city of Philadelphia and several charitable institutions in that city upon his death in 1831. The largest of the bequests ranged from $300,000 for the

construction of canals to $2 million for the establishment of an orphan home (Fox, 1992: 96).

17. Without getting lost in the details, it is important to contextualize the founding of the Lowell Institute in the social and cultural politics of the time. At both the national and local levels, the Brahmins felt that their authority was threatened by the democratic distemper of Jacksonianism and its various populist offspring. Central to the formation and sustenance of democratic populism during the antebellum period was the lyceum movement of popular education. The lyceum movement in New England was a site of much anti-Brahmin discourse around a variety of issues (i.e., Brahmin control of banking, Harvard, and even the disposition of burial plots at Mount Auburn Cemetery) and thus was a source of much irritation to Brahmins such as John Lowell Jr. and fellow clan member Amos Lawrence. The Lowell Institute was conceived by Lowell partially in order to counter the influence of these lyceums, particularly among the middle and upper-middle classes. Moreover, in terms of audience and operation, the institute's lectures were profoundly antidemocratic. Strict rules concerning dress, manner, and audience participation (there was none) were promulgated by John Amory Lowell, the institute's first trustee, to exclude the "ignorant and critical classes of society," who were nothing more than "lean and hungry anti-everythings" (quoted in Story, 1980: 17). Apparently, then, the prosperity of moral virtue promised by Lowell in his will was available only to the materially prosperous, who were not "lean and hungry." Given the desire to incorporate social groupings outside of the Brahmin caste within its matrix of values, as well as its exclusionary and antidemocratic nature, in Gramscian terms the Lowell Institute can be seen as part of a war of position in civil society in which the Brahmins attempted to maintain hegemony within a historical bloc of interclass alliances. Although it is impossible for me to say with certainty whether or not the institute was successful in its larger hegemonic aims, it was successful in exerting hegemonic influence over the lyceum movement in New England between the time of its founding and the U.S. Civil War. As Story (1980: 14–15) points out, by 1860 the Lowell Institute had become the dominant public education organization in the Boston area, having "displaced or absorbed most of the competing lecture organizations."

18. The version of the New Testament I quote is *The New International Version of The Holy Bible* (Colorado Springs: International Bible Society, 1984: 702–703).

19. For an interesting analysis of the figural use of money in the language of both Mather and Benjamin Franklin, see Breitwieser (1984).

20. For an intriguing analysis of Carnegie's rhetoric of self-making that complements the one I offer here, especially as it is embodied in his autobiography, see Decker (1997).

21. As Wall (1970: 819) remarks, "Not all the communities complied with this request, however. Perhaps the Methodists across the way found it a bit presumptuous for a secular institution to arrogate to itself Jehovah's own first command."

22. As Wall (1970: 863–864) points out, Carnegie showed little interest, quite unlike his intense involvement with his other large philanthropic undertakings, in the one institution of higher education that would bear his name, the Carnegie Institute of Technology in Pittsburgh.

23. Even Woodrow Wilson, president of Princeton University, found Carnegie as potential benefactor to be a difficult quarry. In 1902, Wilson, after much pleading and cajoling, managed to convince Carnegie to a pay visit to Princeton in hope of securing funds for a new college residence system, a school of law, and a school of science. After touring the campus and its facilities, Carnegie announced to Wilson and the Princeton trustees (which included a former U.S. president, Grover Cleveland) that "I know exactly what Princeton needs and I intend to give it to her." Wilson and the trustees were to be greatly disappointed, as Carnegie had no intention of giving Princeton what they thought it needed. Rather, he gave Princeton what *he* thought it needed: a lake. Carnegie, as it turned out, harbored a strong dislike of the game of football and its inordinate importance on college campuses. A lake, he reasoned, would encourage the young men of Princeton to take up the more edifying sport of rowing (cf. Wall, 1970: 866–869).

24. For the sake of accuracy, it is important to note that TIAA/CREF is not simply the Carnegie Fund under a different name. As membership in the fund increased to include the vast majority of colleges and universities in the United States, by 1915 it became clear to Carnegie and the fund's trustees that its system of free pensions would soon be economically unfeasible. Consequently, in 1917, the Carnegie Corporation of New York (Carnegie's multipurpose philanthropic foundation) created the Teachers Insurance and Annuity Association of America, which would establish pension programs for faculty and administrators on a contributory basis (Wall, 1970: 879).

25. Although the original charter of the fund specified that only private institutions could apply for inclusion, Carnegie later liberalized its provisions to allow state colleges and universities to join (Wall, 1970: 875). As Wall points out, the fund truly did create a new institutional order of higher education. The effect of the fund, along with the Carnegie Foundation for the Advancement of Teaching, upon higher education in the United States extended far beyond the provision of pensions. The fund became a means by which the Carnegie Foundation could influence far-reaching reforms in curricula, teaching practices, admissions policies, hiring practices, standards for promotion and tenure, and so on. According to Wall (1970: 877), by 1909 the fund and the Carnegie Foundation had become the "national unofficial accrediting agency for colleges and universities."

26. The reference to Adam Smith neckties comes from Terrell Bell, secretary of education during the Reagan administration. In an interview, he reports being "besieged by young men wearing Adam Smith neckties who wanted to dismantle the public education system and replace it with privately owned and managed schools" (quoted in Marcus, 1989: 78).

27. Moreover, as Decker argues, in the context of stories of the self-made man, moral luck was conferred only upon those who embodied the characteristics and values of the white, male, Anglo-Saxon middle and upper classes. Moral luck was denied to white ethnics, women, African Americans, and others in the working classes. For other treatments of the turn-of-the-century mythology of the self-made man, see Cawelti (1965), Stivers (1995), and Wyllie (1956).

6

The "Better Angels" in the End

The paradox of the self becomes explicitly the paradox of narrative plot as the reader consumes it: diminishing as it realizes itself, leading to an end that is the consummation (as well as the consumption) of its sense-making. If the motor of narrative is desire, totalizing, building ever larger units of meaning, the ultimate determinants of meaning lie at the end, and narrative desire is ultimately, inexorably desire for the end. . . . What does [a] story have to tell? The story of an insistence of a desire as persistent as it is incoherent, a desire whose lack of satisfaction gives death as the only alternative, but whose satisfaction would also be death. Here we have figured the contradictory desire of narrative, driving towards the end which would be both its destruction and its meaning, suspended on the metonymic rails which tend towards that end without ever being able quite to say the terminus.
—Peter Brook (1985: 52, 57–58)

All stories, argues Peter Brook in *Reading for the Plot*, tend toward death. The act of constructing a narrative is to engage in the process of mythic sense-making, of conferring shape and meaning upon the temporal and spatial flux of social being. The structure of a narrative—its characters, plot, trajectory, teleology, and the spaces it performs—promise the fulfillment of the desire to know. Compelled by an enigma that inexorably unfolds toward resolution, this desire is the force field that gives energy to the process of telling and listening, writing and reading. The process of narrativity promises that, in the end, all will be revealed and the desire to know will be satisfied. With the consummation of the desire to know at the end of the story, desire dies, awaiting the promise of a new story to bring to life yet again. In this book, I have attempted to construct a narrative about narrative and, by way of this conclusion as ending, I shall reflect upon the desire to know that energizes both narratives. In doing so, however, it is important to note that the ending that my narrative entails is, as Brook argues, contradictory and temporary. In this conclusion, my desire as writer and your desire as reader is both consummated and terminated. Yet this "death" is only temporary, as this ending itself entails new enigmas through which the desire to know will flow. Thus, this conclusion is the manifested destiny of a provisional, rather than a final, telos. If the construction of the moral "truth" of wealth is an ongoing struggle in the social imaginary of Western capitalism, then any solution to the

253

enigma it represents must, in the end, be partial and temporary. That is to say, at best, my analysis can offer no fixed resting point of desire satisfied but only further questions that enhance our capacity to enter into the struggle over the moral "truth" of wealth.

Accordingly, an appropriate way to begin the ending is with Stuart Hall's question concerning the politics of narrative and identity. "Is it possible," he asks, "for there to be identity and action in the world without arbitrary closure—what one might call the necessity to meaning of the end of the sentence?" (1987: 45). If what I have argued in this book concerning narrativity is correct, then the answer is no. Narrativity, as a cultural technology of giving shape to moral identity and of providing a dynamic framework of *phronesis* for moral choice and social action, does indeed require closure in the form of a telos. As a socially constituted and historically specific form of power/knowledge, the closure of narratives can't be anything but arbitrary. Such a closure is one of the primary ways in which narrativity operates as a will to knowledge, truth, and power. However, to say that the closure of narrative is arbitrary does not necessarily mean that it is *final*. It is possible to imagine, to tell, to perform narrative identities containing closures that are contingent and provisional and thereby "open" to other possibilities for social being and becoming that are not always-already inscribed in them as manifested destiny. This contingency is what Brook terms the "paradox of the self" produced by narrativity.

Within the story space of the narrative of fortune of virtue among men of the American upper class, no such contingency is possible, as the emplotment and emplacement of the sovereign individual is absolute and final. The performance of this narrative by men of wealth, I have argued, constitutes a mythic process through which such men are able to make moral sense of their money, power, and privilege. As such, this narrative forms the basis for a rhetoric of selfhood through which the possession of wealth is integrated into a wealthy man's moral identity. Power and property are symbolically transformed into propriety. The desire to know that energizes this narrative is the desire to know one's wealth as being a right, true, and natural part of one's self. More specifically, the consummation of the wealthy masculine self in terms of a coherent moral identity occurs as the narrative unfolds along the "metonymic rails," to use Brook's phrase, of the discursive categories of fortune and virtue. Fortune connotes both a fortune of wealth as well as existential circumstances of chance, contingency, and opportunity. Virtue connotes the behavior and actions through which fortunes of wealth are made and utilized, and fortune as circumstance is transformed into beneficial result. As a metonymic configuration, the narrative of fortune and virtue involves not only the construction of a moral identity for wealthy men as individuals but also the conjuring of a figure who hegemonically reigns supreme in the moral economy of wealth. This moral character is the "better angel" of capitalism, the sovereign self of wealth whose flows of money and desire are territorialized into realms of power and propriety through the accumulation of wealth and its philanthropic dispensation. This flowing of money and desire into domains of sovereignty is encoded as being a sign of virtue, for in the end the "better angel" evinces the primary moral "truth" of wealth, which states that "prosperity has a purpose." This is the "magic" of the territorializing machine of the narrative of fortune and virtue. Within the map of the social produced by this machine, no other ending is possible or desirable.

The desire to know that is evinced in the narrative of this book has also been energized by an enigma, that is, how to make critical sense of the moral sense that wealthy men make of their selves and money through the narrative of fortune and virtue as a form of power/knowledge. I have argued that the moral "truth" of wealth, in contrast to the self-assured ministrations of George Bush and the other "better angels" who I have encountered in producing this book, is not self-evident. Rather, the belief that "prosperity," as signified in the possession of wealth, has a virtuous purpose is a historically and culturally specific feature of the social imaginary of Western capitalism. In order to know how this moral "truth" became enshrined in the moral economy of capitalism, and in order to know how the narrative of fortune and virtue became the dominant story of sovereign selfhood, I have maintained that it is necessary to genealogically examine the conditions of their emergence. I have argued that the moral identity of the "better angels" of capitalism is conjured from a complex field of the confluescent discursive formations of autonomous individualism, citizenship, stewardship, and the market. It is the confluence of these discursive formations that have constituted our knowledge of wealth as the objective manifestation of fortune and of wealthy men as subjects who virtuously transform this object according to will, intention, and desire into realms of sovereignty.

However, the purpose behind investigating the power/knowledge of wealth is not simply to understand its genealogy. My purpose is also to think about the premises and promises of the manifested destiny of the sovereign masculine individual of capitalism in a different way. As John Ransom aptly and succinctly describes the political imperative of the critical analysis of power/knowledge, "If power and knowledge are intertwined, it follows that one way to understand power—potentially to destabilize it or change its focus—is to take firm hold on the knowledge that is right there at the center of its operations" (1997: 23). In deploying the analysis of power/knowledge as a mode of social critique and political action, it is important to remember that power and knowledge are not the same thing. Although they are "intertwined," to use Ransom's word, they are not identical. The can-do-ness of power is contingent upon the know-how of knowledge, and if we come to know the world differently, then that which it is possible to do can change as well. The moral economy of wealth, and its performance of the sovereign individual through the narrative of fortune and virtue, valorizes a particular relation between know-how and can-do-ness. Yet at the very center of its operations are tensions that indicate that there are possible performances of individuality, social engagement, and valorized moral identity that are different than those premised upon the territorializing money machine of appropriation. The rhetorical field of the moral economy of wealth is rent with ambivalences and contradictions and is thus a site of conflict and contestation over the moral "truth" of wealth. There are two particular ambivalences I want to touch upon in bringing this story to its conclusion. The first has to do with the relation between the subject of sovereign individuality and its abjected "other." The second, related ambivalence has to do with civic virtue and community.

One of the central themes of my analysis of the ethical subject of sovereign individuality is that its narrative production and rhetorical performance entail a seductive and compelling metaphysics of presence. Within the narrative of fortune and virtue as a spatial story, the masculine sovereign individual of wealth, power, and propriety stands is ontologically anchored as the virile subject-agent of history: As a moral character, his identity is centered, complete, and coherent across the different registers of spatiality. The sovereign subject rules over psychic, corporeal, material, and moral space as his domain of principality and individuality. Following the argument of Judith Butler (1993), the fullness of his presence and manifested destiny is made possible only upon the excluded presence of the abject from his domain. The abject finds the spaces of the subject inhabitable or unlivable yet is intrinsic to rendering the space of the subject a valorized ethos for the subject. Time and again in my genealogical tracing of the battlelines that have been historically drawn between conflicting definitions of fortune and virtue, I have tried to show how the moral character of sovereign individuality is constituted by his relation of alterity to an abjected "other." The abjected other has taken on many forms: the goddess Fortuna, the *effiminato*, the avaricious, the citizen without honor, the greedy "gainer," the spendthrift, those who do not use their "talents," the slothful, the economically dependent, the weak and flabby inheritor, the miserly, and so on. In each of these forms of the abject, they are defined as being corrupt and enervated precisely because they do not possess the qualities and virtues that the sovereign subject possesses, and, conversely, the subject measures the fullness of his presence against the standard of their lack that renders them abject.

Of all the renderings of the abject, perhaps none is more compelling in terms of performing the metaphysics of presence of the sovereign individual than that offered by entrepreneurs and *homo mercators* Dick Balbus and Troy MacDonnell in Chapter 4. For Balbus, the abject were defined simply as "those without money"; for McDonnell, they were "the indigent." For both Balbus and MacDonnell, the virtuous vocation of *homo mercator* transformed the abject into subjects like himself, "good citizens" whose fullness of presence is succinctly defined by "the ability and desire to make money"; he therefore is able to say "I own this, I am something." For both Balbus and McDonnell, then, good citizenship is wholly defined by the pursuit and possession of money and wealth in the marketplace.

If good citizenship and sovereignty are defined wholly in terms of possessing that which is procured in the marketplace—money, wealth, commodities—then clearly the wealthy are the best citizens of all. Moreover, since the beginning of the 1980s, the resources required for market citizenship have been increasingly concentrated in the hands of the wealthy themselves. When one examines the statistics concerning the distribution of wealth and income in the United States over the past three decades or so, a number of salient features stand out. First, as a whole, the population of the United States has become undeniably wealthier. According to Edward Wolff (1995: 8–10), between 1962 and 1989, the mean wealth of households nearly doubled to approximately \$212,000.[1] Moreover, as conservative intellectuals and their apparatuses of publicity (such as the *Wall Street Journal*) are fond of pointing out, there are now well more than a million households that possess more than \$1 million in assets. According to David Frum of the conservative Manhattan Institute, this prolific increase in wealth has resulted "in history's first mass upper class" (quoted in Todd, 1997: 78). As such, the cornucopia of the marketplace provides the conditions for good citizenship as never before.

However, as Wolff and others argue (Henwood, 1998: 64–68), a closer look at the statistics reveals a more complex picture. A much better measure of what Frum calls the "economic miracle" of wealth creation is median rather than mean household wealth. (For the statistically uninitiated, the mean is simply an average of the value of all household wealth; the median is the point in wealth distribution that divides the population into two equal halves, those who have more than the median and those who have less.) If the mean increases faster than the median, then the gains of wealth are skewed in favor of those above the median. According to Wolff's research, this is precisely what happened, especially in the during the 1980s and early 1990s. After a steady growth between 1962 and 1983, median wealth actually *declined* between 1983 and 1992 to approximately \$51,000 (Todd, 1997: 75). What this means is that the increase in mean wealth is attributed to the gains made by the top quintile (or 20 percent) of the distribution of household wealth. Between 1983 and 1992, as Todd (1997: 76) summarizing Wolff's research writes, "virtually all gains in wealth went to the top 20 percent. The next two-fifths remained about even, and the bottom two-fifths actually got poorer in constant dollars." Moreover, of those gains made by the top 20 percent, almost two-thirds went to the top 1 percent. Although income is much less concentrated than wealth, the trends in distribution reflect the same pattern (Wolff, 1995: 11–12).

Who are the top 1 percent? They comprise about 2.6 million households and have at least approximately $2.5 million of household wealth and approximately $200,000 annual household income. As a group, they have a mean net worth of $7.6 million and a mean income of about $675,000 (Todd, 1997: 73). In terms of net worth, which includes all forms of household wealth, the "gilded 1 Percent," as Todd terms them, accounts for 39 percent of the total. When one looks at financial wealth, or assets that are readily fungible (i.e., they can be converted into cash for consumption, investment, or whatever purposes the owner desires), the top 1 percent as of 1992 possessed approximately 46 percent of the total.[2] The top 20 percent accounts for 92 percent of all financial wealth, which leaves about 8 percent for the bottom four-fifths of all households. As Wolff notes, this upward redistribution of wealth and its concentration in the hands of the top 1 percent has only two historical precedents in the United States: the 1920s and the Gilded Age of the late nineteenth century.

The only facet of net worth where the lower 90 percent of the population has enjoyed a greater growth than the top 10 percent, and especially the top 1 percent, has been debt. More recent data on household worth show that between 1989 and 1995 the debt burden of low-income households (below $25,000) and middle-income households (between $25,000 and $75,000) increased, whereas that of upper-income families declined; the further one goes up the distribution of wealth and income, the more precipitous the decline in debt burden (Henwood, 1998: 67; Kennickell, Starr-McCluer, and Sunden, 1997: 21).[3] Given the stagnation or, until quite recently, the slow growth of real family household income for the bottom 90 percent, as well as the skew in wealth distribution toward the top, the increase in debt has important implications for the kind of "good citizenship" and moral identity valorized by the market.

Quite simply, the sovereign individuality and good citizenship offered by the market is that of the consumer. For the bottom 90 percent of the population, the primary way to make social space habitable as an ethos, and to perform a valorized moral identity, is through consumption. Homes, automobiles, clothes, electronics, vacations, and so on become the measure of the fullness of one's status as a subject and the distance from the abject. In consumer capitalism, the "good life" has become identified with the purchase and consumption of goods. Thus, it is no accident that the liabilities held by the nonwealthy are primarily mortgage and consumer debts, which, in effect, are lended to them by the wealthy themselves. Now, one might aver that the ability to own a house and car, take a vacation, buy a computer for the children, and feed and clothe one's family is not such a bad thing. Of course it is not. But as Juliet Schor argues in her two most recent books, *The Overworked American* (1991) and *The Overspent American* (1998), those without wealth are having to work more and acquire more debt in order to stake a claim in the market as a sovereign subject of consumption. And to the extent that we spend more time and money chasing the chimera of consumer sovereignty—and get deeper into debt—the less time we have to be a rather different kind of citizen than that of the market.

This is a citizen of the community, the moral subject of civil society and the public sphere. This is the kind of citizenship imagined by the tradition of civic republicanism as well as contemporary communitarianism. As I argue above, the civic republican notion of civic virtue was incorporated into the moral economy of wealth as a sign of the magisterial status of the sovereign individual while effacing what the civic republicans understood to be the foundation of good citizenship: economic equality and security. Relative economic equality in turn provides the material basis for friendship, mutuality and concord, and a sense of common interests and the public good. Furthermore, as contemporary communitarians argue, particularly feminists such as Seyla Benhabib (1992), such citizenship also requires empathy, care, and a respect for difference. In this vision of citizenship, one does not seek to appropriate the community as an extension of the self and a principality of sovereign individuality. Such a citizen does not act either as steward, trustee, or entrepreneur of the social. Rather, such a citizen must dialog with and listen to others who are not the same or inferior; he must be willing to be changed by the encounter with others in the community as others are also willing to be changed. This means that the telos of the narrative of social being and becoming is not final but provisional and subject to change. When it is disarticulated from its connections to the understanding of the feminine as chaotic irrationality that must be mastered, this is the twin promise of civic virtue as an ethic and citizenship as a technology of the self. As Barbara Biesecker argues concerning the materiality of rhetoric, "It is in language that the social takes place" (1997: 50). Civic republicanism and feminist communitarianism offer a different language for enabling the social to take place as an ethos of knowing, doing, and living. Within this place, the abject can become subjects whose presence is measured by something other than money and commodities.

According to George Bush, "prosperity has a purpose" because "it allows us to pursue the 'better angels,' to give us time to think and grow. Prosperity with a purpose means taking your idealism and making it concrete through acts of goodness." Yet what this proposition leaves unexamined is the moral "truth" that there should be a positive correlation between wealth, on the one hand, and the capacity for philanthropic beneficence and civic virtue on the other. The problem with this moral "truth" is that its logic grants to those who have prosperity and wealth the privilege, as well as a responsibility, of having the time and money to make their idealism concrete through acts of goodness. This is not to say that the wealthy are the only or even the most capable members of civil society (although this is precisely what the moral economy of wealth proclaims). It is to say that in a capitalist society, where wealth and money is a primary resource upon which one is able to pay attention to the community and participate efficaciously in civil society, then citizenship often becomes a luxury rather than a necessary and intrinsic part of everyday life. Thus, in the end, I offer a new enigma to give new form to the desire to know: Shouldn't we all have the privilege of pursuing and being "better angels"?

Notes

1. Wolff's data on household wealth and income are drawn primarily from the Survey of Consumer Finances (SCF; conducted every three years by the Federal Reserve Board), as well as other sources. See Wolff (1995: 69–72) for detailed discussion of the methodology that he used to arrive at his measures of wealth and income across different data sources. At the time he wrote his book, the 1989 data from the SCF was the most recent available. Todd (1997) summarizes Wolff's analysis of the 1992 SCF.

2. Wolff makes a distinction between net worth and financial wealth. According to Wolff, the *net worth* of a household is "found by adding together the current value of all assets a household own—financial wealth; houses and unincorporated businesses, consumer durables like cars and major appliances, the value of pension rights—and subtracting liabilities—consumer debt, mortgage balances, and other outstanding debt" (1985: 1). *Financial wealth,* a subset of net worth, includes "cash on demand deposits; time and savings deposits, certificates of deposit and money market accounts; government bonds, corporate bonds, and other financial securities; the cash surrender value of life insurance plans, the cash surrender value of pension plans; and corporate stock including money market funds" (Wolff, 1985: 73).

3. It should be noted that the 1995 SCF yielded some very different conclusions to those of Wolff (who used only the 1983 and 1989 SCFs). According to Henwood (1998), the 1995 SCF found very little increase in the concentration of wealth in the 1980s. However, the increase between 1989 and 1995 was dramatic and in terms of scope and magnitude was congruent with trends Wolff found

using the 1983 and 1989 data. The reasons for the discrepancy have to with a change in the methodology of weighting and measuring wealth instituted in the 1989 survey. This makes comparison of the 1980s to the 1990s difficult. Nonetheless, the trends that Wolff analyzed are clearly present in the most recent data. See Kennickell, Starr-McCluer, and Sunden (1997) for a summary of the findings.

References

Abercrombie, Nicholas, Stephen Hill, and Bryan S. Turner. 1986. *The Sovereign Individuals of Capitalism*. Boston: Allen and Unwin.

Adam, Brian. 1990. *Time and Social Theory*. Cambridge, U.K.: Polity.

Alberti, Leon Battista. 1967. *The Family in Renaissance Italy*. Columbia: University of South Carolina Press.

Aldrich, Nelson. 1988. *Old Money: The Mythology of America's Upper Class*. New York: Vintage.

Althusser, Louis. 1970. "The Object of *Capital*." In L. Althusser and E. Balibar. *Reading Capital*. London: Verso.

_____. 1988. "Machiavelli's Solitude." *Economy and Society*, Vol. 17, No. 4 (November): 469–477.

Amory, Cleveland. 1947. *The Proper Bostonians*. New York: Knopf.

Appleby, Joyce. 1978. *Economic Thought and Ideology in Seventeenth-Century England*. Princeton: Princeton University Press.

Arendt, Hannah. 1958. *The Human Condition*. New York: Viking.

Bakhtin, Mikhail. 1981. *The Dialogic Imagination*. Austin: University of Texas Press.

Bal, Mieke. 1984. *Narratology: Introduction to the Theory of Narrative*. Toronto: University of Toronto Press.

Baltzell, E. Digby. 1958. *Philadelphia Gentlemen: The Making of a National Upper Class*. New York: Free Press.

_____. 1966. *The Protestant Establishment: Aristocracy and Caste in America*. New York: Vintage.

_____. 1979. *Puritan Boston and Quaker Philadelphia: Two Protestant Ethics and the Spirit of Class Authority and Leadership*. New York: Free Press.

Barilli, Renato. 1989. *Rhetoric*. Minneapolis: University of Minnesota Press.

Baron, Hans. 1955. *The Crisis of the Early Italian Renaissance: Civic Humanism and Republican Liberty in an Age of Classicism and Tyranny*. Princeton: Princeton University Press.

_____. 1988a. "Civic Wealth and the New Values." In *In Search of Florentine Civic Humanism: Essays on the Transition from Medieval to Modern Thought*. Volume 1. Princeton: Princeton University Press.

_____. 1988b. "Leon Alberti as Heir and Critic of Florentine Civic Humanism." In *In Search of Florentine Civic Humanism: Essays on the Transition from Medieval to Modern Thought*. Volume 1. Princeton: Princeton University Press.

Barthes, Roland. 1973. *Mythologies*. New York: Hill and Wang.

_____. 1977. *Image-Music-Text*. New York: Hill and Wang.

Bataille, Georges. 1988. *The Accursed Share: An Essay on General Economy*. New York: Zone Books.

Bellah, R., et al. 1985. *Habits of the Heart: Individualism and Commitment in American Life*. New York: Basic.

Bender, John, and David Wellbery. 1990. "Rhetoricality: On the Modernist Return of Rhetoric." In John Bender and David Wellbery, eds. *The Ends of Rhetoric*. Palo Alto: Stanford University Press.

Benhabib, Seyla. 1993. *Situating the Self: Gender, Community, and Postmodernism in Contemporary Ethics*. New York: Routledge.

Bercovitch, Serge. 1975. *The Puritan Origins of the American Self*. New Haven: Yale University Press.

Berger, John. 1973. *Ways of Seeing*. New York: Penguin.

Berlin, Isaiah. 1980. "The Originality of Machiavelli." In *Against the Current*. London: Hogarth Press.

Biesecker, Barbara. 1992. "Michel Foucault and the Question of Rhetoric." *Philosophy and Rhetoric*, Vol. 25, No. 4: 351–364.

_____. 1997. *Addressing Postmodernity: Kenneth Burke, Rhetoric, and a Theory of Social Change*. Tuscaloosa: University of Alabama Press.

Billig, Michael. 1991. *Ideology and Opinions: Studies in Rhetorical Psychology*. Newbury Park, Calif.: Sage.

Bolingbroke (Lord), Henry St. John. 1965. *The Idea of a Patriot King*. Indianapolis, Ind.: Bobbs-Merrill.

Boorstin, Daniel. 1987. "From Charity to Philanthropy." In *Hidden History*. New York: Harper and Row.

Bourdieu, Pierre. 1987. "The Biographical Illusion." *Working Papers and Proceedings of the Center for Psychosocial Studies*, No. 14.

_____. 1991. *Language and Symbolic Power*. Cambridge: Harvard University Press.

Braudel, Ferdinand. 1972. *The Mediterranean and the Mediterranean World in the Age of Philip II*. New York: Harper and Row.

_____. 1979. *Civilization and Capitalism*. Volume 2: *The Wheels of Commerce*. New York: Harper and Row.

Breitweiser, Mitchell. 1984. *Cotton Mather and Benjamin Franklin: The Price of Representative Personality*. Cambridge, U.K.: Cambridge University Press.

Bremner, Robert. 1988. *American Philanthropy*. Chicago: University of Chicago Press.

Brook, Peter. 1985. *Reading for the Plot: Design and Intention in Narrative*. New York: Vintage.

Brown, Richard Harvey. 1987. *Society as Text: Essays on Rhetoric, Reason, and Reality*. Chicago: University of Chicago Press.

_____. 1992. "From Suspicion to Affirmation: Postmodernism and Challenges to Rhetorical Analysis." In R. H. Brown, ed. *Writing the Social Text: Poetics and Politics in Social Science Discourse*. New York: Aldine de Gruyter.

Bruner, Jerome. 1987. "Life as Narrative." *Social Research*, Vol. 54, No. 1: 11–32.

_____. 1991. "The Narrative Construction of Reality." *Critical Inquiry*, Vol. 18 (Autumn): 1–21.

Buck-Morss, Susan. 1989. *The Dialectics of Seeing: Walter Benjamin and the Arcades Project*. Cambridge: M.I.T. Press.

Burchell, G. 1991. "Peculiar Interests: Civil Society and Governing the 'Natural System of Liberty.'" In G. Burchell, C. Gordon, and P. Miller, eds. *The Foucault Effect: Studies in Governmentality*. Chicago: University of Chicago Press.

Burchell, G., C. Gordon, and P. Miller, eds. 1991. *The Foucault Effect: Studies in Governmentality*. Chicago: University of Chicago Press.

Burckhardt, Jacob. 1954 (1860). *The Civilization of the Renaissance in Italy*. Vienna: Phaidon Press.

Burgin, Victor. 1987. "Psychical Space and Postmodernism." In *The British Edge*. Boston: Institute of Contemporary Art.

Burke, Peter. 1986. *The Italian Renaissance: Culture and Society in Italy*. Princeton: Princeton University Press.

_____. 1988. "Republics of Merchants in Early Modern Europe." In J. Baechler, ed. *Europe and the Rise of Capitalism*. New York: Basil Blackwell.

Bush, George Herbert Walker. 1988. "Text of Bush's Speech Accepting the Nomination for President." *New York Times*, August 19, p. 13.

Butler, Judith. 1993. *Bodies That Matter: On the Discursive Limits of "Sex."* New York: Routledge.

Caffentzis, Constantine George. 1989. *Clipped Coins, Abused Words, and Civil Government: John Locke's Philosophy of Money*. New York: Autonomedia.

Camic, Charles. 1983. *Experience and Enlightenment: Socialization and Cultural Change in Eighteenth Century Scotland*. Chicago: University of Chicago Press.

Carnegie, Andrew. 1933 (1902). *The Empire of Business*. New York: Doubleday.

_____. 1935 (1885). *Triumphant Democracy, or Fifty Years' March of the Republic*. New York: Doubleday.

_____. 1965a (1886). "An Employer's View of Labor." In E. Kirkland, ed. *The Gospel of Wealth and Other Timely Essays*. Cambridge: Harvard University Press.

_____. 1965b (1886). "Results of the Labor Struggle." In E. Kirkland, ed. *The Gospel of Wealth and Other Timely Essays*. Cambridge, Mass.: Harvard University Press.

_____. 1986 (1920). *The Autobiography of Andrew Carnegie*. Boston: Northeastern University Press.

_____. 1992 (1889). "Gospel of Wealth." In D. Burlingame, ed. *The Responsibilities of Wealth*. Bloomington: Indiana University Press.

Cassirer, Ernst. 1946. *The Myth of the State*. New Haven: Yale University Press.

_____. 1963. *The Individual and the Cosmos in Renaissance Philosophy*. New York: Barnes and Noble.

Castoriadis, Cornelius. 1987. *The Imaginary Institution of Society*. Cambridge: M.I.T. Press.

Cawelti, John. 1965. *Apostles of the Self-Made Man*. Chicago: University of Chicago Press.

Chambers, Iain. 1994. *Migrancy, Culture, Identity*. New York: Routledge.

Chambers, Ross. 1984. *Story and Situation: Narrative Seduction and the Power of Fiction*. Minneapolis: University of Minnesota Press.

Charland, Maurice. 1987. "Constitutive Rhetoric: The Case of the *Peuple Quebecois*." *Quarterly Journal of Speech*, Vol. 73, No. 2: 133–150.

Chase, Susan. 1995. *Ambiguous Empowerment: The Work Narratives of Women School Superintendents*. Amherst: University of Massachusetts Press.

Chitnis, Anand. 1976. *The Scottish Enlightenment: A Social History*. London: Croon Helm.

Clough, Patricia. 1994. *Feminist Thought: Desire, Power, and Academic Discourse*. Boston: Basil Blackwell.

Code, Lorraine. 1991. *What Can She Know? Feminist Theory and the Construction of Knowledge*. Ithaca: Cornell University Press.

Cohen, Jean, and Andrew Arato. 1992. *Civil Society and Political Theory*. Cambridge: M.I.T. Press.

Conquergood, Dwight. 1993. "Storied Worlds and the Work of Teaching." *Communication Education*, Vol. 42 (October): 337–348.

Cousin, Mark, and Althar Hussein. 1984. *Michel Foucault*. New York: St. Martin's.

Culler, Johnathan. 1975. *Structuralist Poetics: Structuralism, Linguistics, and the Study of Literature*. London: Routledge and Kegan Paul.

_____. 1981. "Story and Discourse in the Analysis of Narrative." In *The Pursuit of Signs: Semiotics, Literature, Deconstruction*. Ithaca: Cornell University Press.

Dalzell, Robert F. 1987. *Enterprising Elite: The Boston Associates and the World That They Made*. Cambridge: Harvard University Press.

Dean, Mitchell. 1991. *The Constitution of Poverty: Toward a Genealogy of Liberal Governance*. New York: Routledge.

_____. 1994. *Critical and Effective Histories: Foucault's Methods and Historical Sociology*. New York: Routledge.

de Certeau, Michel. 1984. *The Practice of Everyday Life*. Berkeley: University of California Press

Decker, Jeffrey Louis. 1997. *Made in America: Self-Styled Success from Horatio Alger to Oprah Winfrey*. Minneapolis: University of Minnesota Press.

Deleuze, Gilles, and Felix Guattari. 1983. *Anti-Oedipus: Capitalism and Schizophrenia*. Minneapolis: University of Minnesota Press.

Denzin, Norman. 1996. *Interpretive Ethnography: Ethnographic Practices for the 21st Century*. Newbury Park, Calif.: Sage.

Derrida, Jacques. 1973. *Speech and Phenomena*. Evanston, Ill.: Northwestern University Press.

_____. 1978. *Writing and Difference*. Chicago: University of Chicago Press.

Dickson, P. G. M. 1967. *The Financial Revolution in England*. New York: St. Martin's.

DiMaggio, Paul. 1986. "Cultural Entrepreneurship in Boston: The Creation of an Organizational Base for High Culture in America." In R. Collins, ed. *Media, Culture, and Society: A Critical Reader*. Beverly Hills, Calif.: Sage.

Domhoff, G. William. 1970. *The Higher Circles*. New York: Random House.

_____. 1979. *The Powers That Be: Processes of Ruling Class Domination in America*. New York: Vintage Books.

_____. 1983. *Who Rules America Now?* Englewood Cliffs, N.J.: Prentice-Hall.

du Gay, Paul. 1991. "Enterprise Culture and the Ideology of Excellence." *New Formations*, No. 13 (Spring): 45–61.

Dwyer, John. 1987. *Virtuous Discourse: Sensibility and Community in Late Eighteenth Century Scotland*. Edinburgh: John Donald Publishers.

Edwards, Richard. 1985. "The Proletarianization of the Wage Labor Force." In R. Edwards, T. Reich, and T. Weisskopf, eds. *The Capitalist System*, 3d ed. Englewood Cliffs, N.J.: Prentice-Hall.

Elbaz, Roger. 1987. *The Changing Nature of the Self*. Iowa City: Iowa University Press.

Elias, Norbert. 1978. *The Civilizing Process*. Volume 1: *The History of Manners*. New York: Vintage.

Eliot, Samuel Atkins. 1845. "The Public and Private Charities of Boston." *North American Review* (July): 135–159.

_____. 1860. "The Charities of Boston." *North American Review* (July): 149–165.

Erikson, Erik. 1962. *Young Man Luther*. New York: Norton.

Fairclough, Norman. 1991. "What Might We Mean by 'Enterprise Discourse'?" In R. Keat and N. Abercrombie, eds. *Enterprise Culture*. New York: Routledge.

Farrell, Betty G. 1993. *Elite Families: Class and Power in Nineteenth Century Boston*. Albany: SUNY Press.

Faye, Jean Pierre. 1974. *Migrations du récit sur le peuple juif*. Paris: Belfond.

Feldman, Allen. 1991. *Formations of Violence: The Narrative of the Body and Political Terror in Northern Ireland*. Chicago: University of Chicago Press.

Ferguson, Adam. 1986. *Essay in the History of Civil Society*. Edinburgh: University of Edinburgh Press.

Fisher, Walter. 1987. *Human Communication as Narration*. Columbia: University of South Carolina Press.

Flanagan, Thomas. 1972. "The Concept of *Fortuna* in Machiavelli." In Anthony Parel, ed. *The Political Calculus*. Toronto: University of Toronto Press.

Foucault, Michel. 1972. *The Archeology of Knowledge*. New York: Pantheon.

_____. 1977a. "Nietzsche, Genealogy, History." In *Language, Counter-Memory, Practice*. Ithaca: Cornell University Press.

_____. 1977b. "Two Lectures." In Colin Gordon, ed. *Power/Knowledge: Selected Interviews and Other Writings, 1972–1977*. New York: Pantheon.

_____. 1979. *Discipline and Punish: The Birth of the Prison*. New York: Vintage.

_____. 1983. "The Subject and Power." In P. Rabinow and H. Dreyfus. *Michel Foucault: Between Structuralism and Hermeneutics*. Berkeley: University of California Press.

_____. 1984. "Space, Knowledge, and Power." In P. Rabinow, Eed. *The Foucault Reader*. New York: Pantheon.

_____. 1986. "Of Other Spaces." *Diacritics*, Vol. 16: 22–27

_____. 1988a. "Technologies of the Self." In L. Martin, H. Gutman, and P. Hutton, eds. *Technologies of the Self: A Seminar with Michel Foucault*. Amherst: University of Massachusetts Press.

_____. 1988b. "The Concern with Truth: Interview with Francois Ewald." In L. Kritzman, ed. *Michel Foucault: Politics, Philosophy, Culture: Interviews and Other Writings*. New York: Routledge.

_____. 1991. "Governmentality." In G. Burchell, C. Gordon, and P. Miller, eds. *The Foucault Effect: Studies in Governmentality*. Chicago: University of Chicago Press.

Fox, Kenneth. 1992. "A Businessman's Philanthropic Creed: A Centennial Perspective on Carnegie's 'Gospel of Wealth.'" In D. Burlingame, ed. *The Responsibilities of Wealth*. Bloomington: Indiana University Press.

Franklin, Benjamin. 1840. *The Collected Works of Benjamin Franklin*. Boston: Hilliard, Gray and Co.

Freud, Sigmund. 1919. "The Uncanny." In *The Standard Edition of the Complete Psychological Works of Sigmund Freud*. London: Hogarth Press.

Friedman, Lawrence. 1964. "The Dynastic Trust." *Yale Law Journal*, Vol. 73: 547–592.

Frith, Simon. 1996. "Music and Identity." In S. Hall and P. du Gay, eds. *Questions of Cultural Identity*. Newbury Park, Calif.: Sage.

Game, Ann. 1991. *Undoing the Social: Towards a Deconstructive Sociology*. Toronto: University of Toronto Press.

Game, Ann, and Andrew Metcalfe. 1996. *Passionate Sociology*. Newbury Park, Calif.: Sage.

Giddens, Anthony. 1979. *Central Problems in Social Theory*. Berkeley: University of California Press.

_____. 1984. *The Constitution of Society*. Berkeley: University of California Press.

Gilbert, Felix. 1965. *Machiavelli and Guicciardini: Politics and History in Sixteenth Century Florence*. Princeton: Princeton University Press.

Gilligan, Carol. 1982. *In a Different Voice: Psychological Theory and Women's Development*. Cambridge: Harvard University Press.

Ginzberg, Lori. 1991. *Women and the Work of Benevolence: Class, Politics, and Morality in Nineteenth Century America*. New Haven: Yale University Press.

Goldthwaite, Richard. 1968. *Private Wealth and Renaissance Florence*. Princeton: Princeton University Press.

_____. 1980. *The Building of Renaissance Florence: An Economic and Social History*. Baltimore: Johns Hopkins University Press.

Gordon, Colin. 1987. "The Soul of the Citizen: Max Weber and Michel Foucault on Rationality and Government." In S. Whimster and S. Lash, eds. *Max Weber, Rationality, and Modernity*. London: Allen and Unwin.

_____. 1991. "Governmental Rationality: An Introduction." In Burchell, G., C. Gordon, and P. Miller, eds. *The Foucault Effect: Studies in Governmentality*. Chicago: University of Chicago Press.

Gordon, Avery F. 1997. *Ghostly Matters: Haunting and the Sociological Imagination*. Minneapolis: University of Minnesota Press.

Gramsci, Antonio. 1971. *The Prison Notebooks*. New York: International Publishers.

Greenblatt, Stephen. 1986. "Fiction and Friction." In T. Heller, M. Sosna, and D. Wellberry, eds. *Reconstructing Individualism: Autonomy, Individuality, and the Self in Western Thought*. Stanford: Stanford University Press.

Greene, Ronald. 1998. "Another Materialist Rhetoric." *Critical Studies in Mass Communications*, Vol. 15, No. 1: 21–40.

Greenslet, Ferris. 1946. *The Lowells and Their Seven Worlds*. Boston: Houghton Mifflin.

Gregory, Derek. 1995. *Geographical Imaginations*. Cambridge, U.K: Basil Blackwell.

Greimas, A. J. 1987. *On Meaning: Selected Writings*. Minneapolis: University of Minnesota Press.

Grossberg, L. 1993. "Cultural Studies and/in New Worlds." *Critical Studies in Mass Communications*, Vol. 10, No. 1: 1–22.

Gubrium, Jaber F., and James A. Holstein. 1998. "Narrative Practice and the Coherence of Personal Stories." *The Sociological Quarterly*, Vol. 39, No. 1 (Winter): 163–187.

Gutman, Herbert. 1979. *Work, Culture, and Society in Industrializing America*. New York: Vintage.

Hale, John R. 1977. *Florence and the Medici*. London: Thames and Hudson.

———. 1994. *The Civilization of Europe in the Renaissance*. New York: Athenaeum.

Hall, Peter D. 1982. *The Organization of American Culture: Private Institutions, Elites, and American Nationality*. New York: New York University Press.

———. 1990. "The History of Religious Philanthropy in America." In R. Wuthnow and V. Hodgkinson, eds. *Faith and Philanthropy in America*. San Francisco: Jossey-Bass.

Hall, Stuart. 1986. "On Postmodernism and Articulation: An Interview with Stuart Hall." *Journal of Communication Inquiry*, Vol. 10, No. 2: 45–60.

———. 1987. "Minimal Selves." In *The Real Me: Modernism and the Question of Identity*. London: ICA Documents.

Harré, Rom. 1984. *Personal Being*. Cambridge: Harvard University Press.

Harriman, Robert. 1995. *Political Style: The Artistry of Power*. Chicago: University of Chicago Press.

Harstock, Nancy. 1984. *Money, Sex, and Power: Towards a Feminist Historical Materialism*. Boston: Northeastern University Press.

———. 1990. "Foucault on Power: A Theory for Women?" In Linda Nicholson, ed. *Feminism/Postmodernism*. New York: Routledge.

Hebdige, Dick. 1987. *Cut 'N' Mix: Culture, Identity, and Caribbean Music*. New York: Methuen.

Hennesey, Rosemary. 1993. *Materialist Feminism and the Politics of Discourse*. New York: Routledge.

Henwood, Doug. 1998. *Wall Street: How It Works and for Whom*. New York and London: Verso.

Hinchman, Lewis P., and Sandra K. Hinchman. 1997. *Memory, Community, Identity: The Idea of Narrative in the Human Sciences*. Albany: SUNY Press.

Hindess, Barry. 1996. *Discourses of Power: From Hobbes to Foucault*. Cambridge: Basil Blackwell.

Hirschman, Albert. 1977. *The Passions and the Interests: Political Arguments for Capitalism Before Its Triumph*. Princeton: Princeton University Press.

Hope, V. M. 1989. *Virtue by Consensus: The Moral Philosophy of Hutcheson, Hume, and Smith*. Cambridge, U.K.: Cambridge University Press.

Horne, T. 1978. *The Social Thought of Bernard Mandeville*. New York: Columbia University Press.

Hume, David. 1955a. "Of Commerce." In E. Rotwein, ed. *David Hume: Writings on Economics*. Madison: University of Wisconsin Press.

———. 1955b. "Of Interest." In E. Rotwein, ed. *David Hume: Writings on Economics*. Madison: University of Wisconsin Press.

———. 1963. "Of Avarice." In *Essays: Moral, Political, and Literary*. Oxford: Oxford University Press.

———. 1973. *A Treatise on Human Nature*. New York: Penguin.

———. 1975. *Enquiries Concerning Human Understanding and Concerning the Principals of Morals*. Oxford: Oxford University Press.

Innes, Stephen. 1995. *Creating the Commonwealth: The Economic Culture of Puritan New England*. New York: W. W. Norton.

Jaher, Frederick. 1982. *The Urban Establishment: Upper Strata in Boston, New York, Charleston, Chicago, and Los Angeles*. Urbana: University of Illinois Press.

Jardine, Lisa. 1996. *Worldly Goods: A New History of the Renaissance*. New York: Nan A. Talese/Doubleday.

Jakobson, Roman. 1956. "Two Poles of Language and Two Types of Aphasic Disturbance." In R. Jakobson and M. Halles. *Fundamentals of Language*. The Hague: Mouton.

Jay, Martin. 1994. *Downcast Eyes: The Denigration of Vision in Twentieth Century French Thought*. Berkeley: University of California Press.

Jenkins, Richard. 1996. *Social Identity*. New York: Routledge.

Johnson, Barbara. 1981 "Translator Preface" to Jacques Derrida, *Dissemination*. Chicago: University of Chicago Press.

Jones, Steve. 1992. *Rock Formation: Music, Technology, and Mass Communication*. Newbury Park, Calif.: Sage.

Karl, Barry. 1992. "Andrew Carnegie and His Gospel of Philanthropy: A Study in the Ethics of Philanthropy." In D. Burlingame, ed. *The Responsibilities of Wealth*. Bloomington: Indiana University Press.

Karl, Barry, and Stanley Katz. 1987. "Foundations and Ruling Class Elites." *Daedalus*, No. 116 (Winter): 1–40.

Kelly-Gadol, J. 1977. "Did Women Have a Renaissance?" In R. Bridenthal and C. Koontz, eds. *Becoming Visible: Women in European History*. Boston: Houghton-Mifflin.

Kemp, T. Peter. 1989. "Toward a Narrative Ethics: A Bridge Between Ethics and the Narrative Reflection of Ricoeur." In T. P. Kemp and D. Rasmussen, eds. *The Narrative Path: The Later Works of Paul Ricoeur*. Cambridge: M.I.T. Press.

Kennickell, Arthur, Matha Starr-McCluer, and Annika Sunden. 1997. "Family Finances in the U.S.: Recent Evidence from the Survey of Consumer Finances." *Federal Reserve Bulletin* (January): 1–24.

Kerby, Anthony Paul. 1991. *Narrative and the Self*. Bloomington: Indiana University Press.

Ketcham, Ralph. 1988. *Individualism and Public Life: A Modern Dilemma*. New York: Basil Blackwell.

Kirby, Kathleen. 1995. *Indifferent Boundaries: Spatial Concepts of Human Subjectivity*. New York: Guilford.

Kirkland, Edward C. 1956. *Dream and Thought in the Business Community 1860–1900*. Ithaca: Cornell University Press.

Kolko, Gabriel. 1967. "Brahmins and Business, 1870–1914: A Hypothesis on the Social Basis of Success in American History." In K. Wolff and B. Moore Jr., eds. *The Critical Spirit: Essays in Honor of Herbert Marcuse*. Boston: Beacon Press.

Lachman, Richard, and Stephen Petterson. 1989. "Political Capitalism and Economic Failure in Renaissance Florence." Paper presented at the American Sociological Association Annual Meetings, San Francisco (August).

Lasch, Christopher. 1991. *The True and Only Heaven: Progress and Its Critics*. New York: Norton.

Lears, T. Jackson. 1981. *No Place of Grace: Antimodernism and the Transformation of American Culture, 1880–1920*. New York: Pantheon.

Lefebvre, Henri. 1991. *The Production of Space*. Cambridge: Basil Blackwell.

Lemert, Charles. 1994. "Dark Thoughts About the Self." In C. Calhoun, ed. *Social Theory and the Politics of Identity*. Cambridge: Basil Blackwell.

Linden-Ward, Blanche. 1989. *Silent City on a Hill: Landscapes of Memory and Boston's Mount Auburn Cemetery.* Columbus: Ohio State University Press.

Lloyd, Genevieve. 1984. *The Man of Reason: "Male" and "Female" in Western Philosophy.* Minneapolis: University of Minnesota Press.

Lowe, Donald. 1983. *History of Bourgeois Perception.* Chicago: University of Chicago Press.

Machiavelli, Niccolò. 1965a. *The Art of War.* In *Machiavelli: The Chief Works and Others,* 3 volumes. Allan Gilbert, tr. Durham, N.C.: Duke University Press.

_____. 1965b. *The Discourses.* In *Machiavelli: The Chief Works and Others,* 3 volumes. Allan Gilbert, tr. Durham, N.C.: Duke University Press.

_____. 1965c. *The Prince.* In *Machiavelli: The Chief Works and Others,* 3 volumes. Allan Gilbert, tr. Durham, N.C.: Duke University Press.

_____. 1965d. "Tercets on Fortune." In *Machiavelli: The Chief Works and Others,* 3 volumes. Allan Gilbert, tr. Durham, N.C.: Duke University Press.

_____. 1965e. "Life of Castruccio." In *Machiavelli: The Chief Works and Others,* 3 volumes. Allan Gilbert, tr. Durham, N.C.: Duke University Press.

_____. 1965f. *Florentine Histories.* In *Machiavelli: The Chief Works and Others,* 3 volumes. Allan Gilbert, tr. Durham, N.C.: Duke University Press.

MacIntyre, Alasdair. 1981. *After Virtue: A Study in Moral Theory.* South Bend, Ind.: University of Notre Dame Press.

MacPherson, C. B. 1962. *The Political Theory of Possessive Individualism.* New York: Oxford University Press.

Maines, David. 1993. "Narrative's Moment and Sociology's Phenomena: Toward a Narrative Sociology." *The Sociological Quarterly,* Vol. 34, No. 1: 17–39

_____. 1997. "Inter-Ethnicity and Narrative." Unpublished manuscript.

Mann, Michael. 1986. *The Sources of Social Power.* Volume 1: *From the Beginning to 1760.* Cambridge, U.K: Cambridge University Press.

Mansfield, Harvey. 1996. *Machiavelli's Virtue.* Chicago: University of Chicago Press.

Marcus, Greil. 1989. *Lipstick Traces: A Secret History of the Twentieth Century.* Cambridge: Harvard University Press.

Marcus, George. 1992. *Lives in Trust: The Fortunes of Dynastic Families in Late Twentieth Century America.* Boulder: Westview.

Marshall, Gordon. 1982. *In Search of the Spirit of Capitalism: An Essay on Max Weber's Protestant Ethic Thesis.* New York: Columbia University Press.

Marx, Karl. 1973. *Capital.* Volume 1. New York: Vintage

_____. 1976. *Grundrisse.* New York: Vintage.

Massey, Doreen. 1993a. "Politics and Space/Time." In M. Keith and S. Pile, eds. *Place and the Politics of Identity.* New York: Routledge

_____. 1993b. "Power-Geometry and a Progressive Sense of Place." In J. Bird et al., eds. *Mapping the Futures: Local Cultures, Global Change.* New York: Routledge.

Mather, Cotton. 1966. *Bonafacius: An Essay upon the Good.* Cambridge: Harvard University Press.

Mauss, Marcel. 1967. *The Gift: Functions and Forms of Exchange in Archaic Societies.* New York: Norton.

McCarthy, Kathleen. 1982. *Noblesse Oblige: Charity and Cultural Philanthropy in Chicago, 1849–1929.* Chicago: University of Chicago Press.

_____. 1989. "The Gospel of Wealth: American Giving in Theory and Practice." In R. Magat, ed. *Philanthropic Giving: Varieties and Goals*. New York: Oxford University Press.

_____. 1991. *Women's Culture: American Philanthropy and Art, 1830–1930*. Chicago: University of Chicago Press.

McClaren, Peter. 1995. *Critical Pedagogy and Predatory Culture*. New York: Routledge.

McGee, Michael. 1990. "Text, Context, and the Fragmentation of American Culture." *Western Journal of Speech Communication*, Vol. 54: 274–289.

McGill, Allan. 1985. *Prophets of Extremity: Nietzsche, Heidegger, Foucault, Derrida*. Berkeley: University of California Press.

McKendrick, N., J. Brewer, and J. H. Plumb. 1985. *The Birth of a Consumer Society: The Commercialization of Eighteenth Century England*. Bloomington: Indiana University Press.

McKerrow, Raymie. 1989. "Critical Rhetoric: Theory and Practice." *Communication Monographs*, Vol. 56: 91–111

Miller, David. 1981. *Philosophy and Ideology in Hume's Political Thought*. Oxford: Oxford University Press.

Mills, C. Wright. 1959. *The Sociological Imagination*. New York: Oxford University Press.

Minson, Jeffrey. 1985. *Genealogies of Morals*. New York: St. Martin's.

_____. 1993. *Questions of Conduct*. London: Macmillan.

Mintz, Beth. 1989. "The United States." In Tom Bottomore and Robert J. Brym, eds. *The Capitalist Class: An International Study*. New York: New York University Press.

Montgomery, David. 1979. *Workers' Control in America*. New York: Cambridge University Press.

Morgan, Edmund S. 1966. *Puritan Political Ideas*. Indianapolis, Ind.: Bobbs-Merrill.

Morris, William, ed. 1978. *The American Heritage Dictionary of the English Language*. Boston: Houghton Mifflin.

Munslow, Alan. 1988. "Andrew Carnegie and the Discourse of Cultural Hegemony." *Journal of American Studies*, Vol. 22, No. 2: 213–224.

_____. 1993. *Discourse and Culture: The Creation of America, 1870–1920*. New York: Routledge.

O'Hanlon, Rosalind. 1988. "Recovering the Subject: Subaltern Studies and Histories of Resistance in Colonial South Asia." *Modern Asia Studies*, Vol. 22: 189–224.

Odendahl, Teresa. 1989. *Charity Begins at Home: Generosity and Power Among the Philanthropic Elite*. New York: Basic.

Oldfield, Adrian. 1991. *Citizenship and Community: Civic Republicanism and the Modern World*. New York: Routledge.

Ostrower, Francie. 1995. *Why the Wealthy Give: The Culture of Elite Philanthropy*. Princeton: Princeton University Press.

Parel, Anthony. 1992. *The Machiavellian Cosmos*. New Haven: Yale University Press.

Parry, J., and M. Bloch. 1989. "Introduction." In J. Parry and M. Bloch, eds. *Money and the Morality of Exchange*. New York: Cambridge University Press.

Patch, Harry. 1927. *The Goddess Fortuna in Medieval Literature.* Cambridge: Harvard University Press.

Payton, Robert. 1988. *Philanthropy: Voluntary Action for the Public Good.* New York: Collier.

Pefanis, Julian. 1991. *Heterology and the Postmodern: Bataille, Baudrillard, and Lyotard.* Durham, N.C.: Duke University Press.

Perkins, William. 1966. "On Callings." In E. Morgan, ed. *Puritan Political Ideas.* Indianapolis, Ind.: Bobbs-Merrill.

Pessen, Edward. 1973. *Riches, Class, and Power Before the Civil War.* Lexington, Mass.: D. C. Heath.

Pfohl, Stephen. 1992. *Death at the Parasite Cafe: Social Science (Fictions) and the Postmodern.* New York: St. Martin's.

Phillips, Kevin. 1991. *The Politics of Rich and Poor: Wealth and the American Electorate in the Reagan Aftermath.* New York: Random House.

Pico della Mirandolla, Giovanni. 1948. "Oration on the Dignity of Man." In E. Cassirer et al., eds. *The Renaissance Philosophy of Man.* Chicago: University of Chicago Press.

Pile, Steve, and Nigel Thrift. 1995. "Mapping the Subject." In S. Pile and N. Thrift, eds. *Mapping the Subject: Geographies of Cultural Transformation.* New York: Routledge.

Pitkin, Hannah F. 1984. *Fortune Is a Woman: Gender and Politics in the Thought of Niccolo Machiavelli.* Berkeley: University of California Press.

Plummer, Ken. 1995. *Telling Sexual Stories.* New York: Routledge.

Pocock, J. G. A. 1971. "Civic Humanism and Its Role in Anglo-American Thought." In *Language, Politics, and Time.* New York: Antheneum.

_____. 1975. *The Machiavellian Moment: Florentine Political Thought and the Atlantic Republican Tradition.* Princeton: Princeton University Press.

_____. 1982. "Cambridge Paradigms and Scottish Philosophers." In I. Hont and M. Ignatieff, eds. *Wealth and Virtue: The Shaping of Political Economy in the Scottish Enlightenment.* Cambridge, U.K: Cambridge University Press.

_____. 1985a. "Mobility of Property and the Rise of Eighteenth Century Sociology." In *Virtue, Commerce, and History: Essays in Political Thought, Chiefly in the Eighteenth Century.* Cambridge U.K: Cambridge University Press.

_____. 1985b. "Virtues, Rights, and Manners." In *Virtue, Commerce, and History: Essays in Political Thought, Chiefly in the Eighteenth Century.* Cambridge, U.K: Cambridge University Press.

Poggi, Gianfranco. 1983. *Calvinism and the Capitalist Spirit: Max Weber's Protestant Ethic.* Amherst: University of Massachusetts Press.

Polkinghorne, Donald E. 1988. *Narrative Knowing in the Human Sciences.* Albany: SUNY Press.

_____. 1995. "Narrative Configuration in Qualitative Analysis." In J. A. Hatch and R. Wisniewski, eds. *Life History and Narrative.* Washington, D.C.: Falmer.

Poole, Ross. 1991. *Morality and Modernity.* New York: Routledge.

Probyn, Elspeth. 1993. *Sexing the Self: Gendered Position in Cultural Studies.* New York: Routledge.

Raab, Felix. 1964. *The English Face of Machiavelli.* London: Routledge and Kegan Paul.

Ransom, John. 1997. *Foucault's Discipline: The Politics of Subjectivity*. Durham, N.C.: Duke University Press.

Richards, I. A. 1934. *The Philosophy of Rhetoric*. New York: Oxford University Press.

Richardson, Laurel. 1990. "Narrative and Sociology." *Journal of Contemporary Ethnography*, Vol. 19, No. 1 (April): 116–135.

_____. 1996. *Fields of Play: Constructing an Academic Life*. Philadelphia: Temple University Press.

Ricoeur, Paul. 1984. *Time and Narrative*. Volume 1. Chicago: University of Chicago Press.

_____. 1991a. "Life in Quest of Narrative." In D. Wood, ed. *On Paul Ricoeur: Narrative and Interpretation*. New York: Routledge.

_____. 1991b. "Narrative Identity." In D. Wood, ed. *On Paul Ricoeur: Narrative and Interpretation*. New York: Routledge.

Ritchey, Charles J. 1956. *Drake University Through 75 Years*. Des Moines, Iowa: Drake University.

Robbins, Caroline. 1955. *The Eighteenth Century New Commonwealthmen*. Cambridge: Harvard University Press.

Romanyshyn, Robert. 1989. *Technology as Symptom and Dream*. New York: Routledge.

Rose, Nikolas. 1992. "Governing the Enterprising Self." In P. Heelas and P. Morris, eds. *The Values of the Enterprise Culture*. New York: Routledge.

_____. 1996. "Identity, Genealogy, History." In S. Hall and P. du Gay, eds. *Questions of Cultural Identity*. Newbury Park, Calif.: Sage.

Rubenstein, Nicolai. 1990. "Machiavelli and the Florentine Republican Experience." In G. Bock, Q. Skinner, and M. Viroli, eds. *Machiavelli and Republicanism*. New York: Cambridge University Press.

Ryan, Alan. 1987. *Property*. Minneapolis: University of Minnesota Press.

Schama, Simon. 1991. *Dead Certainties (Unwarranted Speculations)*. New York: Knopf.

Schervish, Paul G. 1990. "Wealth and the Spiritual Secret of Money." In R. Wuthnow and V. Hodgkinson, eds. *Faith and Philanthropy in America*. San Francisco: Jossey-Bass.

_____. 1994. "The Wealthy and the World of Wealth." In Paul G. Schervish, Platon Coutsoukis, and Ethan Lewis. *Gospels of Wealth: How the Rich Portray Their Lives*. Westport, Conn.: Praeger.

_____. (forthcoming). *Principality and Individuality: The Moral Biography of Wealth*. Chicago: University of Chicago Press.

Schervish, Paul G., and Andrew Herman. 1988. *Empowerment and Beneficence: Strategies of Living and Giving Among the Wealthy*. Chestnut Hill, Mass.: Social Welfare Research Institute/Boston College.

_____. 1991. "Money and Hyperagency." Paper presented at "Conference on Money: Lure, Lore, and Liquidity." Hofstra University, Hempstead, New York (November).

Schervish, Paul, Platon Coutsoukis, and Ethan Lewis. 1994. *Gospels of Wealth: How the Rich Portray Their Lives*. Westport, Conn.: Praeger.

Schor, Juliet. 1991. *The Overworked American*. New York: Basic.

_____. 1998. *The Overspent American*. New York: Basic.

Schweninger, Lee. 1990. *John Winthrop*. Boston: G. K. Hall.

Sekora, J. 1977. *Luxury: The Concept in Western Thought, Eden to Smollett*. Baltimore: Johns Hopkins University Press.

Shammas, Carole, Marylyn Salmon, and Michel Dahlin. 1987. *Inheritance in America: From Colonial Times to the Present*. New Brunswick, N.J.: Rutgers University Press.

Shapiro, Michael. 1988. *The Politics of Representation: Writing Practices in Biography, Photography, and Policy Analysis*. Madison: University of Wisconsin Press.

Shapiro, Michael, and Marianne Shapiro. 1988. *Figuration in Verbal Art*. Princeton: Princeton University Press.

Shepardson, Charles. 1995. "History and the Real: Freud With Lacan." *Postmodern Culture*, Vol. 5, No. 2 (January).

Shields, Rob. 1991. *Places on the Margin: Alternative Geographies of Modernity*. New York: Routledge.

Shotter, John. 1983. "A Sense of Place: Vico and the Social Production of Identities." *British Journal of Social Psychology*, Vol. 25: 199–211.

———. 1989. "Rhetoric and the Recovery of Civil Society." *Economy and Society*, Vol. 18, No. 2 (May): 149–166.

———. 1990. "Social Individuality and Possessive Individualism." In I. Parker and J. Shotter, eds. *Deconstructing Social Psychology*. New York: Routledge.

Siegel, Jerrold. 1968. *Rhetoric and Philosophy in Renaissance Humanism: The Union of Eloquence and Wisdom from Petrarch to Valla*. Princeton: Princeton University Press.

Simmel, Georg. 1978. *The Philosophy of Money*. London: Routledge and Kegan Paul.

Skinner, Quentin. 1978. *The Foundations of Modern Political Thought*. Volume 2: *The Age of Reformation*. Cambridge, U.K.: Cambridge University Press.

Smith, Adam. 1976a. *An Inquiry into the Nature and Causes of the Wealth of Nations*. Chicago: University of Chicago Press.

———. 1976b. *The Theory of Moral Sentiments*. Indianapolis, Ind.: Liberty Press.

———. 1978a. *Lectures on Jurisprudence, Report of 1762–1763*, edited by R. L. Meek, D. D. Raphael, and P. G. Stein. London: Oxford University Press.

———. 1978b. *Lectures on Jurisprudence, Report of 1766*, edited by R. L. Meek, D. D. Raphael, and P. G. Stein. London: Oxford University Press.

Smith, Dorothy. 1987. *Everyday Life as Problematic*. Boston: Northeastern University Press.

———. 1991. *The Conceptual Practices of Power: Towards a Feminist Sociology of Knowledge*. Boston: Northeastern University Press.

Soja, Edward. 1989. *Postmodern Geographies: The Reassertion of Space in Critical Social Theory*. London: Verso.

Sombart, Werner. 1967 [1913]. *The Quintessence of Capitalism: A Study in History and Psychology of the Modern Businessman*. New York: Fertig.

Somers, Margaret R., and Gloria D. Gibson. 1994. "Reclaiming the Epistemological 'Other': Narrative and the Social Construction of Identity." In C. Calhoun, ed. *Social Theory and the Politics of Identity*. Cambridge: Basil Blackwell.

Spivak, Gayatri Chakravorty. 1988. "Can the Subaltern Speak?" In C. Nelson and L. Grossberg, eds. *Marxism and the Interpretation of Culture*. Urbana: University of Illinois Press.

Stewart, Kathleen. 1996. *A Space by the Side of the Road: Cultural Poetics in an "Other" America*. Princeton: Princeton University Press.

Stivers, Richard. 1995. *The Culture of Cynicism: American Morality in Decline*. Cambridge: Basil Blackwell.

Story, Joseph. 1980. *The Forging of an Aristocracy: Harvard and Boston's Upper Class, 1800–1870*. Middletown, Conn.: Wesleyan University Press.

Stout, Harry S. 1986. *The New England Soul: Preaching and Religious Culture in Colonial New England*. New York: Oxford University Press.

Sussman, Warren. 1984. "'Personality' and the Making of Twentieth-Century Culture." In *Culture as History: The Transformation of American Culture in the Twentieth Century*. New York: Pantheon.

Tawney, R. H. 1938. *Religion and the Rise of Capitalism*. Harmondsworth, U.K: Penguin.

Taylor, Charles. 1989. *Sources of the Self: The Making of Modern Identity*. Cambridge: Harvard University Press.

Theweleit, Klaus. 1987. *Male Fantasies*. Volume 1: *Women, Floods, Bodies, History*. Minneapolis: University of Minnesota Press.

Tocqueville, Alexis de. 1981. *Democracy in America*. New York: Random House.

Todd, Richard. 1997. "Who Me, Rich?" *Worth* (September): 70–84.

Tribe, Keith. 1981. "The Histories of Economic Discourse." In *Genealogies of Capitalism*. Atlantic Highlands, N.J.: Humanities Press.

Tuck, Richard. 1980. *Natural Rights Theories: Their Origins and Development*. Cambridge U.K.: Cambridge University Press.

Ulmann, Walter. 1967. *The Individual and Society in the Middle Ages*. London: Methuen.

Urry, John. 1995. *Consuming Places*. New York: Routledge.

Useem, Michael. 1984. *The Inner Circle: Large Corporations and the Rise of Business Political Activity in the U.S. and the U.K.* New York: Oxford University Press.

Vanderbilt, Arthur T. II. 1989. *Fortune's Children: The Rise and Fall of the House of Vanderbilt*. New York: Quill/William Morrow.

Veyne, Paul. 1984. *Writing History: Essays of Epistemology*. Middletown, Conn.: Wesleyan University Press.

Vesser, H. Aram. 1989. *The New Historicism*. New York: Routledge.

Vickers, Brian. 1988. *In Defense of Rhetoric*. Oxford, U.K.: Clarendon Press.

von Martin, Alfred. 1963. *The Sociology of the Renaissance*. New York: Harper and Row.

Wall, Joseph. 1970. *Andrew Carnegie*. New York: Oxford University Press.

Weber, Max. 1958. *The Protestant Ethic and the Spirit of Capitalism*. New York: Scribner's.

———. 1966. *General Economic History*. New York: Collier.

Weedon, Chris. 1987. *Feminist Practice and Poststructuralist Theory*. Cambridge: Basil Blackwell.

Weeks, Edward. 1966. *The Lowells and Their Institute*. Boston: Little Brown.

White, Gerald T. 1955. *A History of the Massachusetts Hospital Life Insurance Company*. Cambridge: Harvard University Press.

White, Hayden. 1987. *The Content of the Form: Narrative Discourse and Historical Representation*. Baltimore: Johns Hopkins University Press.

_____. 1996. "Storytelling: Historical and Ideological." In R. Newman, ed. *Centuries' End, Narrative Means*. Stanford: Stanford University Press.

Whitson, Steve, and John Poulakos. 1993. "Nietzsche and the Aesthetics of Rhetoric." *Quarterly Journal of Speech*, Vol. 70, No. 2 (May): 131–145.

Wilden, Anthony. 1987. *The Rules Are No Game: The Strategy of Communication*. London: Routledge and Kegan Paul.

Wolff, Edward. 1995. *Top Heavy: A Study of the Increasing Inequality in Wealth in America*. New York: Twentieth Century Fund Press.

Wood, Ellen Meiksens, and Neal Wood. 1978. *Class Ideology and Ancient Political Theory: Socrates, Plato, and Aristotle in Social Context*. New York: Oxford University Press.

Wuthnow, Robert. 1990. *Communities of Discourse: Ideology and Social Structure in the Reformation, the Enlightenment, and European Socialism*. Cambridge: Harvard University Press.

Wyllie, Irvin G. 1954. *The Self-Made Man in America: The Myth of Rags to Riches*. New York: Free Press.

Xenos, Nicholas. 1989. *Scarcity and Modernity*. New York: Routledge.

Yates, Timothy. 1990. "Jacques Derrida: 'There Is Nothing Outside the Text.'" In Christopher Tilley, ed. *Reading Material Culture: Structuralism, Hermeneutics, and Poststructuralism*. Cambridge: Basil Blackwell.

Zelizer, Viviana. 1994. *The Social Meaning of Money*. New York: Basic Books.

Index